VICARIOUS CONSUMERS

T0304062

Modern Economic and Social History Series

General Editor: Derek H. Aldcroft

Titles in this series include:

Vicarious Consumers
Trans-National Meetings between the West and East in the Mediterranean World (1730–1808)

MANUEL PÉREZ-GARCÍA
Tsinghua University, Beijing, China

This book has been published with a financial subsidy from the
European University Institute.

LONDON AND NEW YORK

First published 2013 by Ashgate Publishing

2 Park Square, Milton Park, Abingdon, Oxon OX14 4RN
711 Third Avenue, New York, NY 10017, USA

Routledge is an imprint of the Taylor & Francis Group, an informa business

First issued in paperback 2016

British Library Cataloguing in Publication Data
A catalogue record for this book is available from the British Library

The Library of Congress has cataloged the printed edition as follows:
Pérez-García, Manuel, 1979–
  Vicarious consumers / by Manuel Pérez-García.
    pages cm.—(Modern economic and social history)
  Includes bibliographical references and index.
  ISBN 978-1-4094-5685-8 (hardcover)—ISBN 978-1-4724-0728-3 (epub) 1.
  Consumer behavior—Spain—History. 2. Consumption
(Economics)—Spain—History. 3. Merchants—Spain—History. 4. Marketing—Spain—History. I. Title.
  HF5415.33.S7P47 2013
  339.4'70946—dc23

                                                                    2013005591

ISBN 978-1-4094-5685-8 (hbk)
ISBN 978-1-138-25465-7 (pbk)

To my father (Manuel), my wife (Marisol), my mother (Encarnita)
and my brothers and sisters (Mariano, Angel, Maria and Encarnita)

Contents

**PART IV   EXAMINING THE 'CONSUMER' AND 'INDUSTRIOUS'
REVOLUTION IN SOUTH-EASTERN SPAIN: THE KINGDOM OF
MURCIA (1730–1808)**

PART V   GENERAL CONCLUSIONS

List of Illustrations

List of Maps

List of Charts

List of Tables

Preface and Acknowledgements

This study is based on socio-economic and cultural factors connected with the material culture of the household, as well as the aspirations of its members for new consumer products. I analyse market activities, demand-side and socio-cultural aspects associated with the introduction of new fashions. Over the centuries, these factors have helped to shape the current consumer globalization of western and eastern societies. The desires, aspirations and choices of individuals are demonstrated to have been inspired by a global movement, in which human and material capital circulated trans-continentally, shifting the patterns of consumption of societies, whose values and traditions were challenged by the acquisition of new material goods. I do not simply analyse those relevant theories applied to material culture and consumption studies related to occidental or oriental societies, such as the 'industrious revolution' or 'trickle-down' approaches, which have been applied mostly in developed economies to explain stages prior to the Industrial Revolution process. Instead, by observing a southern European society, such as Spain, where the industrialization process was slower than in Anglo-Saxon territories, it is possible to determine whether both theories occurred simultaneously or separately; identify what the socio-economic forces and agents that prompted the stimulus for new consumer aspirations were; and understand the cultural consequences that the new modern consumerism brought about.

In this book, the old myths and goals shaped by the political movement of the establishment of new nation-states in the early days of the nineteenth century are deconstructed. The construction of imaginary worlds and unreal communities which the rise of nationalism brought about, and which reinvented traditions created in an invented past, are profoundly dismantled in my research. Prejudices, stereotypes and jibes about what was defined as new, foreign or strange were the primary weapons of the Establishment, and the purpose was to protect the values which the political institutions defined as traditional and pure: the basis for the sought-after nationalistic sentiment. Intercontinental trade is the key feature that needs to be analysed in order to understand the interconnection of cultural models at the dawning of the global era, during the late eighteenth and early nineteenth centuries. Such models were related to distant societies, contributing to the occurrence of a 'global melting pot' and recreating communities whose socio-cultural patterns have certain common facets.

In order to refresh the classic studies on consumer behaviour, it has been considered crucial to employ the trans-national approach, which is the most important analytical tool that enables historians to better understand the global socio-economic movement that extended beyond national barriers. In order to shed light on the bigger questions posed by historians regarding the trans-national movement of people and commodities, as well as the impact of this on smaller territories and communities, it is extremely important to focus on how local economies were transformed by progressive global trends. The study of a given territory, whether western or eastern, developed or underdeveloped, is only a lone star shining in a large constellation of interconnected communities, offering clues that might help us decipher the global process of consumer transformation from the early days until the present. I hope not only to uncover some solutions, but also to identify some questions yet to have been posed. This research has itself proved to be an 'industrious' task and it has navigated trans-continentally to Europe, America and China, in order to seek partial solutions to global problems. I would certainly not have had the courage to undertake this task without the constant and unfailing support of Professor Bartolome Yun-Casalilla during my time at the Department of History and Civilization, European University Institute. We have not only talked, debated and exchanged scientific ideas, but he has also helped me in moments of personal difficulty. For this I am indebted to him and will always be grateful for his help. I must acknowledge professor Yun, as my supervisor, and the members of the jury of my thesis, such as professors Jan de Vries, Gerard Chastagnaret and Lucca Molà, for his comments and remarks during the defence of my thesis at the European University Institute, which has contributed to improving the text for publication.

My year as visiting scholar at the University of California, Berkeley, was certainly one of the most crucial periods in developing my work. I am immensely grateful to Professor Jan de Vries, who was my advisor and mentor at the Department of History and Economics at Berkeley. I must acknowledge Professor Jan de Vries for his patience in assisting me, his comments and remarks, and for introducing me to the academic community at Berkeley and allowing me the honour of collaborating with outstanding Professors such as Christina Romer, David Romer, Martha Olney and Brad de Long. I must not forget the help and assistance of other Professors from Berkeley who have helped transform my lectures, papers and presentations into this book. Professors Richard Herr, David Ringrose, Peter Sahlins, Carla Hesse, Thomas Dandelet and Barry Carr have all contributed to improve my understanding of how to read and interpret the historical discipline.

I need to thank the institutions and persons that have assisted me while I was undertaking research in various libraries and archives, which made this work possible. I would like to mention the administrative staff at: the British Library, the Archive of La Chambre de Commerce et Industrie de Marseille, the Doe and Bancroft Libraries at Berkeley, the European University Institute Library, Biblioteca Iberoamericana 'Octavio Paz' of Guadalajara (Mexico), Biblioteca Nacional de España, Centre de Documentació i Museu Tèxtil de Tarrasa, Archivo Histórico Provincial de Murcia, Archivo Municipal de Murcia, Archivo Municipal de Cartagena and Archivo Municipal de Lorca. I also want to mention my academic exchanges with outstanding scholars such as Glenn Stephen Murray Fantom (University of Valladolid), Rebecca Earle (Warwick University),

Fernando Ramos Palencia (Pablo Olavide University), Ramón Maruri (University of Cantabria), Eloy Martín Corrales (Pompeu Fabra University), François-Joseph Ruggiu (University of Paris IV-Sorbonne) and Lucio Manuel Rocha de Sousa (University of Tokyo). Their comments and questions have been crucial for improving the chapters of this book, as well as for its final outcome. Turning to my early education, special note is needed for those who have fed my passion for the Social Sciences in general, and History in particular, since I embarked upon my degree in History at the University of Murcia. I have become the professional historian I am today thanks to the education I received from the 'Seminario de Familia y Elite de Poder en el Reino de Murcia (ss. XV–XIX)'. Professors Francisco Chacón Jiménez, Juan Hernández Franco and Antonio Irigoyen López are responsible for encouraging my deep interest in learning, undertaking new scientific projects and being in permanent contact with researchers from diverse universities and cultures. From them I learnt that the learning process is a never-ending story. Isolation is a major danger and trap into which a researcher can fall.

No less important for my education as a scholar and individual is the outstanding contribution of my family. The family, as the main nucleus of society, is the social unit in which all values lie. Since I was a child, my interest in learning about cultures, people and the world around me has been inspired by the education I received from my family. I thank my mother, Encarnita, and my brothers and sisters María, Mariano, Encarnita and Angel for being so patient during these years and for being such a united family. And more particularly, my father, Dr Manuel Pérez García, as a scientist, but above all as a person, who taught me the most important lesson I learnt at any university: the 'art of listening' and how to be humble. Without his constant support and help I would not have been able to undertake this research project, especially during the moments of extreme difficulty that I encountered. The trans-nationality of this research took me to a different continent and culture, and it was there that I met my wife. Thank you Marisol for sharing your life with me, for being so patient with me and for opening my eyes to the culture of the 'New World'. The outcome of my research, reflection, understanding and way to approach the life and past cultures and civilizations is the most precious gift for which I will always be grateful to my family.

Manuel Pérez-García,
Tsinghua University, Beijing, China

List of Abbreviations

A.C.C.M.	Archive de la Chambre de Commerce de Marseille
A.H.P.M.	Archivo Histórico Provincial de Murcia
A.M.C.	Archivo Municipal de Cartagena
A.M.L.	Archivo Municipal de Lorca
A.M.M.	Archivo Municipal de Murcia
B.N.	Biblioteca Nacional, Madrid, Spain
C.D.M.T.	Centre de Documentació i Museu Tèxtil, Tarrasa, Spain
M.N.N.	Museo Naval Nacional, Madrid, Spain
M.N.T	Museo Nacional del Traje, Madrid, Spain
p.	Page
pp.	Pages
Scr.	Scribe
Sig.	Signature
Ref.	Reference

Modern Economic and Social History Series
General Editor's Preface

Economic and social history has been a flourishing subject of scholarly study during recent decades. Not only has the volume of literature increased enormously but the range of interest in time, space and subject matter has broadened considerably so that today there are many sub-branches of the subject which have developed considerable status in their own right.

One of the aims of this series is to encourage the publication of scholarly monographs on any aspect of modern economic and social history. The geographical coverage is worldwide and contributions on the non-British themes will be especially welcome. While emphasis will be placed on works embodying original research, it is also intended that the series should provide the opportunity to publish studies of a more general thematic nature which offer a reappraisal or critical analysis of major issues of debate.

Derek H. Aldcroft
University of Leicester

Introduction

The primary focus of this study is consumption and consumer behaviour during the period of transition from the *Ancien Regime* to the modern capitalist era. This topic has been considered in preeminent scholarly works during recent decades. Since McKendrick launched his 'trickle-down' thesis and Jan de Vries' 'industrious revolution' theory, both lines of investigation have marked subsequent studies on consumption. With regard to this research, the Spanish historiography has not given particular attention to this topic. There have, however, been a number of articles, papers and even a few theses that have investigated the patterns of consumption of Spanish society during the *Ancien Regime*. This is our point of departure.

The aim is to undertake a rigorous study on patterns of consumption and possible shifts of consumer behaviour during the second half of the eighteenth century and the early nineteenth century, by analysing the inner dynamics of households of a western Mediterranean area such as south-eastern Spain. During this period, family economies underwent a transformation due to the number of members able to work, as well as their ability to access goods supplied by the market. Jan de Vries considered this issue in his thesis, paying particular attention to the working classes, artisans and peasants, as the engine that propelled the new economic dynamics.

However, an innovative element of my research is the investigation of the role of merchants as mediators and 'vicarious consumers' that stimulated a demand for a large selection of commodities that earlier had not been enjoyed by ordinary people. Therefore, the 'trickle-down' theory will be criticized, as the circulation of certain commodities did not travel vertically between the upper and lower levels of the social hierarchy. The social circulation of goods did not, in fact, follow a methodical dynamic in society. By thoroughly analysing probate inventories, the importance of the role played by merchants, as economic agents who inspired consumers towards new tastes and thus new needs, will be revealed. Families were more market dependent as consumers than market orientated as producers. In addition, this approach is not focused on the study of local markets and particular urban or rural communities as with previous studies. One of the novel points of this work is that the market is emphasized as a common space, where global contacts, meetings and interactions took place. In a world that became increasingly more global, the circulation of people, especially trade communities, merchandise, as well as knowledge and technology, contributed to the transformation of the values and traditions of the new nation-states. The trans-national approach, therefore, allows us to visualize how the shifts in patterns of consumption were linked to socio-cultural influences motivated by regional, national and international connections.

Part I deals with the scholarly debate on consumption and consumer behaviour studies by identifying the main historiographical voids that need to be filled. The results of this research show that the main approaches to consumption that need to be taken into account must include trans-national studies; the internal dynamics of the household economy through the study of probate inventories; the combination of micro and macro studies; as well confirming the necessity for abandoning the obsessive search for the 'origins' of mass consumption societies or 'consumer revolutions'. Thus, in Part I, I outline the historiographical references, as well as the theories, main working hypothesis, sources and methods for the case study: an analysis of consumer behaviour in the western Mediterranean market, by focusing on the area of south-eastern Spain in a global perspective.

Part II looks closely at the controls on consumption exerted by the state, in order to stimulate national production. Agents of the state such as ministers, religious personalities or intellectual figures promoted the rejection of foreign goods and thwarted the acceptance of imported fashions. This social backlash, inspired by global trade, constituted the main element of exclusion towards foreign goods by traditional society. The state saw such imports as evidence of contamination; they represented a threat to the traditional identity of the nation. Stereotypes and prejudices against foreign cultures, which was a global phenomenon as this backlash also occurred elsewhere, for example in England, were therefore employed in the construction of an 'unreal' community and in the building of the new nation-state. This socio-political reaction is linked to the development of international markets. Part III explains how the Mediterranean import-export market was fostering the purchase of commodities due to the settlement in Spain of foreign trade communities, which acted as mediators with local and international markets. The French community of merchants, established in south-eastern Spain, stimulated the market not only for European goods but also for goods from America and Asia.

The demand-side was deeply affected by the role exerted by such commercial groups. In Part IV we can observe, through the study of probate inventories, the distribution of goods among all social groups. In addition, we can observe how household expenditure increased and how the birth of a large middle social class helped merchants to stimulate demand in order to sell superficial goods. In this section we see that in south-eastern Spain, a region lacking a strong artisan and peasant community able to provide merchandise to local towns and villages, goods were supplied from external markets. The appendices, which have been elaborated with the sample of probate inventories, show that merchants substituted the role of artisans and peasants in providing goods. There are some exceptions in which artisans provided manufactured goods with their own labour force. The development of certain urban areas, such as the growth of the port of Cartagena and the construction of its 'Arsenal', as well as the settlement of artisans, most of whom were foreigners, constitute the only cases in which artisan groups stimulated the demand. Nevertheless, the statistics presented in the appendices reveal that this occurred only to a very limited degree.

PART I
The History of Consumption: Debates, Theories, Methods, Sources and Data Bases

Scholars who have analysed material culture and consumption of the *Ancien Regime* have primarily focused on identifying the origins of the consumer society. Recently, the historiography has placed the accent on the comparative and transnational approaches, although these types of studies remain uncommon. It is hoped that this study will fill one of the chief voids in the historiography: the analysis of the patterns of consumption of the *Ancien Regime* through comparative and trans-national perspectives. The introductory part of this book highlights some of the studies about consumption that can be found in the current historiography. It will also introduce the objectives, main hypothesis and questions that have been considered to carry out this research, for example: how patterns of consumption during the eighteenth century in south-eastern Spain changed in light of the activities of trade agents. This region was in permanent contact with important commercial areas such as southern France (Marseille) and northern Italy (Genoa). It is, therefore, crucial to explore how the circulation of merchandise, people and their cultural habits altered consumer behaviour in the western Mediterranean area. The sources used for my study will be introduced and the challenges and advantages posed by each will be discussed. An explication of the methodology employed in this research will show how specific problems can be overcome, and thus respond to the questions raised.

Chapter 1
Studies on Consumption and Material Culture to Date

The study of the development and origin of the 'consumer society' has received increasing attention during recent years. Different approaches to the analyses of consumption in *Ancien Regime* societies have appeared, each attempting to locate the moment of transition in which individuals belonging to different social classes assumed new patterns of consumption, in order to improve their lifestyles, primarily through the acquisition of a wide range of commodities. An interest in understanding this subject developed shortly after the Second World War, and continued into the early 1960s. During this period, 'mass consumption' models started to develop on a wide scale in western European societies. The 1960s witnessed an 'economic boom' in the West, growing from the capitalist and free-market economic model. Most people began to enjoy a certain degree of leisure by purchasing new consumer goods such as televisions, cars and household appliances. The idea of the success of the 'open societies'[1] economic model began to emerge. This scheme offers an optimistic vision of the new possibilities offered by industrial development through the purchase and consumption of new commodities.

The historiography during the 1980s, which was heavily influenced by the positive economic vision of the former decades, stressed the analysis of the origin of 'mass consumption' society in Europe. The approaches assumed by this kind of analysis were influenced by British economic supremacy, which led the different stages of industrial development, exerting a notable influence on patterns of consumption in other European spaces during the period that includes the second half of the eighteenth century, the latter part of the nineteenth century and the beginning of the twentieth century. The former period hosted the opening of the new economic era in Europe. In the course of the latter phase, the different socio-professional groups began consuming commodities linked to an increase in leisure time and higher standards of living. As a result of these studies and focus, a publication by Neil McKendrick, John Brewer and J.H. Plumb, in 1982,

---

[1] This term was adopted by McKendrick, after Rostow, in his optimistic vision of the birth of consumer society. McKendrick, N., 'The Consumer Revolution of Eighteenth-century England', in McKendrick, N., Brewer, J. and Plumb, J.H. (eds), *The Birth of a Consumer Society. The Commercialization of Eighteenth-century England* (London: Europe Publications, 1982), pp. 9–33. See Rostow, W.W., *The Stages of Economic Growth: a Non-Communist Manifesto* (3rd edition, Cambridge: Cambridge University Press, 1990).

influenced the historiography of consumption, as did McKendrick's article about the 'consumer revolution' in eighteenth-century England.[2] The study of the birth of a consumer society in Europe was based on investigations carried out in the main urban areas of the Continent that were also the primary producers of the material goods that generated changes in patterns of consumption.

Some historians have linked the birth of consumer society to the intensification of the British trade exchanges of the eighteenth century.[3] Due to such exchanges a wide range of commodities were introduced from Asia and the American colonies, such as tea, chocolate, cacao, coffee and sugar.[4] The introduction of these goods to society provoked a shift in lifestyle, which altered consumer behaviour. This is evident in probate inventories which begin to include objects in the household such as tea-cups, chocolate pots or textiles (handkerchief, towels) and cutlery, offering a picture of the new tendencies in consumption toward new social habits, hygiene and personal image. Lorna Weatherill produced an important work on this matter concerning new household practices and domestic ornaments, however she only analysed the British side.[5] Thus, according to this interpretation, new social habits emerged, in particular those related to luxury, comfort and the satisfaction of an individual's aesthetic tastes.

John Brewer edited three volumes with Susan Staves, Roy Porter and Ann Bermingham, which constituted an important contribution to studies on consumption.[6] Nevertheless, these books fall into the same trap by studying consumer societies on a local and national scale, without taking into account transnational contacts in a world that became progressively more global. McKendrick's 'consumer revolution' theory occurs within societies that begin to possess an increasing volume of goods that had not previously been enjoyed. These goods extended throughout the market on regional, national and international scales. Due to the rising acquisition of commodities by individuals with different levels of wealth, a 'boom' in consumption occurred:

---

    [2]   McKendrick, N., Brewer, J. and Plumb, J.H. (eds), *The Birth*.

    [3]   Thirsk, J., *Economic Policy and Projects. The Development of a Consumer Society in Early Modern England* (Oxford: Clarendon Press, 1978). Berg, M., 'Commerce and Creativity in Eighteenth-century Birmingham', in Berg, M., *Markets and Manufacture in Early Industrial Europe* (London and New York: Routledge, 1991), pp. 173–201.

    [4]   Shammas, C., *The Pre-Industrial Consumer in England and America* (Oxford: Clarendon Press, 1990).

    [5]   See Weatherill, L., *Consumer Behavior and Material Culture in Britain, 1660–1760* (London and New York: Routledge, 1988).

    [6]   Brewer, J. and Porter, R., *Consumption and the World of Goods* (London and New York: Routledge, 1993). Brewer, J. and Staves, S., *Early Modern Conceptions of Property* (London and New York: Routledge, 1994). Brewer, J. and Bermingham, A., *The Consumption of Culture, 1600–1800: Image, Object, Text* (London and New York: Routledge, 1995).

There was a consumer boom in England in the eighteenth century. In the third quarter of the century that boom reached revolutionary proportions ... For the consumer revolution was the necessary analogue to the industrial revolution, the necessary convulsion on the demand side of the equation to match the convulsion on the supply side.[7]

This phenomenon was referred to by McKendrick as the 'trickle-down' theory, which involved the emulation of the upper classes' behaviour, especially their patterns of consumption, by the middle and lower social groups. This trend for emulation went from the top to the bottom of the social hierarchy and McKendrick establishes that the 'trickle-down' theory can only appear within open societies. These societies have specific features, such as a flexible social hierarchy, a reasonable level of income, as well as established channels and networks for distributing wealth.

Nevertheless, historians argue that this process of 'emulation' changed the patterns of consumption. For instance, Cissie Fairchilds stresses the concept of 'emulation', 'luxury' and 'trickle-down' as valid for the analysis of the introduction of new social manners: 'a lower class prosperous enough to own a few luxuries and eager to follow the latest vagaries of fashion', by which 'populuxe goods were desired as symbols of an aristocratic lifestyle'.[8] We also find critics like Lorna Weatherill, who does not believe the application of such concepts is useful for studies on consumer behaviour.[9] Instead she sees it more appropriate to study the diffusion of goods related to the wealth of social classes. Other scholars such as Amanda Vickery support Weatherill's assessment.[10] There is, therefore, an important distinction to be made when applying the concept of 'emulation' depending on the case study.

In his work on the practices of consumption in the Dutch society of the seventeenth and eighteenth centuries, Jan de Vries indicates that the concept of 'emulation' was applied to English historiography as a result of Harold Perkins' thesis.[11] Perkins argues that the main goal of English merchants was to escape their 'bourgeois' roots and achieve upward mobility on the slippery social ladder. Hence, merchants would emulate the manners, habits and social behaviour of

---

[7]   McKendrick, N., 'The Consumer Revolution', p. 9.

[8]   Fairchilds, C., 'The Production and Marketing of Populuxe Goods in Eighteenth-century Paris', in Brewer, J. and Porter, R. (eds), *Consumption*, pp. 228–48.

[9]   Weatherill, L., 'The Meaning of Consumer Behaviour in Late Seventeenth-and Early Eighteenth Century England', in Brewer, J. and Porter, R., *Consumption*, pp. 206–27.

[10]   Vickery, A., 'Women and the World of Goods: a Lancashire Consumer and her Possessions, 1751–1781', in Brewer, J. and Porter, R., *Consumption*, pp. 274–301.

[11]   Perkins, H., *The Origins of Modern English Society* (London: Routledge and Kegan Paul, 1968). See also De Vries, J., 'Luxury in the Dutch Golden Age in Theory and Practice', in Berg, M. and Eger, E. (eds), *Luxury in the Eighteenth Century. Debates, Desires and Delectable goods* (New York: Palgrave Macmillan, 2003), pp. 41–56.

the nobility. An immediate consequence of the consumption of commodities and luxury goods that could not be acquired by all social groups was the adoption of new 'habitus' and the refined manners of individuals' behaviour. Consequently, people took on a hedonist aesthetic, by showing their preference for a new 'ostentatious'[12] and 'conspicuous' lifestyle through the purchase of a wide range of goods. Conspicuous expenditure occurs when an individual's attitude follows a compulsive tendency for the consumption of a wide variety of goods, most of them unnecessary to meet basic needs. This inclination is marked as a natural feature of human behaviour, where the aim is to emulate and desire the lifestyle of the upper classes:

> The motive is emulation – the stimulus of an invidious comparison which prompts us to outdo those with whom we are in the habit of classing ourselves. Substantially the same proposition is expressed in the commonplace remark that each class envies and emulates the class next above it in the social scale, while rarely compares itself with those below or with those who are considerable in advance.[13]

According to this idea then, each social class envies and emulates the social habits of the group above it, and rarely compares itself with the lowest or very highest classes, which can never be reached. In this vein, Veblen refers to the concept of 'vicarious consumption', the purpose of which is to praise those individuals situated at the apex of the social hierarchy. This new mode of consumption is revealed through the acquisition of selective items such as elaborate clothing or rare, luxurious objects. The 'vicarious agents' are normally those individuals belonging to upper classes or trade sectors that established and popularized new articles to stimulate personal consumption.[14]

These theories, which refer to the consumption of material goods and desire for a better lifestyle through social emulation, had an important impact on the historiography of the 1980s. There is no doubt that one of the pioneers in the study of European material culture was Fernand Braudel. By studying the structures of the quotidian spaces and daily routines of French society he analysed material elements and their slow process of transformation in Europe.[15] Braudel's work

---

[12]   See the chapters 'L'habitus et l'espace des styles de vie' and 'Le sens de la distinction', in Bourdieu, P., *La distinction. Critique sociale du jugement* (Paris: Les editions de minuit, 1979).

[13]   See chapter five, 'The Pecuniary Standard of Living', in Veblen, T., *The Theory of the Leisure Class. An Economic Study of the Institutions* (New York: The Modern Library, 1934), pp. 102–3.

[14]   Gladwell, M., *The Tipping Point: How Little Things Can Make a Big Difference* (Boston, M.A.: Little Brown, 2000).

[15]   Braudel, F., *Civilisation matérielle, économie, capitalisme, XVᵉ–XVIIIᵉ siècle. Les structures du quotidien: le impossible et le impossible* (Tome I, Paris: Armand Colin, 1979).

shows the generalization in Europe of the trend for using cutlery when eating, especially around 1750,[16] which confirms the importance of improved lifestyles, such as how to prepare a banquet for dining in the company of the upper classes.

Braudel's approach significantly influenced the French and Italian history of consumption. While there are few works in the French and Italian historiography, there are nonetheless important references by Giovanni Levi,[17] Paolo Malamina,[18] Maria Antonia Visceglia and Renata Ago.[19] Daniel Roche focuses his attention on an analysis of the clothing of different social groups, studying the use of textiles, colours and embellishment of costumes, which can be examined through probate inventories. The presence of such objects, as elements of distinction among the social actors, is the main evidence pointing to the acquisition of new lifestyles. Roche uses the concept of 'revolution des apparences'[20] to study the French Enlightenment period, when changes in dress took place, playing an important role in the socio-economic and political transformation.

There is an opposing strand of historiographical research that does not accept the application of the concept of a 'consumer revolution', as it does not properly explain the root of economic transformations that occurred on the demand side. In other words, traditional research, based on the 'consumer revolution' theory, does not take into account consumer decisions, when their buying power and level of wealth suffer alterations. These transformations exert an influence on the demand for objects, by shaping, at the same time, new strategies of marketing. The analysis of this fact needs to be included in studies of consumption, as only in doing so can we obtain a full picture of the causes and forces that stimulate the demand side. The study of changes in patterns of consumption has significantly influenced research on material culture. This type of analysis has accounted for transformations in consumption by investigating the economic dynamics that took place within the household unit.[21] This factor substantially influences the market considerations as well as those of the supply of products. Jan de Vries establishes that before the Industrial Revolution an 'industrious revolution' took place, in

---

[16]   Braudel, F., *Civilisation matérielle*, p. 173.

[17]   Levi, G., 'Comportements, ressources, procès: avant la "révolution" de la consommation', in Revel, J. (ed.), *Jeux d'échelles. La micro-analyse à l'experience* (Paris: Hautes Études, Gallimard Le Seuil, 1996), pp. 187–207.

[18]   Malamina, P., *Il lusso dei contadini. Consumi e industrie nella campagne toscane del Sei e Settecento* (Bolonia: Il Mulino, 1990).

[19]   Visceglia, M.A., 'I consumi in Italia in età moderna', in Romano, R. (ed.), *Storia dell'economia italiana. Tomo II. L'età moderna: verso la crisi* (Turin: Einaudi editore, 1991), pp. 219–23. Ago, R., *Il gusto delle cose. Una storia degli oggetti nella Roma del Seicento* (Roma: Donzelli Editore, 2006).

[20]   Roche, D., *La culture des apparences. Une histoire du vêtement XVIIe–XVIIIe siècle* (Paris: Fayard, 1989).

[21]   De Vries, J., 'Between the Purchasing Power and the World of Goods: Understanding the Household Economy in the Early Modern Europe', in Brewer, P. and Porter, R. (eds), *Consumption*, pp. 107–8.

which the factors that involve the demand- and supply-side played an important role. This earlier phase, the 'industrious revolution', opened the door to a whole range of technological changes. For a better comprehension of this technological stage it is necessary for us to understand the role of the household, and especially the function of artisan and peasant families, in stimulating the production and purchase of new material goods.[22]

1.1. The Analysis of Consumption Through the Trans-national and Comparative Perspective

One of the major factors that accounts for the historiographical deficit in analysing the history of consumption and material culture without the approach of global history has been the obsession among scholars for seeking the 'origins' of European consumer societies, which set the stage for the Industrial Revolution process. These researchers have primarily considered the English case when examining economic transformations. Craig Clunas focuses his critique in opposition to John Brewer's thesis, which exerted an important influence on studies that have dealt with the analysis of changes in consumer behaviour. Clunas advocates using a different analysis and approach, which should take into account 'contacts', 'meetings' and 'connections' with external agents removed from national boundaries and geographical limits.[23] Through this perspective, historians could shed light on the problematic search for the origin and nature of technological, socio-economic, political and cultural transformations.

Later research challenges this strong national exceptionality by formulating questions and hypothesis within a global context. There are significant works that put into contact different intercontinental realities through the application of the trans-national perspective, such as the relations between Asia and Europe in the modern period. For instance, we can find studies that deal with socio-cultural exchanges during the modern age, by reviewing the history of China[24] and its relations with European areas. In these types of studies the influence of trade exchanges, in the later socio-economic development of European territories, is examined.

The studies prepared by Anne Raddef are connected with the aforementioned historiographical perspective, by stressing the idea of a global economy that operated throughout Western Europe during the eighteenth century. She

---

[22]   De Vries, J., 'The Industrial Revolution and the Industrious Revolution', *The Journal of Economic History*, vol. 54, no. 2 (June 1994), pp. 249–70.

[23]   Clunas, C., 'Modernity Global and Local: Consumption and the Rise of the West', *The American Historical Review*, vol. 104, no. 5. (December, 1999), p. 1503.

[24]   Adshead, S.A.M, *Material Culture in Europe and China, 1400–1800* (New York and London: St Martin's Press and Macmillan, 1997). Clunas, C., *Pictures and Visuality in Early Modern China* (Princeton: Princeton University Press, 1997).

analyses the Franc-Count, Savoy and Swiss economy at both micro and macro levels, by observing how local economies reacted to changes in wholesale and international commerce, especially as a result of the introduction of abundant types of commodities at ports and on commercial routes.[25] Therefore, according to her theory, the attainment of better standards of living lies in the dynamism and diversity of the domestic economy, which allows the population to afford new items related to personal comfort and leisure.

Through an analysis of new patterns of consumption, Maxime Berg observes the development of trade networks within a global perspective, signalling the importance of the importation of luxury goods from colonies, as a central aspect in the shift of lifestyles.[26] In her opinion, this factor played a more important role for the changes of consumer behaviour than the social emulation of fashions and manners of aristocratic and courtly circles. Within this approach, the current historiography is reviewing the transformation of consumer societies, taking into account the trans-national relations between the Euro-Asian and Atlantic areas through the interactions of the trade exchange networks. These economic circuits stimulated the consumption of exotic goods, such as colonial groceries, exchanges of raw materials for manufactured goods, as well as the introduction of Asian commodities such as Chinese porcelains. Robert Bachelor explores such socio-economic exchanges, by pointing out that the historiography has paid more attention to the 'different births' of consumer societies than to considering the influence of diverse geographic areas on industrial development.[27] He emphasizes that rather than explore the birth of consumer societies, historians should examine consumer habits that were transferred by means of 'trans-cultural' fashions, which were introduced due to successful connections of trade networks.

John Brewer takes into account all these historiographic critiques, by recognizing the historiographic 'error' in the studies of consumption. This error lies in the obsession for searching for the 'birth' of consumer societies, which in his opinion did not take place at the end of the eighteenth century, and in using primarily the Eurocentric perspective as a reference, especially British industrial development.[28] He suggests that this historiographical obsession has blocked the understanding of the process of transformation on consumer behaviour. New

---

[25] Radeff, A., *Du café dans le chaudron. Économie globale d'Ancien Régime. Suisse Occidentale, Franche-Comté et Savoie* (Lausanne: Société d'Histoire de la Suisse Romande, 'Mémoires et documents', 1996).

[26] Berg, M., 'In Pursuit of Luxury: Global History and British Consumer Goods in the Eighteenth Century', *Past and Present*, no. 182 (February 2004), pp. 85–142.

[27] Batchelor, R., 'On the Movement of Porcelains. Rethinking the Birth of Consumer Society as Interactions of Exchange Networks, 1600–1750', in Brewer, J. and Trentmann, F. (eds), *Consuming Cultures, Global Perspectives. Historical Trajectories, Transnational Exchanges* (Oxford and New York: Berg, 2006), pp. 95–121.

[28] Brewer, J., *The Error of Our Ways: Historians and the Birth of Consumer Society*, Working Paper 12 (June 2004), www.consume.bbk.ac.uk, p. 18.

studies need to pay greater attention to the role played by peripheral economies as well as global encounters.[29]

It is therefore necessary to shift the analysis toward the framework of Global History,[30] in which the comparative and trans-national approaches are used to emphasize the exchanges of ideas and new policies made by the new nation-states. The progressive opening and connection of markets, by which different geo-political and territorial areas are linked, plays an important role as a unifying element for the construction of a common economic project between these spaces. The key issue is that the problem of consumption studies should not be analysed through the 'macro' or 'micro' approaches, but historians should consider both scales together by taking into account the 'trans-cultural' and 'trans-critical' perspectives.[31] Therefore, it is not only important to analyse in what way those exchanges occurred, but scholars should also bear in mind the complexity of the diverse socio-economic factors characterized by such interconnections[32].

The history of consumption and material culture is a field in which we find remarkable challenges which historians have to confront by posing a wide range of questions, in order to update preceding works. The historiography of consumption and material culture has yet to have surpassed its major problems, since it has not used the comparative perspective. In light of this problem, Peter Burke makes a relevant critique[33] in his unique contribution to Brewer's volumes on consumption. Burke challenges the classic perspectives on European studies of consumption, by analysing and comparing the different socio-cultural relations beyond Europe, in particular by bearing in mind the reality of Asian colonies. He points out the need for focusing the studies on consumption outside of the European arena. Through this approach, scholars would be able to establish what is pertinent to the occidental sphere, by taking into account all the factors that are interrelated and exert an influence on a more global process of transformation of western and eastern regions. The historian's attention, therefore, would not be focused solely on the exclusiveness of the British case as it has previously been. The imminent consequence of this historiographical void, caused by the obsession with analysing the British case, is the current need to use the comparative perspective to enhance studies on consumption and material culture. However, we can indeed find some works that have taken this approach into account. These

[29]   Brewer, J. and Trentmann, F., 'Introduction. Space, Time and Value in Consuming Cultures', in Brewer, J. and Trentmann, F., *Consuming Cultures*, pp. 1–17.

[30]   O'Brien, P., 'Historiographical Traditions and Modern Imperatives for the Restoration of Global History', *Journal of Global History*, 1 (2006), pp. 3–39.

[31]   Batchelor, R., 'On the Movement of Porcelains', p. 116.

[32]   Pomeranz, K., *The Great Divergence: China, Europe and the Making of the Modern World Economy* (Princeton: Princeton University Press, 2000).

[33]   Burke, P., 'Res et verba: Conspicuous Consumption in the Early Modern World', in Brewer, J. and Porter, R., *Consumption*, 1993. From the same author: *Varieties of Cultural History* (Ithaca, N.Y.: Cornell University Press, 1997).

began to appear towards the end of the 1990s when researchers, influenced by the economic forces of modern globalization, saw that the processes of socio-cultural relations must be studied within a trans-continental framework.

One of the most relevant works on material culture studies, which uses the comparative perspective, was prepared by Steana Nenadic.[34] This author compares the patterns of consumption of middle social groups in Scotland, considering the particular case of the urban areas of Glasgow and Edinburgh during the eighteenth century. Nenadic uses the comparative perspective on a regional scale, taking into account the trade networks that played an important role in the changes in habits of consumption. She conducts her research on a micro-analytical level, contrary to Berg, Clunas and Batchelor,[35] focusing on 'trans-regional' and 'inter-regional' connections, as a dynamic process by which the trade exchanges of both Scottish cities took place. Consequently, through studies with a local approach, comparing two outstanding territories that were connected with other important European cities, historians can analyse how socio-economic and cultural transfers took place, within the broad framework of trans-national history. This approach allows researchers to better understand the process of the construction of the global village, in a world that became more interconnected.

1.2. Studies on Consumption in Spanish Historiography

The Spanish historiography has dealt with studies on consumption, standards of living and material culture. During the 1980s, this topic was practically absent in the historiography. It started to emerge, to some degree, during the beginning of the 1990s, through the organization of congresses and scientific events,[36] as well as the publication of some articles and papers. However, these studies were focused more on the contemporary age rather than on pre-industrial societies. This historiographical vacuum is even more noticeable if we refer to the studies on consumption through the comparison of rural areas with cities. This would enable scholars to understand important aspects such as how patterns of consumption were disseminated, the similarities or differences between agrarian and urban communities regarding new habits and the consumption of goods, the distribution of wealth among nearby regions and how these factors could exert an influence on the transformation of lifestyles and fashions.

---

[34]   Nenadic, S., 'Middle-Rank Consumers and Domestic Culture in Edinburgh and Glasgow 1720–1840', *Past and Present*, no. 145 (November 1994), pp. 122–56.

[35]   Berg, M., *Luxury and Pleasure*. Clunas, C., 'Modernity'. Batchelor, R., 'On the Movement of Porcelains'.

[36]   Fontana, J., 'Nivel de vida, calidad de vida: un intento de estado de la cuestión y algunas reflexiones', in *Actas del XV Simposi d'Analisi Econòmica. Nivells de vida a Espanya, ss. XIX i XX* (Barcelona: Universitat Autònoma de Barcelona, 1990), pp. 1–12.

We do not find an important contribution to this topic until 1994, when the papers of the *International Economic History Congress*, held in Milan, were published. The papers presented at this congress, in connection with studies on consumption for the Spanish late modern age, such as those by Bartolome Yun and Jesus Cruz,[37] are significant for the Spanish historiography. By studying probate inventories, Cruz points out that the adoption of new patterns of consumption was inspired by the acquisition of new political idiosyncrasies during the political period of construction of the new European nation-states.[38] Cruz uses as a reference the study by Carmen Martin Gaite,[39] whose thesis refers to the intellectual debate about whether Spanish patterns of consumption underwent a change due to the influence of specific structural transformations in fashions or behaviour at social gatherings during the eighteenth century. Cruz concludes that the incorporation of the middle social groups into the 'consumer revolution' process was caused by a system of 'cultural assimilation', rather than a sudden improvement in the economic model.

McKendrick's 'consumer revolution' and De Vries' 'industrious revolution' theories began to be taken into account by Spanish historians at the end of the 1990s. Maximo Garcia and Bartolome Yun explored the social diffusion of goods,[40] by deconstructing McKendrick's thesis on patterns of consumption. Their main conclusion is that the process of emulation of consumer habits does not have to follow an upward-downward movement or vice versa. The consumption of new items needs to be framed under the circumstances by which a specific commodity is popularized, by analysing the social agents that stimulate the purchase of goods. In relation to the theories proposed by De Vries, Fernando Ramos Palencia has considered the demand side through his study on the levels of wealth of

---

[37] Professor Yun's paper is focused on the analysis of rural standards of living and material culture in the Duero Valley region. Yun Casalilla, B., 'Peasant Material Culture in Castile (1750–1900): Some Proposals', in Schuurman, A.J. and Walsh, L.S. (eds), *Material Culture: Consumption, Life-Style, Standard of Living, 1500–1900* (Milan: Eleventh International Economic History Congress, September, 1994), pp. 125–36. Cruz, J., 'Elites, Merchants, and Consumption in Madrid at the End of the Old Regime', in Schuurman, A.J. and Walsh, L.S. (eds), *Material Culture*, pp. 137–56.

[38] Cruz, J., 'La construcción de una nueva identidad liberal en el Madrid del siglo XIX: el papel de la cultura material en el hogar', *Revista de Historia Económica* (2003), pp. 181–206. From the same author: *Gentleman, Bourgeois and Revolutionaries. Political Change and Cultural Persistence among the Spanish Dominant Groups, 1750–1850* (New York: Cambridge University Press, 1996).

[39] Martin Gaite, C., *Los usos amorosos del dieciocho en España* (Madrid: Siglo XXI, 1972), p. 22.

[40] García Fernández, M. and Yun Casalilla, B., 'Pautas de consumo, estilos de vida y cambio político en las ciudades castellanas a fines del Antiguo Régimen. Sobre algunas perspectivas del crecimiento económico desde la perspectiva de la demanda', in Fortea Pérez, J.I. (ed.), *Imágenes de la diversidad. El mundo urbano en la Corona de Castilla (ss. XVI–XVIII)* (Santander: Universidad de Cantabria, 1997), p. 276.

Castilian communities, as well as the evolution of household expenditures during periods of crisis and high mortality. Ramos concludes that for the Castilian case, especially in the area of Palencia, an 'industrious revolution' occurred without industrialization.[41]

Later works on studies of consumption have been made using this approach. The most notable example is the book edited by Jaume Torras and Bartolome Yun,[42] in which, for the first time in the Spanish historiography on consumption, standards of living, the acquisition of new fashions and consumer behaviour are all compared by means of the analysis of the Castilian and Catalonian territories.[43] Likewise, the primary centres of commercial diffusion of goods, such as the ports of Barcelona and Santander,[44] were analysed in order to explore the consolidation and formation of a new middle social group that was being enriched by mercantile businesses. In the prologue of the book by Torras and Yun we find an analysis of Spanish studies on consumption and standards of living, in which professor Yun remarks that the historiographical void on this topic should be filled with approaches and analyses that take into account socio-economic and cultural transfers in a comparative and global perspective.[45]

1.3. Contribution to the Topic of Consumption: Main Working Hypothesis

After presenting the historiographical debates and theories in the studies of consumption, it is necessary to indicate the main focus of the case study: the analysis of a non-industrialized area, the Kingdom of Murcia – located in south-eastern Castile – and its connections with the Mediterranean areas, specifically

[41]   Ramos Palencia, F., 'La demanda de textiles en las familias castellanas del Antiguo Régimen: ¿aumento del consumo sin revolución industrial?', *Revista de Historia Económica*, no. Extraordinario, Año XXI (2003), pp. 141–80.

[42]   Torras Elías, J. and Yun Casalilla, B. (eds), *Consumo, condiciones de vida y comercialización. Cataluña y Castilla, ss. XVII–XIX* (Valladolid: Junta de Castilla y León, 1999).

[43]   Moreno Claverías, B., 'La burguesía local de las letras y los negocios a través de los inventarios post-mortem. El Penedés del siglo XVIII', in Torras Elías, J. and Yun Casalilla, B. (eds), *Consumo*, pp. 71–88. For the Castilian rural areas, and especially for the hinterland of Palencia, see: Ramos Palencia, F., 'Una primera aproximación al consumo en el mundo rural castellano a través de los inventarios post-mortem: Palencia, 1750–1840', in Torras Elías, J. and Yun Casalilla, B. (eds), *Consumo*, pp. 107–32.

[44]   Maruri Villanueva, R., 'Vestir el cuerpo, vestir la casa. El consumo de textiles en la burguesía mercantil de Santander, 1750–1850', in Torras Elías, J. and Yun Casalilla, B. (eds), *Consumo*, pp. 159–82. From the same author: *La burguesía mercantil santanderina, 1700–1850* (Santander: Asamblea Regional de Cantabria, D.L., 1990).

[45]   Yun Casalilla, B., 'La historia económica por el lado de la demanda y el consumo: unas reflexiones generales', in Torras Elías, J. and Yun Casalilla, B. (eds), *Consumo*, pp. 9–26.

with southern France. The chief aim is to analyse possible shifts in consumer behaviour from 1730 to 1808. The purpose is to place particular emphasis on the analysis of the consumption of durable and semi-durable goods, which were capable of transferring new cultural identities and patterns of sociability, as well as inspiring the acceptance or rejection of such models by the traditional social classes. In other words, the introduction of objects, seen as new or exotic, could cause a backlash among traditional sectors of society. Scholars, who have not incorporated the trans-national dimension of goods in their historical analysis, have largely disregarded this issue.

The study of merchant groups, especially foreign groups settled in the Kingdom of Murcia, is in my opinion fundamental, since their presence stimulated trade exchanges, as well as growth in the south-eastern Castilian economy during the second half of the eighteenth century. This merchant group was composed primarily of traders who came from France (Marseille, Beàrn), Italy (Genoa, Venice) and Malta. The analysis of merchants is crucial to this investigation, because those individuals, as socio-economic agents, promoted the circulation of goods in society, challenging the traditional customs and increasing household expenditure. These merchants enhanced the communities in which they settled through the transfer of new cultural ideas and lifestyles. The study of these communities, as trans-national groups, is the main feature of the analysis, enabling us to better understand the changes in Spanish patterns of consumption. This foreign social group brought with them new cultural forms and undoubtedly ruffled feathers among traditional society, as they stimulated the purchase of goods seen as 'rare'. It is necessary to thoroughly investigate the socio-cultural influences of these traders and businessmen, as mediators in the introduction of a wide variety of goods, and whether or not new cultural idiosyncrasies occurred in the social hierarchy due to the acquisition of such goods. The case of French merchants, especially traders belonging to the textile sector, will thus be emphasized in order to analyse the introduction of new materials and foreign clothing that could exert an influence on the adoption of new customs, habits and dress.

The introduction of objects into the household, especially luxury items, which include among others, mirrors, clocks, chocolate pots, tableware, napkins, towels and porcelains, played an important role in European societies of the modern age. The consumption of such goods was related to the establishment of new habits and tastes, concern for personal appearance and the private lives of members of the family unit. The introduction of such goods directs the research towards the analysis of their circulation in the household space, especially in the case of south-eastern Castile. The study of the channels of diffusion of these goods, by which merchants exerted their role as mediators in the purchase and sale of commodities, deserves special attention.

In connection with this issue, one of the primary questions to be tackled by this study is what kind of durable and semi-durable goods were consumed by different social groups of a non-industrialized Mediterranean area, such as the Kingdom of Murcia. Special attention is given to urban and rural areas of Murcia, and Cartagena, which was the main port of Castile, where a large range of goods were introduced as a result of commerce with merchants from Marseille. Other important questions related to this issue emerge and we must also consider: how were new patterns of consumption and habits developed in social groups? How did the introduction of new fashions transform day-to-day life? Was a consequence of this the adoption of new socio-cultural idiosyncrasies? In other words, the analysis of contracts carried out by traders, which allowed the introduction of foreign goods and the increase of purchases by individuals with different levels of wealth, is a major aspect of the European economic transformation that needs further investigation. A thorough analysis of this process will provide an answer to the question as to whether the traditional society of *Ancien Regime* Europe was challenged by the adoption of new fashions and habits, those that crossed social, religious and economic boundaries.

These questions can be answered by examining the transformations that emerge in the patterns of consumption of durable, semi-durable and comestible goods, as well as establishing a typology or 'hierarchization' for the purchases of such commodities by social groups with diverse levels of wealth. These questions can be linked by considering them in relation to the consumption and wealth of the family unit. The analysis of the typology of goods purchased, as well as the increase in household expenditure, offers clues about the possible shifts in consumer behaviour. This objective can be achieved by analysing the dowries and probate inventories of families with different levels of wealth, as well as through the examination of manuscripts that reflect the social backlash caused by the transformation of habits of consumption. The study of dowries is particularly crucial as it is through them that it becomes possible to chart new social habits and fashions of material culture. Women played an essential role in the introduction of new fashions, as we can observe by the changes in fashions for dress. Despite the obvious use of these sources for historians, in terms of offering a full picture of the new trends in consumption, Spanish and other European historiographies have not yet focused on these.

Therefore, the main working hypothesis is based on foreign merchants, who settled in Murcia and Cartagena and stimulated a demand among the population for a wide range of commodities, allowing individuals with different levels of wealth to purchase goods that they could not previously afford. The concept of the 'trickle-down' effect will be challenged as upper classes, and especially the aristocracy, were not the sole agents in stimulating the consumption of goods among social groups. This hypothesis is not addressed by Neil McKendrick's apriorism about the emulation of the habits of the upper social classes. Instead, I emphasize the essential role played by merchant groups as mediators and 'vicarious consumers' in the distribution of goods, fuelling the regional economy and stimulating purchases by individuals with diverse levels of income. These merchants exerted an influence on the emulation of patterns of consumption, which did not only flow down the social hierarchy, but also flowed up: 'trickle-up'.[46]

---

[46]   García Fernández, M. and Yun Casalilla, B., *Consumo*, p. 276.

Another primary working hypothesis is designed to determine whether an 'industrious revolution' took place in the south-eastern region of Castile. This will take into account Jan de Vries' thesis which stresses the role played by artisan and peasant groups in the development of the economy, by stimulating the demand for new goods which encouraged self-production and consumption of goods being sold in the market. In this economic circuit, all members of the family unit played a role, often taking part in the production process, as well as performing one or two other jobs at the same time. This saw a growth in the levels of household income as a result. Nevertheless, in this research there is a further dimension to be added to the 'industrious revolution' theory: the merchant groups and their trade networks in the Mediterranean area. This fact may have stimulated the demand side, as a consequence, due to the role played by traders as mediators in the introduction of goods.

This economic expansion is not explained solely by the intensification of artisan and peasant workers, but needs also to take into account the trade links between different Mediterranean areas such as south-eastern Castile and Marseille. These exerted an important influence on consumer behaviour shifts. Raw materials were exported from the ports of Cartagena, Alicante, Valencia and Barcelona to Marseille, and from the latter port, such materials were distributed to artisan industries throughout southern France. Finally, the finished, ready-to-use products fabricated in French industries were re-exported from Marseille to Cartagena and other Spanish ports. These transfers meant that a wide range of goods were made available to south-eastern Castilian territories, thus increasing the demand.

Through this flow of merchandise and human migration, socio-economic and cultural transfers influenced the adoption of new lifestyles in Spain. In the south-eastern region of Castile, and especially in the Kingdom of Murcia, the export-import market functioned efficiently due to the lack of local production of goods, which helped to foster exports of raw materials such as silk and wool, as well as imports of textiles made from these materials. The commercial dynamism which occurred at the port of Cartagena during the second half of the eighteenth century had as a consequence the formation of a national, from Catalonia, Valencia and Madrid, and international merchant group such as the French, Italian and Maltese. It is, therefore, necessary to pose the following questions: what was the role of the merchant groups of Cartagena, who were mostly foreigners, as mediators and promoters of new products? What was their influence on the patterns of consumption of both the elite and ordinary people? What types of commodities, whether they merely met basic necessities or reached levels of 'conspicuous consumption', were introduced by these traders and wholesalers? And finally, in light of the latter question, did a 'revolution' in consumption occur between 1730 and 1808 in the Mediterranean area?

Chapter 2
Sources and Methodology

The study of consumer behaviour during the *Ancien Regime* period, through the analysis of probate inventories and dowries, enables us to answer key questions such as how the circulation of goods brought about changes in patterns of consumption in the Mediterranean area, in particular in the case of south-eastern Castile during the eighteenth century. Bearing in mind the challenges of this research, a comparison of probate inventories and dowries of south-eastern Castile from Murcia and Cartagena will be attempted, in order to examine the circulation of goods among different social groups. In the case of Marseille, the trade records of the 'Chambre de Commerce' offer us a broad impression of the import-export market of goods commercialized from Marseille that appear in Murcia probate inventories. This method will allow us to investigate socio-economic and cultural transfers from France, Marseille, to Spain, Murcia-Cartagena, related to changes in patterns of consumption and the building up of a new national identity through shifts occurring in everyday social habits. Such process is analysed through a micro-scale approach, by making chronological cross-sections between samples of probate inventories and dowries from Cartagena and Murcia, in particular those belonging to the merchant group. By searching for different types of commodities, the possible acquisition of new habits and fashions, transferred in the Mediterranean area due to the constant movement of people, become apparent. Therefore, foreign merchant groups emerge as the main social agents that transformed the material culture of interconnected regions and communities.

The creation of a new database, by using computer programs such as 'Access', will allow us to identify the social circulation of goods. In doing so, trade records from Marseille, as well as probate inventories and dowries from Murcia, can be cross-examined to explore new tendencies in consumption. It has also been very important to incorporate other sources, such as manuscripts and a census record entitled the 'Catastro de la Ensenada'. The latter is a tax source that provides detailed information about the annual incomes of individuals belonging to different socio-professional categories. Treatises and manuscripts written by contemporaries who expressed their opinions on the changes in lifestyle brought about by foreign fashions are also used. An analysis of these texts offers interesting insights about the social reactions to the consumption of certain goods. In general, during the eighteenth century in Europe, a social backlash occurred as result of the global process of diffusion of foreign habits that was to progressively change the traditions and customs of interconnected communities.

2.1. Probate Inventories and Dowries: Some Methodological Problems

In the following pages, the main problems of using probate inventories and dowries, as primary sources, for the analysis of patterns of consumption of the *Ancien Regime* society will be described. In addition, it is important to establish the characteristics, nature and chronology of such sources. For the period that spans between 1730 and 1808, 339 records from different social classes, aristocracy, merchants, artisans, professionals, yeomen, have been examined, taking into account the different levels of wealth of each group. These families were settled in the urban and rural parts of Murcia, as well as the port of Cartagena and its hinterland. The sample of these 339 documents can be broken down into 273 probate inventories and 66 dowries. Dowries must be differentiated into three sub-groups: 'cartas de dote' [letters of dowry], 'escrituras de dote' [registers of dowry] and 'recibos de dote' [receipts of dowry].

Probate Inventories

Probate inventories are the most important source for the study of the economy from the demand-side, as well as for issues related to material culture and consumption during the *Ancien Regime*.[1] By classifying items that appear in probate inventories, we can determine the different patterns of consumption and lifestyles of individuals with differing levels of wealth, professions and social status. Works by Anton Schuurman and Ad Van der Woude[2] show the benefits and pitfalls of using probate inventories. In their book, these sources are studied in depth by describing their different sections, origin, elaboration and the way in which inventories were created. For instance, for the study of the inventories of the French city of Meaux, Micheline Baulant describes how the documents were drawn up: the description of goods found in different rooms in the household, the declaration of family members and the enumeration of debtors and creditors.[3] However, this author remarks that in the document there are notable omissions such as the object's value or whether an item is intended for domestic use or sale. Collaborators of Schuurman's book analyse the different European probate inventories such as those from the Low Countries, England, Germany, France and Greece.

Probate inventories were written at the time of the head of family's death and there are some similarities between European probate inventories; however,

---

[1] See: Torras Elías, J. and Yun Casalilla, B. (eds), *Consumo*; Van der Woude, A. and Schuurman, A. (eds), *Probate Inventories. A New Source for the Historical Study of Wealth, Material Culture and Agricultural Development* (Utrecht: Hes Publishers, 1980).

[2] Schuurman, A., 'Probate inventories: research issues, problems and results', in Van der Woude, A. and Schuurman, A. (eds), *Probate Inventories*, pp. 19–31.

[3] Baulant, M., 'Enquête sur les inventaires après décès autour de Meaux aux XVIIᵉ–XVIIIᵉ siècles', in Schuurman, A. and Walsh, L.S. (eds), *Material Culture*, pp. 141–8.

depending on the area that is analysed, certain nuances or differences emerge.[4] The most significant differences are in the valuation of goods. In Castilian probate inventories, the value of goods is not always provided whereas Catalonian inventories never list the evaluation of commodities. The fact that the value is mentioned in inventories is very important because it allows us to learn about the economic status of the family and its buying power, by examining the purchases of new goods. Also, this feature enables us to classify an individual's level of wealth. There are some common features in Castilian and French [5] probate inventories. For both countries the similarities are present in the preamble, where the origin and nature of the document is described. In this preamble the relatives of the person (such as the wife or husband, parents or grandparents) who contracts the service for the document to be drawn up by a notary may or may not appear. Information such as place of birth, provenance, residence as well as the socio-professional category of the individual may also be described, which allows us to determine his socio-economic status. By examining the possessions listed, we can discern much about the deceased person's lifestyle and whether a transformation in consumer behaviour had occurred. Through the analysis of different individuals which appear in probate inventories such as the notary, witnesses and relatives, we can establish the social network to which the deceased belonged. The individual's social relationships, such as his social circle, friendships or close acquaintances, can be discovered through the witnesses and executors appointed to the deed, since such appointments were entrusted to persons belonging to the social network, family or friends, of the deceased person.

The most important section of the document is the list of possessions. It is important to note that within probate inventories other documents can occasionally appear which facilitate our understanding of the way in which the inventory was made. Such documents might be wills, commercial letters or certificates that show the names of executors, witnesses and notaries who evaluated the possessions. Additionally, in Castilian probate inventories we occasionally find 'declaraciones juradas' [sworn statements], which were made for tax purposes, elaborated during the second half of the eighteenth century, to measure the head of the family's level of income. As Jan de Vries mentions, we can consider probate inventories as the

---

[4] For Catalonian probate inventories, see: Lencina Pérez, X., 'Los inventarios post-mortem en el estudio de la cultura material y el consumo. Propuesta metodológica. Barcelona, siglo XVII', in Torras Elías, J. and Yun Casalilla, B. (eds), *Consumo*, pp. 41–59. Torra Fernández, L., 'Pautas de consumo textil en la Cataluña del siglo XVIII. Una visión a partir de los inventarios post-mortem', in Torras Elías, J. and Yun Casalilla, B. (eds), *Consumo*, pp. 89–105.

[5] However we can find some differences among these probate inventories, by looking at relevant works by: Baulant, M., Piponnier, F., Tryantafyllidou-Baladié, Y. and Veinstein, G., 'Problématique et méthode comunes aux corpus présentés par les chercheurs de l'E.H.E.S.S. de Paris', in Schuurman, A. and Walsh, L.S. (eds), *Material Culture*, pp. 115–26; Baulant, M., 'Enquête', pp. 141–8; Roche, D., *La culture*.

'fixed-photo'[6] of goods, which form the patrimony of an individual at the moment of his death. However, these documents do not show the evolution of the economy of the family unit, in particular the flow of income and how goods were acquired. In other words, this source does not reveal the inner dynamics of the household in selling and purchasing commodities over time.

Some differences do appear, depending on the socio-professional category of individuals who prepare the inventory. Evidence of this is whether in the document the appraiser's name appears, and consequently the detailing of the value and characteristics of each item. The presence of a qualified person, as well as the valuation and detailed description of items, raises the cost of the execution of the probate inventory.[7] Nevertheless, the appraisal of goods is problematic as it is difficult to confirm whether the value assigned in fact corresponds to each item's true value. We should bear in mind that in most cases there is an arbitrary tendency to establish a lower or higher value. At the end of the document we find the sum of the items listed.

Another problem for the analysis of probate inventories of people belonging to certain social groups, such as merchants, is the need to establish the distinction between goods meant for private usage and those which were in fact simply being stored with the intention of later being sold. The location of an item may offer clues as to whether or not it was intended for personal use. In most cases, residences and shops were under the same roof, and we must, therefore, distinguish between both spaces in the inventory. This is made easier where there is a description of all the rooms of the dwelling, such as halls, corridors, living-room, bedrooms, studio, kitchen, attic and so on. Nevertheless, in merchant probate inventories this differentiation between the spaces of the shop and that of the residence is often absent.[8]

Another important issue is the tendency of particular social groups towards a 'specialization of notaries' when having their wills and probate inventories drawn up. This can often help us organize probate inventories belonging to different socio-professional categories when we are dealing with random samples. Individuals belonging to the same social class often used the same notary. This can be explained by the fact that in a particular parish we often find a predominance of persons

---

[6]   De Vries, J., 'Between the Purchasing Power', pp. 98–107.

[7]   Regarding Castile, see studies on the area of Palencia, by: Ramos Palencia, F., 'Una primera aproximación al consumo'; and for the case of the area of Madrid, see Cruz, J., 'La construcción'.

[8]   Cheung and Mui have studied the history of permanent shops and the retailing methods for the distribution of goods in urban and rural areas. See Cheung, H. and Mui, L., *Shops & Shopkeeping in Eighteenth-century England* (London: Routledge, 1989). Ramon Maruri has observed, through his study of the merchants of Santander, that in Spain there was no differentiation between shop and residence. See: Maruri Villanueva, R., *La burguesía*. For seeing how new spaces and distributions of rooms were appearing in the interior of dwellings, see: Cruz, J., 'Propiedad urbana y sociedad en Madrid, 1749–1774', in *Revista de Historia Económica* (1990) no. 2, pp. 239–69.

belonging to the same social group. For example, with the probate inventories of foreigners established in Murcia, most of them were drawn up by the same notary.

Regarding different material goods that appear in probate inventories, the ordination and description of items is generally made in a fairly haphazard way which is often a major problem for the use of these sources in the study of consumer behaviour. Therefore, it has been extremely important to design a specific database with the help of computer software. Employing this technology facilitates our documentation of goods related to the different social classes which make up the sample of inventories.

Depending on the description of each item, we can find the following data in probate inventories: the type or description of the object itself, its origin,[9] the size of the item, colour, its location in the home (the location gives details about the room of the household in which the item is stored), its material, any particular characteristics of the item (in this field there is a detailed description of the object), its condition (state of use or conservation, such as new, old, used, spoilt, [half-used]: 'a medio traer'), quantity and volume,[10] weight,[11] value[12] and coinage used.[13] Such an extensive description may not always be found in probate inventories, and the general rule is that they usually appear listed in a random fashion.

Dowry Letters

Whereas probate inventories are the 'fixed-photo' of the accumulated wealth of the family unit upon an individual's death, dowry letters record the possessions that belong to a new household at the time of marriage. The dowry is a valuable source for investigating patterns of consumption and the introduction of new fashions in the *Ancien Regime*. For this reason, they are an excellent complimentary source to probate inventories.[14] In order to understand the changes and transformations in fashions and lifestyles, the study of dowries helps us to identify how such shifts were taking place. Surprisingly, this subject has not been investigated thoroughly

---

[9]   This entry refers to the region or country from which the object has been imported.

[10]   Objects were counted in units, but also according to their volume or packaging such as in 'boxes', containers, coffers or other types of packages.

[11]   We can find different Castilian weights or measurements such as 'libra' [pound], 'fanegas', 'celemines' and so on.

[12]   In this field the evaluation of the item is detailed, but in some cases does not appear in the inventory.

[13]   For the Castilian example, this is stated in 'reales', 'maravedis' or 'ducados'.

[14]   Zarandieta Arenas, F., 'Riqueza y consumo en la Baja Extremadura en el s. XVII. Análisis a través de las cartas de dote', *Historia Agraria*, 21 (August, 2000), pp. 63–97; García Fernández, M., 'Los bienes dotales en la ciudad de Valladolid, 1700–1850. El ajuar doméstico y la evolución del consumo y la demanda', in Torras Elías, J. and Yun Casalilla, B., *Consumo*, pp. 133–58.

by European historians who have studied consumption. Spanish and Italian scholars are among those to have used this source.[15]

In pre-industrial societies, marriage was an alliance between families rather than a union between two people. Through these alliances both families transferred new material goods to the new household unit. By studying the dowry and 'arras' [possessions that the man contributed to the marriage], historians can quantify the value of goods that appear in these sources and draw conclusions about the level of wealth of both spouses, whose social status may well have been different. This analysis allows us to investigate the evolution and changes to family wealth by examining the types of goods that formed the dowry.

The origin of the dowry comes from the paternal and maternal inheritance and from the family earnings resulting from their own work.[16] This source contains both immovable and movable assets. The dowry was the economic contribution which the women made to the family unit. The husband was entrusted to take care of all these possessions, which he was obliged to return to his wife's family upon her death. The dowry could be made before or after the celebration of the wedding. Therefore, it could appear in different documents such as 'escrituras de entrega de dote' [letters of dowry delivery], 'escrituras de recibo de dote' [letters of receipt of dowry] and 'inventario de dote' [inventory of dowry]. The 'inventory of dowry' is a list of goods that both spouses contributed to the new household. As F. Zarandieta Arenas says, this document is more frequent when a person marries for the second time.[17]

Where there is a reference to the 'delivery' and 'receipt' of a dowry, it means that the document was drawn up by different individuals. The 'delivery of dowry' was ordered to be drawn up by the relatives of the person to whom the dowry was addressed. In most cases, the bride's parents prepared the deed. The 'receipt of dowry' was prepared by the bridegroom, who declared he had received the dowry. This last document was the most common among dowries, and it has proved a very useful source to analyse the wealth of individuals with different socio-economic status, since all items that were transferred to the new family unit appear in this document.

The most common problem when analysing this source is that of recognizing the socio-professional category of the individuals to be married, as a dowry will not always specify the individuals' profession. This makes it more difficult to establish the family's social status. The provenance and origin of relatives (grandparents, parents and spouse) of the bride may sometimes also be detailed

---

[15]   Romanelli, R., 'Donne e patrimonio', in Groppi, A. (ed.), *Storia delle donne in Italia. Il lavoro delle donne* (Bari: Editori Laterza, 1996), pp. 345–67. Ago, R., 'Oltre la dote: I beni femminile', in Groppi, A. (ed.), *Storia delle donne*, pp. 164–82. Torras, J., Duran, M. and Torra, L., 'El ajuar de la novia. El consumo de tejidos en los contratos matrimoniales de una localidad catalana, 1600–1800', in Torras Elías, J. and Yun Casalilla, B. (eds), *Consumo*, pp. 61–70; García Fernández, M., *Consumo*.

[16]   Peristiany, J.G. (ed.), *Dote y matrimonio en los países mediterráneos* (Madrid: Centro de Investigaciones Sociológicas, 1987).

[17]   Zarandieta Arenas, F., 'Riqueza y consumo'.

in the document. Nevertheless, certain goods listed in dowries can often reveal something about the social status of individuals. When we find immovable assets such as houses, agricultural lands and farm tools we can deduce that the individual was a rich landowner. In terms of the items listed in dowries, there is a predominance of textiles such as bed-sheets, clothes, non-manufactured textiles, kitchenware, household furniture, jewellery and coins. The structure and contents of a dowry are often quite similar to that of probate inventories. Regarding the valuation of goods, the dowry gives us more information, as the value of items always appears in Castilian dowries. Moreover, at the end of the document there is a final calculation of the total value of all objects listed.

2.2. The Census of the Marquis of Ensenada

Some of the problems that we may encounter when using probate inventories and dowries can be overcome by cross-referencing sources with tax documents, such as 'Respuestas Particulares del Catastro del Marqués de la Ensenada' [Answers to Doubts found in the Census of the Marquis of Ensenada]. This document allows us to classify individuals and families in relation with their socio-professional category and to evaluate their level of income. The census of the Marquis of Ensenada was made for all Castilian territories. The census corresponding to the Kingdom of Murcia was produced in 1752. This was a tax record, prepared with the goal of compiling a report on the number of inhabitants of Murcia and other populations living in the vicinity. In the report there is a division for each socio-professional category, measuring the annual income of individuals and workers who reside in the household, as well as their ages. The occupational groups considered in my study correspond to the social groups that have been arranged in the sample of probate inventories. Within each category we may find individuals with diverse socio-economic situations. Such groups are composed by: oligarchs (people with a position in the council, those with a noble title or those who own a significant amount of immovable assets in rural areas), merchants (from rich traders and wholesalers who founded important business companies and economic ventures, to small retailers with a 'tienda abierta' [opened shop] in the city), professionals (doctors, notaries or people with an academic career), artisans (within this group we must differentiate between master artisans – individuals at the top level of the working-class, and ordinary artisans – those working for the master artisans).

By using this tax census, we can track the evolution of the income obtained by different social groups. In addition, by cross-referencing the records of the census with probate inventories and dowries we can determine the relation between the buying power of the family and household expenditure. This enables us to evaluate shifts in decisions made by consumers according to their level of income.[18] Nevertheless, we must acknowledge the shortcomings of this source, which is its reliability. In other words, we should bear in mind that as we are dealing with a tax source, in which the annual income is declared, the true income may in fact be higher because if the individual admits to a high income his tax base will rise. The precise income of the taxpayer is not specified.

2.3. The Use of Treatises to Analyse the Social Backlash on Consumption

Although probate inventories, dowries and tax sources can provide a wealth of information about consumption, these sources will be complemented by municipal and national decrees and policies, as well as treatises and manuscripts written by contemporaries, in which we can find the rejection or acceptance of foreign goods in Spanish society, as a result of extensive commerce with French merchants. Important sources have also been found from the city halls of Murcia and Cartagena, as well as from the Crown, which banned the introduction of foreign textiles because the Spanish government thought that this would harm the national economy by thwarting domestic production. The control of consumption exerted by the state is made evident through such measures.

In addition to official policy, treatises written by contemporaries also show us the rejection by Spanish society of new fashions such as French styles of dress. Cardinal Belluga's pastoral letters and treatises offer proof of the rejection of these new fashions. The debate on luxury, superfluous adornments and excesses in consumption was particularly vocal in Castile during the eighteenth century. Eighteenth-century literary sources, such as the manuscripts written by Sempere y Guarinos, as well as Cadalso's *Cartas Marruecas*, among others, enable us to analyse, in depth, the debate which luxury items generated. By citing the opinions and comments of eighteenth-century writers, we can better understand new social tendencies and reactions towards consumption. As such, the focus of this study is not based only on the quantification and typology of goods through examining probate inventories. Literary sources have also been investigated in order to establish the true social image that the consumption of certain commodities brought about, as well as looking closely at societal reactions to the possession of items arriving from abroad.

2.4. The Application of a Database to our Case Study

By using new technologies, such as the 'Access' computer program, it has been possible to create a database that will greatly contribute to economic studies on patterns of consumption and consumer behaviour in European communities. By

---

[18]   Ramos Palencia, F. and Nicolini, E.A., 'A New Method for Estimating the Money Demand in Pre-Industrial Economies: Probate Inventories and Spain in the Eighteenth Century', *European Review of Economic History*, 14 (2009), 145–77.

employing modern methodology, a broad sample of probate inventories (273), as well as dowries (66), has been arranged by making chronological listings of these sources, taking into account the socio-professional category of each individual. Through the examination of certain products, we can determine how lifestyle, consumer behaviour and standards of living changed. The elaboration of a database enables us to answer the questions posed, as well as to properly develop the working hypothesis, which is to derail the 'trickle-down' theory, for the case of south-eastern Castile, related to the emulation of patterns of consumption, as well as to discover whether an 'industrious revolution' took place in that area, through the analysis of the household economy, the size of the family and the number of family members of working age, along with their respective incomes. A thorough analysis of these variables allows us to recreate a fuller picture of the level of wealth, income, buying power and patterns of consumption corresponding to diverse social groups. Likewise, the construction of a database is a relevant tool that enables us to resolve problems related to the analysis of probate inventories. Moreover, we can compare patterns of consumption of families with different levels of income, by examining which types of goods were purchased by which kinds of individuals of diverse socio-economic status.

Our database is composed of the following: 'source reference',[19] 'name',[20] 'marriage',[21] 'relationships',[22] 'items',[23] 'inheritance distribution',[24] 'income'[25] and 'employment'.[26] The use of a database like this enables the organization of the vast quantity of information that compiled from the sample of probate inventories in order to analyse the household economy and consumer behaviour of a given society. There are 10,518 registers linked to goods that are listed in a sample of 273 probate inventories of the territory of the Kingdom of Murcia, and 2,767 records related to items of a sample of 66 dowries for the same community. To deal with such a vast amount of information, the 'Access' database allows us to cross-reference the information of these sources by making queries in order to analyse what types of commodities were consumed according to an individual's socio-professional

---

[19] Here we register the catalogue number of the historic document being used.

[20] This corresponds to the personal data of the person that produced the document. We could call this entry the individual's 'DNA' related to his or her socio-economic status.

[21] This entry is related to the individual's civil status, in which we list all the information, especially the description of goods which appear in the dowry.

[22] By using a computer application with the software 'Heredis', this field enables us to determine the individual's social network. We have listed a community composed of 2,366 persons.

[23] Here, all data and features related to goods that appear in the probate inventories, such as composition, material, colour, price, size and quantity are listed.

[24] Information related to the will, which is sometimes included in the probate inventory.

[25] Information referring to an individual's annual income.

[26] This entry allows us to register the information related to the individual's socio-professional category.

category and how shifts in consumer behaviour occurred over time. We can better understand the usefulness of this methodology by analysing how objects such as chocolate pots, mirrors or luxury textiles were introduced to households with different levels of wealth. We can observe the data according to the possession of different goods that are presented in the Appendices in order to appreciate how this database works. Therefore, through the analysis of this data we can observe how the consumption of such products was primarily inspired by foreign merchants, acting as 'vicarious consumers', in the Kingdom of Murcia. This shows how these socio-economic agents were changing the patterns of consumption towards a new model led by newly acquired tastes and care for one's personal status and image.

Conclusions

In this chapter the main lines of the research have been described. By presenting the major approaches of the historiography during the last few decades on the subject of consumption, I have introduced the ways in which I deviate from these and how I hope to surpass the traditional scholarly works on this topic. By charting such approaches, we can see the major difficulties, or advantages, encountered by European scholars who have analysed the material culture and consumer behaviour of *Ancien Regime* societies. The historiographical voids in fact open up new avenues by which to analyse the topic of consumption by posing different questions and employing different methods to better resolve new issues in studies on consumer behaviour. In recent years, the historiography has put the accent on the comparative and trans-national approaches. This is the point of departure for the following analysis.

Within the framework of trans-national history, classic works on material culture and consumer behaviour are being challenged by a new historical approach. This study explores this new historiographical perspective by detailing the scholarly debate, as well as offering an analysis of how the trade circuits of the Mediterranean area likely altered the demand-side of south-eastern Spain. The main questions for this study are: how commodities circulated in social groups; what the economic impulses were (as well as the social agents) that stimulated the demand; and the possible backlash in society due to the introduction of external fashions. Understanding the birth of the mass consumption society has been a scholarly obsession during recent decades. This study suggests that an analytical approach must be taken in studies on consumption, paying special attention to the socio-cultural and economic transfers which occur when different commodities flow and make contact with different markets. Therefore, one of the key questions for such an approach is to examine the role of merchants, who have a very important influence on consumer decisions. In this case, those choices must be contextualized within the framework of family size in the western Mediterranean area, whether or not such societies were more or less industrialized and whether or not they were mainly dependent on external agents to provide for their necessities.

PART II
Consumption and Stereotypes in Eighteenth-century Mediterranean Europe: the Case of South-eastern Spain

The purpose of this section is to introduce the debates on luxury, control of consumption by the state, as well as the creation of stereotypes that emerged from the socio-cultural circulation of foreign goods and fashions during the eighteenth century. Through the analysis of sources including prohibitions, manuscripts, treatises and written opinion, it is possible to observe the impact these issues had on society. The control exercised by the state on matters of consumption was expressed by the promulgation of rules, decrees and prohibitions, which reflected official dogma on issues such as how society should consume in moderation according to the rules of the Catholic Church, as well as the promotion of the national economy by encouraging the consumption of Spanish goods. These rules fostered the presence of socio-cultural prejudices against foreign fashions, provoking reactions in society against what was considered new and potentially harmful for the nation.

Here the analysis focuses on the rise of consumer societies, in which the individual emerges as a main player, in spite of the state's desire for control. Material goods became widely rooted in western culture in the sixteenth and seventeenth centuries, shaping social and individual subjectivities by means of the 'power of things'.[1] Therefore, people, as autonomous individuals, expressed their own desires and aspirations, confronting the general programme of the state. The symbolism related to the consumption of specific commodities contributed to the creation and redefinition of the national identity. This identity consisted of stereotyping new consumption practices in order to limit the appeal of foreign habits. This material symbolism did not only encourage the creation of national values, it also generated friction between genders. The 'petimetre' model consisted

---

[1]   De Grazia, V., 'Introduction', in De Grazia, V. and Furlough, E. (eds), *The Sex of Things. Gender Consumption in Historical Perspective* (Berkeley: University of California Press, 1996), pp. 1–10.

of a fashionable way of dressing, in which individuals were not only ridiculed for adopting a foreign style, but also for its effeminate connotations. As a counter reaction, the Spanish traditional figure of the 'majo' emerged.

This confrontation was especially significant among the elite class, creating an imaginary community related to the model of the 'petimetre', which was more a fictional figure than a real one. Bearing this in mind, it is possible to analyse the stereotypes of French fashions during the eighteenth century and establish whether such stereotypes were motivated by socio-political issues. The analysis of the *Cartas Marruecas* by Cadalso, amongst other contemporary texts, can shed light on this issue, by showing the Spanish backlash caused by the invasion of French lifestyles. The ways in which people dressed, ate or spoke 'in the French manner' was attacked in the *Cartas Marruecas*. This book was written at the crucial date of 1755, when social prejudices against 'Frenchness' started to emerge in Spanish society. By examining in depth the texts of *Cartas Marruecas*, the reader can appreciate how many practices considered 'traditional' are, in fact, simply inventions, often devised to serve political ends. This tendency was reinforced during the political upheavals in the era of nationalism, when states wanted to reinforce national values. The external appearance of individuals belonging to the new nation-state was a key feature of this movement.[2] The reaction against different ways of dressing and new cultural habits played a very important role in this new spirit of fostering a Spanish national identity.

---

[2]   Hobsbawm, E. and Ranger, T. (eds), *The Invention of Tradition* (Cambridge [Cambridgeshire]; New York: Cambridge University Press, 1983).

Chapter 3
Socio-political Rules and Fashions: the Intervention of the State

The expansion and growth of the market and the progressive connections between national, international and intercontinental trade routes in the Crown of Castile made the acquisition of a wide range of goods possible, as well as the formation of a large middle class with an improved standard of living. This acquisition of goods was linked not only to innovations in the material life of society, but also to changes which occurred in the 'public sphere'.[1] Such social transformations began to appear in both private and public spaces. In the former, the household was the main unit in which the 'pater familias' was responsible for maintaining and controlling the proper development of the family according to Christian beliefs; whereas in the latter, rules and conventions established by the civil and religious community were the main instruments used to control the socio-cultural behaviour of individuals.

Furthermore, this social change was accompanied by a transformation of the economy, in which the market became the core of the financial system, substituting the household as place of wealth and production. The expansion of the market resulted in an increase in the demand for goods, as well as in the multiplication of consumer choices for acquiring different commodities. According to the mercantilist theories and social schemes of the *Ancien Regime*, patterns of consumption must be guided by moderation, respecting the tradition of the nation and refraining from consuming foreign goods, which were considered a threat to the development and improvement of the national economy and production. To secure its goal, the government decreed how society should consume.

The state established local rules and national laws designed to limit the consumption of certain goods, especially those of foreign origin.[2] Thus, women and men had to accept their roles and functions as members of their particular social group, without stepping outside the boundaries established by socio-economic and religious rules.[3] Family can be considered as the main institution

---

[1]   Habermas, J., *The Structural Transformation of the Public Sphere. An Inquiry into a Category of Bourgeois Society* (Great Britain: Polity Press, 1989).

[2]   Morley, D. 'Cultural Transformations: The Politics of Resistence', in Harris, R. and Thornham, M. (eds), *Media Studies. A Reader* (New York: New York University Press, 2000), pp. 471–81.

[3]   Hayek, F., *The Constitution of Liberty* (Chicago: University of Chicago Press, 1960).

where the main consumer choices were made, and the degree of freedom that households possessed in making such choices was shaped by socio-economic constraints, family networks and alliances.[4] Both nuclear and extended families in Mediterranean Europe marked individual decisions, which were firmly rooted in the complexity of family structures. The Catholic Church of Mediterranean Europe, as opposed to the Protestant Church which proclaimed the superiority of the individual soul,[5] praised the sacrality of family and lineage as the main institution which channelled tradition and cultural values according to its teachings. Within this framework, the Church and civil community tended to unify socio-cultural patterns through the limitation on innovations in consumer behaviour. Family ties and bounds defined the social behaviour of individuals, by setting down rules of conduct regarding an individual's manners, habits and language, which composed the 'immaterial culture' inherent to each social group; as well as the 'material culture', which symbolized, through items such as clothing or interior home decorations, the individual's economic status.

This rigid socio-cultural scheme was well defined in the sixteenth and seventeenth centuries.[6] However, in late seventeenth and early eighteenth centuries, the new rationalistic European thought[7] challenged the traditional and classical social categories of the *Ancien Regime*, stressing the fact that the individual was capable of making his/her own decisions. This can be observed through the social reactions to the rules controlling consumption and how people should dress. For instance, in the Spanish case the decree of a national project on how women ought to dress, during the second-half of the eighteenth century, addressed to the 'Board of Noble Ladies', was not accepted. The response of the notable ladies of the country, led by the Countess of Montijo, was that the individual nature of women is to self-distinction through the symbolic meaning of dress.

Therefore, a new tension developed between the general political rules and the establishment of an individual's behaviour when people expressed their social freedom within the 'private sphere'. As such, it is necessary to investigate the projection in social practices of such rules and their theoretical roots, in order to understand the forces that stimulated individuals to make their own choices. The

---

[4]   See the classic work by James S. Dusenberry, *Income, Saving and the Theory of Consumer Behaviour* (Cambridge, Mass.: Harvard University Press, 1949). See also: Anderson, M., Berchhofer, F. and Gershuny, J., 'Introduction', in Anderson, Berchhofer and Gershuny (eds), *The Social and Political Economy of the Household* (Oxford: Oxford University Press, 1994), pp. 1–16.

[5]   Lynch, K.A., *Individuals, Families, and Communities in Western Europe* (Cambridge: Cambridge University Press, 1983).

[6]   Clark, H.C., 'Commerce, the Virtues and the Public Sphere in the Early-Seventeenth-century France', *French Historical Studies*, vol. 21, no. 3 (Summer, 1998), pp. 415–40.

[7]   Israel, J.I., *Radical Enlightenment. Philosophy and the Making of Modernity 1650–1750* (Oxford: Oxford University Press, 2001), pp. 6–8.

analysis of gender factors, in Catholic Europe and in a very traditional society such as Spain, can offer clarification as to whether or not such rules were transgressed, and, if so, we can determine what the new responses and decisions of consumers were. Women were regarded as potential consumers, especially with regard to the introduction of new fashions and goods which went beyond meeting basic necessities.

But how did the Church's teaching in Spain differ from either the Catholic Church elsewhere in Europe or Protestant teaching? It is likely that they did not diverge greatly, but through a careful analysis of texts which certain enlightened intellectuals and other authors wrote during the eighteenth century, we gain a better insight of the possible differences and diverse reactions, as well as the process of assimilation of such teachings. I have considered it pertinent to analyse some Spanish, French and English texts in order to chart the reactions to new fashions in both Catholic and Protestant countries. The forces of repression and teachings may not differ significantly, but the results can vary related to social reactions or the structural transformation of institutions. Here the family unit is crucial to understand such changes, articulation of social protests or the transformation and redefinition of elites.

A good example of diverse reactions in Catholic and Protestant Europe can be seen in Monica Bolufer's works on the transmission of moral values from parents to their children.[8] It is interesting to observe how, through the exchange of letters, in which parents gave 'avis' [advice] to follow the proper Christian and family principles according to their social status, some slight differences between Catholic and Protestant teachings emerged. The texts of Luisa de Padilla, Countess of Aranda, circulated in Spain during 1781 and 1783, expressing the restoration of the family values of the Castilian aristocracy, which had been corrupted by vice and idleness. For such restoration to occur, sons and daughters must follow the tastes and practices of the 'pater familias'. A French noblewoman, Anne-Thérèse de Marguenat de Courcelles, Marquis Lambert (1647–1733), praised the virtues and merits of the status of her family, as well as French politesse rather than focusing on the education of her sons and her role in conjugal life, as the Countess of Aranda stressed. The English aristocrat Philip Dormer Stanhope, Count of Chesterfield (1694–1773), recommended developing cosmopolitan tastes and libertine customs. He understood education as a mimetic practice rather than a servile process of imitation, which was the antithesis of the Christian moralism of the Countess of Aranda.

These pieces of advice are a good example of how the process of absorption and transmission of Christian values, related to material culture and lifestyles, can differ in Catholic and Christian Europe. Thus, it is crucial to analyse in the same way the different approaches of the clergy to new practices of consumption, as well as the

---

[8]   Bolufer, M., 'De madres a hijas, de padres a hijos: familia y transmisión moral (ss. XVII–XVIII)', in Pérez García, M. and Bestard, J. (eds), *Familia, Valores y Representaciones* (Murcia: Universidad de Murcia, 2010), pp. 217–38.

reactions expressed by thinkers and what they wrote regarding the development of new fashions and tastes. By analysing the words and semantic fields of such texts and by placing them in their proper context, the economic, social and religious dimensions of the control of the state on consumption can be fully understood. The study of the meaning of new words or neologisms surrounding the debates on consumption, by spotlighting a new linguistic turn, helps historians to understand better the social transgressions and reactions that occurred through new socio-cultural practices. The analysis of 'mot-clé' [keywords] and 'mot-témoin'[9] [words of evidence] of texts such as those written by Cadalso or the letters exchanged by the Count of Floridablanca and the Countess of Montijo, linked with the new semantic group of the Enlightenment, such as nature, humanity, civility, progress, happiness and economy, offer clues as to why this debate was acquiring more potency, especially among governmental authorities and local elites, who were losing economic and social power. The power of new words and the wide diffusion of texts was the main vehicle by which the state was developing its new political program. The rise of the modern nation-state was manifested through intervention in people's lives, as well as consumer choices.

Catholic Europe embodied such interventionism through the joint action of Church and Monarchy. The texts to be analysed in the following paragraphs represent the discourse of the authorities belonging to the Catholic monarchy. During the eighteenth century, Spanish ministers built barriers in order to regulate the economic and social life, by means of a list of decrees such as restrictions on commerce – taxes, tolls or foreign customs – the promulgation of bans that prohibited the consumption of foreign goods, as well as rules that established the canons for dressing according to the moral virtues of Catholicism.

The progressive acquisition of the individual consciousness can be identified in the literature of the period. Such new perceptions can be found in the personality of Beaumarchais and his most famous plays, *Le Barbier de Seville* (1775), *Le marriage de Figaro* (1785) and *La mère coupable* (1792). The character of Figaro personifies a middle-class person, who attacks the rigid intervention and control of the aristocracy and local authorities over the free development of individuals. Figaro delivers a powerful monologue on this subject to the Count of Alamaviva, an influential and elegant nobleman:

> Non, monsieur le Comte, vous ne l'aurez pas ... vous ne l'aurez pas. Parce que
> vous êtes un grand seigneur, vous, vous croyez un grand génie! ... Noblesse,
> fortune, un rang, des places, tout cela rend si fier! ... Qu'avez-vous fait pour
> tant de biens? Vous vous êtes donné la peine de naître, et rien de plus. Du reste,
> homme assez ordinaire; tandis que moi, morbleu! perdu dans la foule obscure, il
> m'a fallu déployer plus de science et de calculs, pour subsister seulement, qu'on
> n'en a mis depuis cent ans a gouverner toutes les Espagnes ... je m'en dégoûte

---

[9]   Álvarez de Miranda, P., *Palabras e ideas: el léxico de la Ilustración temprana en España (1680–1760)* (Madrid: Real Academia Española, 1992).

et veux courir une carrière honnête … J'apprends la chimie, la pharmacie, la chirurgie, et tout le crédit d'un grand seigneur peut à peine me mettre à la main une lancette vétérinaire![10]

This excerpt illustrates that the notions of reason, the laws of nature and individual development of human beings were strongly at stake in an individual's consciousness. The key words of this text, such as 'grand seigneur' [grand lord], 'noblesse' [nobility], 'fortune' [fortune] and 'rang' [rank] give us a good insight about the new liberal spirit of the eighteenth century by which individuals were seeking social equality. There is a strong confrontation between these words with the semantic group around the term 'grand genie' [grand genius], which includes reason, wisdom and knowledge. These words clearly belong to the new cultural language of the Enlightenment. Figaro attacks the Count of Almaviva with those new words, by expressing that to be born a member of the nobility does not automatically endow one with the virtues of wisdom and reason. In fact, the Count of Almaviva's sole achievement was having been born into the nobility. However, Figaro was educated as a higher 'seigneur' [lord], by learning 'chimie' [chemistry], 'pharmacie' [pharmacy] and 'chirurgie' [surgery], by indoctrinating himself with the knowledge of science. This background provided him with 'le credit d'un grand seigneur' [the credit of a big lord].

3.1. The Emergence of Modern Consumerism versus Religious Interventionism

Within the framework of the Enlightenment and new individual ideas, especially in the Spanish case, the sphere of consumption was mixed with religious, economic, socio-cultural and political issues. By analysing how such ideas were developed, we can better understand the responses and reactions of politicians, cardinals and priests towards new lifestyles and fashions. The backlash these caused among traditional society was directed in particular against new habits in dress. Some European philosophers such as Fontenelle and Bulainvilliers, or the French historian Boureau-Deslandes, were convinced that the power exerted by the new philosophical concepts could be a good instrument to regulate consumption practices.[11] Boureau-Deslandes noted this influence in 1737, when philosophers discovered that debates on education, morals, consumption, luxury, social vices, the arts, economic policy, administration, and 'toute la conduite de la vie'[12] [all conduct of life] were affecting the quotidian life.

---

[10]   Beaumarchais, Pierre-Agustin Caron de, *Le mariage de Figaro*, Préface de Pierre Larthomas (Paris: editions Gallimard, 1984), Acte V, Scène III.

[11]   De Grazia, V. and Furlough, E. (eds), *The Sex of Things*, pp. 1–10.

[12]   Boureau-Deslandes, *Histoire critique*, I, preface, pp. ix–xx. In Israel, J.I., *Radical Enlightenment*, p. 11.

This idea expresses the philosophical concept that the individual cannot freely develop his identity when there is a direct intervention of the state ruling how men and women have to behave. However, in most cases this intellectual debate has been prioritized by scholars instead of understanding the social reality through the analysis of how everyday practices were prohibited by the state. Regulations about how to dress during the eighteenth century were repeatedly ignored. The same prohibitions were, in fact, constantly repeated by both political and religious figures. This issue is the most notable proof that the intellectual debate did not coincide with real social concerns.[13]

Under the umbrella of the debate on luxury[14] which covered moral, social and economic issues, the state led its policies to control consumption. Carmen Martin Gaite has been one of the pioneers in Spanish historiography in studying the debate on luxury as a main feature of the future mass consumption society. However, her approach is to compile a series of testimonies and opinions of the period about a conspicuous elite class, which are linked predominantly with courtly life. Gaite does not distinguish between the differing levels of luxury by separating the political, socio-economic and religious dimension of the debate. Instead, she focuses on such debates as a matter of differentiation between social classes.[15] The debate on luxury goods can be articulated in the following way: there were those who opposed the importation and sale of new commodities, since they saw the compulsive consumption of exotic goods from distant territories as immoral; and there were individuals who supported this sumptuous and abundant consumption as a new way to stimulate economic growth, which, as a result, enabled different social groups to enjoy a wide range of goods.

The debate and distinction between what was defined as a necessity or superficial goods was slightly different in Protestant and Catholic Europe. Mandeville's opinions on luxury are a good example of Protestant Europe views of this debate. According to his writings on the *Fables of the Bees* (1723),[16] the individual's vice and anxiety about frivolities and unnecessary goods has an impact on the prosperity of the nation through the permanent activity of traders. Catholic authorities articulated an opposite opinion; they saw the conspicuous consumption of luxury goods as representative of the degradation of human nature which leads towards idleness and opulence. In fact, they were attacking foreign trade, the economic sector that made possible the introduction and wide consumption of new

---

[13]   Israel, J.I., *Radical Enlightenment*, p. 90.

[14]   Berg, M. and Eger, E., 'The Rise and Fall of Luxury Debates', in Berg, M. and Eger, E. (eds), *Luxury*, 2003, pp. 7–27. Berg, M., *Luxury and Pleasure in Eighteenth-century Britain* (Oxford: Oxford University Press, 2005). Haidt, R., 'Luxury, Consumption and Desire: Theorizing the *Petimetra*', *Arizona Journal of Hispanic Cultural Studies*, vol. 3 (1999), pp. 35–50.

[15]   Martin Gaite, C., *Usos Amorosos*, pp. 25–62.

[16]   Mandeville, B., *The Fable of the Bees, or Private Vices, Public Benefits*, 1723, Douglas Garmen, ed. (London: Wishart and Company, 1934), I, 356; Remark T, pp. 175–6.

and exotic goods. The following texts, which present Catholic views, for the case of Spain, on luxury and conspicuous consumption, can illustrate such differences between Catholic and Protestant Europe. Relevant Spanish religious figures of the eighteenth century, such as cardinal Belluga, saw new fashions, especially among women, as a threat to Catholic morals. Belluga's treatises criticize the adoption of these new styles of clothing. Such criticisms were part of the early phase of the debate on luxury during the eighteenth century, on how to dress the body according to Catholic principles. For example, one of his arguments was that women who wore low-cut dresses revealing their flesh were immoral as such attitudes encourage society towards corruption through the adoption of such profane embellishments:

> la mitad de los pechos fuera, y no pocas más, lo que alguna vez con gran dolor nuestro hemos llegado a ver con nuestros mismos ojos, lo que nos ha lastimado y herido de corazón.[17]

In 1711, Belluga claimed that these fashions were culminating in extreme excesses by means of the adornment of bodices and, hence, unreasonable desires to consume superfluous luxury goods were set as an individual need. Cardinal Belluga wanted the women of the diocese of Murcia to revert to the honest and modest attire that noble ladies had previously worn, 'lleno de honestidad, compostura y modestia'[18] [full of honesty, composure and modesty]. However, roles were changing and dresses were full of superfluous adornment, bright colours and comprised of new exotic materials which showed the individual's desire to consume goods without moderation. The entire treatise is an apologia on the nature of the body, on education, as well as the way in which women must dress in order to observe the Catholic canons of modesty. The appearance of low-cut dresses allowed, in Belluga's opinion, the female body to be seen almost half-naked. His teachings did not differ greatly from other Catholic areas such as Italy, where this custom was also greatly criticized.[19] The Neapolitan philosopher Paolo Mattia Doria believed that the female attitude inherent in all women lead them to vice and corruption. He remarks that the 'libertá di conversare' [freedom of speech] for women, especially in the new social spaces of the eighteenth century such as promenades in gardens, meetings, theatres, feasts, where they appeared in magnificent and provocative dresses, meant more opportunity for intimacy and amorous dalliance outside

---

[17]   A.M.M., Belluga, L., *Carta Pastoral que el Obispo de Cartagena escribe a los fieles de su diócesis a cada uno en lo que le toca, para que todos concurran a que se destierre la profanidad de los trages y varios e intolerables abusos que ahora nuevamente se han introducido* (Murcia, 1711).

[18]   A.M.M., Belluga, L., *Carta sobre trages y honestidad de costumbres* (Murcia, 1715).

[19]   Doria, P.M., *Lettere e ragionamenti* (Naples: Biblioteca Regia Monacensis, 1741), pp. 346, 390, 391.

marriage. So, in order to lead women along the path of virtue and good behaviour according to the morality of Catholicism, Doria recognized that it is essential in this context to 'bene educare le donne' [educate women well]. They must be well taught on matters of love, virtue, human nature and be taught suitable and edifying ideas. The family unit can be considered the most important instrument of society to channel such teachings from parents to sons and daughters, and thus the most important institution to maintain tradition and values.[20] One of the thinkers influenced by Doria's ideas was Giuseppa-Eleonora Barbapiccola, who was a translator of Descartes. She admits, in a letter written in 1726, that most ladies of position waste their time on frivolous pursuits such as discussing the latest fashions and choosing ribbons, but insists that such deplorable inadequacy is not due to their negative 'nature' but their 'wretched education'.

According to the Catholic belief of Mediterranean Europe, religious ministers shared the same anthropological view of the body and canons of beauty. The external appearance of the body was the mirror in which the inner ego was visible for everybody.[21] Following the neo-Platonic tradition of the Renaissance, the external features of the body and the way in which it was decorated represented the interior and visible goodness of the person, best achieved by abandoning all kinds of excesses. Therefore, the ideal of beauty, in the view of such religious ministers, should follow modesty and avoid lavish and conspicuous consumption.[22]

Belluga opens his censure about the excess of 'adornos profanos' [profane ornaments] by asserting that the introduction of these new fashions has a negative consequence on family economies because of unnecessary or superfluous expenditure. Again Belluga refers to the household as a major institution to keep Catholic mores. However, he adds an economic dimension to the debate on fashions declaring that conspicuous consumption can damage religious life, as well as leading to the ruin of family wealth. These passages were intended to be a reformulation of Biblical sources, updated in a new language:

> Comprendiendo debaxo de el nombre de trages, y adornos profanos assi los excesivos, como los provocativos: ya sea lo excesivo en el valor, y preciosidad de los vestidos, con que hombres, y mugeres consumiendo sus caudales,

---

[20]   Bolufer, M., 'De madres a hijas', pp. 217–38.

[21]   Langle de Paz, T., 'Beyond the Canon: New Documents on the Feminist Debate in Early Modern Spain', *Hispanic Review*, vol. 70, no. 3 (Summer, 2002), pp. 393–420. Nahoum-Grappe, V., 'La estética: ¿máscara táctica, estrategia o identidad petrificada?', in Duby, G. and Perrot, M. (eds), *Historia de las Mujeres en el Occidente. Los grandes cambios del siglo y la nueva mujer* (Madrid: ed. Taurus, 2006), pp. 122–41.

[22]   Bolufer, M., *Mujeres e Ilustración. La construcción de la feminidad en la España del siglo XVIII* (Valencia: Institucio Alfons el Magnanim, 1998). Morant, I., *Discursos de la vida buena. Matrimonio, mujer y sexualidad en la literatura humanista* (Madrid: Catedra, 2002).

y arruinando sus familias se visten, o ya en su multiplicidad, magnitud, y sobrepuestos con que los adornan, o ya en las nuevas modas, que unos, y otros con dispendio tanto cada dia inventan ...[23]

Nevertheless, there was an exaggeration in such moral judgments, where the theme was the overlapping features of the religious composure and the desire to display one's good appearance. The appeal of owning a fine outfit was related to the introduction of new fashions and the consumption of desirable objects and ornaments, such as those mentioned by Belluga:

Cortes de los vestidos ... adornos de bajos ... pecheras ... torpes afeytes con otras mil ficciones de su cabeça, y cabello, lazos ... que todo ello lo comprehendemos del nombre profanidad ...[24]

The meaning of such practices of consumption had an anthropological connotation in the way that the body should be dressed, as there is an explicit condemnation of 'superficialidad del ornamento' [superficial ornaments], which leads both men and women to deadly sins. Unnecessary garments were considered 'bienes temporales' [worldly goods] that led to depravation and did not allow women to seek the 'bienes espirituales' [divine goods]. Belluga used the Old Testament, to illustrate his teachings, by quoting Isaiah and Ezekiel's passages:

... Aviendo Isaias a las mugeres de baxo de precepto, y conminacion grave prohibioles la Superfluidad del ornamento; los Apostoles a las mugeres Christianas quanto mas les prohibieran esto mismo? Y despues anade: Tambien se ha de considerar, que si en el antiguo Testamento, donde se prometian bienes temporales, este abuso era pecado mortal, en el nuevo sera horrendo crimen, en que se prometen bienes espirituales, y el camino para ellos es la Cruz, y la penitencia, que no solo en el alma, sino en el cuerpo, y en el ornato se ha de professar.[25]

The excessive use of worldly goods and the abuse of superficial ornaments led women to the cardinal deadly sins: vanity, luxury and gluttony. This feature was also common in other Christian traditions of Europe such as the Calvinist teachings evoking moderation, rather than abstinence, in the use of God's gifts.[26] The human body needed to be built of spiritual goods, rather than material things, in order to seek the soul's salvation. Therefore, the superficiality of ornaments was considered a religious transgression which preachers and religious figures continued to

---

[23]   A.M.M., Belluga, L., *Carta sobre trages*, p. 1.
[24]   A.M.M., Belluga, L., *Carta sobre trages*, p. 1.
[25]   A.M.M., Belluga, L., *Carta sobre trages*, p. 4. Latin de ornatu, fuco mulier. q. I. 15. c. 12.
[26]   Schama, S., *The Embarrassment of Riches* (New York: Knopf, 1985), p. 335.

denounce throughout the eighteenth century. Belluga quotes Ezequiel's passages, referring to the cardinal sins, to denounce the unlimited consumption, haughty ornaments, as well as indecency in dressing the body:

> Los vestidos, y ornato, que les di para su necesidad, lo han convertido en soberbia, y fausto, y en un sobervissimo adorno. Por lo quela yo hare, que su mismo ornato le sirva de ignominia, y quedando en manos de sus enemigos, sirvan al saco de los impios, y tyranos, que lo contaminen. Y apartare mi rostro y especial proteccion de ellos.[27]

Costumes should be simple, modest and orthodox in their embellishment regarding sleeves, ribbons, laces and excessively long plaits. Hence, the principles on how to consume in moderation prevented individual behaviour from challenging official canons. The control of the state on issues of consumption required the help of Catholic institutions in order to regulate individual desires. Belluga's teachings are a good instance of where we can observe control on consumption exerted by the Church in the eighteenth century. Noteworthy comments, following Belluga's stance, appeared about the sins of dressing the body with extravagant ornaments, as well as new revealing fabrics. These elaborate garments, as well as ornate accessories for the hair, put a new focus on different parts of the body. Everything was found in the provocative and indecent style of new fashions:

> ya en las nuevas modas, que unos, y otros con dispendio tanto cada dia inventan: Ya sea lo provocativo … por los inmodestisimos cortes de los vestidos …[28]

This could be considered the prelude of the continuous assessments of the perils that individuals faced regarding worldly goods. As Padre Isla wrote in his famous work, *Fray Gerundio de Campazas*, men had three major enemies:

> el dimonio, mundo y carne; pero las mujeres tienen cuatro: el dimonio, mundo y carne y el deseo de parecer bien.[29]

In his work, Padre Isla frequently mentioned the new tendencies of consumption developed among the Castilian peasantry, due to the taste for exquisite

[27] A.M.M., Belluga, L., *Carta sobre trages*, p. 6, Ezequiel cap. 7. v. 20. Ornamentum monilium fuorum in superbia posuerunt.

[28] A.M.M., Belluga, L., *Carta sobre trages*, p. 1.

[29] De Isla, J.F., *Historia del famoso predicador Fray Gerundio de Campazas, alias Zotes* (1st edition, 1758); we have used J. Jurado's edition made for Gredos editorial, Madrid, 1992. See Yun Casalilla, B., 'Perspectivas para la investigación en historia económica y social de Palencia: Consumo y redes de comercialización', in Calleja González, M.V. (ed.), *Actas del III Congreso de Historia de Palencia* (Palencia: Diputación Provincial de Palencia, 1995), pp. 56–8.

ornamentation that was occurring in quotidian life. But bodily ornaments were not the only objects that were changing individual's tastes. The elegant decoration of the household was also a characteristic feature of personal decisions made by consumers. Padre Isla mentions the porcelains, elegant curtains and colourful textile furniture, among other objects, which were driving individuals towards modern consumerism.[30]

The family is the central institution of civil society in which consumer decisions are made. The increase of household incomes and the development of self-identity towards new tastes, sense of status and social ambition provoked shifts in consumer behaviour. In the process of acquiring commodities, bourgeois women balanced their own sense of individuality against the interests of their families. Women had to make difficult decisions between their own individual interests and the welfare of their households.[31]

The moral discourse on new fashions did not change in 1758 when Padre Isla wrote his work referring to the three human perils that Catholic men and women had to face. Isla's text follows early writings of the eighteenth century, such as those by Belluga:

> ... debaxo del nombre de trages, y adornos profanos: en esta primera parte con el Divino auxilio, que imploramos para la obra, y assumpto tan arduo, que no tiene contra si menos que tres tan poderosos enemigos, como son el Mundo, el Demonio, y la Carne, entramos a demostrar de todo genero de autoridad de la grave malicia, que en todos estos excesos, se halla.[32]

Other members of the religious hierarchy expressed the same attitude Belluga had laid out in his treatise concerning the debate about luxury clothes. The sermon by Don Lucas Campoo y Otazu,[33] on the fifth Sunday after Easter in 1781, is a good example. Again the main social agent he attacked was women, and the main cause of such ridicule was female fashion:

> Sermón contra el luxo y la profanidad en los vestidos y adornos de las mugeres christianas ... Por eso vosotros (continua el Señor) no sois sus palabras, porque no sois de Dios ... como si dixera ... sois hombres carnales y terrenos, os alimentais con los deleytes y placeres del mundo, teneis en ellos vuestras

---

[30]   De Isla, J.F., *Historia*, pp. 181–91.

[31]   Cambell, C., *The Romantic Ethic and the Spirit of Modern Consumerism* (Oxford: Blackwell, 1987). De Grazia, 'Changing Consumption Regimes', in De Grazia, V. and Furlough, E. (eds), *The Sex of Things*, pp. 12–24.

[32]   A.M.M., Belluga, L., *Carta sobre trages*, p. 1.

[33]   Don Lucas Campoo y Otazu was priest and professor of Philosophy and Holy Theology at Santo Tomas de Aquino College, in the city of Malaga. C.D.M.T., CA 299, *Sermón contra el lujo y la profanidad en los vestidos y adornos de las mujeres cristianas* (Málaga, 1781).

mayores complacencias y delicias … el espíritu de Jesu-Cristo y su Santa-Ley
que profesaron, conformandose con ella en todas sus operaciones y costumbres,
se convierten por el contrario al mundo y sus vanidades, se alimentan con el
ayre corrumpido de sus abominables y perversas maximas abrazan el luxo y la
profanidad de sus pompas, la composicion de sus vanos adornos, la inmoderacion
en los trages, en las galas y demas perfiles con que tanto adornan y hermosean
sus cuerpos. Pues, sabed mugeres profanas, que los que son de JesuCristo; y
estas que haceis vosotras, estas obras de luxo y profanidad, y de tanto exceso y
demasia en el adorno de vuestros trages y vestidos, no son obras de JesuCristo, ni
se conforman tampoco con el verdadero espíritu de Su Santa Ley y religion …[34]

Campoo y Otazu follows Belluga's pattern in his criticism, putting the accent
on the vanity and perversion embraced by women, who fed their soul with the
luxurious and profane ornaments of their costumes. Such excess in dressing went
against Catholic teaching which sought to construct the body as a divine temple to
be filled with Catholic values. Campo y Otazu's message did not vary greatly from
Belluga's, nor from other texts that can be found in the early nineteenth century,
such as an edict promulgated by Pope Pio VII in Rome in 1800:

… la iglesia se ha opuesto en todos los campos a la inmodestia de las mujeres en
sus vestidos … Los soberanos pontifices informados de los progresos funestos
que se halla entre el pueblo esta especie de corrupción tomaron de tiempo en
tiempo las propuestas necesarias para ahogar esta locura … su santidad espera
que sus hijos queridos escucharan su voz paternal y no le forzaran a hacer uso
de las penas eclesiásticas … El espera que a vista de sus avisos a las mujeres
observaran la modestia en sus vestidos, la decencia en su porte, y la pureza en su
conducta asi como conviene a unas discípulas del Santo Evangelio …[35]

Moral speeches about the correct type of clothes were not vastly different in the late
seventeenth century and eighteenth centuries. The only thing that differs between
the centuries is the fierce debate in which the clergy condemned new female
fashions as the main cause of male decadence. As such, three important features of
the eighteenth century made the discourse more compelling: the expansion of new
fashions due to the emulation of upper-class behaviour; the market integration
and the wide circulation of commodities; and the industrious activity of artisans
such as tailors who produce these lavish outfits. The result was that different
groups, especially the middle classes, were able to afford fancy goods. In one of
the chapters of Pio VII's decree we find that a fine was imposed on merchants and
tailors who fostered the introduction and manufacture of profane and luxurious
dress:

[34]   C.D.M.T., CA 299, *Sermón contra el lujo.*
[35]   C.D.M.T., CA, 360, *Copia de una bula de su santidad Pio VII sobre la modestia en el vestir*, 1801, Roma.

... los sastres para hombres o para mugeres, los mercaderes de modas o de cintas, en fin todos aquellos que contribuyan con su trabajo a estas modas inmodestas y seductoras no serán exentos de las dichas penas ...[36]

Nevertheless, Pio VII's edict, which sought to encourage sartorial decency, was evidently unsuccessful. The decadence and, at times, indecency of wearing certain garments, in both public and private spheres, is the most notable proof of the failure of religious dogma regarding dress styles. Households, theatres, as well as on the streets and in churches, were the main spaces in which individuals could display their risqué new outfits:

... pues no solamente las casas y las calles sino también los sagrados templos son los teatros en que la inmodestia se ostenta en triunfo; convencido de que es este abuso la fuente de males que cargan sobre la cristiandad ...[37]

Education about indecency and clothing should be given by the 'pater familias', the main social actor passing on these teachings and values. The domestic sphere can be defined as a place of transmission of Christian principles from generation to generation, with the public sphere as the space for displaying the values acquired in the household according to the good manners which express not only good education, but also economic position and social status. The final chapter of Pio's text concludes that it is necessary for the entire body of the Church to instruct people by means of action, starting from the Pope's letters and ending with the words of priests at the pulpit. The ministers of the Catholic Church mobilized their energy and action to fulfil the orders that came from Rome. They used the same language that early eighteenth century priests had used when describing the moral transgressions that were taking place in Spanish society as a result of new female fashions. The key words were: indecency, vanity, luxury, immodesty and extravagance.

3.2. Rescuing the National Economy Through the Regulation of Consumption Practices

The debate on luxury during the eighteenth century was primarily focused on religious transgression, the perils of social emulation among classes[38] and the economic arguments regarding the threat to the national economy of the influx of foreign goods. The commercial patterns, which were being developed during the eighteenth century, through market connections and the circulation of merchandises by traders, enabled liberal social rights, social exchange and private

---

[36] C.D.M.T., CA, 360, *Copia de una bula.*
[37] C.D.M.T., CA, 360, *Copia de una bula.*
[38] Martin Gaite, C., *Usos Amorosos*, pp. 53–4.

property.[39] Commerce contributed to the public good, by spreading wealth in society and making revenue available to the public treasury. However, in the eyes of the government, this pattern was seen as a threat to the development of national industries. The national administration tried to regulate and supervise the trade and consumption of foreign goods through prohibitions. The state agents attempted to control the everyday life of citizens by dissuading any social transgression. The analysis of the following texts is focused on the socio-economic dimension of the debate on luxury.

The aim of censorship during the eighteenth century was to control the circulation of new ideas and material goods contrary to the faith, customs and royal prerogatives. Wearing certain types of clothes not only symbolized the social status of individuals, but also the socio-cultural expression of ideas and thoughts. This demonstrates whether or not individuals were going against social norms and whether they exemplified the development of the modern consumer. Political institutions of the *Ancien Regime* tried to regulate canons on dress styles, which both men and women had to maintain in order to comply with social conventions. In 1729, King Philip V issued a prohibition on excesses in the ornamentation of clothes, which was considered superficial and to have contributed to the ruin of the state economy:

> Pragmática Sanción que su Magestad manda observar sobre trages y otras cosas ... Don Phelipe, por la Gracia de Dios, rey de Castilla ... sabed que por la pragmática promulgada por el señor Rey Don Carlos II ... se dio providencia contra el abuso de trages, y otros gastos superfluos, y con el transcurso del tiempo, y otras ocasiones se ha relaxado la observancia de lo que entonces se ordeno siendo el grave perjuicio del bien de mis vasallos, experimentándose cada día más este inconveniente; y deseando que se observe lo dispuesto en la dicha pragmática, renovándola ...[40]

These prohibitions are further evidence of the intervention of the state in the minutiae of ordinary life, in which the display of certain garments and embellishments was prohibited. This itself is relevant evidence that the middle social classes could now afford commodities they could not obtain before.[41] The progressive democratization in consumption contributed to progressively enlarge the middle class. It fostered the birth of the mass consumption society as we know it today, in spite of the attempts of the government to intervene.

The aim of these laws was to define what was considered good taste and morally acceptable. Political and religious authorities created a social pattern, to which individuals should conform. The Spanish thinkers of the Enlightenment

---

[39]   Clark, H.C., 'Commerce', p. 419.
[40]   C.D.M.T., CA 118, *Pragmática sanción contra los trages y otras cosas* (Madrid, 1729).
[41]   Styles, J., *The Dress of People. Everyday Fashion in Eighteenth-century England* (New Haven and London: Yale University Press, 2007).

were strongly influenced by Ludovico Antonio Muratori with regard to good taste. This influence can be found among the Spanish Enlightenment group of Valencia whose main intellectuals were: Mayans y Siscar, Piquer y Arrufat and Sempere y Guarinos. Sempere y Guarinos translated Muratori's work, in which he stated that good taste is neither individual nor subjective, but it is a kind of universal knowledge which harmonizes all kinds of erudition with a deep understanding of all philosophical systems. Therefore, according to Muratori's ideas and in later Spanish thought,[42] there was a revival of the Renaissance belief, which asserted that 'la belleza' [beauty] is perceived by the soul and not by corporal senses.

The debate on luxury reached its most profound moment when Sempere y Guarinos wrote his work on sumptuary laws in 1788.[43] Sempere y Guarinos believed that the critique of good taste would be more effective if it included the encouragement of education, as well as the ways in which an individual could exert freedom in his choices. But again, Sempere y Guarinos' assessment was based on factors, such as foreign trade, that were having a negative influence on the Spanish economy and did not allow national industries to develop. In all his speeches, he stated that the domestic economy needed complete reform, starting with a shift in consumers' personal choices. Sempere did not see luxury as inherently bad or immoral, nor did he criticize the moral aspects of the new social practices. On the contrary, he believed it could be positive for the economy. He emphasized the economic policies that needed to be reformed, in order to transform national industries. The production of luxury commodities was one of those issues which needed to be developed. He argued that the production of luxury goods on home soil would help stimulate national revenues, insofar as this would help foster an increase in exports whilst reducing the volume of imports. Sempere was more concerned with the nation's economic problems and the decadence of national industries during the latter part of the eighteenth century.

Most religious figures, as we have seen in the previous section, saw luxury as negative and immoral because it brought new social practices that challenged the traditional order. Sempere y Guarinos stands apart from that group. With the publication of his book on sumptuary laws, he strongly criticized the compulsive consumption of luxury goods and the expensive leisure pursuits of the emerging upper-middle social classes that were leading the nation to economic ruin. He advocated the development of luxury as a measure for stimulating the national economy. However, he also drew attention to the negative consequences for the national economy if household expenditure was not kept in moderation:[44]

---

[42] Sánchez-Blanco Parody, F., *Europa y el pensamiento español del siglo XVIII* (Madrid: Alianza Universal Editorial, 1991), p. 146.

[43] Sempere y Guarinos, J., *Historia del lujo y las leyes suntuarias de España* (Madrid: Impr. Real, 1788), p. 48.

[44] Other Enlightenment figures such as Campomanes condemned the vast expenditures that households made in purchasing luxury goods. See Llombart, V., *Campomanes, economista y político de Carlos III* (Madrid: Alianza Universidad Editorial, 1992), p. 261.

... la vanidad, fomentada por el lujo, debe considerarse como mal menor para
impedir uno mayor ... cual sería cesación del trabajo y de la industria y con ella
la ruina del Estado ... las diversiones publicas ... las meriendas y los bailes a
escote y otras muchas diversiones ... quien es capaz de calcular lo que cuesta
sólo este ramo?[45]

The 'Sociedad Económica de Amigos del País' [Economic Societies of Friends
of the Country], one of the main socio-economic institutions of the Spanish
Enlightenment government, expressed the same thoughts on luxury as Sempere y
Guarinos. The 'Sociedad Vascongada de Amigos del País' [Royal Basque Society
of Friends of the Country] amended one of its statutes in 1785 showing that they
were supporting luxury as a concept of progress. The institution saw luxury as the
conspicuous consumption of the rich, who poured their wealth into the consumption
of unnecessary and ostentatious goods. However, as this consumption supported
the labour sector producing these goods, luxury was not perceived as a social evil
because it bolstered the national economy:

Si por voz lujo, se entiende absolutamente el uso voluptuoso y ruinoso de los
bienes, es evidente que no puede hablarse en su favor sin temeridad y escándalo
... puramente político, cual es el de que sus gentes ricas y acomodadas, gastando
sus caudales en consumir géneros costosos para su lucimiento, comodidad y
regalo, fomentan las artes y contribuyen al mantenimiento y honesta ocupación
de los que en ellas se emplean.[46]

Later, during the last decade of the eighteenth century, we find satirical comments
being made by important figures belonging to the upper social classes against the
consumption of luxury commodities. An example is the satirical poem written in
1791 by 'El Licenciado Don Felipe Rojo de Flores, Auditor Honorario de Guerra
por S.M.', who ridicules the wearing of luxury clothing in the society of his period:

En la loca vanidad, pompa engañada
que en tantos males de su
bien redunda,
Funda el hombre su vida mal
fundada,
Sin que el fundamento le
confunda.
Fundandose el hombre de la misma
nada,

---

[45]   Sempere y Guarinos, J., *Historia del lujo*, pp. 48, 203–5.
[46]   Sarrailh, J., *La España ilustrada de la segunda mitad del siglo XVIII* (Madrid:
ed. F.C.E., 1957), p. 244. This issue has been also explored by Martin Gaite, C., *Usos
Amorosos*, p. 34.

Condenado a morir, pues en qué
funda,
Ser hombre, si es mortal, polvo,
si es viento?
Si viento, nada, y nada fundamento?[47]

In this period the debate on luxury took on strong political connotations. Material items considered different or new were met with public scorn, especially by pamphleteers who stereotyped the new fashions. Middle-class snobbery and their emulation of the aristocratic lifestyle is ruthlessly attacked in the poem above. Vanity, pomposity and luxury were thought to be the foundation of the nouveau riche because 'en la loca vanidad ... funda el hombre su vida mal fundada ...' [in the mad vanity ... found the man his bad-founded life ...], in reference to the new lifestyle that people were acquiring through the consumption of new commodities. The superficiality of such goods masked the true nature of the individuals desperate to emulate the old aristocracy. As such, the traditional scheme of the *Ancien Regime* was being attacked by naïve people, who began appearing in stereotypes devised by writers, political pamphleteers and satirists. The stereotype of the French model known as 'petimetre' was created within this socio-political framework, in which conventional society was being challenged.

3.3. The 'Petimetre' and 'Majo' in the Local and International Perspectives

The invention of the satirical and burlesque model of the 'petimetre', which can also be defined as a new expression of individual consumer decisions, was accompanied by a campaign against foreign fashions. This movement was created by political institutions, whose purpose was to control national consumption. The political authorities of the Spanish Enlightenment passed new laws to prohibit the consumption of specific goods, especially those associated with French customs and tastes. As a social reaction to the introduction of French fashions in Spanish society, the classical and 'castizo' Spanish model of 'majo/a', emerged: the so-called 'majismo' phenomenon. Spanish politicians combined moral and economic issues, by creating a political agenda related to the modern nation-state. They also mixed social concepts that defined the tradition, culture and natural customs of the country. Some state policies for controlling consumption consisted in the elaboration of a political project based on the stimulation of domestic industries such as the creation of a national dress made of national materials. The goal was to stimulate the economy by fostering national values through the symbolic power of dress, as well as to create negative stereotypes of foreign fashions and cultures.

---

[47]   C.D.M.T., CA, *Don Felipe Rojo de Flores, Una juiciosa satira contra la profanidad, y luxo con varias noticias historicas relativas a los trages y adornos* (Madrid: Imprenta Real, 1794).

The 'majismo' model emerged as a phenomenon that combined pure values and traditions of the nation, as a reaction against the 'petimetre'. These national values were used by political institutions against the importation of French fashions. Subsequently, this became a political issue due to the French Revolution and, later, with the Napoleonic invasion, it became an instrument of popular rage against French symbols. Hence, this struggle between tradition and modernity became more of a political phenomenon during late eighteenth and early nineteenth centuries.

The emergence of the figure of the 'petimetre' is an example of the participation of men and women in spreading new French fashions throughout Spain during the eighteenth century. Similar models can be found in other European areas. In the second-half of the eighteenth century the British figure of the 'macaroni' emerged,[48] as the precedent of the 'dandy' or 'flâneur',[49] which was a new stereotype of a man with exquisite manners and good taste in clothing. These cultural models were circulating throughout Europe, in Italy, France, Spain and England, as well as in the British colonies of America, when the American Revolution began. The song 'Yankee Doodle Dandy', composed during this period, mentions a man who 'stuck a feather in his hat and called it macaroni'. The meaning of the expression was that Yankees were so naïve that they believe that a feather in the hat was sufficient to qualify a person as a 'macaroni'.[50] This suggests that the expansion of new socio-cultural stereotypes did not occur in isolation, and the 'petimetre'–'majo' struggle was not a localized trend. The whole phenomenon was integrated into a global model, in which individuals were the main actors of inter-cultural transfers, through the circulation of foreign communities and material possessions, in relation to the introduction of new fashions in clothing.

Martin Gaite studied this phenomenon as a particular case that took place in Spain, most notably in Madrid, during the eighteenth century. She suggests that this phenomenon was exclusive to the local elite of Madrid, whose young members introduced ridiculous and extravagant habits from abroad.[51] Scholars have focused the analysis of the social backlash of fashions on the specific circumstances that took place in the courtesan Madrid of the eighteenth century,[52] rather than observing such issues as a matter of global stereotypes that were occurring in

---

[48]   Rauser, A., 'Hair, Authenticity, and the Self-Made Macaroni', *Eighteenth-century Studies*, vol. 38, no. 1, Hair (Fall, 2004), pp. 101–17.

[49]   Auslander, L., 'The Gendering of Consumer Practices in Nineteenth-century France', in De Grazia, V. and Furlough, E. (eds), *The Sex of Things*, p. 90.

[50]   Rauser, Amelia F., 'Hair, Authenticity', pp. 101–17.

[51]   Martin Gaite, C., *Usos Amorosos*, p. 72.

[52]   See studies by: Haidt, R., 'Theorizing the *Petimetra*', p. 34; Bolufer, M., *Mujeres e Ilustración*, p. 200; Subirá, J., '"Petimetría" y "Majismo" en la literatura', *Revista de Literatura*, 4.7–8 (1953): 267–85; Sala Valldaura, J.M., 'Gurruminos, petimetres, abates y currutacos en el teatro breve del siglo XVIII', *Revista de Literatura* (julio–diciembre, vol. LXXI), n. 142, pp. 429–60.

Europe due to trans-national contacts among people and commodities. There is no scholarly work that has centred the analysis of 'petimetres' as a trans-national phenomenon. Once again we find Spanish and Anglo-Saxon studies,[53] which perceive the 'petimetre' as a vain and arrogant figure, by paying special attention to his effeminate character, instead of considering the figure as a product of the stereotypes constructed by politicians, with the aim of developing the program of new nation-states. Through such stereotypes, Spanish politicians wanted to foster a strong sense of nationhood. This issue is related more to the social backlash that was taking place globally, as a result of the progressive development of travel in Europe and America.

The circulation of new ideas and knowledge, as a consequence of the experiences of travellers, was changing traditional habits and transforming national values. Travellers were the major agents who reinforced the construction of socio-cultural stereotypes, as witnesses of life and culture in other lands. Through their travel accounts and descriptions of countries, habits and strange traditions, people could confront their own culture in light of new, exotic and foreign traditions. Travel books that emerged from those voyages offered an insight into the lives of far-off populations and cultures with, in some cases, a fictional perception of reality.[54]

This was the central concept of all nations and social 'milieux', as society was balanced between two different poles: the capacity for adaptation to new cultural models and rigid immobility. The geographic and social isolation of a very traditional society, such as in Spain, meant that the penetration of new ideas and material culture caused a stronger social backlash than in other European areas. As Daniel Roche mentions, four major factors helped shape the main socio-cultural relations that emerged from new human experiences: religion, reason and science, the economic and technological universe and the aesthetic values that emerged from tradition.[55] Hence, the mutation of those values resulted in a strong cultural confrontation.

The circulation of ideas through the new cosmopolitan life and the desire for learning about new geographic areas, cultures and civilizations stimulated the intellectual life of Europeans. However, this cosmopolitanism was also the main vehicle for the diffusion of warped or deformed representations of unknown places, cultures and identities, as well as for the construction of prejudices that went against what was considered new, strange, different or exotic. This cultural sign or mark was in a continual process of formation due to the increase in travel by young people, such as European travels to the ruins of ancient Rome or Pompeii,

---

[53]   Rauser, A., 'Hair, Authenticity', pp. 101–17.

[54]   Crépon, M., *Paysages en mouvement, transports et perception de l'espace (XVIIIe–XIXe siècles)* (Paris: Gallimard, 2005).

[55]   Roche, D., 'Circolazione delle idée, mobilità dele persone: continuità e rotture', in Visceglia, M.A., *Le radici storiche dell'Europa. L'età moderna* (Roma: ed. Viella, 2007), pp. 127–40.

PANTHEON MACARONI.

Illustration 3.1   Philip Dawe, Pantheon Macaroni [A Real Character at the Late
                    Masquerade], printed for John Bowles, 1773. Mezzotint. BM
                    Sat 5221. © Trustees of *The British Museum*, London.

with the desire to learn about ancient cultures and civilizations. What most caught the attention of their fellow citizens was the new language they brought back to their country. The young English Grand Tourists, the so-called 'macaronis',[56] returned with new refined manners that they had learned during their sojourns in Rome, and they expressed these through language as well as extravagant clothing styles.

Young men who had been to Italy on the Grand Tour adopted the Italian word 'maccherone' – a boorish fool, in Italian – and said that anything fashionable or 'à la mode' was 'very macaroni'.[57] Horace Walpole[58] wrote to a friend in 1764 of 'the Macaroni Club, which is composed of all the traveled young men who wear long curls and spying-glasses'. The 'club' was not a formal one: the expression was particularly used to characterize fops who dressed in high fashion with tall, powdered wigs with a 'chapeau bras' on top that could only be removed with the point of a sword. The 'macaronis' were precursors to the 'dandies'[59] who, far from their present connotation of effeminacy, were a more masculine reaction to the excesses of the 'macaroni'.

A very good example of these attitudes is revealed in the letter that the young Jeremy Bentham, an Englishman, notable lawyer and property dealer educated at Westminster, who became a famous utilitarian philosopher, wrote in 1776 to his brother Sir Samuel Bentham, an English naval architect and inventor, when they were 28 and 19 years old respectively. Jeremy Bentham mentions the foolish manners that Fitzherbert's 'macaroni' brother[60] had acquired on his travels around Europe:

---

[56] It has been occasionally argued that the use of 'macaroni' for fashionable British males comes from the Italian maccherone, meaning 'fool', but as the Oxford English Dictionary contends, macaronis were in fact named for the pasta dish that rich young tourist brought back from their sojourns in Rome, the macaroni was known in 1760s as an elite figure marked by the cultivation of European travel. But as *The Macaroni and Theatrical Magazine* explained in its inaugural issue in 1772, 'the word macaroni changed its meaning to that person who exceeded the ordinary bounds of fashion; and is now justly used as term of reproach to all ranks of people, indifferently, who fall into this absurdity'. Rauser, A., 'Hair, Authenticity', pp. 114–15; and *The Macaroni and Theatrical Magazine, or Monthly Register* (October, 1772): 1.

[57] Rauser, A., 'Hair, Authenticity', pp. 101–7.

[58] The English art historian, man of letters, antiquarian and politician. See Haggerty, G., 'Queering Horace Walpole', *Studies in English Literature, 1500–1900*, vol. 46, no. 3, Restoration and Eighteenth Century (Summer, 2006), pp. 543–62.

[59] Norton, R., 'The Macaroni Club: Homosexual Scandals in 1772', *Homosexuality in Eighteenth-century England: A Sourcebook* (19 December 2004, updated 11 June 2005) <http://rictornorton.co.uk/eighteen/macaroni.htm>. See the chapter, 'The Macaroni Club', on Norton, R., *Mother Clap's Molly House: The Gay Subculture in England, 1700–1830* (London: GMP, 1992), p. 302.

[60] The macaroni brother of William Fitzherbert was almost certainly Alleyne Fitzherbert (1753–1839), later 1st Baron St Helens. He was educated at Derby, Eton, and St John's College Cambridge, where he received his B.A. in 1774. After embarking upon a grand tour through France and Italy he was appointed Minister at Brussels (February 1777–August 1782). He then went to Paris to negotiate the peace with the

Fitzherbert's Macaroni Brother, who was in his Brother's Chambers when my
Brother was in mine is made one of the Subpreceptors to the Prince of Wales.
He is said to be a man of sense and knowledge – He is lately come from France
Italy Germany etc. and has the appearance of a great Fribble (I believe you saw
him) but seemed very obliging and well-bred.
    Wilson and I dine chez moi every day. We manage matters very comfortably.
He is studying the doctrine of conveyances and every day at dinner ...[61]

This passage is testimony of the cultural transfers that resulted from the movement of
people among diverse places. This was the effect of a process of selection, choice and
socio-cultural appropriation. The economic and intellectual import-export market
within different European territories was the system of mediation that channelled
and accelerated the success of the transfer of language, food and clothing habits.
This is seen through the acquisition of new linguistic terms such as 'Wilson and I
dine chez moi' [Wilson and I had dinner at my home] as Bentham wrote, astonished,
to his brother, although Benthan in his letters did not ridicule the effeminate manners
of the 'macaroni'. Travel books, diaries and the exchange of letters was the main
instrument that determined the efficacy of these cultural transfers.
    European and Atlantic voyages were rooted in a pedagogical process, by
which people constructed an image of the world, based on places they have visited
and people they have met. Their accounts were created through the construction
of new worlds which travellers had seen. The swift developments in travel
were fostered by different factors such as having a good job, improvements in
the standard of living, commerce and the undertaking of businesses ventures,
migration, pilgrimage or merely a curiosity to learn more about the history, habits
and culture of different countries.[62] The Spanish youths who had travelled to Paris

---

European powers. 1783–87: envoy extraordinary to Catherine II of Russia. 1787: Chief
Secretary to Lord-Lieutenant of Ireland. 1789: envoy extraordinary to The Hague. 1791:
ambassador extraordinary to Madrid, to negotiate a trade agreement; became 1st Baron
St Helens (Irish Peerage). 1794: ambassador to The Hague. 1801: on mission to the newly
acceded Alexander I of Russia; created Baron St Helens in the United Kingdom Peerage.
1803: retired from diplomacy with pension. 1804: Lord of the Bedchamber to George III.
Quotation from: Bentham, Jeremy, '189. To Samuel Bentham 22–23 November 1776 (Aet
28)'. *The Correspondence of Jeremy Bentham: 1752–1776* (ed. Timothy L.S. Sprigge.
London: Athlone Press, 1968), pp. 362–5. Print. *Electronic Enlightenment*, ed. Robert
McNamee et al. Vers. 2.1. 2010 (University of Oxford. 2 June 2010). <http://0-
www.e-enlightenment.com.biblio.eui.eu/item/bentjeOU0010362_1key001cor>. © Electronic
Enlightenment Project, Bodleian Library, University of Oxford, 2008–10. All rights reserved.
Distributed by Oxford University Press. See also the chapter, 'Popular Rage', that Rictor
Norton dedicates to Jeremy Bentham's argument for decriminalization of homosexuality in
the 1770s and 1810s. In Norton, R., *Mother Clap's*, p. 302.
   [61]   Bentham, J., *The Correspondence.*
   [62]   Roche, D., *Humeurs vagabondes. De la circulation des hommes et de l'utilité des
voyages* (Paris: Fayard, 2003).

were also known as 'petimetres', foolish people with extremely elegant manners who wanted to be 'á la mode'. 'Petimetres' or 'currutacos' figures emerged in Madrid and then spread to other urban areas of Spain. The historian Richard Herr wrote the following about the social behaviour of 'petimetres':

> Otros hijos de la aristocracia se permitían el lujo de recorrer países extranjeros, aunque, al parecer, lo único que sacaban en limpio eran unas cuantas modas tontas y el desprecio de sus compatriotas, quienes imitando su tendencia a emplear galicismos, les pusieron el mote de 'petimetres'.[63]

The famous French comedian playwright, Beaumarchais, when he was in Madrid, at the 'Puerta del Sol' plaza, saw such 'petimetres' talking and chatting and exchanging pleasantries and phrases in Italian or French.[64] As a result, Beaumarchais incorporated the 'petimetre' figures in his well-known trilogy *Le Barbier de Seville, Le Mariage de Figaro* and *La Mere Coupable*, a work published in 1782. This author defined the 'petimetre' as an exquisite 'superdandy', who walked in a very measured way and consumed snuff in a very polished manner. The 'petitmetre' or 'currutaco' applied powder to his hair and was seen in urban places as a very effeminate individual:

> … caminar balanceándose sobre las puntas de los pies como un bailarín sobre la cuerda floja, oscilando hacia delante y hacia atrás como si estuviera bebido, ofendiendo el olfato de los viandantes con el aroma de sus ungüentos, sus afeites y perfume.[65]

This new perception of individuals as seen in the public sphere was taking place during the second half of the eighteenth century in Spain, at first in Madrid and later in other urban areas.[66] The display of this kind of fashion through the introduction of a new language and by means of external symbols, such as clothing worn at public ceremonies, was changing the social life in European courts and urban

---

[63] Herr, R., *España y la revolución del siglo XVIII* (Madrid: ed. Aguilar, 1964), pp. 62–3.

[64] Thomas, H., *Beaumarchais en Sevilla*, ed. Planeta (Barcelona: ed. Planeta, 2008), p. 66.

[65] Beaumarchais, Pierre-Agustin Caron de, *Ouvres complètes de Beaumarchais*, Préface de Edouard Fournier (Paris: Laplace, Sánchez et Cie, 1876). In this book Beaumarchais includes his *Memoire sur l'Espagne*, written as a letter, which is addressed to the Duke of Choiseul.

[66] Andioc, R., *Teatro y sociedad en el Madrid del siglo XVIII* (Valencia: Fundación Juan March, Editorial Castalia, 1976), p. 59. Civil corporations were also notable institutions, whose major task was to regulate the socio-economic life of the districts and neighbourhoods, exerting the function of linking the state and its towns. See: Amelang, J.S., *Honored Citizens of Barcelona: Patrician Culture and Class Relations, 1490–1714* (Princeton, N.J.: Princeton University Press, 1986), pp. 28–32.

areas.[67] Thus, a new social interaction was taking place in public spheres such as promenades in the Prado gardens, theatres, bullfights or intimate conferences, among wealthy and industrious artisans, foreigners, the local elite as well as lower social groups.

---

[67] Castle, T., *Masquerade and Civilization: the Carnivalesque in Eighteenth-century English Culture and Fiction* (Stanford, California: Stanford University Press, 1986).

Chapter 4

The Development of Global Models: Transforming Dress as a Means to Control Consumption

A state may exercise a policy in order to direct consumer behaviour towards the acquisition of certain types of goods. This occurred in the various authoritarian states of Europe with a special emphasis in the Catholic territories, such as Spain, during the eighteenth century. Historians and economists should bear in mind the covert collaboration between enterprises and merchants, whether domestic or foreign, in order to create new demands, to renovate fashions and create new needs among consumers. Regardless of whether a particular style was in or out of fashion, the main goal was to stimulate the consumer's psychology, fostering the need to purchase goods seen by the public as new, fashionable, luxurious and exotic. The individual was considered to be an essential target as a potential purchaser of commodities, and in this socio-economic domain the state as a supra-entity sought to curb any compulsive consumer behaviour. This was the main goal of Spanish ministers, during the eighteenth century, as loyal servants of the Monarchy in order to maintain Catholic values and stimulate the national economy.

In the psychology of individuals, within the progressive transformation of consumer behaviour, a fashionable appearance became a necessity rather than a superfluous feature. In this context, continual innovations appear with the creation of new models and stereotypes such as the 'petimetre', 'macaroni', 'dandy' and 'flâneur' during the late eighteenth and early nineteenth centuries, which exceeded the ordinary bounds of fashion. These models emerged as a consequence of the socio-cultural measures that the state employed in order to limit the purchase of foreign goods and avoid the possible contamination of national values. No individuals self-identified as a 'petimetre', 'macaroni', 'dandy' or 'flâneur'. In fact, the Spanish consumed French goods, in particular, or foreign goods, in general, because of the transformation of individual tastes. However, the state, and influential people, used such stereotypes in the public arena, particularly in political pamphlets and books, with the aim of upholding national values and traditions by ridiculing foreign fashions and customs. Such models related to the attempt to construct new and deformed identities that opposed the Spanish national model.

The development of new tastes, the desire for consuming fashionable goods, comfort and leisure time were the key factors that challenged the limits imposed by traditional Spanish values. The meaning of dress, and the ways in which it was used, was the principal element to control. The machinery of the state was working hard when the national project of developing a Spanish national dress began in the second half of the eighteenth century. This constituted the major instance during this period when consumer choices were trying to be controlled. The project was directed at women, as major agents of fashions and social actors, to keep the Spanish traditional values according to Catholic mores. However, was the final rejection of this project by noble ladies evidence that the state could not really control consumption as the self-development of individuals went beyond the political rules?

4.1. Between Fiction and Reality: 'Petimetre' and 'Majo'

The global project of restructuring the socio-economic sphere based on the development of the new nation-states, as well as that of knowledge and thought, in which the construction and reformulation of identities belongs, shows the multiplication of ideas and social actors that shaped the different identities across the European space, or civilization, during the modern age.[1] The conquest or 'colonization' of a new imaginary world,[2] in which those ideas are constructed, was the main argument used by the new nation-states to control the political frontiers and the economic, socio-cultural and religious spheres.

The abundant circulation of travellers' accounts, diaries, books in diverse editions, formats and texts, during the eighteenth and nineteenth centuries, shaped a new socio-cultural and economic market that stimulated the construction of stereotypical images and unreal worlds.[3] The massive quantity of literature regarding voyages,[4] as well as scientific discoveries made in distant lands, stimulated an interest in learning about, and visiting, foreign lands. Books motivated this interest and international travel made satisfying it possible. The desire for learning about new places, people and civilizations is evident from private libraries. From my analysis of probate inventories of south-eastern Spain, in the territory of the Kingdom of Murcia, such interests are evident from the possession of a wide variety of books. These personal libraries comprised: travel books (approximately 13 per cent); books about languages and foreign grammar (approximately 12 per cent); science books (approximately 14 per cent); books on philosophy (approximately 20 per cent); and in the category of 'other'

---

[1]   See the article by Yun Casalilla, B., 'Consumi, società e mercati: verso uno spazio economico europeo', in Visceglia, M.A., *Le radici*, pp. 85–103.

[2]   Gruzinski, S., *La colonisation de l'imaginaire: sociétés indigènes et occidentalisation dans le Mexique espagnol*, 16e–18e siècle (Paris: Gallimard, 1988).

[3]   Chartier, R., *Culture écrite et société: l'ordre des livres, XIVe–XVIIIe siècle* (Paris: Albin Michel, 1996).

[4]   García Mercadal, J., *Viajes de extranjeros por España y Portugal.* In *Siglo XVIII* (vol. III, Madrid: ed. Aguilar, 1962), p. 563.

(approximately 39 per cent), there are a wide range of books such as comedies, Spanish dictionaries and literature.[5]

Literature is the main instrument that brought diverse worlds together. It is the confrontation between the real world and fiction, as result of different people's perceptions of civilizations, cultures, thoughts, languages and traditions. Fiction and reality are the main elements found in books that circulated among different libraries. Texts, comments, treatises and opinions written after reading and being in contact with such writings contributed to the creation of new values and the reinvention of old traditions. The circulation of texts and knowledge formed a new cosmopolitanism and patriotism, as well as the acceptance or rejection of new cultural forms. As a consequence of this process, the conflict between tradition and self-identity and the construction of new imaginary communities emerges. These traditions are reinvented by the power of the introduction of new words in everyday language. The so-called neologisms had very strong political connotations and were used by traditional institutions to develop the political program of the emerging nation-states.

The analysis of certain passages of Cadalso's book, *Cartas Marruecas*, can clarify how the process of confrontation between tradition and modernity occurred. The construction of an imaginary world, an Arcadia dreamt up by modern politicians, far removed from everyday life, was used to reinvent the Spanish tradition. *Cartas Marruecas* represents an early example in the eighteenth century, of the political process of development of the future nation-state. The significance of words and neologisms, throughout the text of this book, represents how such terms were used politically to defend the tradition and values of the nation as opposed to the invasion of foreign habits and manners, which were contaminating the pure national customs.

Luxury goods and new fashions that came from France had a special appeal in Spanish society, especially during the second half of the eighteenth century. Such fashions shaped a new socio-cultural model, which was linked to the enjoyment of all the pleasures life could offer. This foreign model, as viewed by traditional sectors, was considered as a corruption of the pure values of the nation. Hence, political institutions created a stereotype with the aim of considering anything with French connotations as damaging, immoral and of potential harm for the nation. This can be considered as the origin of the modern stereotype, mentioned above, of the 'petimetre', which had both female and male connotations.

The term 'petimetre' comes from the Gallicism 'petit maître', the young man who pays special attention to manners and fashions.[6] This term was associated with the leisured young men and women, originating in the city of Madrid and later spreading to other Spanish cities. In José Cadalso's *Cartas Marruecas*, this figure was recognized as a proud and vain individual, an indolent and lazy person with an

---

[5]   A.H.P.M., protocols, 1730–1808.

[6]   Cadalso, J., *Cartas Marruecas* (Madrid: edition José Miguel Caso, Colección Austral, 1999), 1st edition, 1755, p. 98.

aversion to work. Cadalso, through the North African figure Gazel, reconstructed Spanish and European customs, habits and traditions, as well as the forms of the European language. Gazel reflects on the European and Spanish values, by looking at European civilization through the eyes of an outsider. This character describes new socio-cultural habits that were taking place in eighteenth-century Spain as rare. The adoption of French words and phrases such as 'tournée', 'faire la toileta' or those describing French clothes such as the 'desabillé' or 'bonnets' provoked a reaction among traditionalists who saw the mutation of words, as well as dress, as an attack on time-honoured values.[7] As a result, an antagonistic model emerged, the 'majo', which expressed the 'castizo' identity[8]: traditional Castilian customs and social behaviour, contrary to French fashions.

The legitimacy of this political program depended upon the total obedience of individuals, as devoted members of the state. Any act of disobedience, which could be any unsanctioned individualistic expression, could be considered as a crime against the state. The development of stereotypes is an example of how the machinery of the state was using socio-cultural forms to control people's consumption and hinder the self-identity of individuals.[9] Through Gazel's description of new Spanish attitudes, values and behaviour, Cadalso presented what he saw as the conflict between civilized and uncivilized, by developing concepts with negative connotations that describe the 'other' as the 'stranger'.[10] Ridiculing the 'other' was used to extol national values. The 'stranger' was represented by any French habits and cultural forms that had penetrated Spanish life. The satirical model of the 'petimetre' was constructed to reinforce national values. Traditional sectors and political institutions voiced their own personal fears, worries and anxieties, through the pejorative description of individuals that could be associated with the social values of Spain's nearest political neighbour, and potential rival: France.

Clothes were the most obvious symbol of such features, by which people could mock and ridicule French traditions. France was the main European centre for the creation and recreation of fashions. Therefore, the 'petimetre' was depicted as an individual obsessed with following elegant French fashions and manners. This

---

[7]   Cadalso, J., *Cartas*, 'Letter n. XXXV from Gazel to Benbeley', pp. 128–33.

[8]   Noyes, D., 'La Maja Vestida. Dress as resistance to Enlightenment in Late-18th-century Madrid', *Journal of American Folklore*, 111 (440) (Spring, 1998), pp. 197–217.

[9]   To explore further the process of the construction of nation-states confronted with the development of the self-identity of individuals, who composed the new nation, see: Giddens, A., *Modernity and self-identity* (Cambridge: Cambridge University Press, 1991); Gleason, Ph., 'Identifying Identity: A Semantic History', *Journal of American History*, 69/4 (1983), pp. 910–31.

[10]   See the volume edited on-line (http://www.cromohs.unifi.it/8_2003/cecere.html): Cecere, G., 'L' "Oriente d' Europa": un' idea in movimento (sec. XVIII). Un contributo cartografico', *Cromohs*, 8 (2003): 1–25, in Atti del seminario internazionale: *Immagini d'Italia e d'Europa nella letteratura e nella documentazione di viaggio nel XVIII e nel XIX secolo.*

encouraged widespread criticism and such individuals were seen as unproductive for the nation's economy. They were also criticized for their effeminate attitude, which challenged the masculine model imposed by society.

Illustrations 4.1 and 4.2   'Petimetra' and 'Petimetre'. Colección: Rodríguez, Antonio. Colección General de los Trajes que en la actualidad se usan en España. Principiada en el año 1801. Madrid: Librería de Castillo, 1801. Numéro de serie 1306 y 1308. *Fundación Joaquín Díaz, Centro Etnográfico*, Diputación de Valladolid, Spain.

People who spoke, behaved and dressed in the French style were thus stereotyped as 'petimetre'. The government of King Charles III encouraged young Spanish men to travel abroad and undertake their education in different countries. This was the major feature of the Grand Tour which formerly occurred in France and England, and later in other European countries, and allowed young men to develop their intellectual ability in a variety of subjects such as philosophy, archaeology, geography, history and literature.

Although the historiography of the European Enlightenment has focused largely on England, France and central Europe,[11] during this period, peripheral European territories transformed their own values and traditions, which were manifested through material and immaterial dimensions, by means of the circulation of people, ideas and commodities. Hence, the common identity of European culture was shaped simultaneously in different areas. In the case of Spain, the 'petimetre' model was the expression of both material and immaterial transformations, as a result of the socio-cultural stereotypes that took place in peripheral Europe.[12]

Material transformations can be examined through changes in dress and accessories, and immaterial transformations by means of the acquisition of new socio-cultural manners and habits. This immaterial aspect was manifested through changes in language, such as the introduction of Gallicisms to the Spanish vocabulary, and new manners in social gatherings, theatres, dinners or balls. In Jose Cadalso's *Cartas Marruecas*, written in 1755, we learn about these socio-linguistic mutations:

> En España, como en todas partes el lenguaje se muda a cada paso como las costumbres; y es que, como las voces son invenciones para representar las ideas, es preciso que se inventen palabras para explicar la impresión que hacen las costumbres nuevamente introducidas ... Sólo un sobrino que tengo de edad de veinte años, muchacho que tiene habilidad de trinchar una liebre, bailar un minuet y destapar una botella con más aire que cuantos hombres han nacido de mujeres, me supo explicar algunas voces.[13]

Mentioned in this passage are some of the new ideas and habits which collided with the conventions and traditions of society of this period. The evolution of language influenced new social manners by means of the introduction of French terms. The employment of Gallicisms and 'vocabulaire savant'[14] [the learned vocabulary] shaped the French stereotype of 'petimetre'. This was an invention of literature with a clear political target: stereotyping the 'stranger', considered as the 'other', and building up a new national identity. The introduction of new ideas and words such as 'minuet' was a naïve attitude that older generations could not understand, and one which only those who had travelled in Europe could recognize. This is a good example of the social backlash which resulted from the introduction of new cultural forms in Spain. In the same passage Gazel asked Nuño to read him a letter in which the new ideas, customs and words were written:

---

[11]   Israel, J., *Radical Enlightenment*, pp. 7–8. Hesse, C., *The Other Enlightenment: How French Women Became Modern* (Princeton: Princeton University Press, 2001).

[12]   Sahlins, P., *Boundaries. The Making of France and Spain in the Pyrenées* (Berkeley: University of California Press, 1989). Wolff, L., *Inventing Eastern Europe: The Map of Civilization on the Mind of the Enlightenment* (Stanford, California: Stanford University Press, 1994).

[13]   Cadalso, J., *Cartas*, 'Letter n. XXXV from Gazel to Benbeley', pp. 128–33.

[14]   De Roy, L., *L'emprunt linguistique* (Paris: Edition les Belles-Lettres, 1956).

... Hoy no ha sido día en mi apartamento hasta medio día y medio. Tomé
dos tazas de té. Púseme un desabillé y bonete de noche. Hice un tour en mi
jardín; leía acerca de ocho versos del segundo acto de Zaira. Vino Mr. Lavanda;
empecé mi toeleta. No estuvo el abate. Mandé pagar mi modista. Pasé a la sala
de compañía. Me sequé toda sola. Entró un poco de mundo; jugué una partida de
mediator; tiré las cartas; jugué al piquete. El maitre d'hotel avisó. Mi nuevo jefe
de cocina es divino; el viene de arribar de París. La crapaudina, mi plato favorito,
estaba deliciosa. Tomé café y licor. Otra partida de quince, perdí mi todo. Fui al
espectáculo; la pieza que han anunciado para el lunes que viene es muy galante,
pero los autores son pitoyables; los vestidos horribles, las decoraciones, tristes.
Es menester tomar paciencia, porque es preciso matar el tiempo. Salí al tercer
acto, y me volví de allí a casa. Tomé de la limonada. Entré en mi gabinete para
escribirte ésta, porque soy tu veritable amiga ...[15]

This passage has been also analysed by professors Garcia and Yun.[16] Their
focus is the analysis of the introduction of French fashions in Spain related to
the development of the material culture and the new conception of the household
space. However, our main argument is not only centered on the development of
new lifestyles, leisure and consumption. Through the analysis of such texts and
by looking at specific words, the 'vocabulaire savant', we can appreciate how the
mutation of classic forms of culture and habits shaped new identities linked with
the future nation-states of the nineteenth century.

Three different aspects of the new social life are described in the above
passage: innovative eating habits, clothing and language. These were related to
the naïve behaviour of the nouveau riche and were manifested in social gatherings
and cultural events. For example: how to drink a cup of tea, coffee, liqueur or
lemonade, drinks that were linked with the development of a new refined taste,
as well as how to prepare French recipes: 'Mi nuevo jefe de cocina es divino; el
viene de arribar de París' [My new chef is divine; he came to arrive from Paris].
The attention to dressing with extreme elegance, which was called 'toeleta', was
seen as a refinement in both clothing and personal hygiene. The appearance of new
garments, such as 'desabillé', 'bonete', or interior furniture, such as 'gabinete' or
'buffet', introduced new habits, words and ideas into everyday life. Furthermore,
in this passage we find new descriptions of how to behave at social gatherings,
such as taking a walk or 'tour' in the garden, going to the theatre or playing cards:

Acabó Nuño de leer, diciéndome: -¿Qué has sacado en limpio de todo esto? Por
mi parte, te aseguro que antes de humillarme a preguntar a mis amigos el sentido
de estas frases, me hubiera sujetado a estudiarlas ... Aquello de medio día y
medio ... lo del desabillé ... lo del bonete de noche ... hacer un tour ... no sé
que es Zaira. Mr. de Lavanda ... Empezó su toeleta ... También me dijo lo que

---

15   Cadalso, J., *Cartas*, 'Letter n. XXXV from Gazel to Benbeley', pp. 128–33.
16   See García Fernández, M. and Yun Casalilla, B., *Consumo*, p. 252.

es modista, piquete, maitre d'hotel y otras palabras semejantes … Y lo de matar
el tiempo, siendo así que el tiempo es quien nos mata a todos … me explicó lo
que era misántropo …[17]

The use of these new words was related to a new semantic group that clashed with
traditional habits. The linguistic turn, employed in the analysis of these passages,
proves that a new socio-cultural stereotype was being created by Spanish writers,
who saw, in the use of foreign terms and adoption of increasingly lavish lifestyles
a kind of naïve and superficial attitude contrary to the national tradition:

> Por todo lo cual, dice Nuño, mi parecer y dictamen, 'salvo meliori', es que
> en cada un año se fijen costumbres para el siguiente, y por consecuencia se
> establezca el idioma que se ha de hablar durante sus 365 días … Vocabulario
> nuevo al uso de los que quieran entenderse y explicarse con las gentes de moda,
> para el año de mil setecientos y tantos siguientes, aumentado, revisto y corregido
> por una Sociedad de varones insignes, con los retratos de los más principales.[18]

With this passage, Gazel was claiming that due to the mutation of the Spanish
language, caused by the introduction of Gallicisms, it was necessary to create a
homogeneous vocabulary and dictionary, through which people could understand
these new expressions. The socio-linguistic transfers from France were shaping
the new Spanish cultural idiosyncrasy, altering traditional values.

The analysis of these texts offers substantiation for the main argument: that
the transformation of tradition and values was the main tool used by political
institutions to develop the programme of the nation-state. The control of individual
choices, especially in terms of consumption, was the most important aspect of this
political project. Material goods symbolized the external appearance of people that
composed the nation. This explains the government's criticism of new fashions,
foreign words or the adoption of neologisms, social behaviour, as well as other
tendencies learned from foreign countries that irritated traditional society.

The defence of such sovereignty, especially within the framework of the
building up of nation-states, aimed to redefine the concept of the nation and to
construct an imaginary political community, in which those traditions, identities
and values were inseparable and indissoluble.[19] Therefore, in order to be seen as
patriotic, members of the national community had to reinvent an imaginary world,
both past and present, to reaffirm traditional values. At the same time, they created
fictional stereotypes, such as the 'petimetre', or 'macaroni', related to foreign,
external, new or strange conventions. The 'petimetre' phenomenon occurred
in Spain and the 'macaroni' in Britain. The new national community perceived

---

[17]   Cadalso, J., *Cartas*, 'Letter n. XXXV from Gazel to Benbeley', pp. 128–33.
[18]   Cadalso, J., *Cartas*, 'Letter n. XXXV from Gazel to Benbeley', pp. 128–33.
[19]   Seton-Watson, H., *Nations and States: an Enquiry into the Origins of Nations and the Politics of Nationalism* (London: Methuen, 1977), p. 5.

those fictional stereotypes as being potentially damaging for the construction and reinvention of the new nation-state. As Gellner observes,[20] nationalism is not the awakening of the self-consciousness of the nation, rather it performs as a higher entity to invent unreal communities and a new identity of the nation that have never existed. Consequently, the new communities are not distinguished by their falseness or legitimacy, but they are marked by the style and way they are imagined.[21]

4.2. The National Dress: Construction of a New Identity and Control of Consumption

The policy on consumption, developed by the state during the eighteenth century, was at its height when the government devised a project for imposing a national dress. Once again, clothing represented the material symbol of a political programme which aimed to develop a group consciousness and stimulate national values among citizens. The establishment of a national dress constitutes the last phase of a series of measures issued by Spanish politicians, in conjunction with religious authorities, who combined economic, religious and political arguments in order to control consumption. Both Spanish and Anglo-Saxon historiographies, probably influenced by Carmen Martin Gaite's work, have studied the creation of the Spanish national dress, by analysing particular issues raised by Spanish writers such as Ramon de la Cruz, and the well-known new philosophical concepts introduced in the field of education and the world of ideas by Enlightenment thinkers.[22] However, the issue of the creation of a national style of dress deserves further attention because it was more than just a simple discussion about the superficial ornamentation of women's clothing. It was an issue that went beyond morality, the education of women and the economic development of the country. All of these issues were being used by politicians to shape a sense of nation in the domestic consciousness. The creation of new nation-states in Europe brought about the awakening of nationalisms. The power of dress was the material symbol of the new political program. Nevertheless, in the scholarly articles cited below, we have not found any reference regarding this topic.

---

[20]   Gellner, E., *Thought and Change* (London: Weidenfeld & Nicolson, 1972), p. 169. From the same author: *Nations and Nationalism* (Ithaca, N.Y.: Cornell University Press, 2008).

[21]   Anderson, B., *Imagined Communities: Reflections on the Origin and Spread of Nationalism* (London: Verso, 1983), pp. 17–25.

[22]   See studies by: Martin Gaite, C., *Usos Amorosos*, p. 53; Alvarez Barrientos, J., 'La civilización como modelo de vida en el Madrid del siglo XVIII', *RDTP*, LVI, 1 (2001), p. 153; Leira, A., *Vestido hecho a la inglesa*, Museo del Traje (Madrid: Museo del Traje, 2008), pp. 1–16; Haidt, R., 'Luxury', pp. 35–50; Krauss, W., *Aufklärung III. Deutschland und Spanien* (Berlin: ed. Gruyter, 1996), p. 305.

The main argument of Belluga's message was the upholding of Catholic principles in consumer behaviour, while the goal of Sempere y Guarinos was the development of the national economy and Cadalso's was the defence of tradition and national values against foreign habits. The project of a national dress combined all of these features. The national economy could thus be stimulated by increased production of clothing made from domestic fabrics. Religious principles could be protected by a dress style that embraced Catholic morality. Finally, the exaltation of the country would be represented by a national attire, which could portray tradition and sense of nation.

During the eighteenth century, Spanish society witnessed an expansion in the consumption of foreign goods – see Part IV – and an interest in French culture. This drove traditional society, composed primarily of governmental officials, writers and political 'traitants', to spread a negative perception of those who embraced these fashions. Consequently, the stereotype of the 'petimetre' and 'petimetra' was developed in Spain, especially during the last decades of the eighteenth century, by the creation of negative connotations about everything related to foreign fashions. This issue explains the constant promulgation of prohibitions on specific types of clothing. The 'petimetre' was seen as a picturesque figure, who wore fashionable clothes and adornments such as bracelets, buckles, wristwatches, coloured jackets, waistcoats and breeches; and the 'petimetra' wore low-cut dresses, bracelets, buckles, handbags, fans, coloured costumes and high-heeled shoes.

In relation to the defence of the Spanish tradition and economy, a proposal was made by an anonymous author, probably a lady from the Court of Charles III,[23] which was based on the creation of a national dress for women made from materials produced in the country, without the extravagant and luxurious French adornments. This project was named *Discurso político-económico sobre el luxo de las señoras y proyecto de un trage nacional* [Political and economic essay on ladies' luxury and a plan for a national female dress], and it was expressed as follows:

Al Excmo Señor, Conde de Floridablanca
Señor:
Animada de un verdadero patriotismo dirigido al bien del Estado y de cada individuo en particular, propuse entre los amigos de mi tertulia, gran util

---

[23] The project was presumably signed by a woman with the initials M.O., though it was written by a man. The speech was directed to the Count of Floridablanca, first secretary of the state. See Gallego Abaroa, E., 'La educación de las mujeres en los discursos ilustrados', *Mediterráneo económico*, no. 9 (2006), p. 86. Paula Demerson outlines in her work that probably the author of this project could be Martinez, 'marino' and member of the 'Sociedad Matritense de Amigos del País'. *María Francisca de Sales Portocarrero, Condesa de Montijo. Una figura de la Ilustración* (Madrid: Editora Nacional, 1975), p. 164. See also, Perdices, L. and Reeder, J., *Biblioteca de los economistas españoles de los siglos XVI, XVII y XVIII de Manuel Colmeiro* (Madrid: Real Academia de Ciencias Morales y Políticas, 2005), p. 121.

seria para destruir el pernicioso luxo de las Damas en vestir, señalarles los ayrosos trages, que al mismo tiempo que evitasen la introduccion de las modas extranjeras con que nos arruinamos, caracterizasen la Nacion, distinguiesen las jerarquia de cada una, nos libertasen de las ridiculeces con que casi siempre nos adornamos, solo por ser moda, segun publican quatro extranjeros que nos llevan muchos millones, y fomentasen nuestras Fabricas y Artesanos. Discurso político-economico sobre el luxo de las Señoras, y proyecto de un trage Nacional ... bien entendido que tanto las telas de lana ... como las de seda, oro, y plata que usen las Señoras, deberan ser del Reyno, para lo que podran elegirse aquellas de que tengamos mas fabricas, o proporcionen para hacerlas ...
Capítulo I
Del gravamen que se sigue al Estado y las familias del demasiado luxo en los vestidos
Capítulo II
Se propone como un medio dulce utilísimo para evitar los progresos del lujo el establecimiento de un traje mujeril nacional
Capítulo III
Instrucción para el establecimiento de un traje mugeril nacional
Capítulo IV
Recapitulación de las ventajas que se seguira el uso de un traje mugeril nacional[24]

What emerges from this treatise is the promotion of the national economy, the rejection of luxury clothing related to female and foreign fashions, which went against Catholic tradition, and the fostering of the sense of nation. This was not something new, if we take into account the previous opinions expressed on luxury goods by Belluga, Sempere y Guarinos and Cadalso; as we have seen, each of these authors take a different approach to the debate on luxury. In this treatise, one of the main issues denounced as being negative for the economy was the conspicuous consumption of foreign commodities. Thus, the author insists that to overcome economic decadence, it would be necessary to create a national dress style with articles for women made from national fabrics. This national dress would thus help to develop both local and national industries. In addition, there was a nationalistic twist to this treatise: the wearer of such attire would be seen as a pure and patriotically Spanish individual, opposed to the 'Frenchness' that was invading the country.

The count of Floridablanca entrusted the project to the Countess of Montijo, María Francisca de Sales Portocarrero, who was the secretary of the 'Junta de Damas de Honor y Mérito'[25] [Board of Ladies of Honour and Merit] a group

---

[24] C.D.M.T., CA 361, *Discurso sobre el lujo de las señoras y proyecto de un traje nacional*, Madrid, Imprenta Real, 1788.

[25] The 'Sociedades Económicas de Amigos del País' [Economic Societies of Friends of the Country] were created with the aim of improving the production and economy of the state by means of education. These societies gave lessons on arts, agriculture, economy, industry and commerce. For the case of women, female occupations were structured by

composed of the most important noblewomen. She was put in charge of launching the national dress project to Spanish women. The project included three styles: 'Española' [Spanish], 'Carolina' [Carolinean] and 'Borbonesa' [Bourbonnaise] or 'Madrileño' [Madrilenian] (see Illustration 4.3). Each of these categories comprised other varieties. The first model, 'Española', was to be used for grand occasions; it was designed for the most important ladies. The 'Carolina' model was designed for quotidian use and the 'Borbonesa' could be used according to individual needs or desires.

Illustration 4.3   Three Types of a National Dress Project. Illustrations on the *Discurso sobre el luxo de la señoras y proyecto de un traje nacional*. Madrid: Imprenta Real 1788. C.D.M.T.

The count of Floridablanca and the Countess of Montijo exchanged letters about this new project. The Countess of Montijo's reply sets out the Board of Ladies' firm rejection of the project for a national dress. The main objections raised are the propensity for women to 'stand out', together with the strong conviction that social differences in dress should be maintained, and that the eradication of these differences would have serious social consequences. The Countess concludes that, to carry out a plan of this order, the first step would be to establish an effective model of education to form people's attitudes toward luxury and fashion. In the end, Floridablanca's project came to nothing:

> Respuesta.
> Exmo. S^or. He dado cuenta a la Junta de Señoras del papel de V.E. de 16 del pasado, con que me remite el discurso impreso sobre el luxo de las Señoras, y proyecto de un Traxe Nacional, previniendome, que con este motivo podria la

means of the creation of 'Juntas de Damas de las Sociedades Económicas del País' [Board of Ladies of Economic Societies of Friends of the Country]. See Anes Álvarez de Castrillón, G., *Economía e Ilustración en la España del siglo XVIII* (Barcelona: Ariel, 1981). López Cordón, M.V., 'Familia, sexo y género en la España Moderna', *Studia Histórica. Historia Moderna*, vol. 18 (1998), pp. 105–34.

Junta proponer un premio de Mil rea^s., que V. E. abonaria, al que presente un modelo de un Traxe nacional para las Damas, todo de generos del Pays, el cual reuna la honestidad y decencia, a la gracia y agilidad Española … No toca a la Junta hablar si traen o no utilidad de las leyes sumptuarias en orden a los trajes … y no se halla en estado de investigar un punto que pide profundos conocimientos e instrucción solida en la historia de todos los siglos y Naciones … Ha ceñido la Junta sus reflexiones a la sola esfera de aquellas ideas, de cuyo uso, ni la naturaleza, ni la costumbre le han privado … inclinacion que hay en nuestro sexo a sobresalir, y distinguirse, no mira por objeto principal para salir con este fin ni la preeminencia del nacimiento ni quantas puede haver introducido la política en el orden social de una Monarquía, sino la que viene por la naturaleza en prendas, y dotes de Alma y cuerpo, y como subsidio de esta, la del adorno de los trages … El querer pues que se establezca un trage con el cual la libertad ilimitada que se quite para satisfacer la 1ª inclinación … Y si en los hombres que creen tener nos arraigada la vanidad en quanto a la compostura exterior, seria ardua empresa el de Sugetarlos a solo un trage … Ademas de esto conoce bien V.E. que nunca se podra remediar radicalmente el grave desorden que se experimenta en cuanto a trages y adornos mientras no se mejoren las costumbres por medio de la educación … Sin esto todas las Leyes Suntuarias, seran siempre ineficaces y quedaran expuestas a las vicisitudes de la moda … Todo lo qual me ha ordenado la Junta exponga a V.E. para que lo haga presente a S.M. Dios que a V.E. m. Madrid 5 de Julio de 1788. Exmo. S^{or}. Conde de Floridablanca.[26]

The letter from the Countess of Montijo gives us a clear idea of one of the most important features of the enlightened thought of the time, that is, the defence of the nature of the individual in relation to uses and customs. For this reason she states that the adoption of this project would be 'against nature', because of the 'inclination that exists in our sex to seek to stand out … that which arises naturally from the virtues and gifts of the soul and the body and, deriving from this nature, the adornment of dress, and finally, also deriving from this nature, the difference between classes …'[27] The Countess's argument was based on natural logic that entitled the individual to freely make their own decisions on these matters without any kind of imposition.

This dress style project was intended as an instrument of nationalism against the introduction of foreign fashions. In other words, the programme was contributing towards developing the social-cultural stereotype of the 'petimetre', with a clear political purpose of fostering a national identity. Therefore, the new dress style portrayed a trans-national feature, which transformed everyday life due to the aesthetic and external image inspired by the new clothing habits.[28] By means of the acquisition of foreign dress styles, the individual was seen as a social transgressor.

---

26   C.D.M.T., CA, 241.
27   C.D.M.T., CA, 241.
28   Svendsen, L., *Fashion. A Philosophy* (London: ed. Reaktion Books, 2006).

Stereotypes and prejudices were used against the new styles imported from abroad. Such stereotypes represent an unreal image or deformed vision of the 'other', the individual that comes from afar and has a different socio-cultural behaviour.

Such socio-cultural rejection shaped a deformed imagery, which was cast in the individual's mind. The diffusion of these stereotypes and prejudices was firmly rooted in the construction of nationalisms in early nineteenth-century Europe.[29] This could be seen as a reaction against the French influence in Spanish culture. In eighteenth century Spain, these attitudes did not occur independently from other European territories. Europeans were the primary witnesses and active players regarding what was happening by means of the construction of new nation-states. There was a reinvention of past culture, through the invention of traditions, with the aim of reinforcing the emerging European nation-states. Hobsbawm defined the invention of tradition as:

> a set of practices ... of a ritual or symbolic nature, which seek to inculcate certain values and norms of behaviour by repetition, which automatically implies continuity with the past.[30]

A good example of this process is the national attempts to reconstruct a new reality by means of external appearances. Clothing, therefore, was seen as a national symbol, by which individuals could be distinguished as members of the same race, language, culture, religion and tradition. Such features composed the new aspects of the European territories as nation-states. The same can be said of national projects based upon clothing styles. The defence of traditional values and identities based on clothing, which occurred in eighteenth century Spain, also took place in Scotland. The Scots attempted to preserve their own particular heritage while facing their union with England. The achievement of this goal could only be reached by the reinvention of the origins of the Scots and their traditional mode of dress, by means of the well-known Scottish kilt. These new socio-cultural archetypes were largely invented, but rapidly accepted and approved by the people of Scotland. The traditions that comprise much of Scottish identity are based on eighteenth century forgeries and fantasies, invented by men who felt the need for the Scots to have a culture superior to other cultures found in the British Isles at that time.[31]

The invented aspects of traditions generally come into play when traditions of rather recent historic origin are given fictitious continuity with an historic past of varied accuracy. In fact, some of the most resilient traditions are those based

---

[29]   Anderson, B., 'Introduction', in Balakrishnan, G., *Mapping the Nation* (London: Verso in association with *New Left Review*, 1996), pp. 1–16.

[30]   Hobsbawm, E., 'Introduction: Inventing Traditions', in Hobsbawm, E. and Ranger, T. (eds), *The Invention*, pp. 1–14.

[31]   Trevor-Roper, H., 'The Invention of Tradition: the Highland Tradition of Scotland', in Hobsbawm, E. and Ranger, T. (eds), *The Invention*, pp. 15–42.

upon a largely fictitious history. The fashion systems based on traditions and identities created a fictional world. Some individuals could find in this process a new battle ground to reinforce the construction of new states, by which some privileged people could be part of a powerful new political elite. However, there was resistance among people who considered such a process as a new socio-cultural programme from which they could be excluded. The identification of real and true traditions and customs, based on self-development, authentic customs and free choice of individuals, was the argument that some people used to reject such national projects. Citizens, who presumably were requested to be a part of a common national destiny, repeatedly suffered attacks on their individualism through the intervention of the state.

Regarding the Spanish national project to create a unique female dress style, the final response of the women of the nation, led by the Countess of Montijo, was that adopting this project would be against 'human nature'. A woman's natural tendency to want to be fashionable and stand out in public life, through the use of decorative garments, was the Countess' principal argument against the proposal for an unembellished and plain code of dressing. This was an inherent feature of the differentiation of classes that the female elite wanted to maintain, by preserving their right to dress in elaborate and sumptuous garments. The Countess reinforced this attitude in her letter, by saying that it would be necessary to create a programme to educate women about the awareness of the social class to which they belonged and what was defined as a new fashion or luxury.

Scholars have only focused on the analysis of Countess Montijo's letters on the new Enlightenment tradition of education of society, in this case, on the education of women.[32] This interpretation established that the new liberal ideas introduced by Enlightenment thinkers were changing traditional values. Beyond such traditional interpretations, we find it more relevant to focus on problems regarding the self-development of individuals. Men and women, and in this particular case of female attitudes, were challenging the control exerted by a supra-agent, whose aim was to influence people's decisions. Such an agent, formed from the new nation-state institutions and politicians, pursued the control of religious, economic and social spheres, in which individuals were participating in public life. The Countess' response provides one of the most relevant examples of the Enlightenment related to self-development of the individual, by following tradition and accepted values of virtue, as well as her rejection of the creation of a fictional and unreal image of Spanish women. She followed the thought of Enlightenment thinkers such as

---

[32] See Walton, W., 'Feminine Hospitality in the Bourgeois Home of Nineteenth-century Paris', *Proceedings of the Western Society for French History*, 14 (1987), pp. 197–203; Israel, J., *Radical Enlightenment*, p. 90; Bolufer, M., 'Transformaciones culturales. Luces y sombras', in *Historia de las mujeres en España y America Latina II*, Morant, I. (ed.), Ortega, M., Lavrin, A. and Pérez Cantó, P. (eds) (Madrid: Cátedra, 2005), pp. 479–510; Bolufer, M., *Mujeres e Ilustración*; Morant, I., *Discursos de la vida buena*.

Montesquieu,[33] by saying that individuals should be guided by their own personal habits and customs, although she wanted to preserve the hierarchical patterns of consumption of the female elite. The idea of creating a national dress style was expressed more enthusiastically in the gazettes of the late eighteenth century, when the echoes of the French Revolution resounded in Spain:

> En esta inteligencia parece natural que examinemos ante todas las cosas, quales son las funciones propias, y características de un Petimetre, y este examen, será un equivalente de las medidas que los sastres toman para cortar un sayo adecuado, y proporcionar al cuerpo del sugeto que visten.
>
> Parece según las frecuentes observaciones que diariamente hacemos sobre la conducta de estos caballeritos … concurrir a las funciones publicas, y privadas, y generalmente hallarse en todos los concursos, como por ejemplo a las puertas del Templo, yendo y viniendo de un lado a otro mientras, entran y salen señoritas Petimetras …
>
> En este supuesto, salga ya a la luz la deseada idea del Trage nacional, para los petimetres de España, idea si no me engaño, que será recibida con general aplauso de los Sabios, y maduros Filosofos; pues veran en ella el medio de aniquilar el recurso de tan repetidas invenciones, y tan continuadas vagatelas con que nos sacan el aire los mañosos Estrangeros, obligandonos a consumir por medio de los petrimetres, una infinidad de telas de cedazo y un sin numero de chucherias frivolas, que nos arrancan el dinero haciendo con nosotros lo que hicimos en otro tiempo con los Indios estupidos, de quienes recibimos el oro y la plata en cambio del hierro y vidrio.[34]

The journal of Murcia, *El Correo Literario* [The Literary Post], published an article in 1793 criticizing foreigners, especially French merchants, as 'vicarious consumers' who introduced superfluous goods and frivolities in Spanish society. This foreign community was ridiculed through the grotesque model of the 'petimetre':

> … aire los mañosos Estrangeros, obligandonos a consumir por medio de los petrimetres, una infinidad de telas de cedazo y un sin numero de chucherias frivolas, que nos arrancan el dinero …[35]

The idea of a national dress style was seen as necessary in order to eradicate foreign fashions:

---

[33] Montesquieu, Charles de Secondat, baron de, *Persian Letters*, 1721 (Translated by Mr. Orzell, [Dublin]: London printed, and Dublin re-printed by S. Powell, for P. Crampton, 1731, 3rd edition).

[34] A.M.M., Correo Literario de Murcia, Octubre de 1793.

[35] A.M.M., Correo Literario de Murcia, Octubre de 1793.

salga ya a la luz la deseada idea del Trage nacional, para los petimetres de
España … medio de aniquilar el recurso de tan repetidas invenciones …[36]

However, such a project was not able to succeed since from 1788, when the idea
of the project was launched, to 1793, the political events of the country were
considered a priority. Even though the project was not carried out, it was linked
with the new political discourse to heighten the sense of nation, as it was issued
the year before the French Revolution, in 1788. The article of *El Correo Literario*
was published in 1793, when the War of the Convention against France started.
Therefore, everything connected with French fashion came under strong political
attack through the satirical figure of the 'petimetre', during the period of the French
Revolution as well as during the years of the Napoleonic invasion of the Iberian
Peninsula. But did this strong propaganda against the French model contribute to
the reinforcement of the Spanish phenomenon of the 'majismo'?[37]

Men, 'majos', were recognized by their distinctive costume, broad-brimmed
soft hats, hair nets and long black or brown cloaks.[38] The cloak was worn with
one side flung across the front over the shoulder, and the hat brim often pulled
down, leaving very little of the wearer's face exposed; this menacing posture
was characteristic of the 'majo' style. Women, 'majas', wore a hair net or black
'mantilla', a tight bodice, and a 'basquiña', top petticoat, over a skirt sometimes as
high as mid-calf. Materials were light and flowing, silk and lace if the wearer could
obtain them; the colour was typically black with white and red trimming.[39] Like
men, the 'majas' wore their natural hair, covered but unpowered. They cultivated
the figure-enhancing stance of an arched back, hands on hips and turned-in.[40]

This prototypical image was progressively well received by all social groups.
Such traditionalism and 'casticismo' helped to develop the sense of nation.
Anything that did not fit the schemes of Spanish tradition, especially taking into

---

[36]   A.M.M., Correo Literario de Murcia, Octubre de 1793.

[37]   In Dorothy Noyes' article the term 'majo' is defined as 'masher', a word which
comes from 'amajar' or 'machucar' [to crush]. Popular etymology also associates the word
with 'macho', and the aggressiveness of both sexes of 'majos' was strongly contrasted
with the supposed effeminacy of the 'petimetres'. See, Noyes, D., 'La Maja Vestida',
p. 199. However, regarding the etymology of the word, we are more inclined to accept the
theory that explains 'majo' as coming from the word 'mayo' [May], which is associated
with popular custom in Madrid that people wore traditional dresses in the countryside
during Spring, especially during the San Isidro festival. During this period people enjoyed
traditional Spanish customs in the meadows by the Manzanares River. Goya illustrated
these popular customs in his paintings.

[38]   The typology of clothing defined as the 'majo's' outfit can be found in Cadalso's
epistles. The socio-cultural and symbolic definition of these clothes can be analysed further
in the book by Martin Gaite, C., *Usos Amorosos*.

[39]   Boucher, F., *Histoire du costume en occident de l'antiquité à nous jours* (Paris:
Flammarion, 1965).

[40]   Noyes, D., 'La Maja Vestida', p. 199.

account the political events and turmoil of those years, could be considered as
a transgression against national values. The classical image of Spanish women
wearing a 'chal' or 'mantilla' was well established by then, and remains until today,
as we can still see women using these garments in public events, such as bullfights,
theatres, flamenco concerts or religious processions. Pure Spanish traditionalism
was materialized through this classic clothing. Since the fancy French styles were
eroding the uniqueness of the Spanish culture, the phenomenon of 'majismo' was
developed by critics and used as a satire against Frenchness.

One of the Enlightenment thinkers Clavijo, in his satirical journal *El pensador*
[The thinker], first published in 1763, strongly criticized the superficial and snobbish
behaviour of the 'petimetre'. His essays reflected the ideas of Montesquieu and
Rousseau,[41] since as they did, he expressed that people should be guided by their
own particular whims. He encouraged the 'majismo' model that was rooted in
national customs and traditional habits of Spanish society. Clavijo wrote about the
superficial behaviour of Madrilenian 'petimetres', who composed, or formed, the
Court. He also mentioned the rejection by the 'petimetres' of the traditional and
popular customs of Spanish society:

> adónde se han mudado los hombres ... un gracioso muñeco (petimetre) ...
> ¡Qué bien peinado!, ¡y cómo camina con pasos de rigodón y de minuet! Una
> tienda de dijes trae colgada en cada uno de los dos relojes. ¡Cuántos galones
> y qué ricos encajes! ... se halagan, se acarician, se abrazan, se dan las manos
> en señal de amistad, se besan, se dicen mil Lisonjas ... Es un enemigo de las
> buenas costumbres, a quien dan acogida ciertas gentes de humor extravagante y
> caprichoso, por no decir depravado.[42]

The critics of the 'petimetre' model, and those who favoured the reinforcement of
the traditional 'majismo' style, shared a common purpose: to awaken the national
consciousness, as well as to uphold traditional values against any element that
could contaminate what were considered the cultural roots of the nation. The
struggle between the two socio-cultural models faithfully reflected the desire of
the middle and upper social classes for obtaining greater socio-economic and
political privileges. This issue probably explains why the aesthetic characteristics
of the 'petimetre' and 'majos' became so entangled, since they were types of
substitutive fashions which revealed the snobbism of people and their desire to
emulate. The 'petimetre' stereotype was first patronized by upper social groups
and later reached the middle classes, while the 'majo' style first took hold among
middle social groups and only later did it filter into the attention of the upper

    [41]   Montesquieu, Charles de Secondat, baron de, *Persian Letters*; Rousseau, *Discours
sur l'économie politique* (Geneve: Chez Emanuel du Villard, 1758).
    [42]   B.N., Clavijo y Fajardo, J., *Antología de El pensador* [Texto impreso], 1763
Biblioteca básica canaria; 10, El Pensador, M 6091-1989, I, pensamiento VII, pp. 9, 10,
17, 18.

classes. This can be seen in paintings by Goya, in which he portrayed the 'maja' style in his representations of the Duchess Maria Luisa de Parma. Likewise, the Duchess of Alba can also be seen in traditional attire in his paintings.[43] Therefore, the social dimension of this debate, characterized by the antagonistic models of tradition and modernity, was played out within small groups of the elite.

Illustrations 4.4 and 4.5   'Majo' and 'Maja'. Colección: Rodríguez, Antonio. Colección General de los Trajes que en la actualidad se usan en España. Principiada en el año 1801. Madrid: Librería de Castillo, 1801. Número de serie 1329 y 1421. *Fundación Joaquín Díaz, Centro Etnográfico*, Diputación de Valladolid, Spain.

Notwithstanding, the political aspects of such a class-oriented confrontation was more important than the social debate about the small groups of the elite, as the new political scheme provoked strong national sentiments, as well as a sense of rejection of foreign values. The reaction of society to the decline of the Spanish Empire inspired Enlightenment politicians to legislate towards improving the economic situation of the country. Nationalistic policies and ideas emerged with the aim of preserving the political status of the country. As we have shown, such nationalistic proposals coincided with the project of creating and promoting

---

[43]   See Tomlinson, J.A., *Francisco Goya: The Tapestry Cartoons and Early Career at the Court of Madrid* (Cambridge: Cambridge University Press, 1989).

national dress styles and with the emergence of the socio-cultural 'majismo' phenomenon.

Conclusions

The desire of the government to control consumption and the creation of stereotypes in eighteenth-century Spain had a common purpose: the glorification and preservation of the nation's values, tradition and history. This was the initial step towards instilling a nationalistic feeling in individuals. The state was working towards this goal through a concrete program that had a multifaceted role, as politicians were the main agents used to develop a sense of nation in the psychology of individuals. Prohibitions and decrees regulating how people should consume represented economic measures related to mercantilist countries, designed to augment the public treasury. But they also constituted an effort to control the self-development of individuals who were to behave as loyal servants of the state, a concept more similar to the authoritarian systems of the first half of the twentieth century.

Devotion to the state needed to be guided by rules and conventions governing how individuals should act in both public and private spheres, in order to help integrate national traditions and values as an indivisible unit. Any fissure that could erode the image of the new nation-state, as the supra-agent guiding an individual's destiny, would be eradicated by putting into action the machinery of the state. Therefore, in the common project of the creation of the nation-state, religious, economic and political factors all came into play. Stereotypes and prejudices on the introduction of new fashions were created and propagated to set up a deformed image of what was considered to be new, unconventional, strange or rare.

The stereotyping process was a rapid mechanism that traditional society used for destabilizing any external influence from other countries and cultures in its aim to create a sense of nation. This process was especially important when European countries witnessed the turmoil caused by the political events of the late eighteenth century. The 'petimetre' and 'macaroni' models, representing foreign fashions, were the main examples of the creation of a pejorative image of external fashions and, to discourage these, the major nationalistic attempts consisted of maintaining social conventions and the control of national consumption by creating such burlesque figures.

The social backlash that such models provoked, mainly instigated by the traditional sector of the nation, did not simply seek to suppress novel consumption, but to use such models of fashions to foster and maintain national values through the reinvention of tradition via the development of the 'majo' dress. Such satirical figures exemplified how states created an unreal image of foreign cultures, since they were seen as elements which would contaminate the pure values of the nation. In a world that was becoming more globalized, especially due to the expansion of commerce and travel, nationalistic feelings were employed to form barriers against the invasion of foreign values that could potentially contaminate the nation. Clothing, or indeed any foreign article, represented the symbol of potential transgression against the state. French merchants were the primary 'vicarious agents' in spreading new consumer habits among the Spanish population, as we saw in the *Correo Literario de Murcia* article which denounced foreign merchants as the main cause of the economic decadence of Spain. However, stereotypes, control on consumption and social prejudices were not able to stop global trade, whose influences eventually changed the features of the nation, especially as seen through changes in consumer behaviour.

PART III
French Traders and Western Mediterranean Commerce in a Global Context (1730–1808)

After the war of the Spanish Succession, and during the second half of the eighteenth century in particular, the Spanish economy partially depended on foreign capital. This can be attested by analysing the import-export market of the western Mediterranean area linking the trade between eastern territories of Spain and southern France. The main theme of this section is the analysis of the economic behaviour of the group of French merchants in the Spanish Mediterranean ports. These merchants established important links based on family relations and concepts such as trust and loyalty rooted in the national affiliation of those traders. Being from the same nation was very important in terms of trust and how the information circulated amongst merchants in order to secure a successful deal. They shaped a trans-national community by marrying not only individuals with Italian, French or Maltese origins, but also local people mainly related to trade activities. By analysing these trade networks, it is possible to shed light on important issues such as how foreign merchants created a new market supplying a wide variety of products and how consumers altered their choices in light of the introduction of those commodities.

The introduction of luxury and fashionable commodities challenged the traditional lifestyle and government rules. The analysis of the supply side of the eighteenth-century Spanish Mediterranean economy enables us to study how changes and new trends in consumption were operating. In this section, a detailed study of the statistical series of trade records of the 'Chambre de Commerce de Marseille' allows us to observe international trade between the Mediterranean ports of France and Spain. But this trade was also integrated into a more global context. The port of Marseille, as European gate and trans-national region, was the main marketplace where goods were introduced and spread, especially those which came from the Asian and Atlantic markets. The strength of commercial networks brought, as an immediate consequence, an increase in the consumption of a wide variety of textiles, as well as the introduction of foreign raw materials – cotton, calico, wool and linen – in local workshops, originating from Asia Minor, Levantine areas – Salonika, Smyrrna, Constantinople and Cairo – India and

China. Non-manufactured goods were introduced in French industries, such as Lyon and Grenoble, among others, to manufacture clothing. Then, from Marseille such goods were exported to Mediterranean ports of Spain, from where French merchants usually imported cheap and raw materials such as silk, cotton, wool or barilla, of lesser quality than those from eastern countries. Export of raw materials was the main economic sector of eastern areas of Spain. However, the progressive introduction of Asian raw materials to southern France, the main destination of the sales of eastern Spanish raw materials related to the textile sector, contributed to the fall of Spanish Mediterranean exports during the second half of the eighteenth century. The analysis of the Roux-Frères, one of the most important French companies connected with the foreign commercial elite of the main port of the Crown of Castile, Cartagena, gives us a full view of how these businesses operated. Therefore, Part III in connection with Part IV will allow us to demonstrate that changes in demand in south-eastern Spain mostly occurred due to the thriving French market and the activity of foreign merchants.

Foreign merchant families, as key social actors, stimulated regional economies of the Crown of Castile due to their entrepreneurial attitude by putting the territory in a more global dynamic, in which some other European areas were participating. The relative weakness of a trained labour-force and manufacturing infrastructure made merchants a critical part of the economic engine. The role played by foreign wholesalers and retailers, in satisfying new consumer's needs through the distribution of their products in the market, was critical to advance the national economy.

The introduction of foreign goods reinforced the unbalance in the import-export trade. As we have seen in the previous section, Enlightenment ministers issued mercantile measures, based on protectionism and bans to control consumption. The use of imported foreign goods such as calico, wool, silk, among others, was prohibited. The aim was to stimulate the production of national industries and crafts, as well as the consumption of national products. Although there were some specific cases such as the Catalonian area in the production of textiles, the Castilian society did not specialize in manufacturing items or at least was not competitive enough to avoid the rising entry of eastern goods. The Spanish Mediterranean import-export market that operated in Marseille, as one of the main European centres of business, is the main aspect mentioned in this section in order to understand the shifts in consumer behaviour of the south-eastern Castilian economy, which will be analysed in the following section.

Chapter 5

The Roux-Frères Company, French Trade Networks and the Spanish Mediterranean Import-Export Market

The role played by the merchant groups of Marseille in the western Mediterranean area exerted a very important influence on the change of standards of living and patterns of consumption in south-eastern Spain. They set up businesses extending from the western to eastern regions and they bought and sold both raw materials and manufactured products, making a very extensive circuit of transactions. They founded commercial houses in ports of the Crown of Aragon such as Barcelona, Valencia, Alicante and Majorca, as well as Castilian ports such as Cartagena, Aguilas or Almeria, connected with French (Marseilles, Toulon) and Italian ports (Livorno, Genoa, Venice). They also set up businesses in Maltese, North African (Cairo, Oran and Alexandria) and Adriatic Sea (Dubrovnik) ports in connection with the inland of the Balkans and the Greek region (Thessaloniki). They did not disregard important centres of commerce such as the Asia Minor territories (Smyrna and Constantinople) or Near East Mediterranean ports (Alexandria, Tripoli, Sidon or Acre) – places that linked the Mediterranean market with Asian trade, connecting with the routes of silk and textiles of the Persian and Asian markets[1] (see Map 5.1).

In all of these places, the French merchant groups established their companies introducing and exchanging different sorts of goods. The major factor that facilitated these economic exchanges and trade circuits during the eighteenth century was the general European context of political stability. At the beginning of the century, the end of the war of the Spanish Succession was marked by the signing of 'les pactes de famille' between France and Spain. This pact contributed to European stability. Moreover, the arrival of the Spanish Bourbon dynasty signalled the start of a period of relative peace in the Mediterranean Sea due to the end of Berber attacks on Spanish and French ships, demonstrating equilibrium in relations between the Ottoman Empire and Spanish Government. As a consequence, all of these factors brought a new impulse to the Mediterranean trade in connection with the Asian and Atlantic market.

---

[1] Fukusawa, K., *Toilerie et commerce du Levant d'Alep à Marseille* (Paris: CNRS, 1987). Raveux, O., 'Entre réseau communautaire intercontinental et intégration locale: la colonie marseillaise des marchands arméniens de la Nouvelle-Djoulfa (Ispahan), 1669–1695', *Revue d'histoire moderne et contemporaine*, no. 59–1 (Paris: Belin, 2012), pp. 83–102.

The equilibrium in international relations, required for economic growth, was impeded in some specific cases including: the Habsburg War of Succession and, especially, the plague of Marseille in 1729; the Seven Years' war between France and its American colonies, when Spain joined France in supporting the American Revolution against England; the moment when the French Convention declared war on Spain in 1792 and the subsequent alliance between Spain and France versus England in 1796. All of these socio-political events had an impact on the structure of economic relations during specific periods, causing a downfall in the curves of both the import and export market.[2] Some of these problems were reflected in the decrease of the entries of French ships to the port of Cartagena during the final years of the eighteenth century (see Chart 5.1 below).

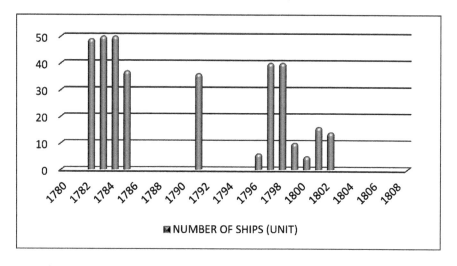

Chart 5.1   Entries of French ships in the Port of Cartagena (1780–1808).
             Source: A.M.C., Libro no. 8 de entrada de embarcaciones francesas
             (1795–98).

French merchant groups were represented by important families such as the Cayron, Champeli Pirraimun, Bicaix, Estrabo, among others, setting up their businesses between south-eastern Castile – Murcia and Cartagena – and southern

---

[2] Related to these political and military events and their impact on the Spanish economic growth, see the works by: Parker, G. and Kagan, R. (eds), *Spain, Europe, and the Atlantic World: Essays in Honour of John H. Elliott* (Cambridge [England]; New York, NY, USA: Cambridge University Press, 1995); Phillips, C.R., *The Treasure of the San José: Death at Sea in the War of the Spanish Succession* (Baltimore: The Johns Hopkins University Press, 2007); Kamen, H., *The War of Succession in Spain, 1700–15* (Bloomington: Indiana University Press, 1969).

France – Marseille, Bearn and Oloron – facilitating a constant circulation of both raw materials and market goods.[3] Spanish raw materials such as silk, cotton and wool were exported from Barcelona, Valencia, Alicante and Cartagena, and the same ports were the main sites of the reception of manufactured clothing and Asian textiles shipped from Marseille (see Map 5.1). French traders who settled in Spain had good links with the French company of Marseille, the Roux-Frères, which facilitated the entry of foreign merchandise to Spanish Mediterranean ports. The main purpose of this company was to secure deals throughout the Mediterranean territory – see Map 5.1. From the sixteenth century, Marseille became one of the main European centres that imported Asian commodities, especially cotton textiles and raw materials from India, Persia and, above all, the Ottoman Empire.[4]

The Iberian Peninsula was one of the major areas that received cotton textiles purchased in Iskenderun and Smyrna, among other places, by traders from Marseille.[5] Asian traders were concerned that the textile trade with the Hispanic Monarchy would provide them with silver coins from Spanish American colonies.[6] This market started to flourish in the sixteenth century and during the seventeenth century reached one of its highest moments of glory – in spite of various disruptions: the plague of 1648, the revolt of Catalonia and the interruption of trade with the Ottoman Empire which caused a serious economic depression.[7] After that moment of economic decadence, recovery arrived in the mid-seventeenth century, and the 1660s was the most prosperous time for the maritime trade connecting the European and Asian market via the Levant. However, after 1686, when the French state intervened by banning the manufacture of calico and Asian textiles in order to revitalize local French silk industries, the short success which southern French industries had by printing calicoes with Asian techniques mastered by the

---

[3] Carrière, Ch., *Négotians Marsellais au XVIIIe siècle. Contribution à l'étude des économies maritimes* (Marseille: Institut Historique de Provence, 1973).

[4] Raveux, O., 'The Birth of a New European Industry. L' Indiennage in Seventeenth-century Marseilles', in Riello, G. and Parthasarathi, P. (eds), *The Spinning World. A Global History of Cotton Textiles, 1200–1850* (London: Oxford University Press, 2008), p. 292.

[5] Martín Corrales, E., 'La importación de telas de algodón levantino y los inicios del estampado en Cataluña', *Revista de Historia Industrial*, 6 (1994), 49.

[6] Matthee, R., *The Politics of Trade Safavd Iran: Silk for Silver, 1600–1730* (Cambridge: Cambridge University Press, 1999). McCabe, I.B., *The Sha's Silk for Europe Silver: The Eurasian Trade of the Julfan Armenians in Sfavid Iran and India (1530–1750)* (Atlanta: Scholars Press, 1999).

[7] Masson, P., *Histoire du commerce français dans le Levant au XVIIe siècle* (Paris: Hachette, 1986). Morineau, M., 'Flottes de commerce et trafics français en Méditerranée au XVIIe siècle', *XVIIe Siècle*, 86–7 (1970), pp. 135–71.

Map 5.1   Trade houses founded by the Roux-Frères Company and the Mediterranean import-export market during the eighteenth century. *Source:* M.N.N., Ref. ge.0017.

Armenian community[8] in Marseille came to an end. Nevertheless, the desire for calicoes and Asian commodities was instilled in consumers and it was the crucial issue that stimulated Marseille's trade with Asian markets during the eighteenth century.

The 1686 ban could be one of the precedents for the following European prohibition of the manufacture and trade of Asian textiles. Within the framework of the mercantile policies in the eighteenth century, states banned the introduction of foreign goods.[9] During the establishment of nationalisms in the nineteenth century, governments promoted the consumption of national products to stimulate domestic industries, as well as to foster national values. This was the origin of an economic system based on the nationalization of consumption. Although the merchant groups from both Spanish and French territories introduced enormous quantities of foreign goods, their respective governments banned the imports of those commodities. In both cases, protectionism was due to the competition of foreigners with the domestic artisan groups. In the case of France, the government wanted to maintain the privileges of the artisan silk and linen industries of Languedoc and Provence,[10] and in that of Spain, the government wanted to maintain the Catalonian area as the main centre of textile production.[11] The consumption of cotton textiles from the Levant started in the Catalonian area during the sixteenth and seventeenth centuries. In order to promote domestic centres of production, the local administrations imposed a strict taxation on the introduction of such textiles,[12] provoking a restriction of the demand due to the high prices.

In 1648, the textile corporations of the city of Barcelona proclaimed that foreign textiles were of inferior quality to those produced in Barcelona.[13] This was one of the earliest (unfruitful) attempts to eliminate competition and stimulate local industries. However, the introduction of Asian textiles to Spain, via the exchange trade with Marseille, augmented during the second half of the seventeenth century and had a very strong impact on domestic centres of production.[14] The attempts to

---

[8] Tékénian, Ch. D., 'Marseille, la Provence et les arméniens', *Mémoire de l'Institut Historique de Provence* (1929), pp. 5–65. McCabe, I.B., 'Global Trading Ambitions in Diaspora: The Armenians and their Eurasian Silk Trade, 1530–1750', in McCabe, I.B., Harlaftis, G. and Minoglou, I. (eds), *Diaspora Entrepreneurial Networks: Four Centuries of History* (Oxford: Berg, 2005), pp. 27–49.

[9] Wallerstein, I., *Modern World System. 2: Mercantilism and the Consolidation of the European World-Economy, 1600–1750* (New York: Academic Press, 1980).

[10] Fukusawa, K., *Toilerie*.

[11] Stein, S.J. and Stein B., *Apogee of Empire. Spain and New Spain in the Age of Charles III* (Baltimore and London: John Hopkins University Press, 2003).

[12] Martín Corrales, E., 'Marseille, Échelle des Toiles Levantines pour l'Espagne, XVIIᵉ et XVIIIᵉ siècles', *Rives méditerranéennes*, 29 (2008), pp. 61–78.

[13] Martín Corrales, E., 'Marseille', p. 2.

[14] Eloy Martín and Joseph Fontana have studied the impact of foreign commerce on the Catalonian area, especially the influence of the French trade. Martín Corrales, E., *Comercio de Cataluña con el Mediterráneo musulmán: el comercio con los 'enemigos de*

ban foreign textiles continued during the eighteenth century, when European trade
became more global. There is material evidence of these futile efforts to dismantle
global and international commerce. Some letters were sent from Versailles to the
'Chambre de Commerce de Marseille' as Spanish diplomats were against the
introduction of foreign textiles.

There was a ban in Spain prohibiting the entrance of English commodities into
Spanish territories in order to stimulate national trade and industry.[15] A letter was
sent from Spain to French statesmen to ensure that merchants from Marseilles
would not introduce any more English commodities to Spain. As we can observe,
the Count of Maurepas sent a letter to different French territories such as Marly,
located in the Île-de-France very close to English ports, and Marseille, where
those English commodities were redistributed to European territories. However,
the Count of Maurepas expressed his opposition to the confiscation of French
shipments by Spanish authorities. Therefore, he strongly advised Marseille
negotiators to undertake proper measures in order to avoid the loss of their
businesses:

> A Marly le 10 May 1740
>
> Vous trouverez cy joint, Messieur, un etrait des ordonnances que le Roy
> d'Espagne a fait rendre, pour deffendre l'introduction dans ses Etats, des
> marchandises d'entrees et fruits d'Angleterre. Il est neccessaire que vous
> en donniez un connaissance aux negociants de Marseille, a fin que ceux qui
> expedieront ces batiments pour les ports de sa M.C. ne s'exposent par aux
> confiscations prononcees par ces ordonnances et qu'ils prennents les precautions
> qui y sout indiquees pour obvier aux difficultes a que les defauta de formalitez
> pourroient occasionner. Je suis, Messieur, tres parfaitement a vous.
>
> Maurepas, 1740, Versailles 10 may, Lettre de Monseigneur, Le Comte de
> Maurepas. M. de la Chambre de Commerce a Marseille, à Marseille. Etraits
> des ordonnances de l'admiraute d'Espagne pour empecher l'yntroduction des
> marchandises et fruits d'Angleterre dans les portes d'Espagne de publies a Cadiz
> au mois de fevrier de 1740 ...[16]

---

la fe' (Barcelona: Bellaterra, 2001). Fontana, J., *El comercio exterior de Barcelona en la 2ª
mitad del siglo XVII, (1664–1699) a través de las importaciones y exportaciones registradas
en su puerto* (Barcelona: Universitat de Barcelona. Facultat de Filosofia i Lletres, 1956),
p. 52–5. The influence of the Marseille trade on Catalonian economy can be seen through
the study of Bergasse and Rambert. Bergasse, L. and Rambert A.G. *Histoire du commerce
de Marseille.* t. IV. *De 1559 a 1660. De 1660 à 1789* (Paris: Librarie Plon, 1954), p. 116.

[15] Nadal i Farregas, J., *Comercio exterior y subdesarrollo. La política comercial y sus
repercusiones en las relaciones hispano-británicas de 1772 a 1914* (Madrid: Instituto de
Estudios Fiscales, 1978).

[16] A.C.C.M., Reference: Serie H, 71. Commerce avec l' Espagne (1700–49).
Prohibition de marchandises venant d' Angleterre.

Such measures were largely disregarded and the European textile trade, especially that connecting southern Europe with the maritime routes of the Levant, continued to flourish during the eighteenth century. In a similar manner, those bans were not implemented by merchants or consumers. Consumers achieved a better lifestyle in south-eastern Spain at the end of the *Ancien Regime* through the purchase of textile, luxury and exotic goods. Manufactured goods such as cloths made of silk as well as Levantine textiles (calicoes, cottons or muslins) still continued to enter the Spanish Mediterranean territory.

The fluent circulation of goods from eastern to western Mediterranean areas facilitated the socio-economic process of globalization within European territories. The trade company of the Roux-Frères is a good example of such a global process. They connected the Mediterranean market with both Atlantic and Asian areas. They introduced goods into European territories not only by means of the import-export market, but also, through the re-export market. In so doing, their businesses were carried out in a circular process by introducing goods from overseas to France. Once such goods arrived there, traders re-exported the commodities throughout Europe, thanks to the action of the companies and branches that they had set up in European ports.

The Roux-Frères was one of the most important trading companies of Mediterranean Europe in the eighteenth and first half of the nineteenth centuries. The company was founded in 1728, with the main aim of connecting both European and Near East markets. The founder of the company was Pierre-Honoré Roux (see Illustration 5.1), who was born in 1695 and died in 1774. He led the company to its highest level of prosperity during the second half of the eighteenth century.[17] The company succeeded the Raymond Bruny Company around 1728, one of the most important trade groups of the Languedoc area, with a high margin of benefits during the eighteenth century. The substantial number of commercial letters of this trading house, which are well-preserved in the 'Chambre de Commerce de Marseille' (in the 'Fond-Roux'), reveals the connections of this company with the different European, Asian and Atlantic markets. Its holdings reached their highest peak in 1791, possessing more than two and a half million 'livres tournois', which is clear evidence of the durability and trust of the company.[18] Their economic structure was based on a secure financial system, which ran upon the bill of exchange payments that had fewer risks than cash deals, to settle long-distant businesses.[19]

---

[17] A.C.C.M, L.IX, Fonds Roux.

[18] Lupo, S., 'Inertie épistolaire et audace négociante au XVIIIᵉ siècle', *Rives Méditerranéennes*, 27 (2007), mis en ligne le 27 juin 2008, Consulté le 10 mars 2010. URL: http://rives.revues.org/2063.

[19] Bartolomei, A., 'Paiements commerciaux et profits bancaires: les usages de la lettre de change (1780–1820)', *Rives Méditerranéennes* [En ligne], Jeunes chercheurs (2007), mis en ligne le 15 octobre 2008, Consulté le 10 mars 2010. URL: http://rives.revues. org/101. See the work by Ann McCants: 'Petty Debts and Family Networks. The Credit

Illustration 5.1   Portrait of P.H. Roux (1774–1843), by Laby. Ref. PGE_PH-
Roux, *Musée de la Chambre de Commerce de Marseille*

Markets of Widows and Wives in Eighteenth-century Amsterdam', in Lemire, B., Pearson,
R. and Campbell G. (eds), *Women and Credit. Researching the Past, Refiguring the Future*
(Oxford: Berg Publishers, 2001), pp. 33–50. Carrière, Ch., *Négotians*, vol. 2, p. 874.

The company business can be traced through the large amount of invoices and merchant payments found in the 'Fond-Roux'. With these documents it is possible to see the contracts that connected Marseille with overseas markets through the port of Cadiz. For instance, the company Sahuc Guillet, from Cadiz, paid off a debt from their bank account to the Roux-Frères in 1784. In 1779 Benito Picardo asked Roux-Frères associates for a banker, who could settle a credit to buy colonial commodities such as cochineal and groceries – cacao, chocolate, sugar and coffee. They also preserved a thriving business circuit in the Mediterranean market, especially with the Levantine routes from which they introduced into Europe via Marseille luxury commodities such as colourful clothes made of silk, cotton or wool from Near Eastern ports – Smyrna, Cairo, Alexandria and Aleppo. The Roux-Verduc network is a very good example of this kind of business.[20] Both merchant groups, through the exchange of letters, shared information about the possible risks and benefits of undertaking such deals. This, progressively, stimulated their benefits at the micro level, as well as the southern European economy at the macro level, as dealers from Spain, Italy, England and central European countries shared, by means of the 'Bourse' [stock-market] of Marseille, the same benefits and information.

A thriving trade circuit was established between southern France and south-eastern Castile by means of this commercial connection between its major ports, Marseille and Cartagena. The manufactured goods which started to appear in south-eastern Castilian probate inventories (see Part IV), in the cities of Murcia and Cartagena, included clothing, bedding and embellishments made of wool, calico – 'indienne' – linen, silk or cotton of very good quality such as cotton muslin – 'mousseline' – and cotton taffeta from Persia.[21] Additionally, most raw materials were brought from eastern Mediterranean ports such as Cairo, Smyrna, Side or Constantinople, places that connected Mediterranean routes with the Asian market. These products were unloaded in Marseille and from there distributed to Languedoc and Provence craftsmen industries, where artisans tried to copy the Asian techniques with the production of such new sumptuous goods. They were primarily purchased by the upper-middle and upper classes. However, the group of merchants to whom we are referring, also bought raw materials of lower quality from nearer markets, such as Castile, at the same time. This is attested to through the exports of raw silk and wool from Cartagena to Marseille registered in the Roux-Frères Company's receipts and invoices during the eighteenth century. As can be observed from the data presented in the following pages we have a complete record of all raw materials which were shipped from the Spanish Mediterranean ports to Marseille (Chart 5.8). The data presented, in addition to the invoices belonging to the Roux-Frères Company that we have examined, are evidence of the thriving movement of merchandise in the port of Cartagena. The main feature of the Castilian market was the export of raw materials and the

---

[20] A.C.C.M, L. IX, 739, lettre du 3 février 1764.
[21] A.C.C.M., L. IX, 870, Fonds Roux-Frères. Correspondant à l'étranger. Espagne.

import of goods made from those raw materials elaborated in French industries. The price of these products (made of Castilian raw materials) was low and the quantity of the ready-made products high. Therefore, large quantities of Castilian raw materials were introduced into the artisan industries of southern France with the aim of copying the original commodities related to the textile sector coming from the Asian market.

The producers of Castilian and, especially, Catalonian raw fibers made of silk, cotton[22] and wool had strong competition in the form of the Asian raw materials that entered Mediterranean ports by means of the Levantine route. Such entries minimized an eventual growth of the eastern Spanish production. Both finished and woven clothes made of calicoes, muslins and Egyptian textiles entered eastern areas of Spain, following the Levantine trade routes, which put the ports of Smyrna, Alexandria or Cairo in contact with Spanish Mediterranean ports – Cartagena, Valencia, Alicante, Barcelona and Majorca – with a major consequence being the decline of purchases of Spanish raw fibers by European textile industries. As we will see in Chapter 6 (see Charts 6.6, 6.7, 6.9, 6.10, 6.11 and 6.12) the data of such entries corresponds to the general numbers of the Marseille trade. The link between both eastern and western Mediterranean ports, which enabled the entry of such goods, was the port of Marseille. The Roux-Frères Company's receipts are notable proof of the deals that were made in the Spanish ports by purchasing those raw materials. In the ports of Cartagena, Almeria, Alicante, Valencia and Barcelona this commercial house bought raw wool from Castilian market places such as Segovia, Granada or Murcia[23] loading such cargo onto their ships. Non-elaborated silk, to manufacture ordinary clothes in French industries, and caustic soda and barilla, to produce the traditional soup from Marseille,[24] were the cargoes shipped from Mediterranean Spanish ports to Marseille. Although the export of the Spanish raw material was one of the most important activities of the Spanish Mediterranean economy, this economic sector was altered in the mid-eighteenth century.[25]

---

[22]   Vicente, M.V. *Clothing the Spanish Empire: Families and Calico Trade in the Early Modern Atlantic World* (New York: Palgrave Macmillan, 2006), p. 6. Martín Corrales, E., 'Marseille'.

[23]   Pérez Picazo, M.T., 'Crecimiento agrícola y relaciones de mercado en la España del siglo XVIII', in *Estructuras agrarias*, 1989, pp. 47–61.

[24]   On July the 15th of 1758 Pierre-Honoré Roux and Frères hired the services of the captain Delsere Escarda Ginochio et Margot to ship from Cartagena and Alicante to Marseille 737 pounds of barilla. The ship belonging to the captain Rossas unloaded in the port of Marseille 176 pounds of barilla from Cartagena. The same year the Roux Company shipped from Cartagena to Marseille 224 pounds of wool by means of the captain Deluant. A.C.C.M. Fonds Roux-Frères, Manifestes des navires entrés à Marseille (1757–71), Référence: L. IX, 1024.

[25]   Angel García Sanz has carefully examined the agrarian structure of Castile during the eighteenth century, through the mercantile policies for stimulating the Spanish exports. Segovia as the main centre of production of wool received such stimulus measures, in order to stop the imminent decadence of the sector, see: 'Estructuras agrarias y reformismo

During the second half of the eighteenth century Cartagena had a fluent commercial flow as the receptor of finished clothes. The port of Cartagena can be defined as a trans-national site, where the interaction between the local community and people from several nationalities such as France, Italy, Malta, England, northern Africa and those from the Levant took place due to commercial exchanges and the circulation of goods. Furthermore, this Spanish harbour can be characterized as a trans-regional area, too, due to its role of supplying the rest of inland Castile. Clean and dirty wool were exported from Cartagena to different Mediterranean places. The origin of the clean wool was Cartagena, Huéscar (Granada), Villanueva de la Fuente or Alcaraz (Ciudad Real), Molina de Aragon (Guadalajara), Villacastin (Segovia); whereas the dirty wool came from the Kingdom of Granada (Maria, Los Velez) and Murcia (Totana, Lorca, Caravaca and Jumilla).[26] This shows the trans-regional links of Cartagena, which put the traditional Castilian wool routes in contact with south-eastern Spain through the process of the exchange of raw materials for ready-to-use products. One of the main destinations of the exported wool from Spanish Mediterranean ports was southern France – Marseilles, Bearn and Oloron Saint-Marie[27] – from which the wool was redistributed to other French regions such as Brittany, Rouen, Normandy and other European countries – Holland or Germany. The wool-market of Castile was connected with European areas playing a very important role in the Spanish Mediterranean economy due to the vigorous activity of French merchants during the second-half of the eighteenth century.

5.1. An 'Interconnected Community': Trade Networks Based on Family Bonds

In the framework of the arrival of the Bourbon dynasty, a large group of French migrants settled in Spain.[28] This group was composed of courtesans, noblemen, artists, lawyers, clerks and merchants. The community that included merchants,

---

ilustrado en la España del siglo XVIII', in *Estructuras agrarias y reformismo ilustrado en la España del siglo XVIII* (Madrid: ed. Ministerio de Agricultura, Pesca y Alimentación, 1989), pp. 629–38. The crisis of the Castilian woollen market has been explored by Melón Jiménez, M.A., 'Algunas consideraciones en torno a la crisis de la transhumancia en Castilla', *Studia Historica. Historia Moderna*, n. 8 (1990), pp. 61–89.

[26] Montojo y Montojo, V. and Maestre de San Juan Pelegrin, F., 'Los comerciantes de Cartagena y su actividad comercial en Huéscar en la segunda mitad del s, XVII', in Díaz López, J.P (ed.), *Campesinos, nobles y mercaderes. Huéscar y el Reino de Granada en los ss. XVI y XVII* (Granada: Ayuntamiento de Huéscar, 2005), pp. 93–109.

[27] A.C.C.M., L. IX, 870, Fonds Roux-Frères. Correspondant à l'étranger. Espagne.

[28] For the French community established in Murcia during the eighteenth century, see the works by: Lemeunier, G. and Pérez Picazo, M.T., 'Les français en Murcie sous l'Ancien Régime (v. 1700–v. 1850). Des migrations populaires au grand commerce', in *Les Français en Espagne a l'époque moderne (XVIe.–XVIIIe. Siècles)* (Paris: CNRS, 1990), pp. 113–14. Salas Auséns, J.A., *En busca del dorado. Inmigración francesa en la España de la Edad Moderna* (Bilbao: Universidad del País Vasco, 2009), pp. 214–24.

as well as a smaller group of artisans, who substituted the group of English and Italian dealers established in Castile during the previous century – see Chart 5.2 – contributed to the economic development of towns and villages. Naturally, the major reason for the substitution of foreign businessmen was that English and Italian merchants supported the Austrian party in the War of Succession, whereas the French merchants remained loyal to the Bourbon cause. However, during the eighteenth century, the role of Italian merchants was important in commercial exchanges inside and outside the Spanish territory.

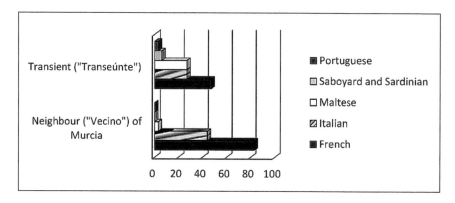

Chart 5.2   Origin of foreign workers of the City of Murcia according to the census of Charles III. *Source:* A.M.M., Charles' III Census of Foreigners, 1764.

In 1764, the census made by Charles III of the foreign population in the Crown of Castile has been a crucial source to support the idea of the importance of the French community in stimulating the south-eastern Spanish economy through the creation of trade networks. The census includes other categories of foreigners, from southern European territories such as Italy, Savoy, Sardinia, Malta and Portugal, who settled in Murcia (see Chart 5.2). The foreign 'vecinos' [neighbours] who established themselves in the Kingdom of Murcia were not the main resource fuelling the economy. An important human capital named in the census as 'transeúntes' [transients] also contributed to set up local markets in a more global economy, in which financial capital, the labour force and merchandises were circulating. The joint function of both foreign neighbours and non-residents stimulated the creation of economic links with other Mediterranean regions.

This French migration featured a wider supply of commodities by the new group of wholesalers and retailers who settled in south-eastern Spain. A new market, especially linked with luxury commodities, was created, provoking progressive shifts in consumer behaviour. The growing Mediterranean import-export market fostered the introduction of products increasing the demand among lower-middle classes. We could affirm that those foreign merchants created a particular market in order to enlarge the demand for merchandise, especially in groups with a modest level of wealth. Their aim was to have an open space to sell commodities that were brought from Asian and Atlantic markets, creating a wider network of customers. Merchants were challenging the traditional socio-cultural and economic values by creating new desires and needs. The introduction of their products motivated individuals toward the acquisition of fashionable foreign items.

The flourishing Mediterranean market was revitalized by the strengthening of networks of traders that resulted from links of trust, loyalty and family relations. Such merchant networks consisted in individuals of the same nationality[29] – French, Maltese and Italian – and kinship (see Charts 5.3 and 5.4). Family ties and bonds featured the social relations among merchants. In the study on family trade in the early modern Atlantic world, Marta V. Vicente asserts[30] that commercial houses and family companies depended on their extended webs of family connections – supervisors, workers, brokers and skippers – to have access to credit, acquisition of technology and purchase of raw materials.

The unpredictable consequences and risks of maritime trade were the main preoccupation of businessmen at that time. In most of cases, only relatives or people of trust were involved in the merchant's enterprise. The national origin of the head of the family's spouse was the same as his ancestors', as well as his entire family network. The elevated percentage of endogamy and co-national marriages among merchants explains that they wanted to ensure the success of their deals, which was mainly based on trust and transparency that were reinforced by the kinship and co-national bonds – see Chart 5.3 and genealogical tree. On the other hand, they required their sons, daughters and family members to run their businesses generation after generation. The technical conditions of shipping and the danger of arrival of periods of war were issues that could put the shipment of goods at risk. Such issues could also make necessary a loan to expand the business at risk, especially if it came from overseas markets.

Family ties and a very precise network of connections, among merchants, could accurately foresee possible risks through the circulation of information. Charts 5.3 and 5.4 were designed from several sources,[31] such as wills, probate inventories and dowries, in which individuals – witnesses and executors – were related to the head of the family. The extended family was widespread among merchants, especially in foreign traders established in south-eastern Castile. Such

---

[29]   Montojo y Montojo, V. and Maestre de San Juan Pelegrin, F., 'El Comercio Cartagenero en el Siglo XVIII', en Rubio Paredes, J.Mª (ed.), *Cartagena Puerto de Mar en el Mediterráneo* (Cartagena: Autoridad Portuaria, 2007).

[30]   Vicente, M.V., *Clothing*.

[31]   Charts 5.3 and 5.4 only refer to individuals who are registered in protocols such as probate inventories, dowries and wills, in relation with the sample of the population that we have worked on belonging to middle social classes. However, this can be thoroughly studied by examining the parish registers.

a large network could assure the achievement of good deals and prolong the life of
the family enterprise thanks to the extended ties of the household.

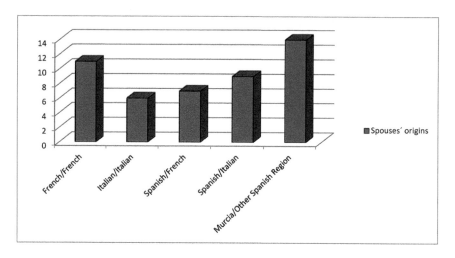

Chart 5.3   Co-national and trans-national marriages among individuals of
             the trade sector in the Kingdom of Murcia (1730–1808). *Source:*
             A.H.P.M., protocols.

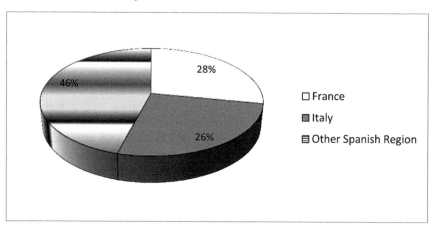

Chart 5.4   Origin of traders established in the Kingdom of Murcia (1730–
             1808). *Source:* A.H.P.M., protocols.

Co-national marriages among the community of foreign merchants were a
relevant factor that explains the reinforcement of such networks. French traders
usually married individuals from the same nationality. Italians, to a smaller
degree, did the same. Spanish traders also tended to marry individuals of the

same origin. There was an important group of businessmen from Barcelona, Valencia,[32] Alicante and Majorca, with the old-maritime commercial tradition of the Crown of Aragon, who founded companies and married individuals from the same region and occupation – see Chart 5.3. Therefore, there are two important components to underline in marriages among merchants. Firstly, national origin is of great importance when they want to enlarge family ties. And the second factor is to marry individuals of the same occupation. This explains why we found an important degree of international marriages among Spanish, French and Italians traders in the Kingdom of Murcia – see Chart 5.3. Thus, such foreign merchants also formed an integrated trans-national network of Mediterranean traders.

Very clear evidence, which shows the relationship between the same national origin and family links among those merchants, is that they founded commercial houses with important margins of profit. Juan Bicaix and Alexadre Durand, both of French nationality, established a commercial house.[33] Don Joseph Cayron had a company in Marseille with Don Jaime Jordan and Don Arnaldo Cayron:

> … igualmente en la ciudad de Marsella y en poder del cuerpo Occo. que llaman el Clero tengo cierta cantidad de mrs. que constan de asiento en mis libros … declaro que tengo Compañía en esta ciudad con D. Jaime Jordan y D. Arnaldo Cairon mis albaceas …[34]

Thanks to the privileged location of the port of Cartagena, the maritime trade of the Mediterranean area exerted free-flowing dynamism on the economy of the Kingdom of Murcia. French and Italian merchants maintained the foreign trade of south-eastern Castile, because Marseille, Livorno, Genoa and Venice were the ports that kept a commercial link with Cartagena. However, the function of these ports was the mediation with the Levant routes. Cartagena supplied the interior of Castile with a high bulk of commodities due to the extended network of wholesalers, retailers and peddlers. The port of Marseille provided goods from Asian and Atlantic markets, not only to Spanish Mediterranean territories, but also to the interior of Europe, such as inner France, Germany, Switzerland, Holland or the Baltic countries.[35] Therefore, both local and international traders, who were settled in Spanish Mediterranean ports, established links with traders from other Mediterranean areas through the creation of an interconnected community based on trust. Such trust lay in kinship and vicinity links, or on national or regional origins.[36]

---

[32] Franch Benavent, R., *Crecimiento comercial y enriquecimiento burgués en la Valencia del siglo XVIII* (Valencia: Institut Alfons el Magnànim, 1986).

[33] A.H.P.M., sig. 2694, escr. Costa Irles, Antonio, sin foliar.

[34] A.H.P.M., sig. 4228, fols. 762r.–768v., escr. Atienza, Juan Mateo.

[35] Perez Picazo, M.T., and Lemeunier, G., *El proceso de modernización de la región murciana (ss. XVI–XIX)* (Murcia: Editora Regional de Murcia, 1984); Montojo y Montojo, V. and Maestre de San Juan Pelegrin, F., 'Los comerciantes'.

[36] Salas Auséns, J.A., *En busca del dorado*, 2009, pp. 214–24.

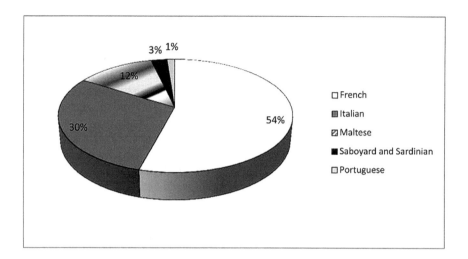

Chart 5.5   Origins of individuals belonging to the secondary sector according
               to the census of Charles III. *Source:* A.M.M., Charles' III Census of
               Foreigners, 1764.

Diasporas, comprising of both national and international merchants,[37] channelled
human and material sources through which migrant labour contributed to stimulate
the economic development of the region and country – see Charts 5.3, 5.4, 5.5.
The Spanish Mediterranean area, from Barcelona to Valencia and the Kingdom
of Murcia, was characterized by the strong presence of Italian merchants in the
seventeenth century. In the eighteenth century that group was substituted by the
French group.[38] Later, due to French turmoil in the early nineteenth century,
the Maltese[39] community acquired more importance. However, we have little
evidence of the commercial activities of Maltese traders prior to the second half

---

    [37]   See works on international migration and migrant labour force by: Gabaccia,
D.R., *Italy's Many Diasporas* (London: UCL Press, 2000). Gabaccia, D.R., Iacovetta, F.
and Ottanelli, F., 'Laboring across National Borders: Class, Gender, and Militancy in the
Proletarian Mass Migrations', *International Labor and Working-class History*, no. 66, New
Approaches to Global Labor History (Fall, 2004), pp. 57–77.
    [38]   Amalric, J.P., 'Franceses en tierras de España. Una presencia mediadora en el
Antiguo Régimen', Villar García, M.B. and Pezzi Cristobal, P. (eds), *Los extranjeros en la
España Moderna* (2 vols. Málaga: Junta de Andalucía, 2003), vol. 1, pp. 23–38.
    [39]   Martín Corrales, E., 'Comerciantes malteses e importaciones catalanas de
algodón (1728–1804)', in *Actas del I coloquio internacional hispano-maltés de Historia*
(Madrid: Ministerrio de Asuntos Exteriores, 1991), pp. 119–62. Franch, R., 'El papel
de los extranjeros en las actividades artesanales y comerciales del Mediterráneo español
durante la Edad Moderna', Villar García and Pezzi Cristóbal, P. (eds), *Los extranjeros*,
vol. 1, p. 54.

of the eighteenth century as their main activity was as itinerant retailers and peddlers.[40]

In Charts 5.6 and 5.7, there is a list of the main occupations of French and Italian traders and artisans who settled in the city of Murcia, as they appear in Charles III's census. This is a notable source that shows how such a foreign community could transfer its knowledge of artisan work as well as stimulating the financial system through commercial activities. The community of French workers was larger than the Italian one, and the occupation of both groups was different. Trade was the main labour sector of the French community and the artisan professions were mainly undertaken by Italians. The main group of merchants, including both wholesalers and retailers, was shaped by the French community, although there was a group of Italian retailers linked, to a smaller degree, to the textile sector.

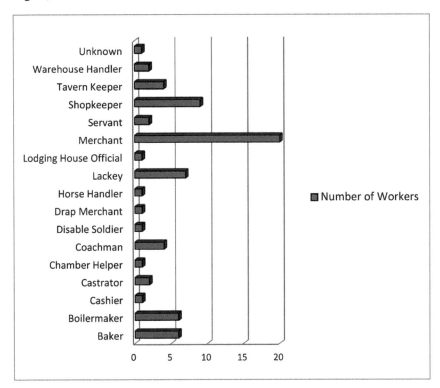

Chart 5.6:   Occupational distribution among the French population of the Kingdom of Murcia according to the census of Charles III. *Source: A.M.M., Charles' III Census of Foreigners, 1764.*

[40]   Vasallo, C., *Corsairing to Commerce. Maltese Merchants in XVIII–century Spain* (Valleta: Malta University Publishers, 1997), pp. 3–4.

Furthermore, there was an important group of Italian and French artisans, which included occupations with a high level of expertise such as pastry chefs, cooks, bakers, shoemakers or stocking makers that improved the local manufacturing of goods. The transfer of artisan habits fed the population's desire for high-quality goods that were consumed by this foreign community. In the Spanish Mediterranean areas, this movement of foreign communities specialising in both long-distance and minor commerce promoted the financial market as most of their business was undertaken through credit sale, which appears on merchant receipts, as well as probate inventories that list the individual's debts.

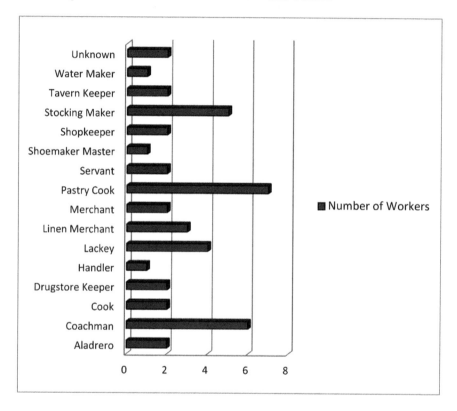

Chart 5.7   Occupational distribution among the Italian population of the Kingdom of Murcia according to the census of Charles III. *Source:* A.M.M., Charles' III Census of Foreigners, 1764

Juan de Orleac's creditors are listed in his probate inventory (Illustration 5.2). He was a French master boilermaker, who lived in the parish of San Pedro, Murcia. His wife was the shopkeeper and his brother-in-law, Juan Cailuz, was a French master boilermaker. Illustration 5.3 shows the capital that is owed to Don Juan de Soria Seller's, master apothecary from Alicante, whose residence was in the parish of Santa Maria of the Cathedral of Murcia. There is evidence of the list of people that needed to liquidate their debts with Francisco Benedicto (Illustration 5.4), who worked as French master artisan and merchant of books and lived in the parish of Santa Maria. Illustration 5.5 is a very good example of how the credit and payment system actually operated in the Kingdom of Murcia. It demonstrates the credit of 3.926 'reales de vellon' conceded from the Cayron-Jordan company, of Murcia, to the Vidal Company of Lorca, for the purchase of a bale of textiles made of 'bayeta' [cloth made fibre].

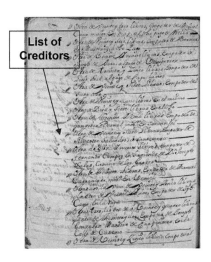

Illustration 5.2   Inventory (a). *Source:* A.H.P.M., protocol 2804.

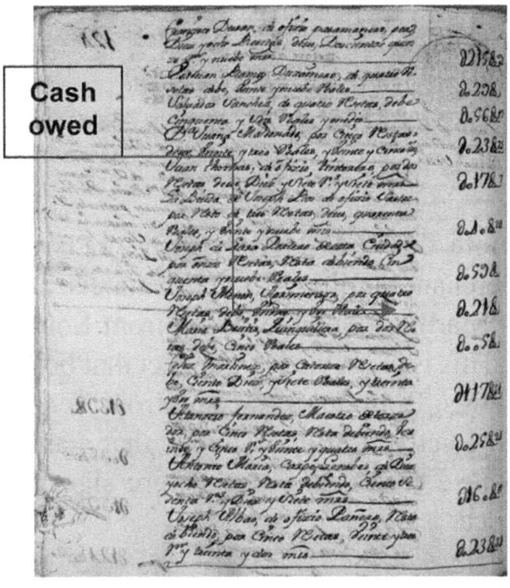

Illustration 5.3   Inventory (b). *Source:* A.H.P.M., protocol 2804.

Illustration 5.4   Inventory (c). *Source:* A.H.P.M., protocol 2811.

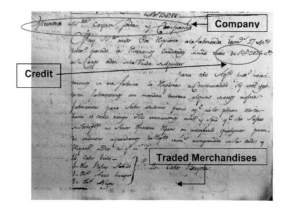

Illustration 5.5   Merchant Letter. *Source:* A.M.L., S. II, 19, Cartas de Antonio
                    Martín de Lorca.

It is important to note that the Cayron family had some important family
connections with the merchant families of Lorca. Francisca Cayron y Bouyon was
married to Don Tomas Martin, a notable trader from Lorca, who also had links
with the Vidal family.[41] This is explained by the fact that both the Vidal and Martin
families had French origins. Both families came from Vence, in southern France.
Thus, we can observe the active traffic of credits that was operating in this area,
connecting families, whose credits and deals were signed in Cartagena, inland
areas of Murcia and Lorca.

---

[41]   A.H.P.M., sig. 4228, fols. 762r.–768v., escr. Atienza, Juan Mateo, Tomo II.

This financial market grew and became successful thanks to the family and co-national bonds on which those dealers based their businesses in order to take fewer risks in their commercial transactions. In addition, those dealers shared information by being in constant contact. It is not unexpected that most of the major groups of French businessmen in the city of Murcia lived within the same parish, the Santa Maria neighbourhood, where they could be in permanent contact. The same occurred with the dealers of Lorca, whose main location was the parish of 'Colegiata de San Patricio'. The concept of vicinity and the strength of family bonds were exceptionally embedded among merchants. Such socio-economic activity had as a result an increase in the families' trade wealth.

The genealogical tree, which we have built up through the merchants' wills and probate inventories, shows how those links were fixed generation after generation, having as a consequence a strong inbreeding of foreign merchant social relationships. The French traders Cayron and Bouyon arranged marriages between their siblings. Similar arrangements were observed among other traders, such as Esttoup, Dachiary and Trifon, who had Italian origins. These marriages had the aim of ensuring the enhancement of the economic life of their companies, making them more profitable.[42]

The predominance of marriages among individuals from the same nationality proves that businesses and family strategies were extremely closely connected in order to maintain their deals and improve their socio-economic status. In some cases, the most flourishing merchants could achieve an ennoblement process obtaining important positions in the council. For instance, the successful deals of Don Antonio Donate, a silk dealer from Italy, allowed him to acquire a position of 'jurado' [a member of the parliament in the council of the city].[43]

Family strategies were key to enhancing businesses. These strategies consisted of expanding influence through interconnected communities, where the outstanding concept of 'paisanaje' or [common identity], which was based on the same geographical origins, was very present. The foreign merchants of the Kingdom of Murcia traced a network among a narrow group of families. It was a way to permit foreigners to find their way when they settled in a new community. Keeping kinship and vicinity allowed merchants to establish a common culture, which eased fluent communication; preserved the flow of information; decreased risk in the business; and, finally, achieved economic success.[44]

---

[42]   A.H.P.M., protocols 3970, 4228.

[43]   A.H.P.M., sig. 2787, fols. 213r.–225v., escr. Espinosa de los Monteros, Francisco.

[44]   Greif, A., *Institutions and the Path to the Modern Economy: Lessons from Medieval Trade* (Cambridge; New York: Cambridge University Press, 2006). Pagano De Divitiis, G., *Mercanti inglesi nell'Italia del seicento: navi, traffici, egemonie* (Venezia: Marsilio editori, 1990). García Fernández, M.N., *Comunidad extranjera y puerto privilegiado: los británicos en Cádiz en el siglo XVIII* (Cádiz: Universidad de Cádiz, Servicio de Publicaciones, 2005). Kaplan, S.L., *Provisioning Paris: Merchants and Millers in the Grain and Flour Trade during the Eighteenth Century* (Ithaca: Cornell University Press, 1984).

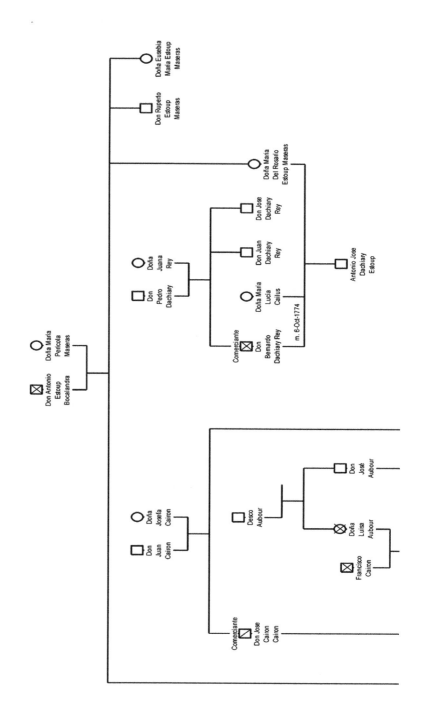

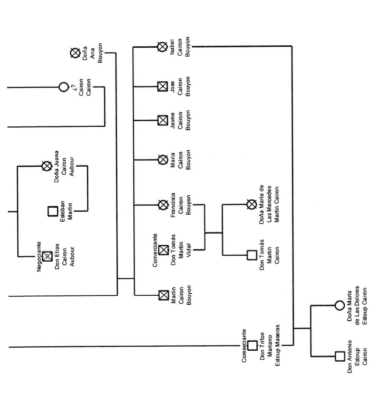

Genealogical Tree

Esttop-Cayron: Presence of Endogamy on Marriages of Merchant Families (Eighteenth to Nineteenth Centuries) *Symbols: Male (□); Female (○); Circulation of patrimony among the family group (X). *Source*: A.H.P.M., protocols, 3970, 4222.

Therefore, local and Mediterranean merchant networks were shaped by extended households, whose family and non-family members had 'paisanaje' and vicinity links in common.[45] Those family ties and social bonds made it possible to preserve family businesses generation after generation, enhancing the household economy. These types of families provided the distribution of knowledge, trade and credit by requiring from their members' loyalty and trust to overcome the randomness of trade affairs – for example, the genealogical tree corresponding to the French dealers Esttop-Cayron, above.

A good example of the trust established by merchants belonging to the same nationality can be seen in Nicolas Esttop Fadeville's probate inventory, dated 28 May 1756. Nicolas Esttop was a silk and grocery merchant, who had a textile shop and inn. He was born in Murcia, but his origins were Italian. His father was a merchant who came to Murcia from Salbaterra and he was married to Ana Bocalandra Docunti, born in Murcia, but with Italian roots due to the origin of her parents – Axel Bocalandria and Bernarda Docunti – both of whom came from Veoli, Genoa. In Nicolas Esttop's probate inventory, Antonio Davide and Francisco Davide, merchants with French origins, appear as witnesses.[46] Nicolas Esttop Fadeville was also the witness for Juana Carpe's dowry contract, which was written on 7 July 1762. Juana Carpe came from Malta and was married to Andres Grech, who came from Malta, being a merchant settled in Murcia.[47] Likewise, in Juan Bicaix's probate inventory, which was made on 3 August 1764, witnesses of French origin appear. This was due to the fact that Juan Bicaix was a French merchant from Beàrn, as were his witnesses. He was a shop owner in company with Francisco Bordonabe and Alexandre Durand. In his inventory, Juan Bautista Salomon, a French dealer, and Claudio Sesane, a dealer from Genoa, merchants of textiles and groceries, were named as appraisers to evaluate Juan Bicaix's possessions.[48]

These references are evidence of the links and social networks that were established among foreign traders who belonged to the same nationality and had settled in the Kingdom of Murcia. The fact that they came from the same region provided tradesmen with a sense of trust in their dealings. We can also deduce that

---

[45]   For the concept of 'paisanaje' and its importance in the trade networks in the eighteenth-century Spanish world, see: Fernández Pérez, P. and Sola-Corbacho, J.C., 'Regional Identity, Family, and Trade in Cadiz and Mexico City in the Eighteenth Century', *Journal of Early Modern History*, 8: 3–4 (2004): 358–85; Gonzalbo, P., *Familias novohispanas: siglos XVI al XIX* (Mexico D.F.: Seminario de Historia de la Familia; Centro de Estudios Históricos, Colegio de México, 1991). Peristiany, J.G. (ed.), *Mediterranean Family Structures* (Cambridge [Eng.]; New York: Cambridge University Press, 1976). Chacón Jiménez, F. and Hernández Franco J. (eds), *Poder, Familia y consanguinidad en la España del Antiguo Régimen* (Barcelona: Anthropos Editorial del Hombre, 1992). Vicente, M. V., *Clothing*.

[46]   A.H.P.M., sig. 3970, sin foliar, escr. Pedro Vasilio Villanueva, 25/06/1756.
[47]   A.H.P.M., sig. 3122, fols. 268r.–270v.
[48]   A.H.P.M., sig. 2694, sin foliar, escr. Antonio Costa Irles, 13/08/1764.

due to the settlement of these social networks, there was a tendency to establish links among persons who belonged to the same socio-professional sector such as silk, grocery or textile merchants.

Within these socio-economic networks, the most important feature that needs to be underlined is that such dealers created a community based on very close social relationships such as marriage, trust, culture, values and nationality. Under such circumstances, they also shared similar patterns of consumption, which they could transfer to other social groups that coexisted with them. The following pages show how these merchants progressively introduced a large volume of commodities from their places of origin. Hence, they were the major economic agents acting as mediators in supplying towns and villages. In connection with this, Part IV will show the shifts in the demand-side due to the intermediation of such traders.

5.2. The Spanish Mediterranean Import-export Market: a Dependency of Foreign Manufactures

Social networks and trade provided a constant flow of merchandise in the Mediterranean area by connecting Europe with the Asian and Atlantic markets. However, this provoked an inequity in Spanish productivity by comparison to other regions such as England and the Netherlands. Eastern areas of Spain had lower productivity than territories of England or the Netherlands, which may reflect the larger investment on technologies, prior to the arrival of large factories, made by the latter countries that favoured the development of local economies. Moreover, north-western Europe may also have had fewer restrictions on their mercantile policies. This issue is revealed through the volume of manufactured goods exported from Marseille to Mediterranean areas of Spain by comparison with some other European territories – see Charts 5.10 and 5.11.[49] The volume of Spanish entries was higher than other European countries with the exception of Italy. Foreign and long distant trade intensified local production and markets, as social networks created by foreign merchants changed the patterns of consumption in both urban and rural populations. This market orientation was the major stimulus that inspired local producers, local elites, entrepreneurs and middle classes for a growing demand of goods that came from the international market.[50] The demand for a wide array of commodities, not only for covering basic necessities, increased throughout Europe. Spain was no exception in such a process. Neither Spanish crafts nor domestic markets could entirely supply such goods. The eastern Spanish market in connection with external economic enterprises of the Mediterranean, Asian and Atlantic regions stimulated the local demand in Spanish Mediterranean areas.

---

[49] A.C.C.M., Statistique. Serie I. Article 29, I.30, I.24, I.31.
[50] Ringrose, D., *Spain, Europe and the 'Spanish Miracle', 1700–1900* (Cambridge: Cambridge University Press, 1996), pp. 135–62.

The task in this section is to show the commercial routes of merchandise in the Levantine and Atlantic markets, which stimulated the Spanish Mediterranean economy. This flow of merchandise in eastern territories of Spain was stronger because of the impossibility of producing the goods that were demanded by local communities. The major consequences of such an economic system were the transfer of cultural values in the Spanish society due to the elevated level of circulation of goods and people, as well as the imbalance in the Spanish Mediterranean import-export market provoked by the high dependency on foreign manufactured goods. The consumption of goods became more global. Merchandise from the markets of Levant and the New World fostered strong levels of trans-nationality, by confronting traditional values, through their widespread introduction in the population. The desire for fancy outfits and garments, labelled as exotic, could only be satisfied by foreign merchants and skilled artisans.[51]

There was commercial dynamism linked with the demographic growth of the Kingdom of Murcia, especially the city of Cartagena, which was one of the main gates of southern Castile for the export-import market, generating a positive curve in the demand of goods. The building of 'Arsenal de Marina' [Navy Arsenal] played a very important role, and allowed Cartagena to be an 'open market'. In the second half of the eighteenth century, the population of Cartagena was 70,000, following the general positive growth of the Kingdom of Murcia (see Table 5.1), which increased from 82,770 inhabitants in 1694 to 252,620 in 1787.[52]

Table 5.1   Census of the Kingdom of Murcia

Census Date	Number of Inhabitants
1694	82,770
1765	195,020
1779	231,006
1787	252,620

Source: Perez Picazo, M.T. and Lemeunier, G., *El proceso de modernización*, p. 136.

The domestic industries of France, Italy and England had more advanced technology than Spain. The centres of Languedoc, Grenoble, Lyon or Dijon, in France, and Bologna and Piedmont, in northern Italy, had a vast quantity of looms to compete with the main English textile centres of Lancashire. The possession of

---

[51]   Although it is well known that Catalonia was the most industrialized area, especially in the production of textiles such as calicoes or cottons by copying Asian techniques, they could not compete with the authentic Asian textiles. See: Thompson, J.K.J., *A Distinctive Industrialization. Cotton in Barcelona (1728–1832)* (Cambridge: Cambridge University Press, 1992).

[52]   Lemeunier, G. and Pérez Picazo, M.T., *El proceso de modernización*.

looms by artisan workers is a very good indicator that reveals the degree of the productive capacity of the textile sector. In the southern Castilian economy there was a progressive decline in the ownership of looms and spinning wheels by silk artisans and weavers, although Valencia, Murcia and Granada were specialized in the production of silk.

Table 5.2   Evolution of ownership of textile tools and number of artisans in the Kingdom of Murcia

Years	Looms	Silk Artisans	Spinning Wheels	Weavers
1738	60	220	200	260
1755	50	145	108	215
1803	30	109	90	90

Source: Perez Picazo, M.T. and Lemeunier, G., El proceso de modernización, p. 190.

As we can see (Table 5.2), there was a progressive fall in the possession of textile tools – looms and spinning wheels – for spinning silk, as well as a reduction in the number of workers in the textile sector. External competition was the main cause for this decline, as well as the lack of domestic investment in new technologies and the limits imposed by the regulations of the artisan guilds. This issue demonstrates that the Kingdom of Murcia was not capable of fostering a process of substitution for the imported goods such as the one that took place in England.[53] Under such circumstances, it was almost impossible to compete with the main textile producers of France and Italy during the eighteenth century. While there was a decline in the number of artisans in the textile sector in most Spanish centres, the population of Dijon that worked on the manufacturing of textiles increased in number and percentage during the eighteenth century. The number of artisans in the textile sector was 597 in 1700, 30 per cent of the global percentage of all occupational sectors. In 1790 the number of workers grew from 597 to 658 increasing by 10 per cent. These numbers are quite significant, taking into account the number of workers registered in the main parish records of Dijon: in 1700, the number of individuals registered was 1,973 and in 1790 it was 2,101.[54]

---

[53]   Maxime Berg noticed the process of substitution that took place in England during the second half of the eighteenth century, when the British textile industries increased their productivity. See Berg, M., 'In Pursuit of Luxury', pp. 85–142.

[54]   Shephard, E.J. Jr, 'Movilidad social y geográfica del artesanado en el siglo XVIII: estudio de la admisión a los gremios de Dijon, 1700–90', in López, V. and Nieto, J.A. (eds), El trabajo en la encrucijada. Artesanos urbanos en la Europa de la Edad Moderna (Madrid: Historia Social, 1996), pp. 37–69.

The same thing also happened in Italy. The population of Turin in 1707 was 33,773. In the census, the number of people that appear as tailors is 376.[55] In the city of Bologna in the early eighteenth century, 236 shoemakers produced 10,858 pairs of shoes per month.[56] North Italy, especially the Piedmont area, witnessed, despite some fluctuations, a positive growth in population, the rates of expansion from 1650 to 1700 being 0.57 and 0.59, from 1700 to1750, 0.28 and 0.24, and from 1750 to 1800, 0.20 and 0.23.[57]

The comparison of these statistics with the data regarding south-eastern Castile confirms the decadence of this area in the production of manufactured goods. Such a lack was overcome by the free-flowing circuit of exchanging raw materials for ready-made items, the export-import market being the main economic resource during the eighteenth century. The connection of markets, provoked by the settlement of affiliations and commercial houses by foreign merchants, was crucial for feeding the global trade of merchandise. Those merchants, acting as mediators in the Spanish Mediterranean market, could better supply the Spanish society than the limitations on production imposed by local institutions. However, there were some areas of growing industries such as the Catalonian area where the crafts of Sabadell, Tarrasa or Lerida manufactured an important volume of textiles made of linen, cotton or wool.

As Thompson[58] has discussed, the inefficacy of direct state intervention such as the guilds or 'Juntas de Comercio' [Boards of Commerce], the tariff restrictions and the promulgation of royal decrees in economic development obstructed Spanish industrialization, whereas some other European countries, such as England, France or the Netherlands, were reaching major stages of economic growth. This demonstrates that the direct intervention by the state, in particular tariff restrictions, had serious consequences for economic development. By contrast, some other European areas such as England, the Netherlands or France started to shift towards such mercantile policies during the last stage of the *Ancien Regime*. England and the Netherlands led the European industrialization process, whereas France tried to follow that pattern by giving more scope to its commercial sector. The French concern for the development of its market is demonstrated by all the privileges that the French state gave to the 'Chambre de Commerce de Marseille',

---

[55]   Cerutti, S., 'Estrategias de grupo y estrategias de oficio: el gremio de sastres de Turin a finales del s. XVIII y principios del XVIII', in López, V. and Nieto, J.A. (eds), *El trabajo*, pp. 70–112.

[56]   Poni, C., 'Normas y pleitos: el gremio de zapateros de Bolonia en el s. XVIII', in López, V. and Nieto, J.A. (eds), *El trabajo*, pp. 153–78.

[57]   Galloway, P.R., 'A Reconstruction of the Population of North Italy from 1650 to 1881.Using Annual Inverse Projection with Comparisons to England, France, and Sweden', *European Journal of Population/Revue Européenne de Démographie*, vol. 10, no. 3 (Sep., 1994), pp. 223–74. See also the work by Siddle, D.J., 'Migration as a Strategy of Accumulation: Social and Economic Change in Eighteenth-century Savoy', *The Economic History Review*, New Series, vol. 50, no. 1 (Feb., 1997), pp. 1–20.

[58]   Thompson, J.K.J., *A Distinctive Industrialization*.

as well as all French trade branches established in Mediterranean territories, such as those founded in eastern regions of Spain.

The economic progress of those European places has its roots in the capacity for market development. Protective taxes created by Bourbon monarchs are significant evidence of Spanish backwardness during the period of European economic growth. There was a lack of political agreement regarding the administrative control of national industry. Examples of this are the measures and decrees dictated by the Bourbons, whose aim was to ban the import of foreign goods and stimulate national production. However, these rules failed in their application. The import of foreign goods continued by means of the action of foreign traders. The imbalance between Spanish imports and exports was marked by the creation of a continuous appetite among the Spanish population for exotic and fancy commodities. Therefore, the progressive shift created in fashion reinforced the social differences in Spanish society, provoking rivalry among those groups who wanted to keep the national traditions and customs. The formation of national stereotypes and confrontation among ideologies, represented by French fashion against the Spanish tradition, was the result of the relative weakness of the Spanish industry in providing national commodities on a large scale.

Catalonia and Valencia were the main territories that specialized in textile production, whose artisan groups were able to initiate a process of substitution of imports. However, the main coastal areas of eastern Spain such as Malaga, Granada, Almeria, Alicante or Cartagena tried to fuel the national economy through the financial market and investments of foreign merchants[59] who supplied goods and stimulated local economies of the Spanish periphery.[60] Chart 5.8 shows

---

[59] See Ringrose, D., The 'Spanish Miracle', pp. 190–204. For the Catalonian and Valencia textile production see works by: Thompson, J.K.J., A Distinctive Industrialization; Piqueras, J., La agricultura valenciana de exportación y su formación histórica (Madrid: Ministerio de Agricultura, 1985), p. 88. However, the majority of Spanish areas such as Malaga, Granada, Almeria, Alicante or Cartagena were not inserted in this process. These territories depended on foreign agents to provide their population with manufactures. See: Lemeunier, G., Perez Picazo, M.T., El proceso de modernización. Martín Rodríguez, M., 'Andalucía: Luces y sombras de una industrialización interrumpida', in Nadal Oller, J. and Carreras, A., Pautas regionales de la industrialización española (siglos XIX Y XX) (Barcelona: Ariel, 1990), pp. 349–51.

[60] Studies on peripheral regions of Europe have insisted upon the external dependence of regions that lacked a deep structural reform on the system of production in order to modernize the national economy. See works by: Gunder Frank, A., 'The Development of Underdevelopment', and 'Economic Dependence, Class Structure, and Underdevelopment Policy', in Cockroft, J.D., Gunder Frank, A. and Johnson, D.J. (eds), Dependence and Underdevelopment (New York: Doubleday, 1972), pp. 3–46. Janos, A.C., 'The Politics of Backwardness in Continental Europe, 1780–1945', World Politics, vol. 41, no. 3 (Apr., 1989), pp. 325–58. For the Spanish case such problems have been deeply studied by Anes Álvarez and Martinez Shaw, who saw the Enlightenment reforms as insufficient measures to undertake a process of modernization on the Spanish economy: Anes Álvarez

the exports of textile raw material such as silk and cotton from the Mediterranean area of Spain to France, through the port of Marseille. Spanish raw silk chiefly came from Valencia, Murcia and Granada, whereas the untreated cotton was mainly exported from Catalonia. We can observe that the imports in Marseille of Levantine raw silk were smaller by comparison to the imports of such raw silk in Marseille from Spanish Mediterranean ports. Spanish raw silk from eastern areas was shipped to Mediterranean ports, where raw silk was distributed to the textile industries of southern France, Languedoc and Provence, and northern Italy, Bologna, Turin and Milan.

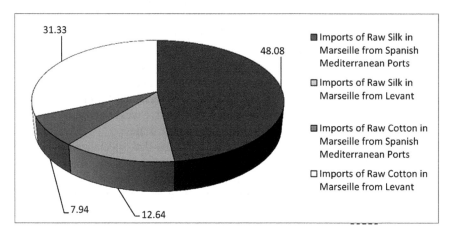

Chart 5.8   Percentages of imports of raw silk and cotton in Marseille (1730–85). Percentages stimated over the total volume of imports. *Source:* A.C.C.M., Statistique. Serie I.

On the other hand, it is also notable that the imports of raw cotton in Marseille from eastern Spanish ports mostly lagged behind the raw cotton coming from the Levant (see Chart 5.8). Only in the second half of the eighteenth century (see the period from 1742 to 1785 which demonstrates the slight rise of Spanish raw cottons and the fall of Levantine raw cottons – Table 5.3), with the French bans on textiles from the Levantine routes, did the imports in Marseille of eastern Spanish raw cotton grow smoothly. But the general tendency was a preference for Asian raw materials. This is outstanding proof that Asian raw cotton became very popular

de Castrillón, G., 'Coyuntura económica e Ilustración', in Rico Manrique, F. (coor.), *Historia y crítica de la literatura española* (4 vols., 1983), vol. 1, Caso González, J.M. (ed.), *Ilustración y Neoclasicismo*, pp. 49–58. Martínez Shaw, C., 'La Cataluña del siglo XVIII bajo el signo de la expansión', in Fernández Díaz, R. (ed.), *España en el siglo XVIII: homenaje a Pierre Vilar* (Barcelona: Crítica, 1985), pp. 55–131.

in European markets, as artisans tried to copy the original Asian textiles, which was a commodity in high demanded due to its quality and affordable prices.[61]

Table 5.3   Average of raw silk and cotton imported in Marseille (1730–85)

	Imports of Raw Silk in Marseille from Spanish Mediterranean Ports	Imports of Raw Silk in Marseille from Levant	Imports of Raw Cotton in Marseille from Spanish Mediterranean Ports	Imports of Raw Cotton in Marseille from Levant	Totals
1730–41	180,635.73 (48.46%)	87,625.54 (23.50%)	30,000 (8.04%)	74,483.79 (19.98%)	372,745.06 (100%)
1742–52	121,024.37 (37.29%)	38,673.46 (11.91%)	36,409.34 (11.22%)	128,365.42 (39.56%)	324,472.59 (100%)
1753–63	66,308.57 (33.15%)	29,023.57 (14.51%)	39,779.19 (19.89%)	64,870 (32.43%)	199,981.33 (100%)
1764–74	40,556.07 (26.46%)	29,303.82 (19.11%)	30,510.23 (19.90%)	52,895.64 (34.51%)	153,265.76 (100%)
1775–85	32,325.37 (24.77%)	33,179.89 (25.43%)	29,963.97 (22.96%)	34,990.68 (26.82%)	130,459.91 (100%)

We have estimated the percentages over the totals of imports for each period and item. *Source:* A.C.C.M., Statistique. Serie I.

The arrival of Levantine raw cotton and silk in Marseille affected the Spanish Mediterranean exports of such material to Marseille. Related to the Spanish Mediterranean market, Marseille traders mainly bought raw cotton from the Catalonian area[62] and raw silk from Valencia, Murcia and Granada. As we can observe in Table 5.3, we have estimated the average entries of Levantine and Spanish Mediterranean raw silk and cotton in Marseille over chronological sections of ten years, thus we can observe, in the long term, how the entry to Marseille of raw materials from the Levant was damaging the entries of Spanish Mediterranean raw materials in Marseille. Although Spanish Mediterranean raw silk remained in demand by Marseille traders – see Chart 5.8 – it was less in demand during the last quarter of the eighteenth century as the progressive import

[61]   The trans-national trade for Asian textiles, whether unprepared or ready to use, has been deeply studied by Riello and Parthasarathi. Riello, G., 'The Globalization of Cotton Textiles: India Cottons, Europe and the Atlantic World, 1600–1800', in Riello, G. and Parthasarathi, P. (eds), *The Spinning World*, pp. 261–87.

[62]   Martínez Shaw, C., 'Los orígenes de la industria algodonera catalana y el comercio colonial', in Tortella Casares, G. and Nadal J. (eds), *Agricultura, comercio colonial y crecimiento económico en la España contemporánea: actas del Primer Coloquio de Historia Económica de España* (Barcelona: Ariel, 1974), pp. 243–67.

to Marseille of Levantine silk was substituting this Spanish raw material. The craze for Asian commodities and the European attempts to imitate the techniques for the production of such items explains the large volume of raw silk and cotton entering Marseille, as southern French industries tried to replicate the exotic Asian textiles.[63]

The import-export trade of Levantine merchandise kept the Spanish balance of payments negative: imports being progressively higher than exports. Although there were some strong attempts to ban the entry of such products with the aim to stimulate the national industries of Spain during the second half of the eighteenth century, the trade of goods from the Levant continued, probably due to the activity of smugglers.[64] Moreover, this had a negative influence on the Catalonian cotton industry. Catalonian textile crafts saw a decline in the production of cotton, as well as in exports to European and Atlantic territories. The competition posed by Asian raw textiles and clothing manufactures, which became more fashionable in European society, did not allow Catalonian fabrics to dominate the textile market in Europe and overseas.[65] Nevertheless, it has been well- demonstrated that there was an important volume of exports of Catalonian manufactured textiles to the Atlantic world, especially to New Spain.[66] The Levantine raw materials and the demand for Asian fabrics in Europe, especially the arrival of Asian silks to France, had a significant impact on the commercialization of eastern Spanish raw materials produced in Barcelona, Valencia and Murcia. This is explained by a shift provoked in the choice of raw materials by the artisans of southern France. In Chart 5.9 we can observe that the current prices of Spanish raw materials such as silk were higher than those from the Levant. This issue should be enshrined in the economic theories of the divergence on prices between Europe and Asia that contributed to the appeal of cheap Asian fabrics, which were exported in high volumes to Europe.[67]

---

[63]   See the work of Beverly Lemire for an examination of the imitation of Asian techniques and how these exotic goods changed European taste: Lemire, B., 'Domesticating the Exotic: Floral Culture and the East India Calico Trade with England, c. 1600–1800', *Textile*, 1/1 (2003), pp. 65–85.

[64]   The sources that we have analysed in the 'Chambre de Commerce de Marseille' do not contain any clue on the smuggling, although professor Martín Corrales has found some traces on this issue in his analysis of the Levant market and its connections with the Mediterranean Spanish ports. See: Martín Corrales, E., 'Marseille', pp. 61–78; Martín Corrales, E., 'La importación de telas', p. 49.

[65]   Delgado Ribas, J.M., 'El algodón engaña: algunas reflexiones en torno a la demanda americana en el desarrollo de la indianería catalana', *Manuscrits: Revista d' Història Moderna*, no. 11 (1993), pp. 61–84.

[66]   Oliva Melgar, J.M., *Cataluña y el comercio privilegiado con América en el siglo XVIII: la Real Compañía de Comercio de Barcelona a Indias* (Barcelona: Universidad de Barcelona, 1987). Thompson, J.K.J., *A Distinctive Industrialization*; Vicente, M.V., *Clothing*.

[67]   Special circumstances such as a cheap labour force, low prices, skilled artisans and cheap and fashionable textiles contributed to the fact that Asian textiles became

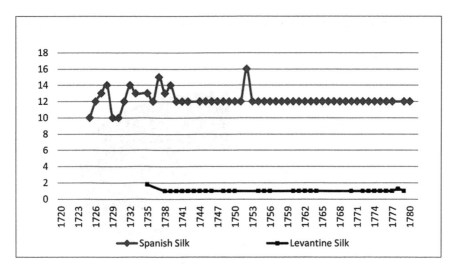

Chart 5.9   Current prices of Spanish and Levantine raw silk in the
              Mediterranean market (1720–80). Unit of price: French 'livres
              tournois'. Volume/Price: 1 pound of silk or cotton / 'x' 'livres
              tournois'. *Source:* A.C.C.M., Statistique. Serie I. Article 29, I.30,
              I.24, I.31.

The cheap labour force and the enormous volumes of cotton, calico and silk from the
Asian market made possible the constant shipping, by European trade companies,
of those raw materials and manufactured products to Europe (in the case of the
French companies from Marseille). The data provided in Charts 5.10 and 5.11
show the value of the imports in Europe from Marseille, with Spanish and Italian
dealers being the main purchasers. The data indicate the failure of mercantilist
states to stop the entry, to Europe, of foreign industrial products from the Atlantic
and Asian markets. The circulation of merchandise in the Mediterranean area via
a wide variety of ships, such as naus, galleons, caravels, pinnaces, brigantine,
polacre, vaisseau, bombard and tartans, made it possible for markets from the New

---

very important for the European economy, and was a significant cause of the economic
divergence between Europe and Asia, as well as the integration of such markets in a more
global context. See works by: Pomeranz, K., *The Great Divergence*. Allen, C.A., 'India in
the Great Divergence', in Hatton, T.J., O'Rourke, K.H. and Taylor, A.M. (eds), *The New
Comparative Economic History: Essays in Honor of Jeffrey G. Williamson* (Cambridge,
Mass.: MIT Press, 2007), pp. 9–32. O'Brien, P., 'The Geopolitics of a Global Industry:
Eurasian Divergence and the Mechanization of Cotton Textile Production in England', in
Riello, G. and Parthasarathi, P. (eds), *The Spinning World*, pp. 351–65. Özmucur, S. and
Pamuk, S., 'Did European Commodity Prices Converge during 1500–1800?', in Hatton,
T.J., O'Rourke, K.H. and Taylor, A.M. (eds), *The New Comparative*, pp. 59–86.

World, Asia and the Old Continent to become globally interconnected.[68] This was the case of the so-called 'caravane maritime'[maritime caravan].[69]

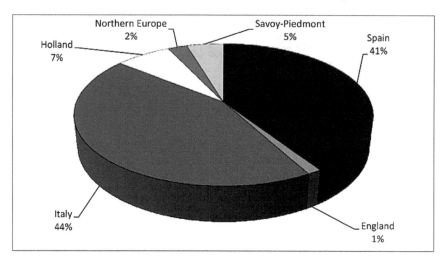

Chart 5.10   Percentages of exports from Marseille to Europe (1730–80). Percentages stimated over the total value of exports. *Source:* A.C.C.M., Statistique. Serie I.

The eastern Spanish export-import trade continued to have a negative balance, as the export of raw materials was lower than the Mediterranean import of ready-made items (see Chart 5.11) which came mainly from France. The progressive entry of Asian raw materials into Europe minimized the former apogee of Spanish Mediterranean raw materials in the European market. Economic agents tried to reactivate the national market and production, by seeking new goods to commercialize.[70] This is the case with natural and botanical products. Moreover, another measure aimed at fuelling the national economy was to imitate the commodities that came from afar: for example, the attempt to emulate and print calicoes.

---

[68]   De Vries, J., 'Connecting Europe and Asia: A Quantitative Analysis of Cape-Route Trade, 1497–1795', in Flynn, D.O., Giraldez, A. and Von Glanhn, R. (eds), *Global Connections and Monetary History, 1470–1800*, 2003 (London: Ashgate, 2003), pp. 35–106.

[69]   Panzac, D., *La caravane maritime. Marins européens et marchands ottomans en Méditerranée (1680–1830)* (Paris: CNRS, 2004).

[70]   Ringrose, D., 'European Economic Growth: Comments on the Noth-Thomas Theory', *The Economic History Review*, vol. 26, n. 2 (1973), pp. 285–92.

Table 5.4   Average of exports from Marseille to Europe (1730–80)

	Spain	England	Italy	Holland	Northern Europe	Savoy-Piedmont	Totals
1730–40	1,545,113.04 (26.06%)	51,014.92 (0.86%)	3,000,462.57 (50.61%)	846,940.42 (14.28%)	340,140.57 (5.73%)	14,437.6 (2.43%)	5,928,047.52 (100%)
1741–51	9,531,954 (33.76%)	170,880.12 (0.60%)	15,777,744.6 (55.88%)	1,930,416.06 (6.83%)	625,915.26 (2.21%)	196,870.8 (0.69%)	28,233,780.8 (100%)
1752–62	11,279,237.6 (51.73%)	51,098.93 (0.23%)	7,073,072.67 (32.43%)	1,380,562.01 (6.33%)	741,766.28 (3.40%)	1,278,222.47 (5.86%)	21,803,960 (100%)
1763–73	9,604,466.24 (43.83%)	422,442.42 (1.92%)	5,798,601.85 (26.46%)	1,667,338.66 (7.61%)	569,758.2 (2.60%)	3,846,795.82 (17.55%)	21,909,403.2 (100%)
1774–84	5,906,560.81 (25.17%)	728,705.95 (3.10%)	11,142,562.4 (47.49%)	2,461,289.63 (10.49%)	364,733.58 (1.55%)	2,856,493.01 (12.17%)	23,460,345.4 (100%)

We have estimated the percentages over the totals of exports for each period and item.

Source: A.C.C.M., Statistique. Serie I.

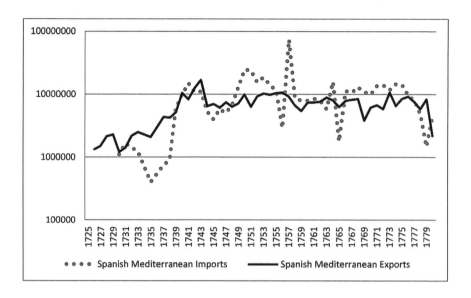

Chart 5.11   Spanish Mediterranean balance of trade in the Marseille market
              (1725–80). Value: in French 'livres'. *Source:* A.C.C.M., Statistique.
              Serie I.

The flow and entry of exotic items via merchants to the national territory
continued, as the basic sectors of domestic economy such as the craft industry and
agriculture required a substantial improvement to substitute the imports.[71] The
Bourbon Monarchy made some attempts to ban the introduction of certain foreign
industrial commodities, especially textiles, but the result was far from positive.
The progressive integration of Spanish and European trade in a more global
context made it impossible to limit the constant entry of Asian and American
goods into the national territory. It is necessary to differentiate these products
among textile products that were half-elaborated and finished in French industries,
ready-made items and raw materials (some of them, especially American raw
materials such as cochineal or foodstuff, were permitted by the Monarchy). It
was mostly industrial products that were banned by the Bourbon Monarchy. The
action of the mercantile rulers was not good enough to limit the rise of the new
consumers' appetites.

Proof of this assertion is the prohibition of Levantine goods, issued by the
Spanish Monarchy in 1782. A letter, forwarded by the Count of Floridablanca to
M. de Lastrin, minister and secretary of France in 1782, described the Spanish
attempt to ban the entry of all kind of Levantine textiles, manufactured and half-
elaborated goods and wheat. The justification offered by Floridablanca was the
danger of plague in Spain if French merchants continued to introduce textiles from

---

[71]   Stein, S.J. and Stein B., *Apogee*, p. 70. Martín Corrales, E., 'Marseille', pp. 1–4.

the Levant. In fact he was referring to the plague of Near East regions that affected the commerce between the eastern and western Mediterranean territories in 1771, but this had occurred a decade earlier, and any risk of contagion had passed.[72] However, beyond the possible risk of contamination in Spain, the prohibition responded to the fact that the Spanish Mediterranean balance of trade was negative and the attempt to stimulate national consumption had failed, as demonstrated in Charts 5.10 and 5.11.

The French authorities, as Monsieur de Lastrin remarked to the Count of Floridablanca, were opposed to the ban on French traders introducing Levantine drapes and other commodities because of the disastrous consequences this measure might incur. The Levant area was one of the major centres of French mercantile trade. Therefore, cutting the flow of this commerce in eastern Spanish society, as a potential consumer of the merchandise traded, could end in the bankruptcy of an important group of French companies:

> Lettre de M. de Lastrin ministre et secretaire de Etat. Prohibition en Espagne des Merchandises du Levant: Annonce de la communication donnée a M. le C. de Vergennes de la lettre de M. le C. de Floridablanca qui annonce l'interdiction en Espagne des marchandises et bleds du Levant
>
> J'ai reçu messieur avec la lettre que vous m'avez ecritte, le 25 du mois derniere, copie de celle de M. de Floridablanca au S. de la Rosa, la quelle vous a été communiqué pour ce consul de S.M. espagnole.
>
> Je vais la transmettre a M. le C. de Vergennes en le priant d'en faire part à M. le C. de Montmorin: cet ambassadeur instruit des motifs de la résolution du Roy d'Espagne, sera en etat de la faire modifier ou revoquer, s'il peut parvenir à demonter au Ministre de Madrid qu'elle est superflue, et qu'elle observe sans objet reel à notre commerce du Levant.
>
> Quant a l'interdiction des bleds a provenant de cette partie, il faut croire qu'on reconnaitra en Espagne que cette deure n'est pas susceptible de contagios. Les formalites aux quelles ont veux soumettre ceux de France, de Sicile, et de Sardaigne céderont toujours aux besoins en supposant que l'execution en fin reellement gênante.
>
> Vous savez messieur que votre depute a ordre de suivre votre reclamation sur le privileges exclusif accorde aux mesageries par l'arret du 9 aout 1781. Je ne la perda point de vue, et je vais me faire rendre compte de la situation où elle se trouve.
>
> Je suis messieur entierement à vous. A Versailles le 9 fevrier 1782.[73]

---

[72] Carrière, Ch., *Richesse du passé marseillais. Le port mondial au XVIIIe siècle* (Marseille: Chambre de Commerce et d'Industrie de Marseille, 1979), p. 48.

[73] A.C.C.M., Référence: Serie H, 73, Commerce avec l' Espagne (1776–91).

Notwithstanding, the commerce based on the export of raw materials continued as it represented the main economic resource,[74] which injected more economic capital into south-eastern territories of Spain – see Table 5.5 and Chart 5.12. Some records have been found about the export of 'vicuña' wool from Spanish America to southern France. There are some registers in the 'Chambre de Commerce de Marseille', which show the commercialization of these high quality fibres produced in Peru – see Table 5.5. By comparison with the raw wool of the metropolitan area, the commercialization of this American product was marginal during the eighteenth century.

Table 5.5   Total volume of imports of wool in Marseille from Spanish Mediterranean ports (1720–80)

	Washed Wool from Segovia	'Vicuña' Wool	Washed Wool	Half-washed Wool	Totals
Totals (Pounds)	6,488,112	561,571	3,966,885	62,753	11,079,321

Source: A.C.C.M., Statistique. Serie I. Article 29, I.30, I.24, I.31.

The washed wool from Segovia exported from the Spanish Mediterranean ports had the highest demand in the textile centres of southern France, as their volume of export to Marseille was the largest – see Table 5.5. Its price was more or less constant after 1738/40 – see Chart 5.13. After that period, there were some fluctuations to the price of the Spanish raw wool, as the Spanish Mediterranean export market was competing, in Marseille, with the British and Asian wools and cottons, especially those from Asia Minor.[75] Since the 1760s, Peruvian wool was also progressively required by European textile centres due to its quality and larger

---

[74]   Oliva Melgar, J.M. and Martínez Shaw, C., 'El sistema atlántico español (siglos XVII–XIX): presentación', in Martínez Shaw C. and Oliva Melgar J.M. (eds), *El sistema atlántico español (siglos XVII–XIX)* (Madrid: ed. Marcial Pons, Madrid, 2005), pp. 11–18. Fenández de Pinedo and Fernández, E. and Bilbao, L.M., 'Exportación de lanas, trashumancia y ocupación del espacio en Castilla durante los siglos XVI, XVII y XVIII', in García Martín, P. and Sánchez Benito, J.M. (eds), *Contribución a la historia de la trashumancia en España* (Madrid: Ministerio de Agricultura, Pesca y Alimentación, 1996), pp. 343–62. García Sanz, A., 'Estructuras agrarias y reformismo', pp. 629–38.

[75]   See the work by Pat Hudson regarding the impact of the British wool on European markets. Hudson, P., 'The Limits of Wool and the Potential Cotton in the Eighteenth and Early Nineteenth-Centuries', in Riello, G. and Parthasarathi, P. (eds), *The Spinning World*, p. 330. Beverly Lemire explores the deep impact of Asian textiles and the process of substitution of Asian cottons for the traditional wool on European demand. Lemire, B., 'Revising the Historical Narrative: India Europe, and the Cotton Trade, c. 1300–1800', Riello, G. and Parthasarathi, P. (eds), *The Spinning World*, pp. 206–8.

size than the metropolitan wool, although its commercialization was small by comparison to Spanish wool. Clothes made of this fabric were very luxurious, and only the rich could afford dresses made of this material. The commercialization of 'vicuña' wool spurred the textile trade with Spanish America.[76]

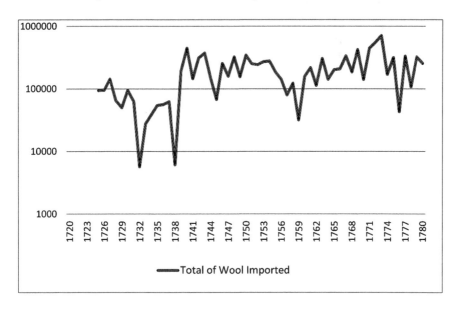

Chart 5.12   Imports of wool in Marseille from Spanish Mediterranean ports (1720–80). Unit of wool: pounds. *Source:* A.C.C.M. Statistique. Etats des Marchandises venant des pays étrangères. Serie I.

Trade in the Mediterranean territory and overseas, especially in the Atlantic area, remained fluent by means of the entrance of a high volume of foreign merchandise in all Spanish Mediterranean ports. The main goods imported in eastern areas of Spain were agricultural products, especially those coming from the Caribbean area, New Spain, New Galicia and New Granada. In fact, they were raw materials that in most cases were re-exported to some other European territories.[77]

---

[76]   Malamud Rikles, C., 'El comercio colonial del siglo XVIII visto como suma del comercio vía Andalucía y del comercio directo europeo', *Journal of Iberian and Latin American Economic History*, año no. 1, no. 2 (1983), pp. 307–22. García Fuentes, L., *El comercio español con América (1650–1700)* (Sevilla: Diputación Provincial de Sevilla, 1980). Walker, G., *Política española y comercio colonial, 1700–1789* (Barcelona: Editorial Ariel, 1979).

[77]   Smith, R.S., 'Indigo Production and Trade in Colonial Guatemala', *HAHR*, vol. XXXIX, 2 (1959); Floyd, S.T., 'The Indigo Merchants: Promoter of Central American Economic Development, 1750–1808', *Business Historic Review*, vol. XXXIX, 11 (1965),

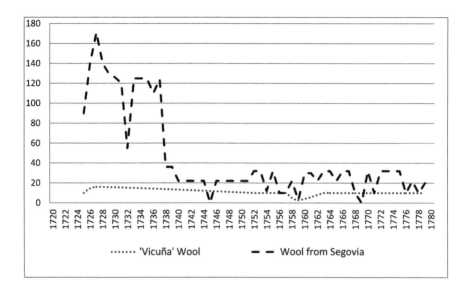

Chart 5.13   Price in Marseille of the wool imported from Spanish Mediterranean
              ports (1720–80). Unit of price: French 'livres tournois'. Volume/
              Price: 1 pound of wool/'x' 'livres tournois'. *Source:* A.C.C.M.
              Statistique. Serie I.

This is the case of raw textile materials such as the cochineal, indigo or 'vicuña'
wool. The industries of eastern Spanish territories could not absorb the entire
supply of such products to produce finished clothes. Foreign commercial houses
re-exported those raw materials to the main textile industrial centres of Europe
which had good commercial connections with Spanish merchants. This is the
reason for the huge amount of registers of cochineal, indigo and 'vicuña' wool,
from America, recorded in the 'Chambre de Commerce de Marseille'. Marseille
traders bought these products from Spanish Mediterranean hands and then raw
materials and dyes were distributed to the textile centres of Languedoc and
Provence to manufacture fashionable clothes.

    This was the system that exploited the formerly neglected natural resources.
By the eighteenth century, the trade of these resources acquired high levels of
development. The data provided in the export of cochineal from Spanish America to
France, via Marseille, corresponded to the registers of the 'Chambre de Commerce
de Marseille'. In the source itself, there is a detailed classification of the imported
cochineal: 'silvestre' [wild], 'fine' [thin], 'mestegue' [mixed], 'en grabeau' [in
beans] and cochineal without denomination, which could be the mature 'grana'

pp. 466–88; Benson, K., 'Indigo Production in the Eighteenth Century', *Hispanic American
Historical Review*, vol. XLIV, 2 (1964); Lee, R.L., 'Cochineal Production and Trade in New
Spain to 1600', *The Americas*, 4 (1947–48).

or [cochineal]. The 'grana' was much imported in Spain because the techniques in preparing the 'grana' were too specific for the Spaniards to emulate. Native Indians were more accurate in the process of preparation and cultivation of the cochineal, which was quite tedious. The main centres for the production of this dyestuff were New Spain, New Granada and New Galicia.[78]

After the conquest the trade of this dyestuff was disregarded by the Spanish, but during the sixteenth century they realized the importance of this agricultural product, which helped to make fashionable and colourful clothes.[79] Although this product was neglected by the government of the period, travellers and missionaries such as the Franciscan friar, Montolinía, understood the importance of cochineal. Before 1550 the Franciscan friar Montolinía wrote:

> ... in these tunas, that are red, the grana is born, that in this language is called mocheztli ... It is a thing of high value because it is bright red. Among Spaniards it is called carmesi.[80]

The bright colour of the 'grana' made the trade of cochineal increasingly important among Europeans. The introduction in Europe of this dying agent was welcomed by dyers, because of the progressive demand, among European society,[81] of clothes dyed with 'grana', as the scarlet colour became closely associated with wealth and royalty.[82] For this reason, Philip II created the post

---

[78] Dalhgren, B., *La grana cochinilla, México* (Mexico: UNAM, 1990). Baskes, J., *Indians, Merchants and Markets. A Reinterpretation of the Repartimiento and Spanish-Indian Economic Relations in Colonial Oaxaca, 1750–1821* (Stanford: Stanford University Press, 2000).

[79] De Alzate y Ramírez, J.A., *Memoria sobre la naturaleza, cultivo y beneficio de la grana* (Mexico: Archivo General de la Nación, 2001). Sánchez Silva, C. and Suárez Bosa, M., 'Evolución de la producción y el comercio mundial de la grana cochinilla, siglos XVI–XIX', *Revista de Indias* (2006), vol. LXVI, no. 237, pp. 473–90. Catherine Larrére asserts that in late eighteenth century some regions from India started to grow the 'grana' in enormous amount. According to this author this dyestuff started to be commercialized in Far East areas as well as Armenian, Turkish and Persian markets. See: Larrére, C., *L' invention de la economie au XVIIIe siècle du droit natural á la physiocratie* (Paris: Prosses Universitaires de France, 1992), pp. 95–140.

[80] Toribio de Benavente (Montolinía), *Historia de los Indios de Nueva España* (Mexico: Salvador Chávez Hayhoe, 1941), p. 197. In Lee, R.L., 'Cochineal Production and Trade in New Spain to 1600', *The Americas*, vol. 4, no. 4 (April 1948), pp. 449–73.

[81] Houghton in his analysis of consumption of dyestuffs in England places the indigo or 'añil' in first position followed by the 'granza', cochineal, 'orchilla y musgo', 'curcuma', wood from Campeche and 'goma laca'. See Houghton, H., *La cochinilla. Memoria demostrativa de las causas que han producido la decadencia de este renglón de comercio en los últimos años. Publicada por la Sociedad Eonómica de Amigos del País de Gran Canaria* (Gran Canaria: Imprenta de la Verdad, 1887), p. 84.

[82] Born, W., 'Scarlet', *Ciba Review*, I (March, 1938), p. 226. Friis, A., *Alderman Cockayne's Project and the Cloth trade* (London: Oxford University Press, 1927).

of 'juez de grana', which became highly lucrative, as cochineal production increased.

However, the eighteenth century witnessed the major flow of commercialization of cochineal from New Spain to Europe. The data provided by John Fisher in his work on the trade of Spanish America,[83] as well as the data of this research, on trade between the Mediterranean area of Spain with the New World, demonstrate the high commercialization of this dyestuff in Europe during the eighteenth century.

Table 5.6   Imports of cochineal in Marseille from Spanish-America (1720–80)

	Cochineal	Cochineal 'en grabeau'	Cochineal 'fine'	Cochineal 'mestegue'	Cochineal 'Silvestre'	Totals
Total Volume (Pounds)	2,451,550	27,978	794,546	554,586	134,381	3,963,041
Total Value (in French 'livres')	66,981,900	276,995	13,897,779	10,188,815	832,002	92,177,491

Source: A.C.C.M., Statistique. Serie I. Article 29, I.30, I.24, I.

This product contributed to spur the European demand for a wide variety of dresses and garments made of bright 'carmesí' or [scarlet]. The volume of imports of all cochineal traded from the New World to the industrial textile centres of France, reached almost 4,000,000 pounds between 1725 and 1780. The average price of cochineal per unit was around 15 and 20 French 'livres', occasionally fluctuating in the late 30s and early 50s, which can be explained by the interruption of trade relations with France in 1729 because of the plague of Marseille and the colonial turmoil during the mid-eighteenth century. The import of both cochineal and 'vicuña' wool rose as their prices, especially related to the latter in comparison with other types of wool, fluctuated during the eighteenth century (see Charts 5.13 and 5.15). Other types of wool and dyestuff saw uncompetitive prices; while Atlantic commodities such as the 'grana' cochineal and 'vicuña' wool goods were in growing demand in Europe due to the characteristics of this fibre, as well as the bright colours provided by the 'grana' (see Charts 5.12 and 5.14).

---

[83]   Fisher, J., 'The Imperial Response to "Free trade": Spanish Imports from Spanish America, 1778–1796', *Journal of Latin America Studies*, vol. 17, no. 1 (May, 1985), pp. 35–78.

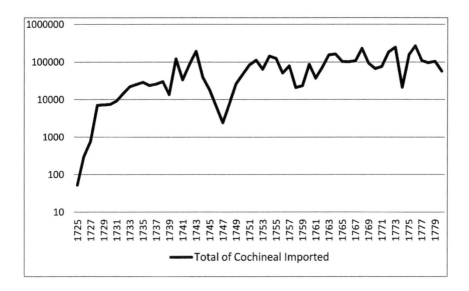

Chart 5.14   Imports of cochineal in Marseille from Spanish-America (1725–80).
              Unit: in pounds. *Source:* A.C.C.M., Statistique. Serie I.

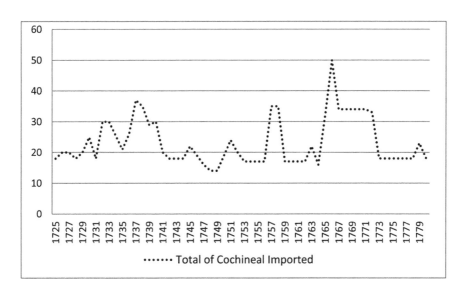

Chart 5.15   Price in Marseille of cochineal imported from Spanish-America
              (1725–80). Unit of price: French 'livres tournois'. Volume/Price:
              1 pound of cochineal / 'x' 'livres tournois'. *Source:* A.C.C.M.,
              Statistique.

Chapter 6
The Circulation of Trans-national Goods from Marseille to Spain

The trade records of the 'Chambre de Commerce de Marseille' list the commercialization of non-finished and finished goods from Asia, agricultural goods, such as sugar, chocolate, coffee and cacao, from French colonies of America, as well as tea and coffee from Yemen, India and China. The trade of these goods shaped the majority of the wholesale market of southern Europe. There is a satisfactory description of goods traded in different European areas, as well as the volume of each item and its price – in French 'livres tournois' or 'soleils'. The sources of the 'Chambre de Commerce de Marseille' are extremely useful as they allow us to measure the trends in the wholesale market for the western Mediterranean area. However, these sources do not represent the totality of the flow of the market. They are simply an indicator of the mercantile relationships among European countries within the Mediterranean, Atlantic and Asian market. Through the analysis of this source it is possible to observe that the volume of goods commercialized from Marseille to Europe, mainly to eastern Spain, grew during the eighteenth century. The effect of this constant circulation of goods was an alteration in the patterns of consumption of the Spanish population, as Murcia and Cartagena were the main locations for reception and distribution of goods in the south-eastern area. Certainly, merchants exerted a very strong influence on the shifts in consumer behaviour. In ports or bazaars, people could admire the luxury commodities brought from abroad. In those peripheral areas the transmission and changes of socio-cultural patterns occurred rapidly due to the free-flowing circulation of merchandise, people and financial resources.

In the case of Spain, the ports of Barcelona, Valencia, Majorca, Alicante or Cartagena were potential areas for the sale of products by French merchants. The routes of the trans-Mediterranean market facilitated the circulation of luxury merchandise, spurring the eastern Spanish demand. During the late seventeenth and early eighteenth centuries, the Béarnaise and Provencal migration to the Spanish Levant area contributed to reinforcing such trans-Mediterranean commercial flows. It is crucial to add to such circuits the trans-Pyrenean trade routes, which also fostered the Spanish-French import-export market. The industrious labour of rural workers from villages in southern France, such as those located in Bearn and Oloron[1] as well as rural communities in Provence

---

[1] Salas Auséns, J.A., *En busca del Dorado*, pp. 214–24.

such as Languedoc,[2] Puy, Lyon or Grenoble, contributed to the increase in textile commercialization. In those areas, Spanish raw materials were sold to manufacture clothing. Finally, French merchants were the mediators in selling such products in Spain. Outstanding merchant families such as Bremon, Camon, Cayron, Hourtane, Solicofre,[3] Selon, Schlimer, Desmoulins or Bicaix,[4] who installed their trade companies in southern France – Marseille – and the Spanish Levant – Majorca,[5] Valencia and Murcia – are good examples that prove the continued exchange of raw materials for manufactured goods between Spain and France during the eighteenth century. Chart 6.1 shows the data concerning the export of aprons from Marseille to Spain, manufactured in Puy en-Velay, a village located in the Massif Central of France. In this area there was a specialization in producing textiles with materials such as thread and silk. The weavers from these places introduced flowery figures in the borders of the carefully spun apron thread. This is a good instance of the exchange of raw materials for finished clothes.

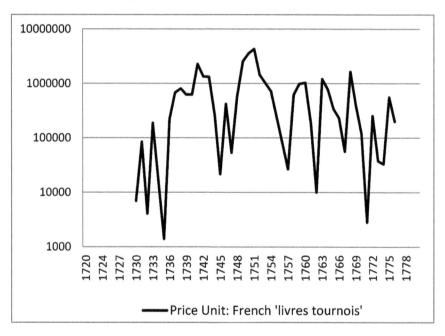

Chart 6.1   Exports of aprons from Marseille to Spain (1720–80). *Source:* A.C.C.M., Statistique. Serie I.

[2]   Thompson, J.K.J., *Clermont-de-Lodève 1633–1789. Fluctuations in the Prosperity of a Languedocian Cloth-Making Town* (Cambridge: Cambridge University Press, 1982).
[3]   Montojo y Montojo, V. and Maestre de San Juan Pelegrin, F., 'El comercio'.
[4]   A.H.P.M., Sig. 2694, sin foliar, escr. Antonio Costa Irles, 13/08/1764.
[5]   Bibiloni Amengual, A., 'Mallorca i els ports europeus: la comercialització de l'oli (1667–1702)' *Randa*, no. 25, (1989), pp. 17–46.

During the eighteenth century there was an important demand for these types of clothes in Spanish Mediterranean society. The imports of aprons increased until 1751, when they began to decrease. This explains why the demand for this commodity was created before 1750, as a consequence of the introduction of French fashions in Spain. The total volume of aprons imported to Spain from Puy between 1730 and 1780 was 583,524.98 pounds; the total value of aprons imported was 30,894,356 French 'livres'.[6] Silk was the main fibre used for elaborating aprons. It was exported from the Mediterranean area of Spain such as Valencia, Murcia and Granada, as well as Asia. With this raw material the French textile industries of Auvergne such as Puy-en-Velay produced a significant amount of finished clothes that were sold in eastern regions of Spain. The same occurred with clothes made of cotton. The half-prepared Catalonian cotton, as well as the cotton from the Levant area, was imported to the textile centres of Languedoc, Auvergne and Provence. After the process of fabrication, the ready-to-use products were exported from France to Spain, via Marseille.

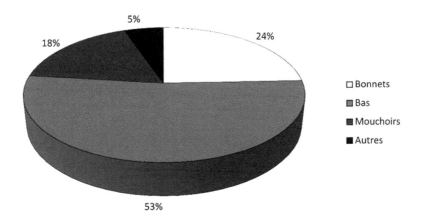

Chart 6.2   Exports of clothes made of cotton from Marseille to Spain (1720–80). *Source:* A.C.C.M., Statistique. Serie I, Articles: 21, 22, 23, 24.

In Chart 6.2 we find the main cotton products exported from Marseille to Spain. These were French 'bonnets' [hats], 'bas' [stockings], 'mouchoirs' [handkerchiefs] and 'autres' [other garments] which included 'bourses' [purses], 'ceintures' [belts] and some other textile adornments made from cotton. Table 6.1 shows both the total volume of imports of these items, in Mediterranean regions of Spain, and their total value. These were some of the main clothes commercialized by French

---

[6]   Source: A.C.C.M., Statistique. Serie I, Articles: 21, 22, 23, 24.

merchants, which shaped new fashions and tastes in the Spanish Mediterranean society. The high offer of this type of clothing – see Chart 3.18 – is perfectly correlated with the rising demand of garments made of a wide range of fibres such as silk or thread, as we will see in the next section by examining probate inventories. Stockings, 'bonnets' and 'mouchoirs' were highly popular in eastern Spain because people from the middle and upper social classes wanted to be 'á la mode française' [French fashion].

Table 6.1   Exports of clothes made of cotton from Marseille to Spain (1720–80)

	'Bonnets'	'Bas'	'Mouchoirs'	'Autres'	Totals
Total Volume (in pieces)	17,821.5	38,439.5	12,930	3,881	73,072
Total Value (in French 'livres')	74,835.5	179,443.5	133,027	20,939	408,245

Source: A.C.C.M., Statistique. Serie I, Articles: 21, 22, 23, 24.

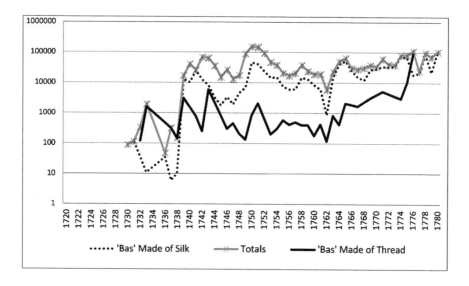

Chart 6.3   Exports of 'bas' [stockings] from Marseille to Spanish Mediterranean ports (1720–80). Volume: in pounds. *Source:* A.C.C.M.

Table 6.2   Exports of clothes made of silk from Marseille to Spanish Mediterranean ports (1720–80)

	'Bonnet'	'Bas'	'Mouchoir'	'Autres'	'Etoffe'	'Ruban'	'Gant'	Totals
Total Volume (pounds)	17,956	811,371	324,444	2,538	1,236,418	195,397	5,439	2,593,563
Total Value (in French 'livres')	818,328	29,115,575	87,941	36,526	44,280,525	10,848,074	176,760	85,363,729

Source: A.C.C.M., Statistique. Serie I, Articles: 21, 22, 23, 24.

Table 6.3   Exports of hats from Marseille to Spanish Mediterranean ports (1720–80)

	'Castor'	'Commun'	'Demy-Castor'	'Paille'	'Poil et Laine'	'Soie et Laine'	Totals
Total Volume (pounds)	5,685	37,920	1,660	38,257	1,409,627	113,184	1,606,333
Total Value (in French 'livres')	158,275	47,280	16,019	80,610	6,939,144	565,920	7,807,248

Source: A.C.C.M., Statistique. Serie I, Articles: 21, 22, 23, 24.

As one of the major raw materials in Spanish-French commercial exchanges, silk played a very important role in the manufacture of clothes in French artisan centres.[7] Clothes made of silk occupied an important position in the export market from France to Spain – see Chart 6.4 and Table 6.2.

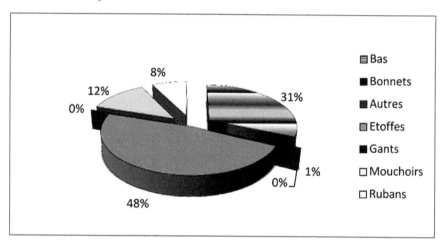

Chart 6.4   Exports of clothes made of silk from Marseille to Spanish Mediterranean ports (1720–80). *Source:* A.C.C.M., Statistique. Serie I.

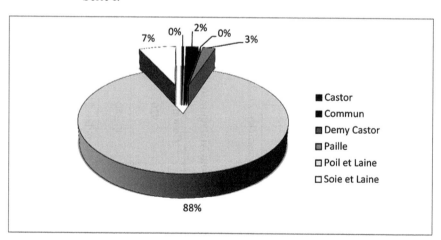

Chart 6.5   Exports of hats from Marseille to Spanish Mediterranean ports (1720–80). *Source:* A.C.C.M., Statistique. Serie I.

[7]   Chapman, S.D. and Chassagne, S., *European Textile Printers in the Eighteenth Century. A Study of Peel and Oberkampf* (London: Heinemann Educational Books, 1981).

Hats were also exported in high quantities from Marseille to eastern Spain. They were made of textiles or leather, and sometimes both. Regarding leather, the material was 'castor' [beaver] skin, 'commun' [ordinary skin], 'demy-castor' [half-beaver], and we also find hats made of 'paille' [straw]. The fibres that were usually used to manufacture hats were silk and cotton. Hats made of silk and wool were frequently exported, followed by hats made of mixed materials such as wool and leather – see Chart 6.5 and Table 6.3. The hat industry was based in southern France, the main centres of production being Tarn-et-Garonne, located in the Midi Pyreneans, Espéraza, in Languedoc, Toulouse and the Béarnaise area of Oloron-Sainte-Marie.[8] Jean-Marc Olivier has identified that the only route of that trade and circulation of merchandise was the trans-Pyrenean.[9] However, as Charts 6.1 to 6.5 demonstrate, there was an important commercialization and circulation of those goods in the Mediterranean territories of Spain through the port of Marseille. Therefore, both trans-Pyrenean and trans-Mediterranean markets contributed to export from southern France to eastern Spain not only goods, but also new fashions and cultural identities, transferred through the circulation of people and commodities.

6.1. The Craze for Asian Textiles: the Building up of 'Global Commodities'

The trans-Pyrenean and trans-Mediterranean markets were not the only ones providing luxury goods and new fashionable articles to the eastern territories of Spain. The trans-continental circuits of trade, connecting the Asian and European market through maritime routes, fostered the circulation of luxury merchandise on a wider scale. French trade companies such as the Roux-Frères established commercial branches in the main ports of the Levant such as Smyrna, Tripoli, Side, Antioch and Alexandria. A permanent embassy, composed of Marseille merchants, was established in Constantinople, and enhanced the development of a free-flowing relationship between French and Levantine traders. Since the seventeenth and early eighteenth centuries, European merchants from England, Holland and France settled their customs duties and counters in buildings called *khans*: large rectangular edifices where business and commercial exchange took place. These *khans* were a way to establish materially an autonomous and collective commercial life, which guaranteed the economic freedom of each European nation. The exception to paying

---

[8]   Passama, J., *La chapellerie toulosaine au XIXe siècle* (Mémoire de maîtrise réalisé sous la direction de Jean-Marc Olivier, Université de Toulouse 2-Le Mirail, 2002). Christol, C., *L'industrie chapelière dans le haut vallée de l'Aude aux XIXe et XXe siècles* (Toulouse: Mémoire de maîtrise réalisé sous la direction de Rémy Pech, Université de Toulouse II-Le Mirail, 1995).

[9]   Olivier, J.M., 'Les exportations transpyrénéennes d'horlogerie franco-suisse et d'articles de Paris vers l'Espagne (XVIIIe–XIXe siècles)', in Minovez, J. and Poujade, P. (eds), *Circulation des marchandises et réseaux commerciaux dans les Pyrénées (XIII–XIX siècles)* (Toulouse: CNRS-Université de Toulouse Le Mirail, 2005), pp. 31–8.

taxes, the non-intervention of the Ottoman authority and the freedom of export and import of merchandise was stipulated on a moral and legal level in signed charts.[10]

Illustration 6.1   Reception par le grand Vizir d'un ambassadeur de France a Constantinople. Peinture. Attribuée à A. de Favray. Milieu XVIII° s. Ref. PGE 00425 *Musée de la Chambre de Commerce de Marseille.*

In the French case those regulations encouraged economic development and stimulated the commercial life of the country, especially taking into account that its major competitors, the British Levant Company and the Dutch VOC, preferred to look at the routes of the East Indies rather than the connections of the Levantine Mediterranean with the Near East.[11] In a certain way, both companies disregarded the trade of Levantine merchandise, especially the cotton and woollen clothing

---

[10]   Fukusawa, K., *Toilerie*, pp. 71–2.

[11]   Haudrère, P., *La compagnie française des Indes au XVIIIe siècle (1719–1795)* (4 vols, Paris: Librairie de l'Inde, 1989), vol. 1, p. 467. Cuenca Esteban, J.J., 'Comparative Patterns of Colonial Trade: Britain and its Rivals', in Prados de la Escosura, L. (ed.), *Exceptionalism and Industrialization: Britain and its European Rivals, 1688–1815* (Cambridge: Cambridge University Press, 2004), pp. 35–66.

trade, in order to expand the trade of their domestic wool beyond Europe, which eventually failed due to the strong competition of Asian fabrics.[12] They were more focused on the spice route, trying to exchange their national fabrics for spices from the East Indies.[13] This issue made the Mediterranean commercial traffic, especially concerning the Levant area, a French scenario of commerce.

The French consulate regime, which fostered commercial exchange, was consolidated during the eighteenth century. The main positions were those concerning the embassy of Constantinople followed by the appointment of other consulates such as Cairo, Thessaloniki, Alger and Aleppo. Those consulate positions became hereditary among trade families.[14] For instance, the Honoré Guez and Company, Honoré Richard Company and Honoré Pagan in association with the Roux-Frères Company[15] occupied those important positions during the eighteenth century.[16] For this reason, the Roux Company of Marseille, led by Pierre-Honoré Roux and after by Jean-Baptiste-Ignace, was one of the main companies of the worldwide port of Marseille with trade relations with the Near and Far East, Barbary, Europe and the French colonies of America.[17] The connection with those places brought about a constant circulation of luxury goods such as porcelains from China, raw textiles, drapes of a high quality and finished clothing from Asia. This economic circuit enabled merchants to commercialize goods through the well-known silk route. They also introduced sugar, cacao and chocolate from the American colonies, tea from the Levant and India and coffee from Yemen (see Map 6.1).

---

[12]   Braude, B., 'International Competition and Domestic Cloth in the Ottoman Empire, 1500–1650: a Study in Underdevelopment', *Review Fernand Braudel Center* 2/3 (1979), pp. 437–51. Floor, W., 'Economy and Society: Fibres, Fabrics, Factories', in Bier, C. (ed.), *Woven from the Soul, Spun from the Heart: Textile Arts of Safavit and Qajar Iran 16th–17th centuries* (Washington DC: Textile Museum, 1987), pp. 20–32. Bowen, H.V., *The Business of the Empire: the East India Company and the Imperial Britain, 1756–1833* (Cambridge: Cambridge University Press, 2006), pp. 246–7.

[13]   Ferrier, R.W., 'An English View of Persian Trade in 1618', *Journal of the Economic and Social History of the Orient*, vol. XIX, part. II (1976), pp. 182–214. From the same author: 'The Armenians and the East India Company in Persia in the Seventeenth and Early Eighteenth-Centuries', *The Economic History Review*, 2nd series, vol. XXVI, no. 1 (1973), pp. 38–62. Glamann, K., *Dutch-Asiatic Trade 1620–1740* (Copenhagen-La Have: Nijhoff, 1958), pp. 13–15. Steensgard, N., *The Asian Trade revolution of the Seventeenth-century. The East India Companies and the Decline of the Caravan Trade* (Chicago: University of Chicago Press, 1973), pp. 367–97.

[14]   Fukusawa, K., *Toilerie*, pp. 73–4.

[15]   Roux, F. Ch., *Les Echelles de Syrie et de Palestine au XVIIIe siècle* (Paris: Paul Geuthner, 1928). Davis, R., *Aleppo and Devonshire Square. English Traders in the Levant in the Eighteenth Century* (London: Macmillan, 1967).

[16]   A.C.C.M., L. IX, 773–5, Lettres des divers correspondants à Alep.

[17]   A.C.C.M., L. IX, 773, Lettre d'A. Geoffroy, procureur de J.-J. Badaraque, 17 février 1775.

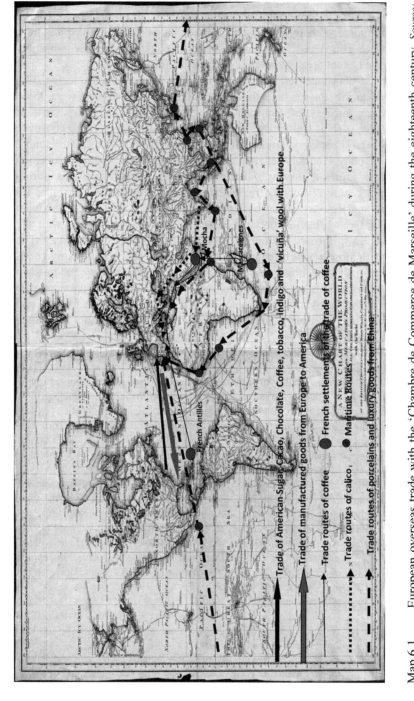

Map 6.1   European overseas trade with the 'Chambre de Commerce de Marseille' during the eighteenth century. *Source:* M.N.N., Madrid, Spain, Ref. 0001, A, 0006.

As demonstrated by the data on textile import-export corresponding to the western Mediterranean area, Marseille was one of the main centres of export of textiles to the Spanish Mediterranean ports, as well as the gate of entry of luxury commodities from Persia and the East Indies via the Levant area.[18] There was a constant flow of circulation of silk in the Mediterranean territories towards the French artisan centres.[19] The merchants of Marseille[20] played a central role in the re-export market of drapes made of silk such as 'etoffes' and 'dorures fines' – see Chart 6.6 – whose origin was Persia, the East Indies and China, as well as the products made of Spanish and Far Eastern silk.[21] A good example of this issue is the 'bas' [stockings] made of different kinds of silk – see Chart 6.7 – in the industries of Provence, Languedoc[22] and particularly those located in the Rhône Alpine region such as Lyon. Such stockings were basically made of 'etamine' and 'filoselle'. The 'etamine' was a sort of silk 'jaspée' [marbled] or 'virée' [with double silk layers]. This type of silk was also imported from the East Indies to Marseille, the silk being of two ells of length and 7/16 of width.[23]

However, the exports of stockings made of 'etamine' to Mediterranean regions of Spain was quite marginal in comparison with those made of 'filoselle' – flowered and dyed silk from the Levant.[24] The most likely reason for the major export of silk of 'filoselle' was that it was a pre-dyed product. It is important to understand that the dying technique was difficult for the European dyers to emulate.[25] The imports of the Asian ready-dyed product to Marseille reduced the cost of production of French textile manufactures, as the dying technique was costly and complicated for French drapers.

The 'dorures fines' are drapes from China which were unknown in Europe during the first half of the eighteenth century. They are composed of embellished satin with gold and silver flowers made of paper cut in long and narrow threads.

[18]   Peyrot, J., 'Marseille, porte d'entrée des soies aux XVIIe et XVIIIe siècles', in *Marseille sur les routes de la soie*, Actes de la table ronde organisée par la Chambre de Commerce et d'Industrie Marseille-Provence et l'Université de Provence (Marseille: Chambre de Commerce et d'Industrie Marseille-Provence, 2001), pp. 61–76. Tryantafyllidou-Baladié, Y., 'Le marché de la soie au Proche-Orient et son importance pour les industries françaises du XVIIe au XIXe siècle: le rôle du port de Marseille', in *Marseille*, pp. 282–300.

[19]   Boulanger, P., 'Marseille, escale des soies à l'orée du XVIIIe siècle', in *Marseille*, pp. 47–65.

[20]   Eymard-Beamelle, M.J., 'Les tissus de soie ouvrée à Marseille (XVIIe–XVIIIe s.)', in *Marseille*, pp. 1–46.

[21]   Eymard-Beamelle, M.J., 'Les tissus', pp. 18–19.

[22]   Buti, G., 'Marseille, l'Espagne et la soie au XVIIIe siècle', in *Marseille*, pp. 229–53. Villard, M., 'Aspects des industries de la soie en Languedoc aux XVIIe et XVIII siècle', in *Marseille*, pp. 177–93.

[23]   Eymard-Beamelle, M.J., 'Les tissus', p. 19.

[24]   Eymard-Beamelle, M.J., 'Les tissus', p. 20.

[25]   See the section 'French Textile Printing and Fashion Before 1759', in Chapman, S.D. and Chassagne, S., *European Textile*.

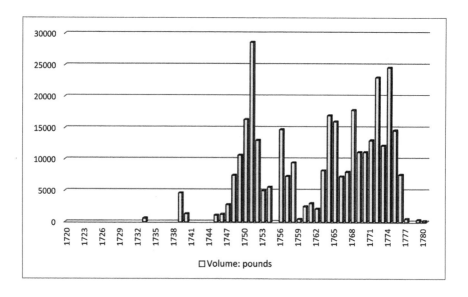

Chart 6.6   Re-exports of 'dorure' from Marseille to Spanish Mediterranean
             ports (1720–80). *Source:* A.C.C.M., Statistique. Serie I, Articles:
             21, 22, 23, 24.

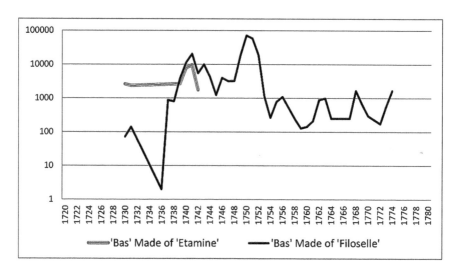

Chart 6.7   Re-exports of 'bas' [stockings] made of diverse types of silk from
             Marseille to Spanish Mediterranean ports (1720–80). Volume: in
             pounds. *Source:* A.C.C.M., Statistique. Serie I, Articles: 21, 22, 23,
             24.

The commercialization of this type of silk in the Mediterranean market, as well as their introduction into the Spanish Mediterranean ports was very notable during the eighteenth century, especially during the second half, when in 1750 almost 30,000 'pièces' of 'dorures fines' were exported from Marseille to Mediterranean areas of Spain – see Chart 6.6.

On the other hand, the data provided in the charts make it very evident that the fascination for luxury items and the shape of exotic fashions was spurred by the circulation of a wide range of textile commodities.[26] I have separated those items into different typologies, for instance, white drapes made of cotton such as 'demittes', 'escamittes', 'battanonis' and 'ajamis', in order to properly analyse the evolution of the Mediterranean import-export market. The latter was blue and it was elaborated with the technique of indigo. The difficulties of the dying process could be the main factor, as well as the major importation of 'filoselle' [dyed-silk] in comparison with undyed silk, which explains that the volume of dyed-cottons such as 'ajamis' imported in Europe were higher than the whites cottons such as 'demittes' or 'escamittes'. The re-export of blue cotton – 'ajamis' – from Marseille to eastern Spain was highest in 1750 when around 50,000 'pièces' of 'ajamis' were introduced to Mediterranean ports of Spain. The import of 'demittes', 'battanonis' and 'escamittes', during most decades of the eighteenth century, were fairly constant, at no more than 10,000 'pièces' – see Chart 6.8.

The 'demittes' came via the routes of Smyrna, Seyde and Cyprus, whereas the 'ajamis' and 'battanonis' came from the routes of Aleppo.[27] The 'demittes' reached elevated levels of production in Rosette, Egypt. They were used especially for corsets. The 'demittes' were exported in large quantities from Marseille to Spain, Portugal and Italy. The 'ajamis' were exported from Persia and Cairo to France. In Lyon, dresses and skirts were made with this cotton, as well as clothing made of silk,[28] and then these finished textile products were re-exported to Mediterranean ports of Spain.

---

[26] Related to the entry of both non-finished and finished clothing in Spain from the market of Levant, connected with French trade, we must note that smuggling could exert an important influence. This issue could probably demonstrate the entry of textile merchandises in the second half of the eighteenth century, when the Bourbon monarchy ruled bans on commercialization of some foreign textiles into the national territories. See: Martín Corrales, E., 'Marseille', pp. 61–78; Martín Corrales, E., 'La importación de telas', p. 49.

[27] Fukusawa, K., *Toilerie*, p. 19.

[28] Miller, L.E., 'Paris-Lyon-Paris: Dialogue in the Design and Distribution of Patterned Silks in the Eighteenth Century', in Fox, R. and Turner, A.J. (eds), *Luxury Trades and Consumerism in Ancien Régime Paris: Studies in the History of the Skilled Workforce* (Farnham: Ashgate, 1998), pp. 139–68.

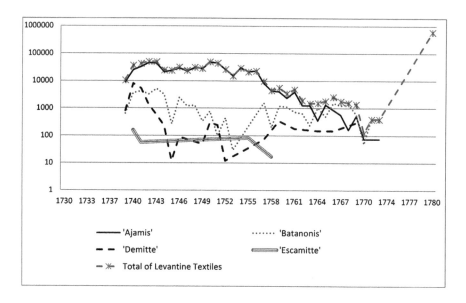

Chart 6.8   Re-exports of Levantine clothing from Marseille to Spanish
             Mediterranean ports (1730–80). Volume: in 'pièces'. *Source:*
             A.C.C.M. Statistique. Serie I.

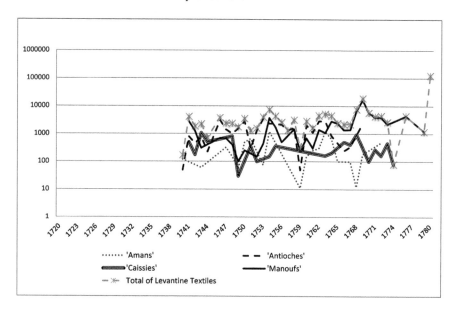

Chart 6.9   Re-exports of Levantine clothing from Marseille to Spanish
             Mediterranean ports (1720–80). Volume: in 'pièces'. *Source:*
             A.C.C.M. Statistique. Serie I.

Other textiles, known as blue drapes, were the 'amans' and 'antioches', from the scale of Aleppo, and they were exported to Marseille and re-exported to eastern Spain. The 'antioches' were exported as white drapes with the 'caissies' and 'manoufs', which were textiles made of cotton.[29] The main place of manufacture of 'caissies' and 'manoufs' was Egypt. The volume of export of these drapes to the Spanish Mediterranean territory, via Marseille, was very important, as 'manoufs' were the most numerous exported items related to this group. The volume of export of 'manoufs' was almost 16,000 'pièces' in the late 1760s and early 1770s – see Chart 6.9 – whereas 'antioches', 'amans' and 'caissies' maintained a constant volume of no more than 4,000 'pièces' during the century. In terms of comparison with the first group – 'ajamis', 'demittes', 'battanonis' and 'escamittes' – the second group was less numerous. However, the introduction of this type of clothing consolidated the taste for exotic goods, especially Asian goods, fostering the acquisition of new fashions. The third group of textiles from the Levant are the drapes called 'toiles blanches', 'toiles de montagne' and 'toiles diverses'. The 'toiles blanches' are drapes of high quality from Side and Aleppo as well as Egypt, highly commercialized in Levantine routes during the eighteenth century.

'Toiles diverses' are those of a different origin and they could be dyed or white clothing.[30] The volume of export of those drapes was the most significant, with the 'toiles diverses' reaching an amount of some 600,000 'pièces', c. 1750, and the 'toiles blanches' and 'toiles de montagne' having the highest quantity of exports, 100,000 'pièces', during the second half of the eighteenth century. The volume of exports of these drapes was very irregular during that period, fluctuating from 100,000 'pièces' to 600,000 pounds – see Chart 6.10. As a final group of clothing of the Levantine market, we have included 'musselines' [muslins] and 'indiennes' [calicoes], which were one of the main textiles demanded by the European and south-eastern Spanish society during the eighteenth century. Calico, a fine cotton cloth painted in attractive flowery motif designs, was originally from India and its exotic name recalled the Indian town of Calicut.[31] However, the coarser cotton called muslin has its origins in the Iraqi town of Mosul.[32]

---

[29] Fukusawa, K., *Toilerie*, p. 20.

[30] Fukusawa, K., *Toilerie*, p. 19.

[31] Parthasarathi, P., 'Cotton Textiles in the Indian Subcontinent, 1200–1800', in Riello, G. and Parthasarathi, P. (eds), *The Spinning World*, pp. 17–41. Dale, S.F., *Indian Merchants and Eurasian Trade, 1600–1750* (Cambridge: Cambridge University Press, 1994), pp. 46–55. Veinstein, G., 'Commercial Relations between India and the Ottoman Empire (Late Fifteenth to Late Eighteenth Centuries): A Few Notes and Hypothesis', in Chaudhury, S. and Morineau, M. (eds), *Merchants, Companies and Trade: Europe and Asia in the Early Modern Era* (Cambridge: Cambridge University Press, 1999), pp. 95–115.

[32] Faroqhi, S., 'Ottoman Cotton Textiles. The Story of a Success that did not Last, 1500–1800', in Riello, G. and Parthasarathi, P. (eds), *The Spinning World*, pp. 89–103. Vicente, M.V., *Clothing*.

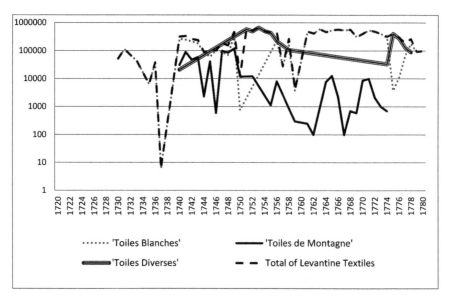

Chart 6.10   Re-exports of Levantine clothing from Marseille to Spanish
              Mediterranean ports (1720–80). Volume: in 'pièces'. *Source:*
              A.C.C.M., Statistique. Serie I.

These commodities were highly demanded by European society due to their
excellent features such as permanent colour, ease of washing, low-price[33] and
fashionable appeal for both domestic interiors and clothing.[34] However, the
volume of imports in Mediterranean areas of Spain of both items was inferior in
comparison with the other Asian textiles introduced from the Levantine market.
Finished clothing made of calico reached its highest volume of import, at 16,000
'pièces', during the first half of the eighteenth century, whereas for the same
period, the major import of muslins was less than 1,500 'pièces' annually – see
Chart 6.11. The fall in Spanish Mediterranean imports of calicoes during the
eighteenth century, by comparison with the other Asian textiles, was due to the
banning policy of the Spanish institutions.

    Nevertheless, 5,000 'pièces' of finished clothing made of calico, entering
Spanish Mediterranean ports per year, is not a quantity to underestimate,

---

    [33]   Broadberry, S. and Gupta, B., 'The Early Modern Great Divergence: Wages, Prices
and Economic Development in Europe and Asia, 1500–1800', *Economic History Review*,
59/1 (2006), pp. 2–31. Chaudhuri, K.N., *The Trading World of Asia and the English East
India Company 1660–1760* (Cambridge: Cambridge University Press, 1978). Wallerstein,
I, Decdeli, H. and Kasaba, R., 'The Incorporation of the Ottoman Empire into the World-
Economy', in Slamo lu-nan, H. (ed.), *The Ottoman Empire and the World Economy*
(Cambridge: Cambridge University Press, 1987), pp. 88–100.
    [34]   Lemire, B., 'Domesticating'.

especially if we recall that the entrance of this foreign product competed with national fabrics such as Castilian wool and Catalonian cotton[35] – see Charts 5.8 and 5.9 in Chapter 5. When the export of clothing made of calico from Marseille to Spanish Mediterranean ports increased in early 1730, the export of Spanish cotton and wool dropped – see Charts 5.8, 5.9 (Chapter 5) and 6.11 (this chapter). The banning policy contributed, in the short term, to a decrease of the entry of foreign goods, but, in general, it did not prevent the introduction of calicoes and some other foreign commodities, as we have shown in the data of the export of Asian and French commodities to Mediterranean areas of Spain.

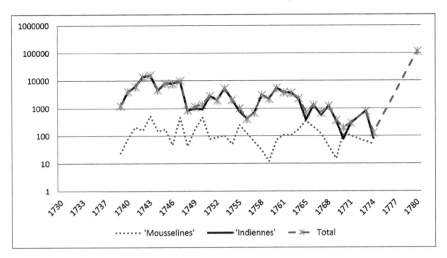

Chart 6.11   Re-exports of Indian and Persian clothing from Marseille to Spanish Mediterranean ports (1730–80). Volume: in 'pièces'. *Source:* A.C.C.M., Statistique. Serie I.

Those prohibitions on the commercialization of calicoes became very common in European countries during the eighteenth century.[36] This period turned into a state of uncontrolled excitement because of the progressive introduction of Indian imports such as the textiles mentioned above. The mercantile measures particularly

---

[35]   Martín Corrales, E., 'Marseille'; Thompson, J.K.J., *A Distinctive Industrialization*.

[36]   Rothstein, N., 'The Calico Campaign of 1719–1721', *East London Papers*, 7 (1964), pp. 3–21. Keirn, T., 'Parliament, Legislation and the Regulation of English Textile Industries, 1689–1714', in Davison, L., Hitchcock, T. and Shoemakers, R.D. (eds), *Stilling the Grumbling Hive: the Response to Social and Economic Problems in England, 1689–1750* (Stroud: Allen Sutton Press, 1992), pp. 1–24. O'Brien, P.K., Griffith, T. and Hunt, Ph., 'Political Components of the Industrial Revolution: English Cotton Textile Industry, 1660–1774', *Economic History Review*, 46/3 (1991), pp. 395–423. O'Brien, P.K., 'The Geopolitics'.

focused their attention on the banning of calico and muslin, especially in the case of Spain. This could be the reason why the quantities of muslin or calico exported to eastern Spain were minor when compared to other textiles from the Near East such as 'ajamis', 'antioches' or 'toiles blanches':

> Habiendose expedido una Real-Pragmatica sanction en fuerza de ley, su fecha en Aranjuez a veinticuatro de junio próximo pasado, por la que se prohíbe absolutamente la introducción de Muselinas en el Reyno, cuyo tenor a la letra es como sigue. Don Carlos, por la Gracia de Dios ...
>
> ... SABED, que habiéndose experimentado los graves perjuicios que la introducción y consumo de muselinas ha causado y causa, asi de las fabricas de estos reinos, que por falta de consumo de sus texidos se haya en decadencia, como a mis reales haberes en las continuas entradas fraudulentas, a que da lugar el corto lugar que ocupa este genero, y la facilidad de introducirlo con otras piezas de texidos de mayor volumen, y también en la extracción de caudales, que es consiguiente se haga, con notable daño de la balanza de Comercio del Reyno; se me represento por mi consejo-pleno en consulta de dieciséis de enero de mil setecientos sesenta y nueve, con vista de la que dirigi a la Junta General de Comercio, lo conveniente que seria la absoluta prohibición de las muselinas y otros texidos de algodón y lienzos pintados, ya fuesen fabricados en Asia, o en Africa, o ya imitados en Europa ... y haberse acreditado muy en breve los perjuicios que experimentan las fabricas de Cataluña ...
>
> ... por la qual prohibo la entrada asi por Mar como por tierra de las muselinas bajo comiso del genero, carruajes y bestias ...
>
> PUBLICACION.
>
> En la villa de Madrid a quarto dias del mes de Julio de mill setecientos setenta ...[37]

Such mercantilist policies did not prevent the Asian and French exports to Mediterranean territories of Spain. The ban on calico and muslin was the main aim of the Spanish Government. In 1767 Charles III, in the ordinances of the manufacturers of calicoes of Catalonia, ruled that only authorized workers could dye and print calicoes, because there were a lot of people in the country that printed and worked with calico textiles without any patterns. The prohibition clearly mentions that all calico must have the pattern of the Crown. In other words, the authorities were trying to 'nationalize' the product. The impact was that foreign products had gone beyond the realm of the merchant groups as well as the conspicuous elite. Therefore, European governments tried to domesticate those products, in an unfruitful attempt to imitate and assimilate the complex techniques of the manufacturing of such

---

[37] C.D.M.T., CA 168, *Notificación de la Real Orden prohibiendo la entrada de muselinas*, Barcelona, 1770.

products.[38] The main strategy devised by European authorities[39] was to substitute the imported commodity for another similar version with a national pattern.

The king, in the same ordinances, in chart XII, recognized the high quality of the finer and more delicate calicoes produced outside Catalonia, which were introduced to Spain from far-off territories. He ruled that only authorized people could work with foreign calicoes and he strictly prohibited experimentation with new dyes and colours. The major reason for this ban was to foster the Spanish production of calicoes, because the national artisan centres could not compete with the fine and colourful calicoes that entered the different kingdoms via the Levantine market. Consequently, in those ordinances, it was established that in the buying-selling process all calicoes should have a national pattern in order to eliminate the introduction of foreign calicoes:

XI.

Respecto a que muchos pintan indianas sin tener forma de fabrica, ni las oficinas que se requieren para su perfeccion, de que resulta que los pintados salen falsificados, en grave perjucio del publico, y descredito a las fabricas que observan la debidas reglas: ordeno, que no puedan estampar, o pintar indianas, ni otros lienzos persona alguna que no sea habilitada por fabricante …

XII.

No habiendo en estos reinos fabricas de telas de hilo finas, ni tampoco de algodón, que igualen a las de los reinos extraños, podrán valerse de ellas, y estamparlas, o pintarlas los fabricantes de indianas aprobados, como observen las reglas que establecen estas ordenanzas para las indianas que se fabrican en este reino.

XVII.

Mediante que no provienen de las fabricas los muchos engaños que experimentan los que visten indianas, en cuanto a los colores, y si de algunos ambiciosos y poco temerosos de Dios, que las venden de segunda, y tercera mano, sin detenerse en asegurar por colores fuertes los que son sencillos, y aun suponiendo por haberlas comprado por tales en las fabricas, y esto quedaría sin averiguación cortándose algún pedazo de la parte de donde esta, o debe estar la marca: mando, que ninguna persona de las que venden indianas pueda tener en su poder piezas, ni pedazos de ellas sin la marca, y manifestación de colores …[40]

---

[38]   Raveux, O., 'Espaces et tecnologiques dans la France méridionale d'ancien régime: l'example de l'indiennage marseillais (1648–1793)', *Annales du Midi*, 116/246 (2004), pp. 155–70.

[39]   Martín Corrales, E., 'Marseille'; Thompson, J.K.J., *A Distinctive Industrialization*; Lemire, B., 'Domesticating'; Riello, G., 'The Globalization'. Styles, J., 'Product Innovation in Early Modern London', *Past and Present*, 168 (2000), pp. 124–69. Montgomery, M., *Printed Textiles: English and American Cottons and Linens, 1700–1850* (New York: Viking Press, 1970).

[40]   C.D.M.T., CA 155, *Ordenanzas para los fabricantes de Indianas de Cataluña*, 1767.

The ban on the introduction of foreign Indian cottons to Spain likely explains the progressive decrease in calico imports. The Mediterranean ports of Spain were the main destination of the exports of clothing made of calico from Marseille during the first half of the eighteenth century. From the early 1750s onwards, the main destinations of calicoes, corresponding to this market, shifted from Spain to Italy and Piedmont – see Chart 6.12 – where calicoes imported from Asia could be easily re-exported to central Europe by Marseille merchants.[41]

From the 1750s to the early 1770s the volume of exports of calicoes to England increased. However, Italy maintained its position as a major buyer of Asian calicoes related to the French market – see Chart 6.12. In terms of comparison with other places in Europe, we have included Holland and northern Europe. In the latter area, the merchants of the 'Chambre de Commerce de Marseille' included the Baltic and Hanseatic territories, where the introduction of calicoes was quite marginal as we can observe in Chart 6.12. The small amount of exports to England, Holland and northern Europe is explained by the fact that central and, in particular, northern Europe was a market dominated by Dutch and English merchants during the seventeenth and eighteenth centuries.[42] These merchants were more focused on controlling the commercialization of cotton from the Atlantic market, especially those from the American colonies.[43] The constant rivalry between England and Holland, to control the northern European market,[44] is remarkable proof that there were few possibilities for French merchants to introduce their products in this area.

---

[41]   Mazzaoui, M.F., 'The First European Cotton Industry. Italy and Germany, 1100–1800', in Riello, G. and Parthasarathi, P. (eds), *The Spinning World*, pp. 63–88. Epstein, S.R., *Freedom and Growth: The Rise of States and Markets in Europe, 1300–1750* (London: Routledge, 2000).

[42]   For an overview of the expansion on cotton manufacture in northern Europe see: Duplessis, R.S., *Transitions to Capitalism in Early Modern Europe* (Cambridge: Cambridge University Press, 1997). Vermaut, J., 'Structural Transformation in a Textile Centre: Bruges from Sixteenth to the Nineteenth Century', in Van der Wee, H. (ed.), *The Rise and Decline of Urban Industries in Italy and the Low Countries (Late Middle Ages-Early Modern Times)* (Louvain: Louvain University Press, 1988), pp. 187–206.

[43]   Egnal, M., *New World Economies: The Growth of the Thirteen Colonies and Early Canada* (New York: Oxford University Press, 1998). Banks, K.J., *Chasing Empire across the Sea: Communications and the State in the French Atlantic, 1713–1763* (Montreal and Kingston: MacGill Queen's University Press, 2002). Duplessis, R.S., 'Cottons Consumption in the Seventeenth and Eighteenth-century North Atlantic', in Riello, G. and Parthasarathi, P. (eds), *The Spinning World*, pp. 227–46.

[44]   Ormrod, D., *The Rise of Commercial Empires. England and the Netherlands in the Age of Mercantilism, 1650–1770* (Cambridge: Cambridge University Press, 2003). O'Brien, P., 'Mercantilism and Imperialism in the Rise and Decline of the Dutch and British Empire, 1688–1815', *De Economist*, 148 (2000), pp. 469–501.

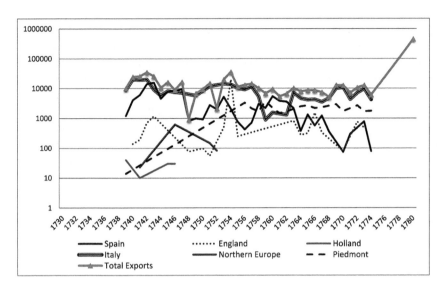

Chart 6.12   Exports of clothing made of calico from Marseille to Europe
              (1730–80). Volume: in 'pièces'. *Source:* A.C.C.M., Statistique.
              Serie I.

As a result of the ban on the introduction of Asian calicoes in Spain, the imports
of this fibre dropped, after 1767, whereas they rose in Italy and England. Although
the prohibition of foreign textiles was quite common in European territories,
merchants and workers, especially from England[45] or Holland,[46] devised some
strategies such as the emulation of Indian products with European substitutes or a
lax application of customs rules. It was a way which enabled traders to evade those
bans and foster a process of 'import substitution'.[47]

Regarding the evolution of calico prices per unit acquired in the wholesale
market from the early 1740s until the late 1770s there was a tendency to keep
the prices constant. There was very little fluctuation in prices during the 1730s
and 1740s. These prices correspond with the list of the current prices of such

[45]   Gauci, P., *Emporium of the Worlds. The Merchants of London 1660–1800* (London:
Hambledom Continuum, 2007). Hancock, D., *Citizens of the World. London Merchants
and the Integration of the British Atlantic Community, 1735–1785* (Cambridge: Cambridge
University Press, 1995).

[46]   Wright, H.R.C., *Free Trade and Protection in the Netherlands, 1816–1830*
(Cambridge: Cambridge University Press, 1955). De Vries, J., 'The Decline and Rise of the
Dutch Economy, 1675–1750', in Saxonhouse, A.G. and Wridley, G. (eds), *Technique, Spirit
and Form in the Making of Modern Economic: Essays in Honour of William N. Parker*
(Greenwich: JAI Press, 1984), pp. 149–89.

[47]   Sicknger, R.L., 'Regulation or Ruination: Parliament's Consistent Pattern of
Mercantilist Regulation of the English Textile Trade, 1660–1800', *Parliamentary History*,
19/2 (2000), p. 229.

a commodity, which was issued by the Marseille commercial and financial newspapers, the prices being related to the wholesale import-export market. As one of the biggest ports in France and the warehouse of the Mediterranean territory, Marseille had a huge amount of both material and human resources, unrivalled in the western Mediterranean area.[48] The merchants of Marseille, as well as the industrial entrepreneurs, located in southern France, had a well-drawn economic network of information and transparency.[49] This system allowed them to organize themselves and to protect their interests by knowing firsthand the commercial newspapers published by traders of Italian city states and the Lyonnaise fairs.[50] Hence, they fixed the price of the commodities traded in the ports of the Mediterranean market, in order to re-export the products to the European wholesale market by selling them, mainly, in European capitals. The uniformity of these prices, as we can see in Charts 6.13 and 6.14, is due to the organized effort of European merchants, who resided in Marseille, whose purpose was to negotiate a flat and affordable price. The 'Bourse', whose seat was in the 'Chambre de Commerce de Marseille', was the institution that fixed the price of commodities in the stock market. Bargaining for a good price enabled foreign merchants to supply to diverse countries by ensuring the sales of their products. For instance, the Roux Company settled businesses in eastern Spain, trading with products that they acquired on the Mediterranean market and Levantine routes. European dealers might have had an agreement to set a flat price for calicoes purchased in Marseille with the main European nations after 1750, as can be observed in Charts 6.13 and 6.14.

England, Holland, Italy, the Hanseatic and Baltic countries and Piedmont established a buying price of 12 French 'livres', the price during earlier decades being higher and more fluctuant than after 1750 – see Charts 6.13 and 6.14. Whereas for Spain the price kept a constant rate of 20 French 'livres' – see Chart 6.13. The higher buying cost may explain why the Spanish acquisition of calicoes progressively fell after 1750. The purchase, especially, by Italian, Piedmontese and English traders rose once they obtained a buying price that was lower than the Spanish merchants.

---

[48]   Carrière, Ch., *Négotians*. Rambert, G. (ed.), *Histoire du commerce de Marseille* (8 vols., Paris: Plon, 1949–1966), vol. 1. Masson, P., *Histoire de commerce français dans le Levant aux XVIIIe siècle* (Paris: Hachette, 1986).

[49]   Rosenthal, J.L., 'Credit Markets and Economic Change in Southeastern France 1630–1788', *Explorations in Economic History*, 30: 129–57 (1993).

[50]   McCusker, J.J. and Gravesteijn, C., *The Beginning of Commercial and Financial Journalism. The Commodity Price Currents, Exchange Rate Currents and Money Currents of Early Modern Europe* (Amsterdam: Neha, 1991), pp. 363–9, 439–43. Asthor, E., 'Recent Research on Levantine Trade', *Journal of European Economic History*, II (1973), 187–206, XIV (1985).

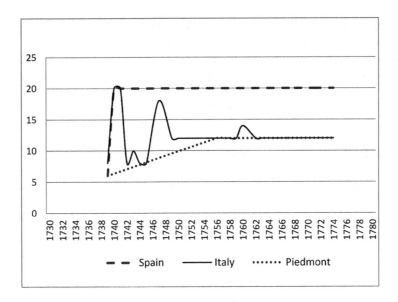

Chart 6.13   Price per unit of items made of calico exported from Marseille to southern Europe (1730–80). Unit of price: French 'livres tournois'. Volume/Price: 1 pound of calicoes / 'x' 'livres tournois'. *Source:* A.C.C.M., Statistique. Serie I.

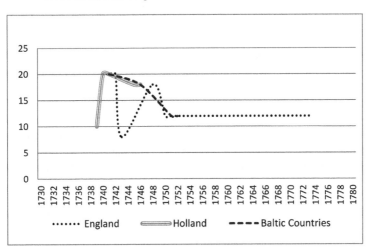

Chart 6.14   Price per unit of items made of calico exported from Marseille to northern Europe (1730–80). Unit of price: French 'livres tournois'. Volume/Price: 1 pound of calicoes / 'x' 'livres tournois'. *Source:* A.C.C.M., Statistique. Serie I.

Charts 6.13 and 6.14 correspond to wholesale market prices, which did not fluctuate because they were imposed by the 'Chambre de Commerce de Marseille', after negotiations with foreign traders in order not to cause any damage to Marseille businessmen.[51] Therefore, it was not necessary to deflate the prices as they related to the complete index prices fixed from 1730 to 1780. Such price deflation kept a similar steady trend for the whole period.

6.2. The Commercialization of Colonial Groceries from Asia and America

Long-distance trade to America and India spread the consumption of hot beverages to Europe. European consumers witnessed the introduction of new beverages from Asian and American colonies, which inspired economic and socio-cultural changes.[52] The European mercantilist policies fostered the consumption and commercialization of hot beverages and drinks made of exotic herbs and plants. Natural products and exotic commodities had some important connotations that involved the Bourbon policy of the eighteenth century. Their economic policies had, as their main goal, the introduction of products from the colonies to the metropolitan territory in order to enrich the colonial commerce of the Crown and keep the balance of payments positive. Another important factor which involved the introduction of these exotic commodities was the acceptance or rejection of the consumption of such goods by society. The definition of what was understood as good 'gout'[53] [taste], in the framework of not transgressing the cultural and moral norms, played a very important role in the circulation and acceptance of the trade and consumption of such commodities.

This analysis has focused on the economic implications of trading with these commodities from the Atlantic and Asian markets and what the main purpose of European territories in commercializing these goods was. Fleets and shipments can be analysed to observe the agents, institutional spaces, knowledge-skills and territories that participated in the European project to trade in natural objects. These shipments were an obvious effort of the mercantilist policy to stimulate the national economy of European countries.[54] The data that we provided shows the real expansion and diffusion of such goods in western Europe, especially

---

[51]   Carrière, Ch., *Négotians*. McCusker, J.J. and Gravesteijn, C., *The Beginning*.

[52]   Clarence-Smith, W.G., 'The Global Consumption of Hot Beverages, c. 1500 to c. 1900', in Nützenadel, A. and Trentmann, F. (eds), *Food and Globalization. Consumption, Markets and Politics in the Modern World* (London: Cultures of Consumption Series, 2008), pp. 37–55. Prance, G. and Nesbitt, M. (eds), *The Cultural History of Plants* (New York: Routledge, 2005).

[53]   Portier, R., 'Goût', in Delon, M. (ed.), *Dictionnaire européen des Lumières* (Paris: P.U.F., 1997), p. 510.

[54]   De Vos, P., 'Natural History and the Pursuit of Empire in Eighteenth-century Spain', *Eighteenth-century Studies*, vol. 40, no. 2 (Winter, 2007), pp. 209–39.

in the Mediterranean market, corresponding to the merchants' businesses of the 'Chambre de Commerce de Marseille'.

Such traders introduced chocolate, cacao, different kinds of sugar from the French colonies of America, as well as tea and coffee from Levantine routes. The chief European territories, where those commodities were re-exported from the port of Marseille, were Spain, Italy, England and Holland. It is well known that the monopoly of the tea trade and some other natural Asian goods corresponded to the British East India Company and the Dutch VOC. However, in the process of commercialization and distribution of these exotic goods the French merchant played a very important role.

The new stage of commercial growth, unfolding in the late seventeenth and early eighteenth centuries, was driven by the new marketing measures conducted by the hard-working merchants of Europe, who supplied commodities that awoke the desire and appetite for luxury goods. The rising consumer demand for agricultural goods such as, sugar, spices, tea, coffee and colonial tobacco caused European nations to undertake new projects in order to enrich the national treasury. Such measures were especially related to Enlightenment projects, whose aim was to benefit from the economic resources of the land.[55] The Enlightenment dignitaries were concerned with knowledge of geography and natural history in order to search for agricultural resources to improve the economic reserves of the nation.[56]

The search for import substitution was not only undertaken in the textile sector, as we have seen with the European attempts to find substitutes for Indian calicoes. In Spain, there was a project undertaken by the Royal Botanical Garden, whose main purpose was to find an American substitute for Asian tea. Hence, the Spanish Enlightenment leaders tried to spread the commercialization and diffusion of 'Bogotá' tea.[57] The important amounts of the imported cacao and coffee from Yemen and American colonies, via the Levantine and Atlantic routes, by means of the merchants from Marseille, reveal the failure of the Spanish institutions to spread the consumption and trade of tea. The limited success of 'Bogotá' tea in upper-class gatherings is explained by the fact that they found it more a medicine than a commodity of 'gout' or taste. For them it was not a pleasant drink.

During the eighteenth century, the amount of traded tea in the Spanish Mediterranean ports was quite marginal, 11,796 pounds, by comparison to

[55] Shammas, C., 'The Revolutionary Impact of European Demand for Tropical Goods', in Morgan, K. and McCusker, J.J. (eds), *The Early Modern Atlantic Economy* (Cambridge: Cambridge University Press, 2000), pp. 163–85.

[56] Withers, Ch. W.J., 'Geography, Natural History and the Eighteenth-century Enlightenment: Putting the World in Place', *History Workshop Journal*, no. 39 (Spring, 1995), pp. 136–63.

[57] Figueroa, M.F., 'La 'expedición' de la naturaleza americana: sobre unos gustos metropolitanos y algunas recolecciones coloniales', *Anuario de Historia de América Latina*, 45 (2008), pp. 297–324.

the commercialization and consumption of some other commodities such as cacao, 3,513,979 pounds, from Veracruz and the Antilles (Saint-Domingue and Martinique), and coffee, 1,164,207 pounds,[58] from Yemen and the Antilles – see Charts 6.15 and 6.16. This is remarkable proof which shows, in relation with hot beverages, that chocolate was quite successful in Spanish society and became the 'national beverage'. The trade and consumption of coffee was progressively introduced in Spain, mainly coffee from the American French colonies and, in a secondary position, Arabian coffee. The attempts of French merchants to trade with tea or opium – see Chart 6.16 – had very little success, especially because those commodities were a monopoly in the hands of the East Company of Indies and the VOC, which were the two major trade companies of the spice routes.

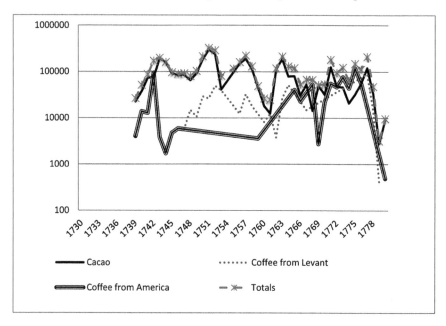

Chart 6.15   Exports of agricultural goods from Marseille to Spanish Mediterranean ports (1730–80). Volume: in pounds. *Source:* A.C.C.M., Statistique. Serie I.

French merchants encountered the same problem when they tried to expand their businesses in selling tobacco – see Chart 6.16 – in the Spanish Mediterranean territory, because they had to face two factors: firstly, the deals with tobacco in Spain were a monopoly in the hands of the Spanish Crown and, secondly, French merchants had to confront the English, Dutch and Portuguese smuggling of

---

[58]   A.C.C.M., Statistique. Etats des Marchandises sorties aux pays étrangères, Serie I, 24.

tobacco.[59] Whereas English traders introduced it from their American colonies, especially from Virginia, the Portuguese dealers[60] commercialized the tobacco from their territories of Brazil and Dutch traders from Guyana.[61]

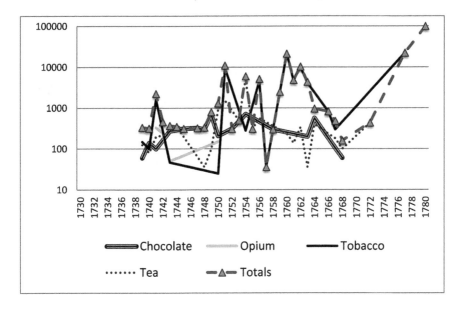

Chart 6.16   Exports of agricultural goods from Marseille to Spanish Mediterranean ports (1730–80). Volume expressed in pounds. *Source:* A.C.C.M., Statistique. Serie I.

In Western Europe, Marseille merchants were quite successful in trading and spreading the consumption of cacao, coffee and chocolate. For this market, the potential buyers of cacao and chocolate were Italy, in the first place, followed by Spain and Piedmont. I have introduced the data registered in the 'Chambre de Commerce de Marseille' that shows the English, Dutch and north European

---

[59]   Pijning, E., 'Passive Resistance: Portuguese Diplomacy of Contraband Trade during King John V's Reign (1705–1750)', *Arquipelago-Historia*, 2ª serie, II (1997), pp. 171–91. Escobedo Romero, R., 'El contrabando transpirenaico y el monopolio de tabacos español durante el s. XVIII', in Minovez, J.M. and Poujade, P. (eds), *Circulation*, pp. 119–32.

[60]   Trivellato, F., *Cross-Cultural Trade in the Early Modern Period* (New Haven: Yale University Press, 2009). Hancock, D., 'The Trouble with Networks: Managing the Scots' Early-Modern Madeira Trade', *Business History Review*, 79 (2005), pp. 467–91. Price, J.M., *France and Chesapeake. A History of the French Tobacco Monopoly, 1674–1791* (Ann Harbor: The University of Michigan Press, 2 vols, 1973).

[61]   Crespo Solana, A., *América desde otra frontera. La Guayana holandesa (Surinam): 1680–1795* (Madrid: Consejo Superior de Investigaciones Científicas, 2006).

(Hanseatic and Baltic countries) purchases of cacao – see Chart 6.17 – coffee – see Chart 6.18 – and chocolate – see Chart 6.19 – to compare them with southern Europe.

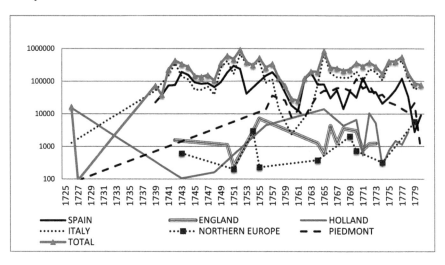

Chart 6.17   Exports of cacao from Marseille to Europe (1725–80). Volume: in pounds. *Source:* A.C.C.M., Statistique. Serie I.

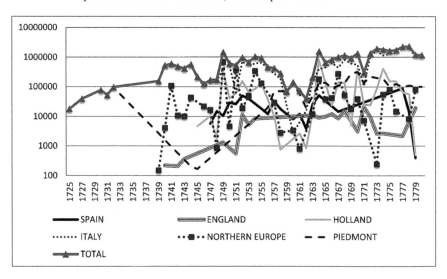

Chart 6.18   Exports of coffee from Marseille to Europe (1725–80). Nominal Price: in French 'livres'. *Source:* A.C.C.M., Statistique. Serie I.

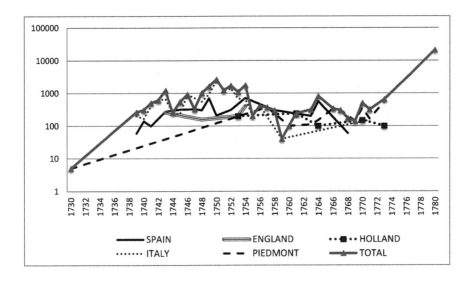

Chart 6.19   Exports of chocolate from Marseille to Europe (1730–80). Volume: in pounds. *Source:* A.C.C.M., Statistique. Serie I.

The comparison with those European territories shows again, as occurred with the trading of Asian textiles, that French merchants from Marseille had few opportunities to place their commodities from overseas in northern Europe. This was due to the stiff competition between England and Holland to control the central European market when both the West and East India Companies were the major commercial institutions.[62] It is important to note that Holland had access to Atlantic trade via the North Sea, contributing to the economic growth of central and Eastern European countries.[63] During the seventeenth century, coffee, tea, tobacco, sugar and cacao became popular at the same time. Chocolate as a

    [62]   Hamilton, E.J., 'The Role of Monopoly in the Overseas Expansion and Colonial Trade of Europe before 1800', *American Economic Review* (1948), 38 (2), pp. 33–53. Israel, J., *The Dutch Republic: its Rise, Greatness and Fall 1477–1806. Volume I: The Oxford History of Early Modern Europe* (New York: Oxford University Press, 1995).
    [63]   The rise of the Dutch economy due to its control of north-western European trade and its connections with the Atlantic world has been studied in deep by De Vries and Van der Woude. See: De Vries, J. and Van der Woude, Ad., *The First Modern Economy: Success, Failure, and Perseverance of the Dutch Economy, 1500–1815* (Cambridge: Cambridge University Press, 1997). De Long, Shleifer or Acemoglu have explored how absolutist institutions could have exerted a control over the trade and the economic growth of European countries. De Long, J.B. and Shleifer, A., 'Princes and Merchants: European City Growth before the Industrial Revolution', *Journal of Law and Economics*, vol. 36, no. 2 (Oct., 1993), pp. 671–702. Acemoglu, D., Johnson S. and Robinson J., 'The Rise of Europe: Atlantic Trade, Institutional Change, and Economic Growth', *The American Economic Review*, vol. 95, no. 3 (Jun., 2005), pp. 546–79.

beverage was very popular in Spain, France and Italy, as well as in north-western European territories such as Holland or England. However, chocolate was mainly in the hands of Spaniards because of their Latin American dominions, followed by the French due to the American plantations of cacao in the Antilles.

The English and Dutch, who became obsessed in trading coffee, as demonstrated by the establishment of numerous coffee houses, shifted towards the consumption of tea in order to reinforce the trade with China and India. In particular English society saw the virtues and effects of chocolate corresponding more to a beverage with medicinal and nourishing faculties than a pleasant drink:

> ... travellers and physicians, do agree in this, that Cacao Nut has a wonderful faculty of quenching thirst, allaying hectic heats, of nourishing and fathing the body. Mr. Gage acquaint us, that he drank chocolate in the Indies ... and he scarse knew what any disease was in al time, he growing fat ... Mr. Hughes ... says our English Seamen are very greedy of it when they come into any Indian port ... Mr. Hughes himself grew very fat in Jamaica ... so he judges: it may be proper for some breeding women, and those persons that are Hypocondriacal, and Melancolly ...
>
> The industrious author of the Vinetum Britannicum makes a Quare, whether the Kernel of the Wallnut may not supply the defect of the cacao, if well ground.
>
> Dr Grew thinks, that for those that drink chocolate at Coffee-Houses without any Medicinal respect, there is no doubt, but that of Almonds finely beaten, and mixed with a due proportion of Spices, and Sugar, may be made as a pleasant a drink as the best chocolate.[64]

The property of quenching thirst and nourishing the body made chocolate become an important drink in the new dietary habits. In the passage above, written by John Chamberlain in 1682, he noticed that some dignitaries, when visiting English colonies in the Caribbean Sea such as Jamaica, became fat, as they ate chocolate to relieve the symptoms of certain diseases. This was the major use of chocolate in the past. However, the last paragraph of the text reveals that people had noticed the pleasant taste of chocolate when mixed with sugar and spices, introducing new recipes.[65]

Europeans were slow to adopt the habit of drinking coffee for several reasons: as a Muslim drink it was viewed as heretical, and the Turkish fashion for this hot,

---

[64]   Chamberlayne, John, *The Natural History of Coffee, Chocolate, Thee, 1682. The Making of the Modern World* (London: Printed for Christopher Wilkinson, 1682 – Gale, Cengage L., UCBerkeley Library, 2008), pp. 17–19.

[65]   Pennell, S., 'Consumption and Consumerism in Early Modern England', *The Historical Journal*, vol. 42, no. 2 (Jun., 1999), pp. 549–64. Coe, S.D. and Coe, M.D., *The True History of Chocolate* (London: Thames and Hudson Ltd, 1996). Murcott, A., Mennell, S. and van Otterloo, A.H., *The Sociology of Food* (Aldershot: Sage Publications, 1992), pp. 1–34.

black, bitter drink did not attract European palates. Moreover, this rare caffeine spice was very expensive. Indeed, coffee did not start to be widely consumed until the last quarter of the eighteenth century.[66] As Kenneth Pomeranz mentions, central European regions, via Austria, were the areas where coffee was propagated by the Turkish unintentionally, after their failure in the siege of Vienna in 1683, when the Turks departed, leaving their coffee bags.[67] The owner of the first Viennese coffeehouse thought of adding honey and milk to coffee, which was more appealing to the Europeans. But coffee still remained an exceptional product due to its high price.

The Marseille commercial companies dealt with this commodity, having an advantage over the British and Dutch East India Companies. The permanent embassies that French traders had in the Levantine routes, such as Cairo and Alexandria, allowed them to easily ship coffee cargoes from Yemen. They also traded coffee from the French American colonies, the Antilles, as well as the French African colonies of the Mascarene Islands of Bourbon (La Réunion), Maurice and Rodrigues, close to the coast of Madagascar.[68] In the early days of the coffee trade, the Arabian Peninsula had the monopoly on exporting this commodity, Mocha and Yemen being the main centres of production.[69] French merchants tried to spread the consumption of coffee in Europe by combining new recipes and making this product more pleasant to drink. The new qualities of this beverage were very well appreciated by Europeans, who progressively started to consume more of this drink.

Formerly, Europeans, as we have seen in the previous discussion of chocolate properties, considered coffee to be more of a medicine than a pleasant casual drink. British merchants were the first to deal with Arabian coffee through the East India Companies in the late seventeenth and early eighteenth centuries. For this reason, they spread the idea that the nature and coffee qualities were as follows:

> As for the qualities and nature of coffee, our own country man, Dr Willis, has publish'd a very rational account, whose great reputation and authority are of small force; he says, that in several headachs, dizziness, lethargies, and catarrhs,

---

[66]   Pomeranz, K. and Topik, S., *The World that Trade Created: Society, Culture and the World Economy, 1400 to the Present* (New York: M.E. Sharpe, 1999).

[67]   Pomeranz, K. and Topik, S., *The World*, p. 81.

[68]   Carrière, Ch., *Négotians*, pp. 38–41.

[69]   *Le café en Méditerranée. Histoire, anthropologie, économie XVIIIe–XXe siècle.* Actes de la Table ronde de l'Institut de Recherches Méditerranéennes et de la Chambre de Commerce et d'Industrie de Marseille (Marseille: Institut de Recherches Méditerranéennes, Université de Provence, 1980). Clarence-Smith, W.G., 'The Spread of Coffee Cultivation in Asia, from the Seventeenth to the Early Nineteenth Century', in Tuchscherer, M. (ed.), *Le commerce du café avant l'ère des plantations colonials* (Cairo: Institut français d'archéologie orientale, 2001), pp. 371–84. Mauro, F., *Histoire du café* (Paris: Editions Desjonquères, 1991).

where there is a gross habit of body, and cold heavy constitution, there coffee may be proper, and sucessfull; and these cafes he sent his patients to the coffee-house rather than to the apothecaries shop ...[70]

Illustration 6.2   Coffee was first introduced to western Europe in the mid-17th century and quickly became extremely popular; the first recorded coffee-house outside the Ottoman Empire opened its doors in Venice in 1645 and the first one in England opened in Oxford five years later. The coffee-houses of 17th- and 18th-century Europe were places of socializing, business, and the exchange of news and gossip. *Source:* www.turkishcoffee world.com.

Coffee was also seen as an anti-aphrodisiac beverage:

Olerious, who says, that the Persian are of an opinion that coffee allays their natural heat, for which reason they drink it, that they may avoid the charge, and inconveniences of many children ... some of them have come to the Holstein physician of that embassy, for remedies to prevent the multiplication of children ...[71]

---

[70]   Chamberlayne, John, *The Natural*, p. 4.
[71]   Chamberlayne, John, *The Natural*, p. 5.

The European imports of coffee mainly came from the Arabian territory.[72] However, in the early 1820s, coffee trees were planted on the Bourbon island (la Réunion), Martinique and Saint-Domingue, from which French merchants exported coffee to Europe. From that time onwards coffee became a luxury colonial drink rather than a medicine. England had few possibilities to receive French coffee, as we can observe in Chart 6.18, because when coffee trees were introduced in the French Antilles, this plant was also introduced in the British colony of Jamaica. In addition, it is important to mention that coffee from Saint-Domingue was cheap and of very good quality, and was consumed by Europeans in high quantities; but the Mocha coffee continued to be the most popular among consumers. Through the mediation of the merchants from Marseille,[73] coffee from the Antilles conquered the western Mediterranean market. The Dutch VOC was devoted to the coffee from Mocha, as well as the whole north European market.

Regarding the price per unit of these commodities (cacao, coffee and chocolate) stipulated by the European merchants in agreement with the 'Chambre de Commerce de Marseille', as well as the prices of textiles as mentioned in previous pages, cacao was the only agricultural product that did not fluctuate significantly after the Seven Years' war, when the exports of cacao to Spain dropped, whereas in Italy and Piedmont such exports rose. In the European market, the rate of the cacao price fluctuated between 30 and 6 'soleils' (1 French 'livre' = 20 French 'soleils') – see Chart 6.21. This statement is favoured by W.G. Clarence-Smith's[74] affirmation that Spanish tariffs were reformed after the British victory in the Seven Years' war in 1763. This caused the cost of cacao beans to fall sharply in both the metropolitan and colonial markets[75] – see Charts 6.21 and 6.23.

The price of chocolate exported in bars fluctuated constantly, and Italy was one of the main consumers. Price fluctuations could be explained by the strong competition between the Spanish and French chocolate exports. Dealers of the 'Chambre de Commerce de Marseille' were trying hard to open the business of chocolate in European markets. The chocolate price rate fluctuated from 10 to 40 French 'soleils' – see Chart 6.20. The price of coffee fluctuated the most from the 1720s to the end of the Seven Years' war. The rate of the stipulated buying price of this commodity varied from 10 to 45 French 'soleils' – see Charts 6.22 and 6.24. The strong competition with Arabian coffee, which was mainly commercialized in Europe by the traders from Marseille, as well as the British East India Companies

---

[72]   Braudel, F., *Les structures du quotidien. Civilisation matérielle, économie et capitalisme XVe–XVIIIe siècle* (Paris: Armand Colin, 1979), p. 223.

[73]   Paris, R., *Histoire du commerce de Marseille de 1660 à 1789*, vol. 5, *Le Levant* (Paris: ed. Gaston Rambert, 1957), pp. 559–61.

[74]   Clarence-Smith, W.G., 'The Spread', p. 41.

[75]   Burnet, J., *Liquid Pleasures, a Social History of Drinks in Modern Britain* (London: Taylor and Francis, 1999), pp. 52–6. Clarence-Smith, W.G., *Cocoa and Chocolate, 1765–1914* (London: Routledge, 2000).

and the Dutch VOC, could be the cause of the variations in the wholesale price of coffee.

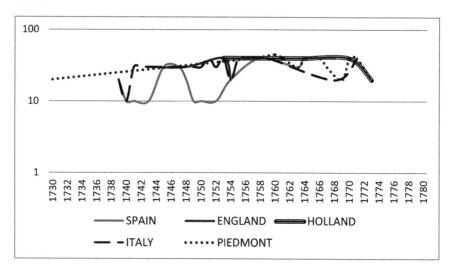

Chart 6.20   Price per unit of exported chocolate from Marseille to Europe (1725–80). Nominal Price: in French 'soleils'. *Source:* A.C.C.M., Statistique. Serie I, Articles: 21, 22, 23, 24.

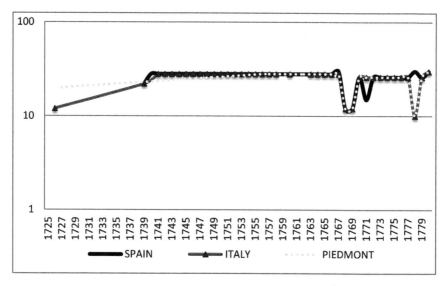

Chart 6.21   Price per unit of exported cacao from Marseille to southern Europe (1725–80). Nominal Price: in French 'soleils'. *Source:* A.C.C.M., Statistique. Serie I.

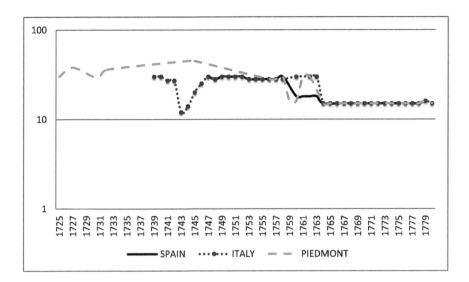

Chart 6.22   Price per unit of exported coffee from Marseille to southern Europe (1725–80). Nominal Price: in French 'soleils'. *Source:* A.C.C.M., Statistique. Serie I

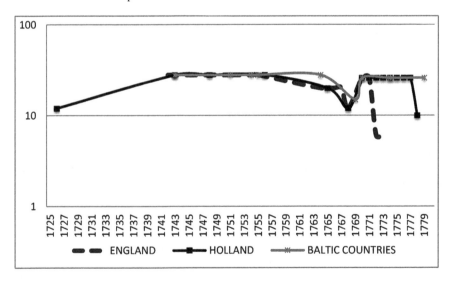

Chart 6.23   Price per unit of exported cacao from Marseille to northern Europe (1725–80). Nominal Price: in French 'soleils'. *Source:* A.C.C.M., Statistique. Serie I.

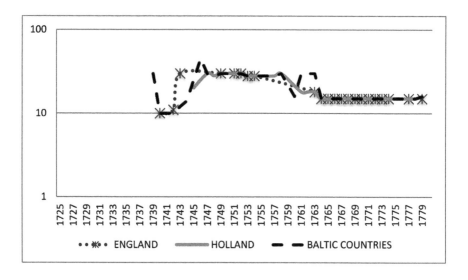

Chart 6.24   Price per unit of exported coffee from Marseille to northern Europe
               (1725–80). Nominal Price: in French 'soleils'. *Source:* A.C.C.M.,
               Statistique. Serie I.

Conclusions

The activity of international traders in the western Mediterranean territory
constituted a potential factor that stimulated the local economies of eastern Spain
through the commercialization of foreign commodities. This was the case of south-
eastern Castile, where the population had to be supplied by foreign commerce due
to the limited existence of a strong artisan group, like that of southern France
(Languedoc) or northern Italy (Piedmont), with a high production of goods in
order to substitute the imports. This economic process was undertaken by the
British economy during the eighteenth century. Most of the Spanish Mediterranean
territory, especially the south-eastern areas, depended on foreign trade to supply
goods to the population.

     The relative weakness of Spanish Mediterranean production was seen as a
potential opportunity for traders, especially those from France, to expand their
businesses. In addition, the eastern Spanish production of raw textile materials such
as silk, wool or cotton was taken as an advantage for French traders to establish
companies in the Spanish Mediterranean territory. The exchange of raw materials
for ready-to-use products, most of them manufactured in southern French industries
or Near East territories, contributed to keeping the Spanish Mediterranean balance
of payments negative. Thus, French traders established socio-economic networks
over the Mediterranean market, and the eastern Spanish territory was one of the
main areas in which they sold their products. Such networks allowed them to

expand their market, through the creation of an interconnected foreign community, in which co-national marriages, trust, culture and values were used to transfer and share new patterns of consumption.

The commercialization of products made of Asian raw materials, which were manufactured in the French textiles industries of Lyon, Grenoble or Bearn, as well as finished clothing from Asia and agricultural products from Levantine and Atlantic routes, represents both the international and global connections of the Mediterranean market. The Spanish coastal regions, such as the port of Cartagena, in south-eastern Spain, participated in this global market. Through the analysis of the continuous entry of foreign products by studying the registers of the 'Chambre de Commerce de Marseille', especially focusing on the textile sector, we can see that the Spanish Mediterranean population was attracted by foreign and exotic commodities. The high commercialization of French and Asian textiles, but also agricultural goods such as chocolate, cacao, coffee or tea, in the Spanish Mediterranean market is a notable proof of this trend.

A thorough examination of the supply-side in the western Mediterranean market allows us to understand the shifts that occurred in the consumer behaviour of south-eastern Spain, which will be analysed in the next section. Therefore, we can emphasize that the action of international dealers, as main economic agents and 'vicarious consumers' of goods, stimulated regional economies, supplying the population with a wide variety of commodities and creating a new demand. This contributed to transferring new fashions and change in socio-cultural values and identities. The strategic role of the Kingdom of Murcia and Cartagena, as the main port of southern Castile for the trade with the Mediterranean territory, was essential in international commerce, as well as for the supply of new products. The permanent circulation of people and merchandise in this 'trans-Mediterranean' area caused traders to become the key agents in the changing tastes and patterns of consumption.

PART IV
Examining the 'Consumer' and 'Industrious' Revolution in South-eastern Spain: the Kingdom of Murcia (1730–1808)

The establishment of family merchant networks in the geography of the Spanish Mediterranean was the key factor that led to a wide diffusion of goods in late eighteenth-century Spanish society. But what were the economic impulses that displaced the old habits and inspired the acquisition of more elegant and sophisticated lifestyles, which constituted the so-called origins or birth of modern mass consumption societies? The scholarly explanations of those changes have been based on arguments about the technological advance and change of traditional economies that occurred during the Industrial Revolution. The literature on that debate is extensive and it is not my task to repeat that discussion.[1] However, as we have seen in the previous chapter there are some reasons to believe that changes on the demand-side were motivated by certain deep transformations on the supply-side. Prior to those technological and industrial changes there was a global extension of the trade networks and businesses, whose aim was integrated markets in order to increase benefits. This international and intercontinental business entailed the creation of a large-scale market for the wider consumption of goods. Port cities were the main locations for the entry of new goods from afar, which rapidly caught the attention of both retailers and consumers. I will show how goods were spread among different social groups and the mediators who changed the demand-side, analysing whether or not the 'industrious revolution' and 'trickle-down' theories took place in the southern European economy.

The playing out of these factors implied the so-called 'industrious revolution', but what happens when the intervention of governmental institutions are unhelpful for the process of modernization? Certainly some areas of the Spanish economy can be identified as industrious such as the Castilian inland – Segovia or Palencia –

---

[1]   Clark, G. and Vand Der Weerf, 'Work in Progress? The Industrious Revolution', *Journal of Economic History*, 58, no. 3 (1998), pp. 830–43. Mokyr, J., 'Demand vs. Supply in the Industrial Revolution', *Journal of Economic History*, 37 (1977), pp. 981–1008.

with a huge agricultural production of wool textiles, the area of Catalonia – Sabadell produced an important quantity of cotton and the area of Tarrasa and Lerida had a significant output of linen – the area of Granada and Valencia produced silk – and the region of Murcia was specialized in the agricultural production of silk, 'barilla' and wool. Essentially, there was a specialization in producing raw materials which tended to increase both family labour and income. The only way to encourage household purchases was to establish a commercial circuit in order to exchange raw materials for finished products. This is what explains the success of merchant families established in the Kingdom of Murcia and its port, Cartagena, and those of Mediterranean ports such as Marseille, Genoa, Malta and the Levant.

Part III has demonstrated that the only way to overcome those constraints on production and stimulate society to purchase goods which could not be acquired in the national market, was to establish a connection with foreign wholesale markets. These markets were the only ones that could supply new retailer and consumer necessities. Nuclear and extended families had an important influence on the diffusion of goods in both urban and rural areas. From the moment in which large volumes of commodities entered the nearby areas of harbours, a merchant circuit was established among wholesalers, retailers and peddlers, who were the main socio-economic agents that made goods circulate throughout the territory, being sold in both first- and second-hand markets. A very organized geographical network was created to locate the products in the market and households were the main consumption unit that fostered the circulation of items and their diffusion.

In Part IV, a view of the new necessities created by merchants taking part in local, national and international trade circuits will be offered. The increase in the consumption of goods during the eighteenth century, especially during the second-half, entailed changes in household economies for a new refined taste and elegant manners in everyday life. Nonetheless, traditional Spanish social groups identified such necessities as a transgression, instead of recognizing that people who wore new and fancy clothes were potential consumers of a large-scale market, which supplied commodities that domestic industries could not satisfy. Therefore, the aim is to study (despite the social backlash and prejudices of the period) to what extent a change in the patterns of consumption occurred; to identify the social mechanisms behind such changes; to observe the social trends of diffusion, examining whether or not the 'trickle-down' theory can be applied; and finally, to understand the economic effects on the relations of the different social groups with the market. A systematic analysis of dowries will offer us some clues about the acquisition of new fashions and reveal how commodities were circulating in household economies with different levels of wealth and how the purchase of market goods was progressively growing. Women were the main agents that changed fashions and introduced new lifestyles. Changes in clothes, as well as interior decorations, were due to women's desire for sumptuous and delicate goods, ignoring the modesty and sobriety that the religious hierarchy promoted, and acquiring all types of ornament and jewellery.

Chapter 7

Consumer Behaviour in South-eastern Spain: Channels of Diffusion, Household Economy and Fashions

The analysis of probate inventories deals with the investigation of the goods that are listed in the source itself. Through the study of probate inventories, the purpose is to analyse whether or not the demand of goods increases among the different social groups, taking into account the channels of distribution that encouraged the purchase of goods and the social actors that fostered the demand-side. By examining this large sample of data we can see the evolution of the demand for a wide range of goods in the domestic unit. The aim for analysing probate inventories is to study selected goods in a sample of 273 inventories (see Tables 7.1 and 7.2), which have been arranged into two periods during the eighteenth century spanning between 1730 and 1808. The first period runs from 1730 to 1769 and the second from 1770 to 1808. The reason for this division is to examine the distribution of selected goods within the social groups during the period studied, as well as analysing the socio-economic factors that altered the levels of consumption in the household economy over the century. The period chosen can highlight the evolution of the demand-side: in 1720–30, there was a disruption of the French market due to the plague in Marseille; in 1750–69, after a period of peace and stability, broken by the Seven Years' war, some disturbance occurred in the Mediterranean market resulting from the struggles between France and England; finally, in the last decade of the eighteenth century and the first decade of the nineteenth century the French-Spanish turmoil had negative effects on the economy, in the short term, such as the drop in the demand-side and the rise in prices.[1]

Probate inventories among different social classes have been collected in order to analyse the progressive adaptation of fashions, how consumers became aware of these fashions shifting their pattern of consumption and what the channels of distribution that stimulated this demand were. Through the analysis of probate inventories of south-eastern Spain, it is possible to observe the growing

---

[1] This general framework has been thoroughly analysed by Carrière and Fukusawa, who demonstrated the negative effects of the plague of Marseille of 1720–30 and the European wars in the maritime commerce of the western Mediterranean areas: Carrière, Ch., *Négotians*, vol. I, pp. 466–566; Carrière, Ch., *Richesse du passé marseillais*, pp. 24–30. Fukusawa, K., *Toilerie*, pp. 123–43.

consumption of French commodities that took place in this area. The study of this socio-economic process helps us to understand the real grounds for the social stereotype of the 'petimetre'. Therefore, we can also determine whether such foundations were solid or whether they were just a process in accord with the socio-political turmoil after the French Revolution and during the Napoleonic invasion, which generated a repulsion of French culture. Or did a taste for French commodities simply exist and was the interpretation of 'petimetre' only a socio-political construction? Scholars have often analysed the listed commodities of probate inventories in a random fashion, but this only gives details on the evolution of the stock and does not offer any information about the progressive acquisition of fashions and, consequently, the new perception and identification for those socio-cultural styles by society. The immediate consequence of this question is the introduction of the modern concept of the stereotype, which is in relation with the social distinction given by the 'power of things', in other words, by the social status achieved through the consumption of particular commodities. In using probate inventories, our aim is to determine how the taste for foreign commodities and traditional styles identified as Spanish or national were propagated among social groups since in most cases people that wore clothes associated with the 'majo' and 'petimetre' did not identify themselves as 'majo' or 'petimetre'. It is necessary to look at how commodities were spread in social groups and whether those goods were corresponding with foreign modes.

Secondly, the analysis of probate inventories organized by different social groups gives us some clues as to the appearance of new tastes in comfort, well-being and acquisition of refined manners in social gatherings by means of the purchase of fine items – such as clothes or furniture. This issue can be explored by examining particular items in probate inventories such as mirrors, chocolate-pots, coffee-pots, tea-pots, jackets, chain watches, clocks, books, jackets, fashionable wear, calicoes – 'indienne' or 'indianas' – shoes, chinaware, porcelains, tea-cups and so on. The link of the international trade, studied in Part III, which altered the demand-side through the introduction of commodities from distant markets, such as American or Asian groceries and exotic textiles, provoked some shifts in consumer behaviour. By analysing the relation between the global commerce and consumers, we can observe the real consequences, through the demand-side, of the interaction of the market on consumers' decisions. Trade networks, composed by foreign merchants, stimulated such shifts through the transfer to local people of their cultural values and patterns of consumption.

Both questions coincide with each other because the acquisition of foreign commodities, as well as the consumption of certain household furniture, was related to the compulsive snobbery about comfortable and fashionable goods. There could be an increasing tendency in societies of the western Mediterranean Europe to want 'exotic' and high quality goods, which drove society to strive for a better lifestyle. Through the analysis of household commodities, of a given society such as in the case of the Spanish Mediterranean area – Murcia and its harbour, Cartagena – which was subjected to that new process of consumption among different social groups, we can accurately determine the diffusion of those fashions throughout the eighteenth century. Furthermore, we can establish in which social groups the consumption of clothing, household furniture and beverage utensils – for chocolate, coffee or tea – occurred. Hence, we can better approach important topics on consumption studies such as the progressive diffusion or 'democratization' in society of consuming new and desirable luxury goods. In order to answer these questions I have employed a method that has not been used before, which is to analyse in the sample of probate inventories whether or not that new process of consumption was in relation with the 'industrious revolution' and/ or 'trickle-down' theories.

The general narrative and shifts of consumer behaviour from the seventeenth century onwards can be attested through the circulation of Atlantic goods, in Europe, such as groceries – tea, coffee, sugar, tobacco and chocolate[2] – and some new textiles and clothing from the Asian market.[3] In the second half of the eighteenth century, and even in the early nineteenth century, consumer transformation was higher, having as an immediate effect the increase of the consumption of objects associated with genteel dining and social display in public life. Regional elites, as well as the large middle social group of both rural and urban spaces, integrated international fashions and new lifestyles. The changes of patterns of consumption, witnessed during the eighteenth century in Europe,[4] were associated with the rise of the gentility and an increase in incomes, which enabled people to afford the purchase of commodities (see Appendix E, p. 273) that were consumed far more than during the previous century. Spain was no exception[5] and the geographic area that we have studied, the Kingdom of Murcia, shows some signs of this progressive consumer transformation.

I have analysed a sample of 273 probate inventories corresponding to families of both urban and rural areas of two major cities of the Kingdom of Murcia – Murcia and the port of Cartagena – see Appendix G and H, pp. 287, 313. The sample includes different social groups with their respective levels of income, paying particular attention to the middle social class, in two chronological periods: from 1730 to 1769 and from 1770 to 1808. It is important to note that the social distinction I have made in the sample of inventories corresponds with

---

[2]   McCants, A., 'Poor Consumers as Global Consumers: the Diffusion of Tea and coffee Drinking in the Eighteenth Century', *Economic History Review*, 61/S1 (2008), pp. 172–200. Shammas, C., *The Pre-Industrial*.

[3]   In relation to the commerce of Asian textiles in Europe see the work by Riello, G. and Parthasarath, P., *The Spinning World*.

[4]   To observe such changes in European territories, see the works by: De Vries, J., *The Industrious Revolution. Consumer Behavior and the Household Economy, 1650 to the Present* (Cambridge: Cambridge University Press, 2008); McKendrick, N., 'The Consumer Revolution'; Berg, M., 'In Pursuit of Luxury', pp. 85–142; Brewer, J., *The Error*.

[5]   The rise of household incomes and its relation with the acquisition of better lifestyles has been carefully examined by Fernando Ramos Palencia for the Spanish case: Ramos Palencia, F. and Nicolini, E.A., 'A New Method', pp. 145–77.

decisions that historians have to make when they are analysing an extremely divided and hierarchical society such as the *Ancien Regime*. Therefore, it is essential to organize the sample of probate inventories, arranging it into different social groups, in order to explain the origins, developments and duration in different regions and places in which new processes of consumption were taking place. As Kriedte, Medick and Schlumbohm established in their study of peasant societies of Europe, a given society such as the Swiss, with a different typology of peasantry – 'petit ouvriers' [small workers], 'ouvriers industrielles' [industrial workers], 'petit propietaires' [small landlords] or 'propietaires urbains' [urban landlords][6] – makes it more difficult to analyse the impact of the 'longue durée' of the economic process if one does not explore the social structure or use instruments to classify social groups.

The sample of inventories has been arranged in seven social groups from the top to the bottom of the social pyramid: local oligarchy, merchants, landowners, master artisans, professionals, artisans and yeomen. This sample is made according to urban and rural occupations with the aim of obtaining a representative sample of inventories with respect to the entire population. Local oligarchy corresponds with elite individuals such as noblemen with titles, persons with important positions in the council – 'regidor' or 'jurado' – church – 'beneficiados' or posts in the cathedral – or high-ranked positions related to maritime institutions such as those of the city of Cartagena – captain or general of the army. The merchant group includes jobs related to the trade sector, especially wholesalers, people that have funded important commercial ventures and established trade companies and retailers. Landowners include individuals associated with the rural sector that possess important holdings of land and crops in rural areas and urban peripheries, where the main orchards were located. It is essential to note that in the Kingdom of Murcia, especially due to the extension of the 'lugares de huerta' [orchards], rural areas were very close to the urban centres, a feature that facilitated the commercialization and distribution of goods.

Master artisans are the easiest group to classify as they were craftsmen with the title of master. Professionals are the group with the fewest records in the archive of inventories as they are rarely found; among these were doctors, bachelors, lawyers or clerks. Artisans include all professions related to the manufacture occupations, those which the *Ancien Regime* society classified as 'manuales y viles' [manual and vile], such as weavers, carpenters, bakers, bricklayers, upholsterers, locksmiths, blacksmiths, silversmiths and so on. The rural working class is the most complex

---

[6]   To organize a typology of peasants and 'petit ouvriers' these authors made the decision of 'parler de work-peasantries' in order to examine the diffused category of the rural working class. See Kriedte, P., Medick, H., Schlumbohm, J., 'Proto-industrialization: bilan et perspectives. Démographie, structure sociale et industrie à domicile modern', in Leboutte, R. (ed.), *Proto-industrialization. Recherches récentes et nouvelles perspectives* (Gèneve: Librairie Droz S.A., 1996), p. 56.

group of *Ancien Regime* society to classify as Kriedte, Medick and Schlumbohm have discussed. In this group all types of farming occupations that appear in the sample are included such as 'jornaleros' or 'labradores' [yeomen] – see Tables 7.1 and 7.2 below referring to the sample of inventories.

Table 7.1   Sample of probate inventories for the Kingdom of Murcia (1730–1808)

Social Status	1730/69	1770/1808
Local oligarchy	17	17
Merchants	16	17
Landowners	23	23
Master Artisans	11	11
Professionals	4	4
Artisans	26	26
Yeomen	38	40
Total	135	138 = 273

Source: A.H.P.M., protocols.

Table 7.2   Sample of probate inventories for the Kingdom of Murcia in urban and rural areas (1730–1808)

	Place	1730/69	1770/1808	Total
Murcia	**Urban**	34	38	72
	Rural	32	32	64
Cartagena	**Urban**	31	36	67
	Rural	38	32	70

Source: A.H.P.M., protocols.

Using the temporal division, which goes from 1730 to 1769 and from 1770 to 1808, allows us to analyse two important features regarding the transformations on patterns of consumption: changes which occurred over time, and the social distribution of commodities in rural and urban areas of south-eastern Castile. What we find is a mechanism of change and, therefore, it is necessary to look for similarities and differences in consumer structures at diverse locations and levels. We identify patterns for specific goods, periods, places and the dominant groups in the socio-economic process of diffusion and those which were less influential for motivating shifts in consumer behaviour.

7.1. An Econometric First Approach to Measure the Consumer Behaviour in South-eastern Spain

For analysing the study of consumption I have established, as a necessary pattern, the relationship between two important variables: purchasing power and standard of living in the territory of south-eastern Spain. A careful empirical analysis of probate inventories is offered in order to study changes in the household economy.[7] I attempt to integrate the discourse between historians and economists and shed light on some important questions that scholars have pursued in recent decades, for example: was the family budget the only constraint for expenditure or was there a new distribution of the household labour force not depending only on the 'pater familias' income, allowing the family to obtain more commodities, especially as an outcome of the role played by the work of women and their ability to provide more commodities for the household? For an accurate analysis of the possible changes in consumer behaviour it is essential to examine the topic beyond this simple equation: rising wages entail a growing demand, as Gilboy explains in his thesis on the demand shifts:

> In order that a shift in the demand schedule may occur, individuals must be able to buy more units of a commodity at the same price, or the same amount of the commodity at a higher price … the entire schedule must shift upward, indicating a greater buying power.[8]

It is necessary to add other important variables to this rigid economic model, such as how purchasing power is affected by relative prices and salaries in order to understand changes in the demand-side, whether or not it narrows, and whether or not there are enough substitutive commodities on the market.[9] For this reason, in my analysis I have integrated those variables to explain why, when and how new consumer behaviour took place in a pre-industrial south European economy.

---

[7]   I express my gratitude to Fernando Ramos Palencia who has allowed me to see his PhD dissertation and has helped me with the complicated econometric methods to analyse the Castilian consumer behaviour: Ramos Palencia, F., *Pautas de consumo familiar y mercado en la Castilla preindustrial. El consumo de bienes duraderos y semiduraderos en Palencia, 1750–1850* (Facultad de Ciencias Económicas y Empresariales, Departamento de Historia e Instituciones Económicas y Economía Aplicada, Universidad de Valladolid, unpublished PhD, 2001).

[8]   Gilboy, E.W., *Wages in Eighteenth Century England* (Cambridge: Cambridge University Press, 1932).

[9]   Modigliani, F. and Brumberg, R., 'Utility Analysis and the Consumption Function: an Interpretation of Cross-Section Data', in Kurihara, K., *Post-Keynesian Economics* (New Brunswick: Rutgers University Press, 1954).

I have dismissed the rigid interpretation of that process, such as an increase of incomes entails rising consumption and low level of revenues make the demand-side steady depending on the variation of global demand in relation to the relative incomes.[10] Even though disposable income is one of the main determinants in consumption and, therefore, no other variable – wealth or interest rate – plays a key role,[11] the global demand is more affected by a sociologic determinism in which a portion of income spent is fortuitous for certain commodities, more linked with luxury and leisure time, and another is constant, linked with goods to satisfy basic necessities. Hence, a drop in the level of incomes would be estimated as transitory and it would not affect the pattern of consumption,[12] which can be observed through the stock of the durable consumption goods listed in the inventory. This sociological determinism is driven by concepts such as desire, taste, fashion, attitudes and emulation, furnishing both economic and cultural spheres of the family unit, moving the individual beyond his budget and feeling at the same time a particular attraction for certain commodities whose goal is not to cover primary necessities. Now individuals' desire is to see the family in a state of well-being. Surely, a dependent variable to achieve such an aim is the constant fluctuation of prices, which exert a direct influence on purchasing power.

With the economic indicators we have available for our study – the list of both Castilian general prices and wages through the index elaborated by Reher-Ballesteros,[13] and the Marquis de la Ensenada census which gives us an estimation of social classes' purchasing power and distribution of income – we are able to portray the purchasing power of social groups for a specific territory of south-eastern Spain, the Kingdom of Murcia, as well as to track inequalities through occupational sectors. Unfortunately, this census was made in 1756 and provides only an immobile and static picture of social group incomes, which can only be interpreted for the short term. However, this source is crucial as it enables us to visualize the purchasing power not only of the population as a whole, but also for social strata, and, in particular, for consumer behaviour as we have analysed through our sample of probate inventories.

---

[10]   Modigliani, F., *The Collected Papers of Franco Modigliani*, (eds) A. Abel, S. Johnson (Cambridge, MA: MIT Press, 1980–89). Dusenberry, J.S., *Income*.

[11]   Keynes, J.M., *The General Theory of Employment, Interest and Money* (London: Macmillan, 1936).

[12]   Friedman, M., *The Theory of the Consumption Function* (Princeton: Princeton University Press, 1957).

[13]   Reher, D.S. and Ballesteros, S., 'Precios y salarios en Castilla la Nueva: la construcción de un índice de salarios reales', *Revista de Historia Económica* (XI) (1993), no. 1, pp. 101–51. For Castilian prices see also: Hamilton, E.J., *American Treasure and the Price Revolution in Spain, 1501–1650* (Cambridge, MA: Harvard University Press, 1934). From the same author: *War and Prices in Spain, 1651–1800* (Cambridge, MA: Harvard University Press, 1974).

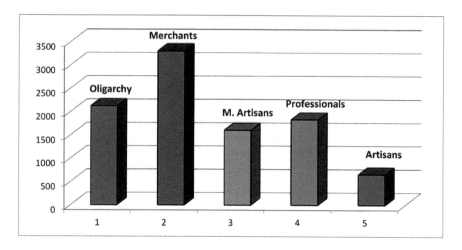

Chart 7.1   Estimated average of annual incomes in 'reales'. *Source:* A.H.P.M.,
             Respuestas Particulares al Catastro de la Ensenada (1752–55),
             Hacienda, L. 3845.

Chart 7.1 illustrates the estimated average of earnings per annum corresponding
to different social groups whose consumer choices and expenditure have been
analysed in the sample of probate inventories, divided by occupational and social
categories.[14] Peak earnings were reached by the merchant group and the lowest
level by the artisan group. Strikingly, the oligarchy – rich clergymen, noblemen
and notable people with important political positions in institutions such as the
council, church, court or army – were traditionally those with the highest economic
power, but in the second half of the eighteenth century were progressively losing
their economic supremacy.[15] As can be observed in Chart 7.1, master artisan,
professionals' incomes remained stable, on average. These estimates of annual
incomes allow us to measure inequality in the distribution of income by means of
the Gini index. As the data of incomes are only for the year 1756, it is not possible
to track inequalities and measure them over time. However, I have computed the

---

[14]   The number of cases studied is 273, related to the whole sample of probate
inventories, in which we specified the total number corresponding to each socio-professional
category. We have arranged this chart through individuals that appear in our sample of
probate inventories (see Table 7.1), whose annual income is also detailed in the Marquis
de la Ensenada's census. Thus, we have been able to estimate the average of incomes for
different socio-professional categories.
[15]   However, this way of estimating the average of annual incomes can be biased,
as most of socio-professional groups of the *Ancien Regime*, especially those related to
the oligarchy, were extremely unequal according with their socio-economic status. Such
inequality can be attested from Charts 7.2 to 7.6. This issue can also be applied to those
groups who lived in urban or rural areas, their annual incomes being different depending
on where they lived.

inequalities for that particular year in order to have a basic measurement regarding what was occurring during the second half of the eighteenth century in households with diverse socio-economic levels.

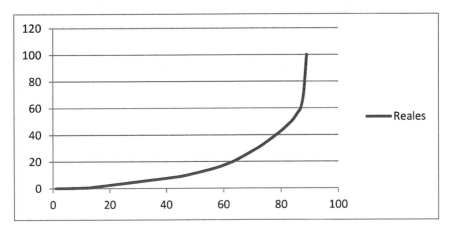

Chart 7.2   Lorenz curve for local oligarchy incomes. *Incomes in 'reales'.

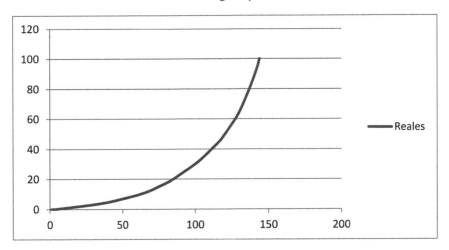

Chart 7.3   Lorenz curve for merchant incomes. *Incomes in 'reales'.

As can be seen from Chart 7.2 to Chart 7.6 the higher inequalities in the distribution of incomes correspond with upper social groups such as the oligarchy and merchant classes, then inequalities become slightly less pronounced among the middle social groups – master artisans, professionals and liberals, and artisans.[16] Thus, the wealth

------

[16]   For drawing the curve of Lorenz, which shows the inequalities of the level of incomes among social groups, we have calculated the Gini index through the computation

is more homogeneously distributed in the last group, whose purchasing power was
more affected by the shifts in prices during the eighteenth century. The oligarchy
hardly noticed any important variation in its buying power; nevertheless this group
had important economic losses by comparison to the merchant group whose level
of income was higher and purchasing power barely fluctuated during the second
half of the eighteenth century. However, in the long term, all social groups were
affected by a steadly increasing tendency in their buying power. Such acceleration
is more notable after the first half of the nineteenth century; the second half of the
eighteenth century was the period in which this tendency started.

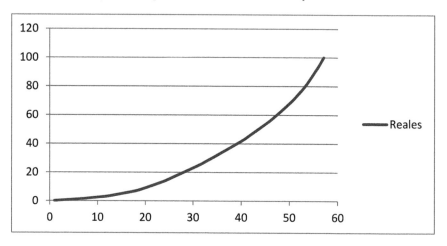

Chart 7.4   Lorenz curve for master artisan incomes. *Incomes in 'reales'.

There was more wealth, but it was distributed with increasing inequality in
urban economies such as Murcia or Cartagena in which there was a dependency
on both agricultural and imported goods. This produced a consumer elite whose
expenditures for basic necessities took up a relatively small portion of their
incomes, and whose demand for quality imports was surprisingly constant even in
periods of economic recession. Hence, unequal income distribution heightened the

---

of the accumulative sum of income (p) related to each social group and the number of
individuals that have such income; where 'q' is the percentage of the accumulative
frequencies of income related to each socio-professional category:

$$I_G = \frac{\sum_{i=1}^{n-1}(p_i - q_i)}{\sum_{i=1}^{n-1}p_i}$$

See Pérez López, C., *Estadística Aplicada a través de Excel* (Madrid: Universidad
Complutense, 2002), p. 236.

effect of urban elasticities of demand, strongest in middle social groups, while the elite group maintained a similar inelesticity for imported commodities.[17]

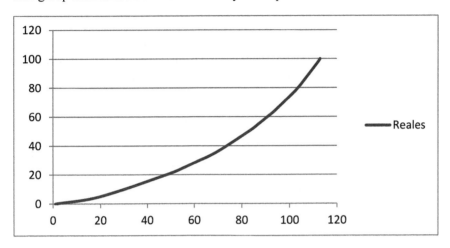

Chart 7.5   Lorenz curve for professional incomes. *Incomes in 'reales'.

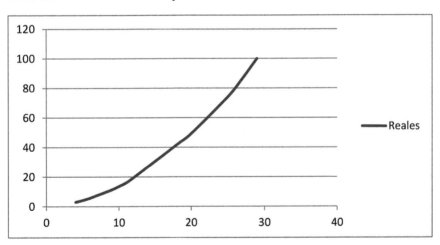

Chart 7.6   Lorenz curve for artisan incomes. *Incomes in 'reales'. *Source:* A.H.P.M., Respuestas Particulares al Catastro de la Ensenada (1752–55), Hacienda, L. 3845.

---

[17]   See the work by David Ringrose, who noticed similar effects in the economy of Madrid and its influence in the Spanish territory: Ringrose, D., *Spain.*

These indicators show that the south-eastern Spanish eighteenth-century population, especially the middle social groups, began enjoying better lifestyles and increased their household expenditure for beverages such as tea, coffee and chocolate[18] – see Appendix F, p. 279 – which allowed people to enjoy better nutrition, therefore increasing their life expectancy. Household earnings were also absorbed by groceries and goods related to the textile sector. However, due to the progresive adoption of better standards of living and the steady level of purchasing power in south-eastern Spain, during the second half of the eighteenth century, a third group of commodities, luxury items, such as sumptuous clothes, domestic furniture and interior embellishment, also had an important influence on household expenditures – see Chart 7.13.

The regression analysis model offers us an accurate method to analyse choices and shifts occurring in household consumption, which can be measured by means of inventories, as well as the value of durable and semi-durable commodities. For that purpose, we have used the OLS method, calculating t-statistic and standards of error by white method robust for heteroscedasticity.[19] We determine the variables

---

[18]   McCants, A., 'Poor Consumers', pp. 172–200.

[19]   See Deaton, A., 'Demand Analysis', in *Handbook of Econometrics*, Griliches, Z. and Intriligator, M. (eds) (Amsterdam: North Holland, 1994). Ramos Palencia, F., *Pautas de consumo*, p. 87. The development of econometric models, which collects consumption data, poses some problems of a statistical nature. One of the most important features is the possible presence of heterocedasticity, which may arise, once basic needs are fulfilled. Therefore, families with high incomes have a larger surplus of wage that can be saved or spent to a greater or lesser extent. Thus, to estimate a model that collects data on consumption it would be natural to expect that the figures, for consumer spending on goods, had a higher variance or dispersion in families with higher incomes than in those with lower ones. Econometrically means greater dispersion of the residuals as increases the value of the endogenous variable set. Heteroscedasticity does not destroy unbiased properties and consistency of estimators obtained by ordinary least squares (OLS). However, these estimators (those with a smaller variance or dispersion) are efficient even asymptotically (that is, when the sample size is large enough), which undermines the credibility to establish confidence intervals and contrast of scenarios using the statistical t and F. In fact, if we estimated by means of OLS allowing the presence of heteroscedasticity, we could not find a statistically significant coefficient when in reality it would exist. In sum, in the case confirmed of the existence of a heterocedastic disturbance and as additional condition, results, of other erroneous specification contrasts do not reveal other weaknesses in the econometric model, therefore we should consider a new estimate. In principle, if we know the structure of the shocks of the model, this estimation is least squares generalized, whose estimates have a smaller variance than those obtained by OLS provided that the estimate of the variance-covariance matrix of the disturbance is obtained consistently. Unfortunately, the structure of the disturbance is rarely known with precision. Given this predicament, the most common procedure to reduce the heteroscedasticity of the econometric model is the logarithmic transformation of the variables used. This is possible because the transformation compresses the scale that measured such variables. Also, an advantage of the logarithmic transformation is that the coefficient (slope) of the explanatory variable measures the elasticity of the exogenous variable on the explanatory variable

for the chronologic period from 1730 to 1808 due to their flexibility of estimation, which is a feature that characterized the bulk of current empirical works on production, costs, utility and demand-side, with a trans-logarithmic function[20] that develops a second order Taylor's series around the point $\ln X = 0$ obtaining:

$$\ln X \approx B_0 \sum_{i=1}^{M} (\frac{\partial \ln X}{\partial \ln a_i}) \ln a_i + \frac{1}{2} \sum_{i=1}^{M} \sum_{j=1}^{M} \left(\frac{\partial^2 \ln X}{\partial \ln a_i \ln a_j} \right) \ln a_i \ln a_j$$

In this model all derivatives are evaluated on the point of the expansion of the series. If we identified these derivatives as quotients applying the symmetry of 'a' partial derivatives, f(x) will be expressed in this way:

$$\ln X = B_0 + B_1 \ln a_1 + \ldots + B_M \ln a_M + \partial_{11} \left(\frac{1}{2} \ln^2 a_1 \right) + \partial_{12} \ln \partial_1 \ln \partial_2 + \rho_{22} \left(\frac{1}{2} \ln^2 a_2 \right) + \ldots + \partial_{MM} (\frac{1}{2} \ln^2 a_m)$$

If δ_{ij} is zero, it comes down to a Cobb-Douglas function with a constant unitary elasticity of substitution. This function is based, as we see, on a simple double-logarithmic transformation of all variables used, with the exception, obviously, if dummy variables are applied. The primary objective is to find determining factors on the consumption of durable and semi-durable goods, so that knowing the evolution of variables associated with family size, wealth, gender of the individual or the type of occupation we can determine the behaviour of spending on durable goods belonging to the family unit, an issue for which there is little scholarly statistical evidence. The main point sheds light on the influence of different groups of commodities –

---

or endogenous, that is, the percentage change in the exogenous variable to a percentage change in the regressor. To a lesser extent, as it is well known, another problem that may arise is the presence of autocorrelation, which is associated with the existence of cycles or trends in the endogenous variable of the model (in this case domestic consumption) and the omission of relevant explanatory variables. Autocorrelation occurs when the disturbance of the econometric model is correlated with some of the regressors. It could be measured, the degree of autocorrelation, through the known Durbin-Watson statistic. Values close to 2 mean the absence of autocorrelation. Finally, multicollinearity can also arise between different explanatory variables included in the model. By considering the following working hypothesis, obviously, wealth and consumer income are determining factors in consumer spending. However, it might be that when we get information on income and wealth, these two variables are correlated, since individuals with greater wealth are those who generally have higher incomes. Therefore, although theoretically the wealth and income help to explain consumer behaviour, in the sample it can be relatively difficult to discern the influence of each variable in household spending.

[20] Berndt, E. and Christensen, L., 'The Translog Function and the Substitution of Equipment, Structures, and Labour in US Manufacturing, 1929–1968', *Journal of Econometrics*, vol. 1, no. 1 (1973), pp. 81–114. Deaton, A. and Muellbauer, J., *Economics and Consumer Behaviour* (New York: Cambridge University Press, 1980).

textiles, luxury goods and beverage items – which exert an influence on consumer choices that take place in households for the period from 1730 to 1808. In the textile group we have organized cloth items into categories as well as household goods such as curtains, upholstery or decorative items. In the luxury goods category we have included domestic items such as mirrors, clocks, porcelains, chinaware, books and buffets. Regarding items for beverages, this group includes all kinds of domestic utensils – coffee, tea or chocolate-pots, 'jícaras' [bowls], 'salvillas' [trays] or cups – used for serving drinks such as chocolate, coffee or tea in social gatherings: the so-call British 'tea-hour' whose Spanish equivalent is the 'chocolate-hour'. The equation of the econometric model can be expressed as follows:

$$\text{Ln Household Consumption} = A_0 + A_1 \text{LnBeverage items} + A_2 \text{LnLuxury items} + A_3 \text{LnTextile items} + A_4 \text{LnPrices} + A_5 \text{LnWealth} + A_6 \text{Urban Development} + A_7 \text{Gender} + A_8 \text{Agrarian Sector} + A_9 \text{Oligarchy Sector} + \varepsilon_t$$

I have obviously put together the different categories of commodities such as textiles, luxury goods and items for beverages using 1756[21] as index year for depreciating their price. By using the OLS method I have firstly estimated the prices of textiles purchased (see Table 7.3) and secondly the volume of textile consumed (Table 7.6), therefore I have measured textiles as a dependent in logarithmic variable. The goal is to compare the degree of dependency of textiles consumed in the household unit with the expenditure on luxury items and goods for beverages. This idea challenges the scholarly argument that as wealth increases, the expenditure on durable and semi-durable goods decreases.[22] Our argument is the opposite, the per capita expenditure (in 'reales')[23] and volume of consumption (in units) in the families of south-eastern Castile increased, as household wealth rose, being the highest expenditure for household commodities related to social groups with middle level wealth – see Tables 7.4 and 7.5. Therefore, the multiplication of a wide range of textile expenditures, especially in the second half of the eighteenth century, and the logarithmic adjustment – attributed to the modern consumer as opposed to the semi-logarithmic curve, characteristic of the traditional consumer – increases the expenditure of other groups of household commodities, revealing a shift in consumer

---

[21] 1756 was more or less a stable year with the absence of any sort of economic crisis, epidemic disaster or politic turbulence such as war. See Reher, D.S. and Ballesteros, E., 'Precios'.

[22] Carole Shammas estimated the consumption of durable and semi-durable goods in pre-industrial societies in England and the North American colonies between 1500–1800. Shammas, C., *The Pre-Industrial*. Alice Jones accounted per capita consumption in American British Colonies concluding that consumers' durable goods of household furnishing and equipment for consumer use decrease as wealth increase. Jones, A., *Wealth of Nation to Be* (New York: Columbia University Press, 1980), p. 110.

[23] For the estimation of the per capita expenditure we have estimated, for the whole period, the average of the ratios among textiles, luxury and beverage goods with the family size.

behaviour, where rising consumption is characterized by comfort, new tastes and desires, resulting in better standards of living and lifestyles[24].

In the regression analysis of Table 7.3, we have used as explanatory variables the level of wealth and urban development, groups belonging to agrarian occupations – named in the table as 'sector' – and gender component. Thus, the dummy values have been given to urban development (unit values if an individual lived in an urban area, and zero for people who lived in rural areas), agrarian group (unit values if an individual belongs to rural occupations and zero if individual belongs to another social group) and gender component (unit values if the individual is male and zero if the individual is female).[25] Even though the statistical results are not as good as we would like, they do show a robust consistency among them when we introduce the explanatory variables described above. The results obtained in Table 7.3 show that although R^2 figures are low, there exists a positive correlation in all estimations as regression statistics and the analysis of variance demonstrates, consequently, there is an elastic demand for luxury items as people find rapid substitutions among that group. The relations among the possession of textile commodities such as fine upholstery and embellishment items as well as luxury commodities such as mirrors, clocks, and porcelains are positively related as they indicate a tendency toward comfort and better lifestyle. In a lesser degree the same occurs with the possession of items related to the use of drinks in social gatherings such as tea, coffee or chocolate utensils – pots, cups, trays (see Table 7.3).

Table 7.3   OLS estimates of household consumption, Southern Castile (Spain), 1730–1808. Dependent variable in logarithmic: price (in 'reales') of textiles possessed. (Continues over the page.)

Regression Statistics	
Coefficient of correlation	0.6576
R^2	0.4325
R^2 adjusted	0.3809
Standard Error of Estimate	1.1049
Observations	73.0000

[24]   Regarding the Spanish case this idea was foreseen by Ramon Maruri and Andrés Hoyo Aparicio, in whose study for the northern Spanish case, the area of Santander, shows that a wide range of textiles, consumed in the household during the eighteenth and nineteenth centuries, multiplied the consumption of other commodities, especially household items, entailing a better lifestyle in the family unit. See 'Pautas de consumo textil en una sociedad rural: Liébana (Cantabria), 1760–1860', *Revista de Historia Económica*, Año XXI (2003), no. extraordinario, pp. 107–39.

[25]   We have to bear in mind that all these estimations have been made through probate inventories. As we work with the stock of products, which does not allow us to know the flow of purchases within the household, the conclusions that we arrive are very approximate.

Analysis of Variance

	Freedom Degree	Square Sum	Square Average	F-Statistics	F critic value
Regression	6.0000	61.3964	10.2327	8.3825	0.0000
Residuals	66.0000	80.5680	1.2207		
Total	72.0000	141.9643			

	Coefficient	Standard Error	T-Statistic	Probability	Inferior 95%	Superior 95%	Inferior 95,0%	Superior 95,0%
Interception	2.2609	1.2598	1.7946	0.0773	-0.2544	4.7762	-0.2544	4.7762
Wealth	0.1823	0.1275	1.4291	0.1577	-0.0724	0.4369	-0.0724	0.4369
Luxury Item Prices	0.2206	0.0932	2.3660	0.0209	0.0345	0.4068	0.0345	0.4068
Beverage Item Prices	0.0705	0.0791	0.8908	0.3763	-0.0875	0.2285	-0.0875	0.2285
SECTOR	-0.2182	0.3378	-0.6459	0.5206	-0.8926	0.4562	-0.8926	0.4562
URBAN	0.2908	0.3479	0.8359	0.4062	-0.4038	0.9855	-0.4038	0.9855
GENDER	-0.5235	0.2965	-1.7656	0.0821	-1.1155	0.0685	-1.1155	0.0685

Table 7.4   Household expenditure (in 'reales') 'per capita' according to level of wealth (1730–1808)[26]

Wealth Groups	Textile Items	Luxury Items	Beverage Items
0 > 10000	59.15	52.42	25.33
10000 > 50000	163.83	133.16	88.35
50000 > 100000	88.88	44.84	15.63
> 100000	240.54	595.93	233.21
Total	138.10	206.59	90.63

Source: A.H.P.M., probate inventories.

Table 7.5   Household consumption (in units) 'per capita' according to level of wealth (1730–1808)

Wealth Groups	Textile Items	Luxury Items	Beverage Items
0 > 10000	1.34	0.45	0.36
10000 > 50000	1.28	0.44	0.45
50000 > 100000	2.04	1.25	1.93
> 100000	3.54	7.92	5.70
Total	2.05	2.52	2.11

Source: A.H.P.M., probate inventories.

Thus, R^2 is close to 0.50, which means that approximately 50 per cent of all expenditure on textile consumption in the household could be explained by the level of wealth, the choices on consumption of textiles denoting that textile commodities absorbed more of the household budgets than luxury and beverage items, as well as the degree of urban development, the main occupation of the breadwinner and the gender component. Another relevant interpretation that could be made from the value of commodities – see Table 7.3 – is that the expenditure on textiles does not depend only on the level of wealth but also to other factors such as the purchase of luxury goods and the gender component – women were the main agents that introduced new fashions and contributed to develop a new sort of domesticity in the household. Hence, the consumption

---

[26] The group of textile items includes French textiles such as 'Bretaña' textiles, 'briaçu', 'cabriolé', textiles made of 'Cambray', textiles made of 'crea', 'desavillé', textiles with the French trade mark that is signalled in the inventory and textiles made of 'tripé'. In this group we have also include the traditional 'basquiñas' [top petticoat], 'chals' [shawls], jacket, 'coafia' [hair net], 'jubon' [doublet], suits and mantillas. Related to the luxury items we have included chinaware, household cloth made of 'indianas' [calicoes], porcelains, mirrors, books and clocks. In the third group, beverage items, the following items are included: chocolate-pots, tea-pots, coffee-pots, 'salvillas' [trays], 'jícaras' [bowls] and cups.

of luxury goods as well as utensils for beverages also depended on the same factors as the consumption of textiles. There was a high tendency, especially in the second-half of the eighteenth century, in which the gender variable plays a very important role in relation with new domestic practices. It is unsurprising that a significant amount of female inventories contain a strong relation between the purchase of textiles and that of household furniture and ornaments. The logarithmic adjustment curves of the prices of luxury and beverage goods, as well as wealth, show the positive correlation among those variables and the consumption of textiles, which is a feature that characterizes the consumer of pre-industrial society with the economic trends of the modern era, in which individuals could progressively enjoy of a wide variety of commodities having multiple choices and increasing the per capita consumption – see Charts 7.7, 7.8 and 7.9. According to the data available in the regression analysis, the predictions estimated show a growing trend in the household expenditure. But this does not mean that a 'consumer revolution' took place, as McKendrick[27] described in the industrial transformation of the English society. Nevertheless, individuals of south-eastern Spain with diverse levels of wealth purchased more goods, stimulating thus local economies.

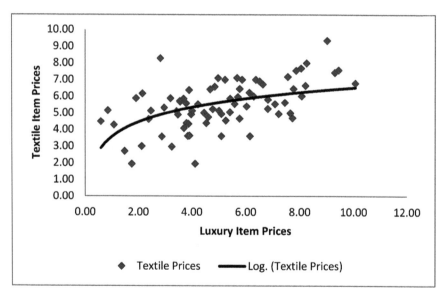

Chart 7.7   Adjusted regression curve of the price of luxury goods (1730–1808)

---

[27]   McKendrick, N., 'The Consumer Revolution'.

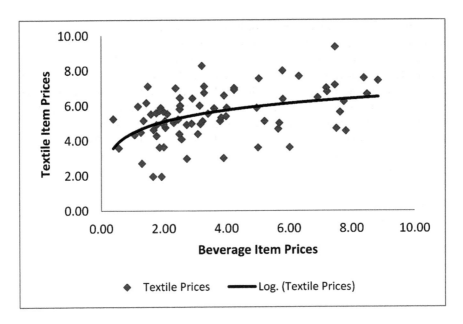

Chart 7.8   Adjusted regression curve of the price of beverage goods (1730–1808)

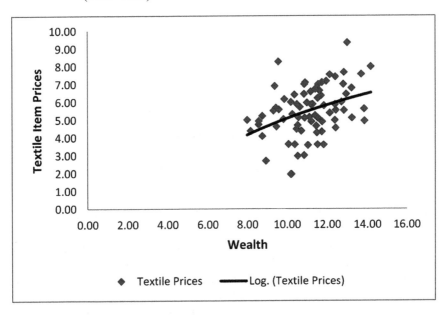

Chart 7.9   Adjusted regression curve of wealth (1730–1808)

In the estimation of the quantity of items purchased – see Table 7.6 – we have taken into account the same explanatory variables used for that of household expenditure with the addition, in this case, of the family size. As we can observe – in Table 7.5 – there is a positive correlation in the rising consumption of units per capita related to family size and the level of wealth of the household unit. The economic interpretation of the model shows that there is a positive correlation between consumption of textiles and the rise in purchase of household furniture and utensils for beverages – see Charts 7.10, 7.11 and 7.12 – in which the family size, gender, occupation, wealth and place of residence – whether rural or urban – are the key factors for a full comprehension of the new model of consumer behaviour. Although the statistical data is not as complete as economic historians would like, the results are consistent and show that the rising consumption of textiles in the family unit, with a given level of wealth, entailed a positive expenditure on luxury items for embellishing the home, as well as utensils for enjoying the 'chocolate hour' during social gatherings. This implies that an increase in stock or in the quantity of goods inventorized would effectively mean an increase in levels of consumption.

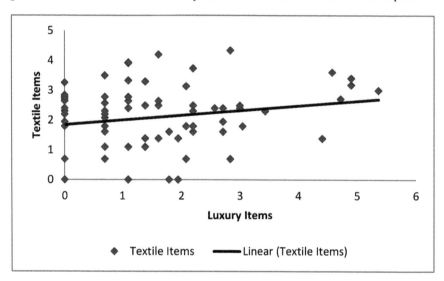

Chart 7.10   Adjusted regression curve of volume of luxury items (1730–1808)

New attitudes towards lifestyles, a role essentially played by women, as inventories of their possessions show, corroborate the idea that comfort began to take hold in pre-industrial societies, which thus entered a new stage of slow economic transformation.[28] Another relevant feature is the urban development of the location in which the family lives. The special characteristic of the Kingdom of Murcia is that

---

[28]   See the case of the Castilian interior, the area of Palencia, studied by Ramos Palencia, F. and Nicolini, E.A., 'A New Method', pp. 145–77.

rural areas of cities of Murcia and Cartagena, especially 'lugares de campo y huerta', are very close to urban places, a crucial factor which increased the consumption of rural families for urban goods. This issue made it possible for rural families' expenditures, such as those absorbed by household textiles made of 'indianas', to reach a similar level to urban areas during last decades of the eighteenth century.

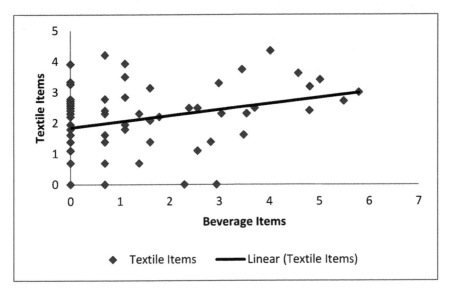

Chart 7.11   Adjusted regression curve of volume of beverage items (1730–1808)

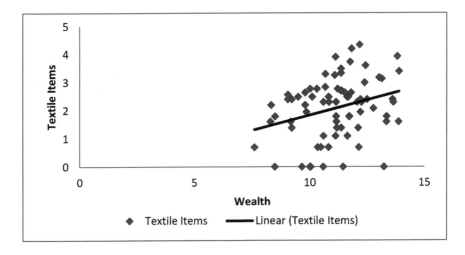

Chart 7.12   Adjusted regression curve of volume of wealth (1730–1808)

Furthermore, it is important to note that the geographic factor, due to the closeness of both rural and urban areas in the Kingdom of Murcia, was not the only cause contributing to improve the household lifestyle and rise in family consumption. As can be seen in the adjusted regression curve – Charts 7.16 and 7.19 – wealth, as an explanatory variable, exerted a positive influence in relation to the purchase of textiles over time. The low relative prices, especially in the second half of the eighteenth century, eased the positive weight of the correlation of wealth-consumption, fostering the progressive concentration of wealth of social groups with diverse economic resources. Certainly, this was one of the major features that characterized the development of a 'sense of domestic enviroment', meaning that a larger proportion of the family budget could be spent on industrial articles such as textiles and other durable and semi-durable goods, as we saw above in articles such as luxury goods and utensils for beverages.

There is a very small variation of real wealth, especially during the decades of the second quarter of the eighteenth century, which was stable in the absence of economic crisis or any turmoil that could have caused any fluctuation in prices. The role of wealth, real assets and financial power of individuals in determining consumption was becoming a substantially important factor. If we add to this the role of wealth and the function played by permanent incomes – see Chart 7.1 – the consumer choice hypothesis could be plausible, in which the consumer was the rational agent that maximized the utility of commodities allocated to the flow of economic resources to a given pattern of consumption during the life cycle.

We see a gradual increase in the consumption of semi-durable goods with rising levels of capital – see Table 7.3 and Appendix E, p. 273. Nevertheless, in relative terms – see Table 7.4 and 7.7 – when a household's wealth increases the shifts in consumption among family members are more static since they tend to reflect traditional consumer behaviour. This occurs in families where their consumer choices are more traditional and less open to modernity – linked with foreign values and the consumption of new objects. This implied that families with less wealth, and therefore smaller incomes, had a marginal propensity to consume durable goods in higher proportions than those families with higher levels of income. Consequently, wealth – expressed here as the total sum of general assets reported in a probate inventory – has a major bearing on the final consumer decisions regarding the purchase of new goods. This fact ratifies the results of the estimated demand function for pre-industrial household economies.

Table 7.6   OLS estimates of household consumption, Southern Castile (Spain), 1730–1808. Dependent variable in logarithmic: volume textiles possessed

Regression Statistics

Coefficient of correlation	0.479362891
R^2	0.229788781
R^2 adjusted	0.148099712
Standard Error of Estimate	0.994453635
Observations	74

Analysis of Variance

	Freedom Degree	Square Sum	Square Average	F-Statistics	F critic value
Regression	7	19.47296107	2.781851582	2.8129685	0.012601939
Residuals	66	65.26991016	0.988938033		
Total	73	84.74287123			

	Coefficient	Standard Error	T-Statistic	Probability	Inferior 95%	Superior 95%	Inferior 95,0%	Superior 95,0%
Interception	-0.44736469	1.022527872	-0.437508553	0.6631709	-2.48890743	159417805	-2.48890743	1.594178054
Wealth	-0.069123875	0.137889705	-0.501287397	0.6178368	-0.34443554	0.20618779	-0.34443554	0.206187791
Luxury Items	0.236746049	0.101126359	2.341091393	0.0222575	0.034840761	0.43865134	0.034840761	0.438651338
Beverage Items	0.203983868	0.103423193	1.972322284	0.0527652	-0.0025072	0.41047493	-0.0025072	0.410474933
Family Size	0.284836432	0.178496078	1.595757373	0.1153206	-0.07154248	0.64121535	-0.07154248	0.641215346
Urban	0.019025421	0.288924018	0.06584922	0.9476969	-0.55782999	0.59588083	-0.55782999	0.59588083
Gender	-0.2530697	0.268781461	-0.941544478	0.3498595	-0.78970919	0.28356979	-0.78970919	0.283569795
Sector	0.38297054	0.31660763	1.20960616	0.230745	-0.24915698	1.01509807	-0.24915698	1.01509807

Table 7.7   Percentages over average of household consumption according to
               the family size (1730–1808)

Wealth Groups	Textile	Luxury Goods	Beverage Goods
0 > 10000	2.30	1.87	1.64
10000 > 50000	2.43	0.82	0.29
50000 > 100000	0.63	0.30	0.07
> 100000	0.37	0.79	0.48
Total	2.43	1.87	1.87

Source: A.H.P.M., probate inventories.

The wide range of textile commodities consumed in households of south-eastern
Castile is proof that an individual's expenditures were not only governed by income
constraints in the last decades of the eighteenth century, which we could define as
a period of rising consumption.[29] People also started to show an interest in finding
satisfactory cheap substitutes.[30] The rising consumption of 'indianas' – 'indiennes'
or 'calicoes' – is a very good example of that substitution process. Chart 7.13
shows the high presence of textiles, followed by luxury and goods for beverages,
in south-eastern Castilian households. We have estimated the percentages related
to the textile, luxury and items for beverage listed in the inventories, with the total
records listed in the sample numbering 10,491.

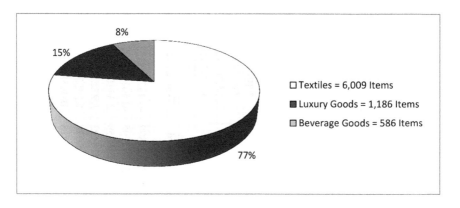

Chart 7.13   Presence of diverse goods in south-eastern Castile households
               (1730–1808). *Source:* A.H.P.M., probate inventories.

---

[29]   See the works by: Hoyo Aparicio, A. and Maruri Villanueva, R., 'Pautas de consumo',
pp. 107–39; Ramos Palencia, F. and Nicolini, E.A., 'A New Method', pp. 145–77.
[30]   See Berndt, E.R. and Christensen, L.R. 'The Internal Structure of Functional
Relationships: Separability, Substitution, and Aggregation', *The Review of Economic
Studies*, vol. 40, No. 3 (July, 1973), pp. 403–10.

People could dress in beautiful, colourful clothes and embellish their homes with curtains, carpets, upholstery and tapestries. These social inclinations involved shifts in consumer behaviour and were an important force that made demand rise during individuals' life cycle, leading towards a slow, but progressive, pattern of acceleration in global demand. Families with modest levels of wealth were involved in the process of rising consumption, and began to purchase cheap items emulating the expensive possesions of the middle-upper classes – see Appendix F, p. 279.

Although social impulses, which make the demand curve upwards or downwards, are quite difficult to measure in order to determine dependent variables that have an influence on the demand-side, a very important factor that fuels the demand of goods of an individual during his/her life-course is the presence of a labour force in his/her household. It has been shown that individuals with more than two incomes in their household have a wide range of commodities listed in their inventories, especially commodities with an inelastic demand such as luxury items like porcelains, clocks or high quality textiles and groceries such as tea, coffee or sugar. For instance, Don Vicente Galiana, merchant of textiles in the city of Murcia, had 13,200 'reales' as annual income and his spouse, as a shopkeeper, contributed to the household economy, thus increasing the household income.[31] His inventory reveals a variety of the above-mentioned commodities.[32] Don Pasqual Soria Seller, master apothecary, with 3,000 'reales' as annual income, had all his family members, five in total, working in the apothecary shop,[33] which means that due to the intensive labour of some households with modest revenues, they could thrive and achieve a lifestyle similar to those of higher economic levels. Don Pasqual Soria's inventory[34] lists commodities such as jewellery, porcelains and fine textiles as an example of the importance of the influence of the household reallocation of economic resources serving to stimulate the demand of goods.

7.2. Examining the 'Industrious Revolution' Theory in the Kingdom of Murcia (1730–1808)

By analysing the probate inventories of artisan and peasant groups – see Appendix A, p. 241 – we can determine whether the industrious revolution took place in south-eastern Spanish society, examining the consumption of particular goods such as household furniture, luxury goods and clothing. Related to the artisan groups there was, in some periods, less consumption of certain goods by comparison to those

---

[31]   A.H.P.M., Respuestas Particulares al Catastro de la Ensenada (1752–55), Hacienda, L. 3845.

[32]   A.H.P.M., sig. 2703, fols. 1r.–64v., escr. Costa Irles, Antonio.

[33]   A.H.P.M., Respuestas Particulares al Catastro de la Ensenada (1752–55), Hacienda, L. 3845.

[34]   A.H.P.M., sig. 2804, fols. 84r.–153v.

purchased by the rest of population – see Appendix A, p. 241. In this particular case, the industrious revolution did not take place. Through the comparison of the average goods consumed by artisans and the rest of population, even though certain goods were mostly consumed by such artisan groups, we could not say that there was an industrious revolution on a large scale within this social sector – see Appendix A, p. 241. However, from our data of probate inventories, we can deduce that there were certainly some symptoms of an industrious revolution, as in some cases artisans stimulated the consumption of specific goods such as some French textiles ('duray' or 'desavillé') or traditional clothes ('basquiñas', 'cofias' or 'mantillas') in the second half of the eighteenth century, and household furniture, only in the first half of the eighteenth century.

The general tendency was a progressive fall in consumption of these goods by artisans when compared with the rest of the population during the second half of the eighteenth century, thus we cannot strongly affirm that the industrious revolution took place on a significant scale in south-eastern Castile. We have to take into account that most of these products came from the market, which is a fact that does not entail an industrious revolution, and did not provoke an increase in production. Most of these goods belong to the textile sector, and south-eastern Spain, especially the area of Murcia, was not specialized in the production of textile products. Moreover, as we have seen in Part III, the possession of looms and industrial artefacts – see Table 5.2 – to manufacture textiles decreased in Murcia during the eighteenth century. This demonstrates that only goods from the market could satisfy the local demand. For instance, regarding some French commodities such as 'briaçu' [a French garment knotted with silver buckles as described in probate inventories], textiles made of 'cambray'[35] and items with the French 'trade-mark', the volume of consumption was higher by craftsmen in the first half of the eighteenth century. Nevertheless, a shift occurred in the second half of the century and a higher consumption of these goods by the rest of population distanced that of the artisan group – see Appendix A, p. 241.

Some other French commodities such as 'cabriolé', 'pompadour' [French high-quality fabric] or textiles made of 'trué' were consumed more by the rest of the population during the first half of the century. But a shift occurred during the second half of the century: the consumption of these French commodities was higher among the artisan groups. The purchase of 'desavillé'[36] and textiles made of 'duray' did not exist at all in the first half of the eighteenth century, but in the second half of the century, craftsmen's inventories listed more of those items than the inventories of the rest of the population – see Appendix A, p. 241.

---

[35]   For the description of all of these items and materials see the glossary (p. 374) and Dávila Corona, R.M., Duran y Pujol, M. and García Fernández, M., *Diccionario histórico de telas y tejidos. Castellano-Catalán* (Valladolid: Junta de Castilla y León, Consejería de Cultura y Turismo, 2004), pp. 66, 76, 106, 197.

[36]   See Boutin-Arnaud, M.N. and Tasmadjian, S., *Le vêtement* (Paris: Éditions Nathan, 1997).

On the other hand, 'buffets' and textiles made of 'crea' were predominantly listed in craftsmen's inventories, and the consumption of these two commodities reveals that in this particular case most of the goods came from the market, by means of French traders, and not from the local productive forces, which demonstrates that the industrious revolution did not occur – see the data of Appendix A, p. 241.

Regarding the other category of commodities, 'majo's' attire, the results of our data sheet – Appendix A, p. 241 – show little variation by comparison to the category of French commodities. Garments such as 'basquiñas' [top petticoats], 'chals' [shawls], mantillas and suits were listed in higher amounts in craftsmen inventories than in other social groups' inventories during the entire century, whereas items such as jackets, 'cofias' [hair nets] and 'jubones' [doublets] were listed less in artisan's inventories during the period from 1730–69. This pattern changed in the last decades of the eighteenth century, when artisans listed more of these commodities. Therefore, toward the last quarter of the eighteenth century there was a clear predominance among craftsmen for consuming the 'majo's' outfit.

In the case of items relating to household furniture, such a prevalence did not exist by comparison to the previous category of goods; only mirrors, household cloth made of 'indiana',[37] clocks and 'jicaras' [bowls] were consumed in higher volumes by artisan groups than other social categories. Chinaware, porcelains, items from China, books or other utensils for drinking beverages such as tea, coffee or chocolate were consumed in lesser proportions or were simply not consumed – see Appendix A, p. 241. Through the analysis of the social circulation of these categories of commodities related with clothing and interior decoration, which were related with French and traditional fashions, a new tendency toward taste and comfort was achieved entailing a better lifestyle. So can we establish, categorically, that the industrious revolution took place? We can surely affirm that there was a constant shift regarding consumer's choices, but was the artisan labour force the stimulus for the rising consumption of the above-mentioned commodities? We can gain some insight through Jan de Vries' explanations of the industrious revolution theory, which related to Becker's theory of the allocation of time:[38]

> ... proposing that a household that purchases market-supplied goods subject to a resource constraint of money income, and combines these goods with the labour and other resources of the household to produce what Becker call 'Z' the more basic commodities that directly enter the household utility function. The purchased goods should be thought of as ranging from items requiring very little household labour before they are transformed to the consumable 'Z' commodities (say tea), to those (say sheep) that require extensive labour

---

[37]   See Riello, G. and Parthasarath, P., *The Spinning World*, p. 411.

[38]   Becker, G., 'A theory of the Allocation of Time', *The Economic Journal*, 75 (1965), pp. 493–517.

before the transformation (to clothing) is complete. Correspondingly, the 'Z' commodities should be thought of as items of utility.[39]

Considering this affirmation, it could be said that in a south-eastern Spanish territory, the Kingdom of Murcia, an industrious revolution did not occur, though the foremost pillar of this theory, the artisan group, led shifts in changing tastes and patterns of consumption – see Appendix A, p. 241. Most of the goods that were consumed came from the market, but it did not provoke an increase in local production – see Chart 5.2. Our sample of inventories confirms the reduction in the possession of looms and textile artefacts, as well as domestic production of textiles such as linen, passing the percentage of looms in artisan households from approximately 12 per cent (for the period of 1730–69) to 3 per cent (from 1770 to 1808). The production of domestic linen in artisan workshops passed from approximately 17 per cent (from 1730 to 1769) to 12 per cent (from 1770 to 1808).[40] Such indicators are very low, showing that the productive forces of the household did not experience an increase. Thus, we can say that households became more market-dependant as consumers, but did not become more market-orientated as producers.

Examining probate inventories of the sample, as we have mentioned earlier, some goods, which could be defined as 'Z' commodities such as those related to interior decorations, clothing and drinks, have been found in higher proportions in artisans' inventories. Therefore, the precedent shifts in tastes seen in inventories of the inhabitants of the Kingdom of Murcia were linked with the composition of 'Z' commodities in artisan households, which shaped the supply-side in relation with affordable prices, as well as the elasticity in the demand of some goods when finding substitutive items. Some of these articles, textiles or household adornments

---

[39]   De Vries, J., 'Between the Purchasing', p. 256. Professor De Vries defined 'Z' commodities those which were produced at home intended for domestic use. Notwithstanding, in an economy like south-eastern Spain most of those commodities were not transformed at home, especially textiles. An important portion of goods were acquired from the external market. We keep the name 'Z' commodities, because they maintain the utility function as most of those items, mainly textiles, keep the elastic demand existing for an important number of substitutive goods. These commodities were certainly purchased from the market, but not to transform them as ready products – with the household labour, the majority of these goods entered into the household as manufactures. However, some local artisan families that kept looms and artifacts – it is necessary be aware of the falling possession of looms during the eighteenth century in the Kingdom of Murcia – were able to manufacture with their labour force raw materials, therefore, to produce some commodities for domestic use. But this is not the general case. See De Vries, J., *The Dutch Rural Economy in the Golden Age, 1500–1700* (New Haven: Yale University Press, 1974).

[40]   These percentages have been estimated over the total sample of inventories, 273, and the 74 inventories corresponding to artisans, observing the looms and artefacts listed in such inventories for the periods that go from 1730 to 1769 and 1770 to 1808. A.H.P.M. protocols from 2,786 to 11,375.

were substituted using imitations as they were expensive luxury commodities or goods that in earlier decades ordinary people could not afford.

The port of Cartagena is a paradigmatic example of market integration of the Spanish Mediterranean area, which provided commodities to the population in higher proportions than previous times – see Appendix G and H, pp. 287, 313. The relation of the artisan sector with commercial businesses of the Mediterranean area is one of the most relevant features of this market that could suggest a possible industrious revolution, which in fact did not occur – see Appendix A, G and H, pp. 241, 287, 313. The rising volumes of commodities related to clothing, interior decoration and colonial groceries in craftsmens' inventories made possible an economic flow in which those goods did not only increase or create the supply, but also stimulated consumption. This issue shows a positive tendency of particular local artisan workshops and merchant businesses, prompting an increase in consumption on the part of households close to this economic network.

The other socio-economic factor of the industrious revolution lies in the peasant population and is linked with the acquisition of new agrarian technological changes leading to an intensified land use, which sparked an increase in the agricultural production and population growth. The industrious revolution of areas such as north-western Europe or the British American colonies is characterized by an increase in the number of hours worked by peasant groups, who sacrificed their leisure time and dedicated more time to agricultural production – see Chart 7.14. Thus, the introduction of those new technologies as well as the intensification of working hours allowed the agrarian class to acquire a wider range of commodities, the so-called Z-commodities, which enabled peasants to achieve a better standard of living. Therefore, the rise of the marginal productivity of the agricultural sector permitted society to have access to the Z-commodities.[41] Nevertheless, how can we explain that, in some European areas such as the Mediterranean regions of south-eastern Spain, the agrarian group could enjoy of a wider variety of goods, which they did not have access to in previous times?[42] In this regard, it is necessary to be aware that structural changes in technology and to the productivity of the

---

[41]   We will not enter into the old debate of how fast or slow agricultural change was taking place in some parts of Europe. We simply mention the main features of economic transformation of pre-industrial Europe to contextualize and give further explanation of how the industrious revolution could happen, in some particular areas, without a technological and structural transformation of the agrarian sector. The process of the industrious revolution when the agrarian group has a predominant role is very well explained by De Vries, J., *The Industrious Revolution*, pp. 73–5. The ancient literature regarding the European agricultural development can be found in the following notable works: Le Roy Ladurie, E., 'L' histoire immobile', *Annales. Economies, Sociétés, Civilizations*, 29 (1974): 673–92; Abel, W., *Agricultural Fluctuations in Europe* (London: Menthuen, 1980); Slicher van Bath, B.H. *The Agrarian History of Western Europe, 500–1850* (London: Edward Arnold, 1963); Boserup, E., *The Conditions of Agricultural Growth* (Chicago: University of Chicago Press, 1965).

[42]   See Pérez Picazo, M.T. and Lemeunier, G., *El proceso de modernización*, pp. 148–201.

agricultural sector led to the intensification of agriculture in industrialized areas, and this was the precondition to drive the economy towards modern economic growth. We must recall that both agricultural and artisan sectors are the main pillars of the industrious revolution theory. On the other hand, what occurs when one of these factors is missing? Can we still call the economic process an industrious revolution or we must simply amend the industrious revolution theory for the territory of our case study?

Surely, in Spain and most Mediterranean areas during the eighteenth century, especially in the second half, no agricultural change came about by the intensification of working land, acquisition of new agrarian technologies or the rise of productivity.[43] In south-eastern Spain, on the Mediterranean area, quite the opposite occurred. The agrarian class began to enjoy extensive sorts of commodities due to the secular conditions of the almost inexistent European wars, agrarian and demographic crisis – see Appendix B, F, G and H, pp. 249, 279, 287, 313. Thus, most of the population, especially that located in the Spanish Mediterranean areas, had assured a minimum of commodities for subsistence. This is the well-known global context that the Spanish historiography highlights. Nevertheless, our goal is to explore how the agrarian group and other economic agents such as craftsmen could have access to Z-commodities, bearing in mind that the industrious revolution did not occur in the Kingdom of Murcia.

---

[43]   David Ringrose summarizes clearly the failures of eighteenth-century economists and propagandists such as Campomanes and Jovellanos when those intellectuals presented their ideas on the reform of land and property as the keys to revitalize the Spanish economic life. There was a clear attempt to release markets in selling land and commodities as major aspects to stimulate agrarian labour and find solutions to problems of productivity and food supply. However, to make effective those plans, such changes had to be accompanied by the abolition of the large bulk of private 'mayorazgos' [entailed-states] in the hands of the majority of the tenant class, collective ownership of land and pre-emptive grazing privileges. These ideas circulated in official circles during the second half of the eighteenth century, reflecting a conjunction of mercantilist, physiocratic and liberal doctrine. As Professor Ringrose remarks, at the official level such ideas were not applied systematically until the 'bourgeois revolution' in the 1830s, a fact that avoids an earlier modernization of the Spanish agrarian sector. However, this important factor did not constrain the steady expansion of the rural population, a fact reflected in the growing participation of the agrarian class in absorbing the demand for goods primarily led to urban areas during the second half of the eighteenth century despite institutional coercions. See Ringrose, D., *Spain*, p. 169; Aranguren, J.L., *Moral y sociedad: La moral social española en el s. XIX* (Madrid: Cuadernos para el Diálogo, 1970), p. 42; Smith, R.S., 'English Economic Though in Spain, 1775–1848', *South Atlantic Quarterly*, vol. 67 (1968), pp. 306–37; Pedro Rodríguez, Conde de Campomanes, *Apéndice a la educación popular de los artesanos y su fomento*, 5 vols. (Madrid: Imprenta de D. Antonio de Sancha, 1775–1777); Clavero, B., *Mayorazgo: propiedad feudal en Castilla, 1369–1836* (Madrid: Siglo XXI, 1974); Fontana, J., 'La Desamortización de Mendizábal y sus antecedentes', in García Sanz, A. and Garrabou, R. (eds), *Historia agraria de la España Contemporánea*, vol. 1: *Cambio social y nuevas formas de propiedad (1800–1850)* (Barcelona: Crítica, 1985), pp. 219–44.

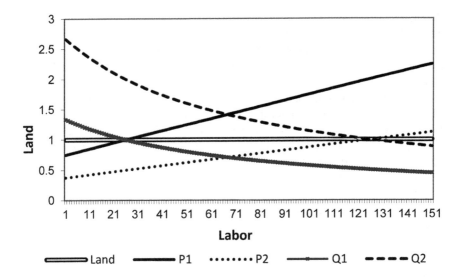

Chart 7.14   The intensification of agricultural production. *Source:* De Vries, J.,
The Dutch, p. 18. P_1: increase of population. P_2: increase of population.
Q_1: increase in the agrarian productivity. Q_2: increase in the agrarian
productivity.

In fact, what Jan de Vries foresaw did happen: an extension of the agricultural
model of intensification drawn up by Boserup. This extension was the intensive
participation of households, in particular those of the agrarian sector, interacting
with markets rather than shaping an exclusive network with the land. We can
confirm the absorption of agrarian work by non-agricultural activities due to the
possibilities of the market conditions, specialization in particular sectors and the
increase in per capita output. Those features can be corroborated in the particular
case of the management of land in the Mediterranean area of Spain, in particular
in the Kingdom of Murcia, and the economic process of acceleration of the port
of Cartagena. The construction of the 'Arsenal' of Cartagena in the second half of
the eighteenth century led to a specialization of the economic sector particularly
in activities related to maritime jobs, mercantile and commercial businesses,
such as the shipping of groceries and textiles. Therefore, we see a progressive
development of local artisan workshops, merchant and trade networks, especially
the second-hand market and peddler connections, which absorbed the agrarian
sector making it participate in those activities.

These assumptions are confirmed in the data sheet of probate inventories
(see Appendix B, F, G and H, pp. 249, 279, 287, 313) in which we can see, in
the records of rural areas of Cartagena, that there was increase in purchases of
some Z-commodities such as textiles made of 'indiana', 70.12 per cent over 67.64
per cent (see Appendix H, p. 313) during the eighteenth century in agrarian

inhabitants. This was related to the absorption of agrarian workers by the artisan and local trade sector, as shown by the increase in consumption of 'indiana' in craftsmen inventories. In addition, the consumption of particular goods in rural areas of Cartagena, during the second half of the eighteenth century, was higher by comparison to the urban areas.

Hence, in the particular case of the agrarian class, the industrious revolution did not occur either in Murcia nor in Cartagena (see Appendix B, p. 249), though the purchase of Z-commodities by inhabitants of rural areas rose progressively (see Appendix G and H, pp. 287, 313), but this fact was more due to local artisan and trade networks than a growth in agrarian labour. In peasant communities of the Kingdom of Murcia the industrious revolution did not take place (see Appendix B, p. 249), though it is true that during the eighteenth century there was a high production of raw material, silk and wool, which was used in exchange for textile manufactures. This production was orientated to supply external markets, especially those located in Mediterranean Europe such as France or Italy, and did not make available to local peasant household the necessary material to convert into ready-to-use manufactures for domestic use.

Furthermore, the lack in acquiring sufficient technology to extend the production in the entire manufacturing sector is also seen in the decline in possession of looms, as well as other artefacts for working, in both artisan and peasant groups during the eighteenth century in all territories of the Kingdom of Murcia[44] – see Table 5.2. This did not supplant the extension of the household as a small factory and foremost unit of production and self-consumption. As we have attested in artisan probate inventories (see Appendix A, p. 241), economic expansion was only experienced in very few craftsmen households, in which the particular conditions of the local market as well as the organization of the household members, and their distribution of individual incomes, allowed artisans to enjoy Z-commodities and to find the proper substitutes of market-purchased goods.

In probate inventories, textile manufacture such as 'de la tierra' [from the land], 'del país' [from the country], 'casero' [domestic], 'basto y ordinario' [rough and ordinary] fabrics are found – see Chart 7.15. The appearance of those items in both artisan and peasant probate inventories denotes whether or not there is a strong domestic production, related to the degree of traditional and productive structures linked with self-consumption. As we can see in the data sheet of probate inventories, the frequency in which those items appear in records of south-eastern Castile is quite low. 'Basta y ordinaria' silk [rough silk] appears in approximately 2 per cent of records, 'casero' linen [domestic linen] in approximately 12 per cent of records and 'de la tierra' fabrics [fibres from the territory] in only 1 per cent of registers analysed. These percentages are quite small, which indicate that the

---

[44]   Pérez Picazo, M.T. and Lemeunier, G., *El proceso de modernización.*

transformation of fabrics in manufactures into households of the Kingdom of Murcia occurred in a very small portion of the global consumption of cloth.[45]

In Chart 7.15, we can see how those kinds of fabrics comprised a very small fraction of the domestic usage by comparison to other materials such as linen, silk or wool which were exported to industries in southern France and re-exported as ready-to-use products from France to Spain – see Chapter 3. This lack of manufacturing production was the main reason for the significant amount of foreign textiles – especially French materials – introduced to Spanish ports as ready products. In addition, national textiles made of Catalonian cotton,[46] attested in the progressive usage in individual wardrobes, shows the popularization of that industrial fibre – see Chart 7.15. Cotton was increasingly consumed to the detriment of silk.[47]

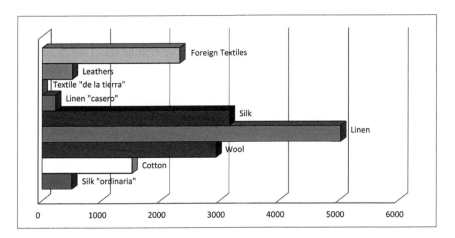

Chart 7.15   Textile preferences in south-eastern Spain inventories (1730–1808). Measure: Units. *Source:* A.H.P.M., probate inventories.

The use of silk experienced a decline because of its high price, and the fact that cotton was an innovative product, a symbol of industrial modernization, relatively cheap and also a symbol of hygiene because it was easier to wash. Some scholars have argued that the use of cotton was a factor in the decline of mortality rates in

[45]   The same pattern has been detected by Ruíz Gómez in his studies on the textile industry from Cantabria: Ruíz Gómez, F., *Fábricas textiles en la industrialización de Cantabria* (Santander: Universidad de Cantabria-Textil Santanderina, S.A., 1998). See also: Hoyo Aparicio, A. and Maruri Villanueva, R., 'Pautas de consumo', pp. 107–39.

[46]   Martín Corrales, E., 'La importación'. Martín Corrales, E., 'Marseille'.

[47]   Sytles, J., 'What Were Cottons for in the Early Industrial Revolution', in Riello, G. and Parthasarathi, P. (eds), *The Spinning World*, pp. 307–26. Hudson, P., 'The Limits'.

England during the eighteenth and nineteenth centuries.[48] This fabric is registered in inventories with different valuations. For instance, Juan Bicaix, merchant, with 140,464 'reales', Mira Roque, yeoman, with 4,000 'reales' or María Quilez, landowner, with 59,854 'reales' of wealth have all registered in their respective inventories cloths made of cotton.[49] As we can observe from the figures above, leather wear occupied a very small portion of individual choices.

We can certainly say that there was a market orientation, and that a shift from market contact and sale of commodities to supplement the household demand took place. Merchant activities were still the main sector which stimulated the demand-side. New goods were the basis for the rise of household incomes, a feature that translated into the acquisition of better standards of living. Cartagena, as the main Castilian port, supplied goods to inner areas of Castile such as Murcia, Albacete or Madrid, and was also one of the main Mediterranean territories that integrated diverse markets from Europe, Asia and the Americas. Therefore, the market orientation of this south-eastern Spanish territory was shaping a new economic microcosm by means of the circulation of commodities, foreign financial and human capital, leading the region to important economic development.

In the process of emulation, artisans copied commodities brought from Asian markets by means of imitating the techniques of production in order to spread these types of goods among middle and lower social classes. They were, thus, trying to create a new market and generate a demand for exotic products, with the goal of spreading their business. The immediate consequence of the creation of such a demand was the social 'democratization' in consumption and the expansion of new fashions. According to this hypothesis, from the merchant's point of view there were no limits in the social hierarchy regarding the promotion and sale of products. It made no difference to them if they were spurring a social transgression, as the consumption of exotic and sumptuous goods was believed to be limited only to the upper social tiers. Their goal was to introduce products to different social groups, simply because traders wanted to extend the demand for those commodities in order that their businesses might prosper. The acquisition of original and unique goods was predominant among the elite and local oligarchy who wanted to emulate the conspicuous consumption and lifestyle of the aristocracy. However, as we will see in the following pages, the elite were not the only group to foster a process of emulation in the patterns of consumption of the lower social groups. The merchant group, especially French dealers, played the role of 'vicarious agents', leading new trends of consumption in other social

---

[48]   Rule, J., *The Vital Century: England's Developing Economy, 1714–1815* (London; New York: Longman, 1992).

[49]   A.H.P.M., sig. 2946, fols. 14r.–16r., escr. Gilarte, Pedro. A.H.P.M., sig. 4281, fols. 415r.–453v., escr. Bocio y Belda, Francisco. A.H.P.M., sig. 2694, sin foliar, escr. Costa Irles, Antonio.

groups – see Appendix F, p. 279. Therefore, the process of emulation did not follow a vertical pattern from upper to lower classes.

The adoption of new lifestyles and patterns of consumption was influenced by the size of Mediterranean families, especially in the case of Spain, during the second half of eighteenth and early nineteenth centuries. In northern Europe, mainly in the Netherlands, an industrious revolution occurred, as Jan de Vries has aptly described, due to the role played by artisan and peasant families, whose size was mostly nuclear and who were more entrepreneurial in nature, working for market supplies and increasing household incomes.[50] On the other hand, in the case of southern Europe, and analysing Spain, the nuclear size of the family was not so predominant, in spite of the fact that David S. Reher[51] in his study of Castilian families established that the main size of these families was nuclear, applying the theories of the Cambridge group.[52]

As we have shown by means of the merchant social networks and their genealogical tree – in Chapter 3 – there was not an exclusivity of the nuclear family in Spain during late eighteenth and early nineteenth centuries. Instead, there was a very important role played by the extended family, especially in southern Castile, or multinuclear family within the home. In Mediterranean families there was a tendency for the coexistence of different generations in the same residence.[53] This issue can be attested in families that exerted an important influence on both the supply and demand-side. Merchant groups participated in this process as suppliers and consumers. Their family size progressively grew due to the coexistence of different generations in the household. In these families the predominance of endogamy had an important influence in terms of shaping the Spanish economy, with the major goal of tenant families being the transmission of land and property to the next generation with the aim of avoiding the loss of primary family assets. Thus, the economy was strongly dependent on the land management, which was a constraint for expanding the economic development, with the labour force of the country being less productive and more dependent on the lease contracts for land made by local powers.[54]

The existence of the extended or multinuclear family was an important part of Castilian society, especially among the middle social class. The Spanish economy was more dependent on external agents than on its entrepreneurial abilities to

---

[50]   De Vries, J., *The Industrious*.

[51]   Reher, D.S., 'Family Ties in Western Europe: Persistent Contrasts', *Population and Development Review*, vol. 24, no. 2 (Jun. 1998): 203–34.

[52]   Laslett, P. and Wall, R. (eds), *Household and Family in Past Time* (Cambridge: Cambridge University Press, 1972).

[53]   Delille, G., *Le maire et le prieur: pouvoir central et pouvoir local en Méditerranée occidentale, XVe-XVIIIe Siècle* (Rome: Ecole française de Rome; Paris: Editions de l'Ecole des Hautes Études en Sciences Sociales, 2003). Viazzo, P.P., 'What's so Special about the Mediterranean?', *Continuity and Change*, 18 (2003), pp. 111–37.

[54]   Ringrose, D., *Spain*, p. 169.

increase labour forces for industry. This issue shows why foreign merchants played such important role in the Spanish economy and why, due to their interaction with Mediterranean and overseas markets, they shaped Castilian consumer behaviour. Hence, for both artisan and peasant families there was not a deep industrious revolution, but due to the industrious foreign businessmen, mostly French, who installed their companies in Spanish territories, local demand was, nevertheless, stimulated.

The educational process of Mediterranean families based on traditional values as well as a carefully shaped moral identity, was a feature, especially in extended families, which fostered individuals to consume commodities whose external meaning did not transgress their conventional patterns in both social and cultural spheres. The good taste,[55] which defined what was good, bad or acceptable in the *Ancien Regime* society, was constantly present in the family model. In Spain during the eighteenth century, the social backlash could occur due to the introduction of foreign commodities with different cultural symbols.

Table 7.8   Distribution of offspring having the same breadwinner's occupation as collected in probate inventories of the Kingdom of Murcia (1730–1808)

Social Group	No. of Inventories	Inventory Distribution (%)
Merchants	33	36.36
Yeomen	78	76.92
Master Artisans	22	31.81
Artisans	52	21.15
Total	185	48.64

Source: A.H.P.M., protocols – wills and probate inventories.

Table 7.9   Distribution of family size as collected in probate inventories of the Kingdom of Murcia (1730–1808)

Social Group	No. of Inventories	Inventory Distribution (average)
Merchants	33	4.00
Yeomen	78	4.64
Master Artisans	22	5.74
Artisans	52	4.73
Total	185	4.64

Source: A.H.P.M., protocols – wills and probate inventories.

---

55   Adams, C., *A Taste for Comfort and Status. A Bourgeois Family in Eighteenth-century France* (Pennsylvania: The Pennsylvania State University Press, University Park, 2000).

We have found an important percentage of families, whose members worked in the same breadwinner's job, over the sample of 273 protocols that have been analysed. Table 7.8 shows the estimated percentage of families that work in the same family business, whose percentage reached approximately 49 per cent, almost half of the population analysed. This issue explains why there was a strong endogamous component among working families whose aim was to transmit companies, in merchant families, or workshops, in artisan groups, in order to ensure their economic survival.

Table 7.9 shows the estimated average family size among occupational groups, which is almost the same among all categories collected, which contributed to maintain enough offspring to continue the family business. This was one important feature which led to the appearance of a large middle social group, in south-eastern Castilian society, with an improved standard of living. Clearly the agrarian sector predominates in the southern Spanish economy, therefore most descendants continued to work on the farm or orchard in which the breadwinner was employed. This also happened in the port of Cartagena during the eighteenth century, in which most people, who previously worked in agricultural activities, worked in jobs related to the maritime sector.[56] The increase of middle- and lower-social group incomes allowed families to afford the purchase of commodities, which could not be obtained earlier, changing the family lifestyle. Hence, we can state that a shift of incomes and purchases was occurring, in south-eastern Castilian families, and this was an indicator of the new consumer behaviour.

In addition, middle social groups combined two tasks, as artisans and merchants with 'tienda abierta' [open-shop] in the urban space, either Murcia or Cartagena.[57] In Cartagena merchants effectively had two jobs, as shopkeepers and traders or artisans, especially related with the maritime sector.[58] A similar situation characterized the urban area of Murcia. However, here more workers combined artisan and commercial jobs related to the textile sector, producing raw materials – especially silk – and thereafter selling the product.[59] This is particularly

---

[56]   There was a growing development of works related to the maritime sector: D. Pedro Antonio Pereti Pinneti worked as 'factor de provision de bienes de la Real Armada' [agent of provision of goods of the Real Navy]; D. Jose Liza worked as well as 'factor de galeras de la Real Armada' [agent of galleys of the Real Navy], in 1770. A.H.P.M., sig. 11375.

[57]   In the city of Murcia there was an important group of merchants with open-shops. Foreign merchants – Juan Bicaix, Nicolas Esttop Fadeville or D. Juan Francisco Estrabo Camon – were the most numerous group. A.H.P.M., sig. 2694, 2787.

[58]   We have found some examples in Cartagena that demonstrate this issue. In 1781, Mateo Sicilia Celdran was an artisan and retailer at the same time and D. Santiago Matalona Lauero, whose origins were from Naples, was a merchant and shopkeeper in 1801. A.H.P.M., sig. 5492, 6214.

[59]   Some people worked as an artisan and as a retailer at the same time: in the year 1796 the artisan Maria Teresa Farfan y Martinez; in 1782 Antonio Gallego Lopez was silk weaver and retailer in the rural area of Murcia; in 1755 the Italian silk weaver Antonio Donate, whose family group worked as silversmith and merchants. A.H.P.M., sig., 2378, 2352.

relevant because goods could be spread throughout both rural and urban areas more easily. Specific items could be more extended in the social hierarchy, especially among people that desired more commodities. As a consequence, in both cities of Cartagena and Murcia there was a tendency towards the democratization for purchasing items in larger bulk, which formerly were available to wealthy people. These family networks reinforced local market integration to provide goods in towns and villages. The expansion of inter-regional trade networks was a crucial factor that changed consumer behaviour.

This issue is demonstrated by the rising consumption of beverages such as chocolate, tea and coffee by families with different levels of wealth – see Appendix E, p. 273. Chocolate was certainly a drink with higher consumption among all social groups and became very popular among the middle groups. Its consumption, attested to in the sample of inventories of south-eastern Castile, shifted from 31.06 per cent, for the period 1730–69, to 59.25 per cent, for 1770–1808, which means that its purchase augmented household expenditures, especially affecting artisan and peasant families – see Appendix F, p. 279. These beverages were necessary for everyday life. The list of numerous pots, bowls, cups and trays in probate inventories suggests intensive use. Moreover, the description of petty debts related to the purchase of chocolate, sugar, tea and coffee indicates that colonial products were bought commonly and in small quantities for immediate consumption, like the most basic groceries.[60] The consumption of tea was quite marginal among the population studied, even among the upper classes, as people did not find it a particularly pleasant drink, mainly due to the fact that it was primarily used for medicinal purposes – see Appendix E, F, G and H, pp. 273, 279, 287, 313. Coffee consumption increased by 6 percentage points in expenditure, especially in the upper-middle and upper groups – see Appendix H, p. 313. Its consumption did, however, become increasingly popular, the most popular varieties coming from Moka and French American colonies due to the high quality and superior taste – see previous chapter, in which beverage import data shows that coffee was unloaded in significant volumes in Spanish ports.

The rising consumption of the aforementioned drinks is a useful indicator that people were improving their standards of living, spending an important portion of their incomes on these groceries. During the second half of the eighteenth century, the population was enjoying better living conditions, reflected in the rising use of different foods, enabling a higher life expectancy, although births and deaths remained at a high level. The improved system of commmunication and transportation, evident from the arrival of notable volumes of colonial products

---

[60] Professor McCants showed in her study that the consumption of colonial products such as tea, chocolate or coffee in Dutch households was quite marginal during the seventeenth century, with the VOC's sales at 4.1 per cent. However, in around 1730 they represented some 25 per cent and became the second most important sale category for the company. Chocolate consumption began earlier but its spread was slower and less pervasive. Coffee came later than tea and was soon as common. See McCants, A., 'Poor Consumers', pp. 172–200.

from Mediterranean, Asian and Atlantic markets – see the previous chapter – to Spanish ports, allowed better internal redistribution; consequently, household purchases of food increased. Therefore, groceries such as chocolate, coffee or tea were commodities for which households decicated an important portion of their budgets[61] – see Chart 7.13 – especially due to the stability in nominal prices of such products as well as the rise of real incomes of middle social classes, especially artisans and yeomen. This pattern is confirmed by the probate inventories (see Appendix E, F, G, H and I, pp. 273, 279, 287, 313, 321) which illustrate that the eighteenth century signalled the beginning of better standards of living and a short-term decline of mortality rates, a trend which was accentuated in the second half of the nineteenth century and the beginning of the twentieth century.

7.3. Criticizing the 'Trickle-Down' Theory in the Kingdom of Murcia (1730–1808)

In the previous section we have seen econometric methods, which help us to build price indexes, purchasing power, family incomes or expenditures for goods. However, these methods are only a tool that gives us a broad picture of the evolution of the demand-side. If we add to these economic variables certain sociological explanations, such as the interpretation of the consumption of specific goods which had strong social symbolism, then we can better understand how the demand equation was affected by social variables. I have tackled this problem by studying in the sample of probate inventories whether or not the trickle-down theory occurred in a southern European economy.

Although McKendrick's explanation about consumption was very contro-versial, it is a valuable theory to analyse socio-economic and cultural changes during the transition from the eighteenth to nineteenth century. In essence the theory is based on the presence of a 'consumer revolution'[62] prior to the Industrial Revolution, as well as the existence of significant changes in the habits of consumption among the European population during the second half of the eighteenth century. In order to explain his hypothesis of the 'consumer revolution', McKendrick asserts that at the moment in which the supply-side is equal to the demand-side, and with the existence of a strong elasticity of the demand to absorb the goods that are supplied, then the immediate consequence is a 'boom' on consumption. Thus, there is access by the different social groups to the new goods which are supplied by the market.

---

[61]   See the work by Mokyr, who analyses per capita data for tea, coffee, sugar and tobacco to estimate the overall standard of living: Mokyr, J., 'Is There Still Life in the Pessimist Case? Consumption during the Industrial Revolution, 1790–1850', *Journal of Economic History*, XLVIII (1998), pp. 69–92. See also: Shammas, C., 'The Eighteenth-century English Diet and Economic Change', *Explorations in Economic History*, 21 (1982), pp. 254–69.

[62]   McKendrick, N., 'The Consumer Revolution', pp. 9–33.

Such a 'boom' on consumption was followed by the purchase of goods by the large middle class, emulating the consumer behaviour of the upper social groups. The 'trickle-down' effect would explain emulation in tastes and patterns of consumption from the elite group to middle classes – merchants, artisans, yeomen. This emulation embraced an upward social mobility within the middle social classes applying McKendrick's theory. But in our view, he is mistaken when he asserts that a consequence of the consumption of new goods was social mobility. This misunderstanding is produced by his faulty association between consumption and the emulation of upper-class habits. The emulation does not bring about a social mobility of an upward nature. Nevertheless, by means of the consumption of new goods, the middle classes try to imitate the 'modus operandi' of upper social groups – aristocracy, gentry – in order to acquire a refined 'habitus' or similar lifestyle.

By focusing on London society, scholars[63] have associated the industrial development and the growth of consumption with the following factors:

- The centralized market of the main European urban centres (London, Amsterdam or Paris).
- The remarkable growth of the populations of these cities, especially London which grew from some 200,000 inhabitants in 1600 to 900,000 in 1800.
- The influence of London's shops, lifestyle and the influence of its fashions to modify the consumer behaviour.
- The commercial techniques in development of the shops in London and their new marketing, distribution and advertisement models.
- The increase in demand of new goods (clothes, candles, manufactured cutlery, furniture, etc. ...) by wives who worked with their husbands.

But we should ask why in some territories and urban places such as eighteenth-century south-eastern Spain, which were not industrialized and saw slower economic development than industrialized northern European regions, there was a process that at first glance could be similar to the so-called 'trickle-down' effect? To answer this, it is necessary to examine some of the characteristics of the 'trickle-down' concept. For instance, there was not a 'consumer revolution' or a 'boom' on consumption, which were factors related more to the developed economies of the modern world. In our opinion, the concept of the 'revolution des apparences'[64] gives a more valuable definition to this socio-economic process which produced an increase in the demand of commodities. Hence, it is better to affirm that in eighteenth-century Spain, a progressively growing tendency in the demand-side was taking place, which started to reach its apex in the second half of the nineteenth and twentieth centuries. This positive tendency in consumption

---

[63]   McKendrick, N., 'The Consumer Revolution'. Borsay, P., *The English Urban Renaissance. Culture and Society in the Provincial Town, 1660–1770* (Oxford: Oxford University Press, 1989), pp. 315–19. Cheung, H. and Mui, L., *Shops*.

[64]   Roche, D., *La culture*.

allowed people to decorate their homes, as well as their bodies, with a wide range of goods.

The role played by the port of Cartagena in the distribution of commodities towards inner areas of the Kingdom of Murcia, such as the cities of Murcia and Lorca and its neighbouring villages, was the main feature that stimulated the process of emulation among the social classes. The foremost protagonists of that process were merchants established in the region, from rich wholesalers to ordinary retailers as well as peddlers. Shops, stationary and itinerant markets as well as publicity, such as fashion almanacs, were the main marketing instruments of that commercial network. Retailers with stores such as Juan Bicaix, in the city of Murcia, and Don José Policano, in the city of Cartagena, promoted the sale of commodities that characterized their trade activity.[65] Moreover, rich merchants such as the Vidal Company, established in the city of Lorca, had connections with small retailers, shaping an effective network, fostering the demand for a wide variety of commodities, especially textiles – see Illustrations from 7.1 to 7.3. In such illustrations we can observe the detailed descriptions of the sales of foreign textiles, from French and Asian markets, by the groups of French merchants. Merchant inventories form the most valuable and striking evidence that challenge the 'trickle-down' theory. As can be seen in the results of the sample – see Appendix C and D, pp. 257, 265 – traders were the 'vicarious consumers' that promoted their products, as well as playing their own role as commercial agents. Merchants were not mere suppliers; they were also active consumers stimulating the desire and demand for the goods that were being promoted. Surely the noble elite were not the main social agents in spurring new consumer behaviour or the only group that generated a pattern of emulation from above to below in terms of social tiers. The consumption of a wider, and in some instances, new variety of clothing which fostered those shifts on consumer behaviour of society in south-eastern Spain took place as a result of the role played by dealers, especially French dealers, in promoting their own commodities. The textile sector stimulated the demand, from wealthy to ordinary people (see Appendix E, F, I, pp. 273, 279, 321), and the consumption of textile items, adjusted to a logarithm function (see Charts from 7.10 to 7.12), was the factor that raised the demand as seen through the wide supply and variety of clothing available.

The great demand for textiles – see Appendix F, p. 279 – from diverse origins is related to the supply of textiles from both Levantine and European markets, as shown by the trade records of the 'Chambre de Commerce de Marseille'. This, also, can be seen through records such as the commercial letters of the Vidal Company[66]

---

[65] A.H.P.M., sig. 2946, fols. 14r.–16r., escr. Gilarte, Pedro. A.H.P.M., sig. 5487, fols. 20r.22v., escr. Alzaraz Serrano, Gines.

[66] The Vidal Company, whose origins came from France, established also family connections in Catalonia, as one their main peninsular site of their businesses. A.M.L., protocols 771, 991, 1077, 1187. See: Muset i Pons, A., *Catalunya i el mercat español al segle XVIII: Els traginers i els negociants de Calaf i Copons* (Barcelona: ed. Abadía de

located in the city of Lorca.[67] This company commercialized 'zangalete' [textile made of silk whose origin is Persian and Byzantine], bought by the Vidal Company from the Lyonnais Zellveguer Company in September of 1789. In 1792 Monsieur Zellveguer ordered a shipment, from Marseille to Cartagena, of dyed and colourful 'zangaletes' as well as textiles made in Cambray, textiles made of 'crea' and white textiles, which were products sold by the Vidal Company. The transaction was brokered by Loui Ferrand who was the agent responsible for overseeing the arrival of the merchandise in proper condition in Cartagena, as well as guaranteeing the payment from the Vidal Company:

> ... aurez la bonte de me faire preparer de ce qui aura mieux, observant que la toile tinte ayant la couleure vive, de l'autre un peu blanc ... de me faire l'expedition pour Cartagene a la consignation de Loui Ferrand: 4 pieces toile a la peyne 2/3; 2 pieces de toile a la peyne 5/8; 2 pieces de toile Ymperiale; 4 pieces de sangallete rosse; 2 pieces de sangallete aurore; 2 pieces de sangallete porcelaine; 2 pieces de sangallete noir; 3 pieces de cambray; 3 pieces de crea; 3 pieces de crea semi largue; 3 pieces de crea etroite; 6 pieces de toile platille finee; 6 pieces de allemagnette; 10 pieces de rouente; 6 pieces de mouchoir de fil fond blanc a bordure rouge; 6/8 pieces de toile en cru ordinaire.[68]

Illustrations 7.1 and 7.3 correspond to a sample of colourful textiles made of 'sayas', silk, 'granas', muslins and taffetas, bought in 1790 and 1791 by the Vidal Company from Monrepos Lacosta Company, in Valencia, while the French dealers, Cayron Company of Murcia,[69] acted as intermediaries in the transaction. Illustration 7.2 shows a sample of textiles made of silk bought in July of 1789 by the French Jordan-Cayron Company with offices in Murcia. This company had numerous deals and a circuit of transactions which ran from Marseille, following the Spanish Mediterranean area, down to Murcia. The Jordan-Cayron Company was one of the mediators of the Vidal Company purchases. The Vidal Company needed a good, trustworthy intermediary, as the distance covered once the merchandise was unloaded in Cartagena, from the port to inner areas such as Murcia or Lorca, was long and difficult because of the dangers of the road. Thus, they signed credits with Jordan-Cayron to ensure the arrival of merchandise from Cartagena to interior areas in which the Vidal Company had businesses:

Montserrat, 1997), pp. 238–60. See also the work by Pérez Picazo and Lemeunier, who studied the diasporas of Catalonian traders over the peninsular territory: Lemeunier, G. and Pérez Picazo, M.T., 'Comercio y comerciantes catalanes en la crisis del Antiguo Régimen murciano', Primer Congrés d' Història Moderna de Catalunya (vol. 1, Barcelona: Universidad de Barcelona, 1984), pp. 747–56.

[67]   A.M.L., Cartas de Antonio Martín de Lorca, S. II, 19.
[68]   A.M.L., Cartas de Antonio Martín de Lorca, S. II, 19.
[69]   A.M.L., Cartas de Antonio Martín de Lorca, S. II, 19.

Respondemos a la referida de vmd. 14 corriente dejamos creditados de 162 rs de una bala de indianas que en 8 de octubre ultimo desembolsaron y dejaron de pasarnos aviso de 124 rs. por sus igualmente desembolsos al lino, pieles, y 16 rs entregados a ese colegial Martinez y de resultas les dejamos adeudados por principio de cuenta 11354 ... que su citada nos acompaña dimanando la diligencia a nuestro perjuicio en lugar de los 2665 rs. que por equivocacion nos cargan solo debe ser de 2655 rs.[70]

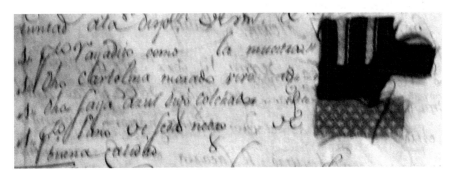

Illustration 7.1   Sample of 'sayas'. *Source:* A.M.L.

This important volume of business was stimulated by the rising demand of textiles as confirmed in probate inventories – see Appendix F, p. 279 – in which commodities circulated easily among households with different levels of wealth – see Appendix E, p. 273. The wide variety of textiles supplied – see Charts from 7.16 to 7.24[71] – mostly by French traders was one of the foremost features of a pre-industrialized economy that fostered the emulation process among different social groups. Wool and linen were the materials preferred by consumers; while silk purchases suffered a decline because of the growing demand for Asian textiles. Domestic or European cotton was not in high demand by households (see Chart 7.22), by comparison to Asian cottons (see Chart 7.16), as well as other fibres such as canvas (see Chart 7.19) or leathers (see Chart 7.17). The origins of the textiles were Asia, France – both with a wide range of materials – and Italy, with Italian exports to Spain being quite marginal during the eighteenth century. Thus, ordinary people could easily purchase cheap cloths or imitations of fine and low-priced textiles emulating, consequently, the privileged lifestyles of the nobles. Vidal-Cayron's business as well as the rising demand for and supply of Asian textiles – see Appendix E and I, pp. 273, 321 – constitute certain proof of the power of emulation as manifested in urban life. The city was the major centre in which the desire for acquiring goods developed new consumer behaviour. The

---

[70]   A.M.L., Cartas de Antonio Martín de Lorca, S. II, 19.
[71]   The volume of consumption is measured in units.

fascination for incorporating lasting, exotic and fancy Indian cloths – see Chart
7.16 – was the main attraction reflected in European consumer's minds:

> Europe was attracted to Indian decorative textiles on account of their cheapness
> and technical excellence (especially their fast and brilliant dye-colours), not
> their qualities of design.[72]

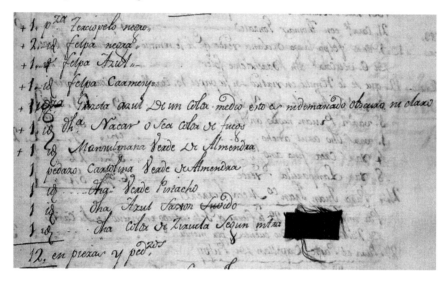

Illustration 7.2   Sample of silk. *Source:* A.M.L.

The strategic position of clothing in consumer demand could be related to its
accessibility.[73] In this progressive process of rising demand, people of modest
earnings could embrace new fashions and experience some changes in their
lifestyles. Benoît Garnot noticed this process in which new consumer behaviour
was taking place in the provincial town of Chartres:

> Numerous habits of daily life change in eighteenth-century Chartres. The world
> of consumption is in the process of being born. The people of Chartres come to
> possess more and more goods.[74]

---

[72]   John Irwin, quoted in John Styles, 'Product Innovation', p. 136.
[73]   De Vries, J., *The Industrious*, p. 140.
[74]   Garnot, B., *Un déclin. Chartres au XVIIIe siècle* (Paris: Editions de L.T.H.S.,
1991).

Illustration 7.3   Sample of 'granas', muslins and taffetas. *Source:* A.M.L.

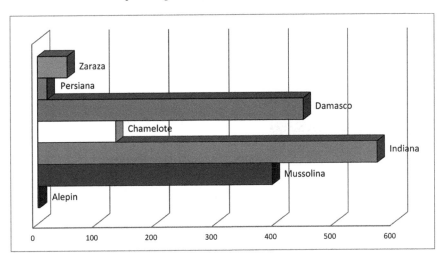

Chart 7.16   Asian textiles in south-eastern Spain inventories (1730–1808). Measure: Units.

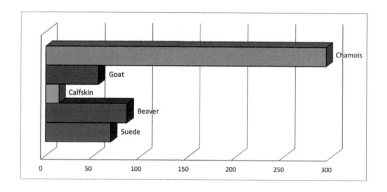

Chart 7.17   Leather materials in south-eastern Spain inventories (1730–1808).
              Measure: Units.

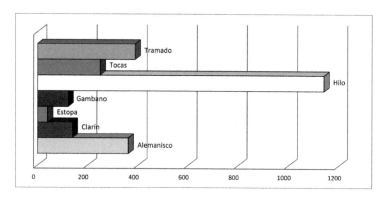

Chart 7.18   Linen textiles in south-eastern Spain inventories (1730–1808).
              Measure: Units.

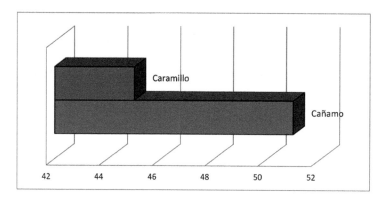

Chart 7.19   Canvas textiles in south-eastern Spain inventories (1730–1808).
              Measure: Units.

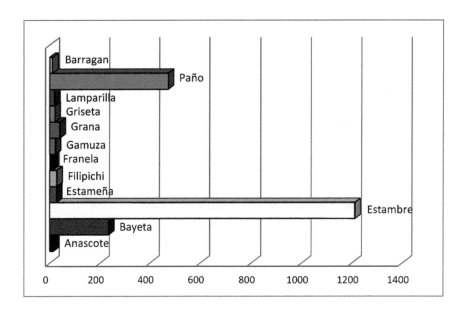

Chart 7.20   Woollen textiles in south-eastern Spain inventories (1730–1808). Measure: Units.

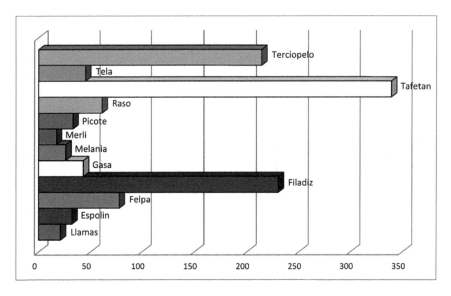

Chart 7.21   Silk textiles in south-eastern Spain inventories (1730–1808). Measure: Units.

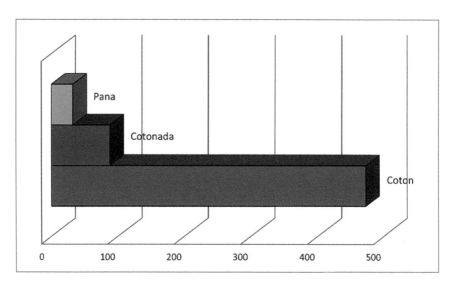

Chart 7.22   Cotton textiles in south-eastern Spain inventories (1730–1808).
              Measure: Units.

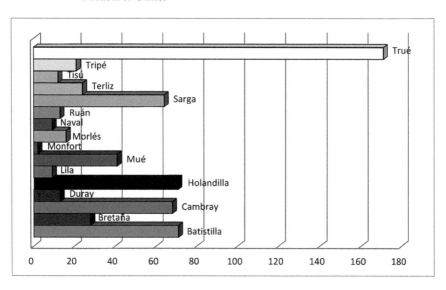

Chart 7.23   French textiles in south-eastern Spain inventories (1730–1808).
              Measure: Units.

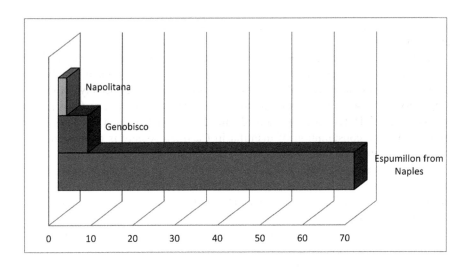

Chart 7.24   Italian textiles in south-eastern Spain inventories (1730–1808). Measure: Units.

The urban areas of Murcia and Cartagena and their rural surroundings were not excluded from this process in which middle social groups started to participate in economic life as potential consumers. Certainly, in those areas the 'trickle-down' effect occurred as we can see by comparing local oligarchy and merchant probate inventories with the probate inventories of the remainder of the population – see Appendix C and D, pp. 257, 265. Nevertheless, as we have mentioned, local oligarchies were not the sole social agents in spreading new patterns of consumption. This emulation process also started from middle social groups such as merchants, a feature that diverges from McKendrick's theory.

   Consequently, in this new process of consumption, in which most of population was benefiting from rising purchases of commodities, there were some exceptions which explain why the emulation process did not go from up to down in the social hierarchy. As we have seen in previous scholarly works, the general pattern of social emulation has been analysed from the elite to the middle classes and ordinary people – see Appendix C and D, pp. 257, 265. There were some exceptions, especially relating to the diffusion of traditional Spanish garments and the above-mentioned French textiles. If we observe the results offered by the sample of probate inventories – see Appendix C and D, pp. 257, 265 – commodities identified as part of the 'majo's' attire such as 'basquiñas' [top petticoat], 'chal' [shawl], jackets, 'cofias' [hair nets], 'jubon' [doublet], mantillas and suits were consumed more by the local oligarchy than the rest of population during the first half of the eighteenth century. A shift occurred, however, in the second half of the century, when the rest of the population purchased higher volumes of these commodities than the oligarchy. Comparing merchant inventories (Appendix D, p. 265) with those related to other social groups, purchases related to the 'majo's' attire – items such as jackets, mantillas or suits – were higher in the oligarchy group than merchants.

Therefore, the 'trickle-down' effect did not occur in this particular case since merchants, one of the potential agents in promoting the consumption of goods, did not participate in the process of emulation of traditional clothes. Likely, artisans – Appendix A, p. 241 – were the group that fostered the consumption of this group of commodities. Herein, the assertion advanced by Máximo García and Bartolome Yun[75] about the consumption of mantilla in Castilian society is confirmed as a symbol of Spanish popular fashion which did not follow a process of circulation from upper to modest groups. The same happened in Cartagena and Murcia, which means that there was a strong popular culture that opposed resistance to high-class fashions, or rather there was a social confrontation against the 'strange' or 'foreign' things whose symbolization clashed with traditional culture.

Notwithstanding, the paradigmatic case of merchants as 'vicarious consumers' can also be found in the circulation of novel garments such as jackets, waistcoats, bow-ties, trousers, frock-coats (Illustration 7.4) and tail-coats (Illustration 7.5) – see Tables 7.10 and 7.11. In this case results could not be clearer. The spread of those new items, symbols of modernization of the dress style, did not follow an upward to downward trend. Traders were the main agents in stimulating the social diffusion and consumption of those articles. If we compare the results of the period from 1730 to 1808, merchants' probate inventories list a higher quantity of those goods than those of the oligarchy. So, the affirmation by Fine and Leopold[76] is thus confirmed regarding the case of the social diffusion of the frock-coat, as merchants were the foremost mediators in fostering the demand in the rest of the population for this fine and modern commodity. Therefore, the emulation of new lifestyles and social manners did not start from the noble oligarchy. Some scholars have remarked that those commodities did not enter wardrobes of different social tiers until 1817–20.[77]

However, the inventories studied in the sample show a diverse result. Jackets penetrated household wardrobes in the decade of 1790, though in some inventories this item marginally appears in 1733. The waistcoat progressively appears from 1774 onwards. So, the jacket and waistcoat were gradually replacing the 'casaca' and 'chupa', not from 1817, but even earlier: from the last quarter of the eighteenth century. However, the 'corbatin' – bow-tie – dated prior to the appearance of jackets and waistcoats. The bow-tie is mostly listed in inventories from 1730 onwards, and its usage rose after 1750. Related to the jacket and waistcoat, there is another garment which stands out as symbol of the process of

---

[75] García Fernández, M. and Yun-Casalilla, B., 'Pautas de consumo', p. 276. Regarding the British context, the 'frock-coat' was a garment that was spread from lower to higher tiers of society. See Fine, B. and Leopold, E., 'Consumerism and the Industrial Revolution', *Social History*, no. 15 (1990), pp. 151–79.

[76] Fine, B. and Leopold, E., 'Consumerism'.

[77] Hoyo Aparicio, A. and Maruri Villanueva, R., 'Pautas de consumo textil'.

modernization of clothing: trousers. This item was progressively substituting the 'calzon' [breeches] in the beginning of the nineteenth century, representing, as Davidoff and Hall mentioned, one of the most spectacular changes in the transition from the traditional to the modern world.[78]

Table 7.10   Examining the 'trickle-down' effect through the consumption of innovative clothes by the local oligarchy in the Kingdom of Murcia (1730–1808)

Sample (=*273)	Jackets (%)	Waist-coats (%)	'Corbatines' [Bow Ties] (%)	'Pantalones' [Trousers] (%)	'Levitas' [Frock Coats] (%)	'Fracs' [Tail Coats] (%)
Local Oligarchy (=*34)	3.12	6.25	12.50	3.12	0.00	0.00
Rest of the Population (=*239)	3.40	12.34	4.25	0.85	0.85	0.42
Total	3.37	11.61	5.24	1.12	0.74	0.37

Source: A.H.P.M., probate inventories.

Table 7.11   Examining the 'trickle-down' effect through the consumption of innovative clothes by merchants in the Kingdom of Murcia (1730–1808)

Sample (=*273)	Jackets (%)	Waist-coats (%)	'Corbatines' [Bow Ties] (%)	'Pantalones' [Trousers] (%)	'Levitas' [Frock Coats] (%)	'Fracs' [Tail Coats] (%)
Merchants (=*33)	15.15	30.30	15.15	6.06	3.03	3.03
Rest of the Population (=*240)	2.13	8.97	3.84	0.42	0.42	0.00
Total	3.74	11.61	5.24	1.12	0.74	0.37

Source: A.H.P.M., probate inventories.

Jackets, waistcoats, bow-ties and trousers shaped new dress styles, representing the symbol of the rising modernization of the economy. Contrary to what Ramon Maruri and Andres Hoyo observed in the rural regions of northern Spain, Cantabria, in which the elite were the 'vicarious consumers' as the process of

---

[78]   Davidoff, L. and Hall, C., *Family Fortunes: Men and Women of the English Middle Class 1780–1850* (London: Hutchinson, 1987).

Illustrations 7.4 and 7.5   'Currutaco' wearing a 'levita' (frock-coat) and
'petimetre' wearing a 'frac' (tail-coat), with breeches
and shoes from Mahon. Colección: Antonio Rodríguez.
Colección General de los Trajes que en la actualidad
se usan en España. Iniciada en el año 1801. Madrid:
Librería de Castillo, 1801. Número de Serie 1316 y
1435. *Fundación Joaquín Díaz, Centro Etnográfico*,
Diputación de Valladolid, Spain.

diffusion and emulation in that area followed an above to below pattern in the
social hierarchy.[79] In our case, for a region of south-eastern Spain, the Kingdom
of Murcia, the agents of diffusion were not noble elite, but merchant groups,
whose mediation in stimulating the consumption of new goods was followed
by a well-designed strategy of marketing. The introduction of others items such
as the 'levitas' [frock-coat] and 'fracs' [tail-coats] followed the same model of
circulation, with traders being the social group that introduced these new clothes.
The general pattern regarding the consumption of other commodities such as
fine and luxury French goods ('desaville', 'pompadour' textiles or 'cabrioles'),
household furniture (mirrors, items with the French trade-mark, chinaware, items

_____

    [79]   Hoyo Aparicio, A. and Maruri Villanueva, R., 'Pautas de consumo textil', p. 116.

from China, hangings and upholstery made of 'indianas') and utensils such as cups, trays or pots for drinking chocolate or tea undoubtedly followed an upwards to downwards trend in the social hierarchy (see Appendix C, p. 257). Coffee was the only exception as it was popularized by artisan groups – see Appendix A, p. 241. Through the progressive modernization of clothing and household furniture, new refinement and social manners were established in society, forming the material expression of the upcoming modern times.

Regarding the consumption of French textiles such as those made of 'bretaña', 'briaçu', 'cambray', 'crea' and 'duray' – see Appendix D, p. 265 – these were popularized due to the interaction of merchants, who spread the consumption of these articles throughout society. In addition, the popularization process in consuming other commodities did not follow the upwards to downwards pattern from wealthy to ordinary people. For instance, the consumption of porcelain had merchants as its main promoter – see Appendix D, p. 265. Foreign trade stimulated the circulation of this item in Europe, allowing European families to obtain grandeur or exquisite refinements. Porcelain is a very good example which shows the development of new tastes for goods, whose uniqueness was feeding the desires for luxury goods among society.[80] Entrepreneurs were an important agent in motivating consumer behavioural changes, as these intermediaries embodied modern socio-economic development governing the power of fashion and producing new needs in society[81]: 'once set, the windmill of fashion rolls as if it were self-activating'.[82]

The process by which commodities circulate in society is not simple and the motivations in emulating the patterns of consumption is much more complex than the generalized model of the flow of merchandise, which has been traditionally analysed through the trend of emulation from upper to lower social groups. The model could even be more problematic. Looking at the results of our registers – see Appendix A, B, C, D, pp. 241, 249, 257, 265 – the diffusion of consumption regarding particular durable goods such as household furniture – buffets or clocks – books or domestic utensils for having drinks – in this case the consumption of coffee – in gatherings does not follow a trend from upper, middle to lower social tiers. Regarding these particular objects, the tendency goes from the local oligarchy, and then falls down to middle-lower groups – craftsmen – with the merchant group being the last social agent in which these items circulate. Therefore, the process of the flow of goods is seen as a circular trend.

---

[80]   Batchelor, R., 'Modernity'. Clunas, C., 'On the Movement of Porcelains'.

[81]   Levi Martin, J., 'The Myth of the Consumption-Oriented Economy and the Rise of the Desiring Subject', *Theory and Society*, 28 (1999), p. 425. Corneo, G. and Jeanne, O., 'Segmented Communication and Fashionable Behaviour', *Journal of Economic Behaviour and Organization*, 39 (1999), pp. 371–85; 'Conformism, Snobbism, and Conspicuous Consumption', *Journal of Public Economics*, 66 (1997), pp. 55–71.

[82]   Simmel, G., 'Fashion', *International Quarterly*, 10 (1904), pp. 130–55. Svendsen, L., *Fashion*.

This tendency is likely to be present in economies with an important presence of elite groups as the primary actors of the political and socio-cultural life of the territory. This would mean that the joint function of a working class, not very well defined, and merchant group, as a force that potentially might spearhead the economic development of the region, promoted the supply of goods and services. This shortfall in the provision of commodities by craftsmen, in sectors of production such as textile or household furniture, due to the lack of manufacturing, was filled by commercial activities. Hence, by establishing a financial system based on credit, merchants assured the supply of household needs as well as stimulating new consumer desires.[83]

---

[83] Levine, D., 'Consumer Goods and Capitalist Modernization', *Journal of Inter-disciplinary History*, 22 (1991), pp. 67–77.

Chapter 8
The Trans-cultural Circulation of New Fashions in Urban and Rural Spaces

South-eastern Spain, and in particular the Kingdom of Murcia, is relatively small in size by comparison to other territories of Spain. However, the geography of the region and its natural resources gave the Kingdom a special dynamism in terms of its economic exchanges. The main cities – Murcia, Cartagena, Lorca or Caravaca – located in the four corners of the Kingdom of Murcia ensured the broad distribution and supply of goods to the population. In the eighteenth century, Murcia was the main political centre in which the local oligarchy, composed by small groups of notable families, ruled the city and controlled the agrarian resources of the rural hinterland of Murcia. The city was also a very important commercial centre, in which the main trade companies, mainly French, were established. The district of 'huerta y campo de Murcia' [the countryside of Murcia] was located outside the ancient boundaries of the medieval city. The proximity between the urban and rural areas of Murcia made possible a rapid circulation of goods among these nearby areas.

The city of Cartagena presents similar features to Murcia, related to the political and socio-economic structure, but has a special identity completely different to Murcia. The port of Cartagena has been defined as the best natural port of the Mediterranean area, and main site of the entry of Mediterranean and foreign products to Castile. It has also an important military function as in 1728 it was declared as a military base of the Mediterranean maritime zone, as well as one of the three shipyards used by the Spanish Royal Marine during the eighteenth century. The characteristics of the port of Cartagena, and its vicinity to the city of Murcia and rural areas, made possible the efficient distribution of goods. The dynamism of the cities of Cartagena and Murcia was complemented by the role played by the cities of Lorca and Caravaca, as important inner areas of the Kingdom of Murcia that communicated with the Kingdom of Granada (Andalucia). Thus, the commercial axis of Murcia, Cartagena, Caravaca and Lorca stimulated important trade transactions that resulted from the activity of the foreign merchants who settled in these territories. Within this framework the Kingdom of Murcia can be defined as a small constellation of towns and little villages, in which the inter-regional trade, due to the proximity between urban and rural areas, facilitated the supply of goods to the population. Obviously, regional differences and local peculiarities emerge due to the characteristics of different social groups belonging to each town or village.

The city of Murcia was the main urban area in which people displayed new clothing and dress styles related to seeking comfort and enjoying leisure time. But this happened not only in households of upper social groups. In the middle social groups, as well as in the lower ones, there was a progressive tendency towards this new, improved lifestyle. In Cartagena, the commodities that were unloaded at the port, and then commercialized, caught the attention of various social classes. These goods were then distributed to urban and rural areas. Thus, in the following pages some contrasts in consumption according to the proximity to urban and rural areas will be seen. The consumption of luxury commodities, textiles and groceries rose surprisingly in the rural areas of Cartagena, and this is an indicator that shifts in consumer behaviour did not only take place in cities and small towns. People did not simply emulate the patterns of consumption of the urban local oligarchy; their choices of consumption were led by the intensification of trade networks and advertising campaigns. Here the role played by peddlers appears to have been crucial for such shifts in taste.

Dowries are the main source that historians have for analysing the spread of new fashions. Women were the main social agents in the diffusion of new fashions, both in public and private spheres, such as walks and promenades, theatres, bullfights or in the domestic spaces as protectors of the family's values and reputation. The dowry sheds light upon the multifaceted role of women as individuals combining tradition and modernity. This source lists goods that can be defined as traditional – such as religious medals, wedding rings, crucifixes, or religious books (the Bible, Lives of the Saints, histories of the Church and so on), but also items that seem quite modern such as low-cut dresses, extravagant jewellery, suits, lingerie or modern shoes. In other words, dowries listed goods considered to be novelties, which interested and attracted consumers. As a consequence, there was a reaction among the more traditional sectors of society that sought to defend the catholic values of the state. The differentiation of urban and rural spaces offers us some clues on how these new fashions circulated among towns and villages.

8.1. Towns and Rural Communities: the Influence of the Geographical Variable in the Circulation of Goods

The process of how changes in consumption were operating can be best understood by analysing the channels of distribution of goods in certain areas. In the particular case of the Kingdom of Murcia, it is crucial to separate its two major rural areas – 'huerta y campo' of Murcia and 'campo' of Cartagena. Secondly, the focus of our analysis is centred on the circulation of goods in the urban areas of both territories. This enables us to analyse how marketing and trade systems were operating via the sale of new commodities in shops, bazaars and second-hand markets, by reaching potential customers in rural areas and the main cities of the territory – see Map 8.2. The urban area of the port of Cartagena in which commodities entered has been analysed, as well as their distribution in rural communities. Secondly, I have compared the level of distribution and consumption of goods in inner areas such as the city of Murcia and its surrounding villages – see Appendix G and H, pp. 287, 313.

As we can observe, in the tables of Appendix G and H (pp. 287, 313), during the eighteenth century the attraction for some commodities fluctuated, especially during the second half of the century, with the privileged location of Cartagena being crucial for the sales and promotion of goods to its population. This feature explains why some goods, such as textiles made of 'indianas', were more popular in the urban area of Cartagena and its rural surroundings than the city of Murcia and its neighbouring area. However, other commodities such as chinaware and other exotic goods from China such as fans, porcelains or furniture were more popular in the city of Murcia. The purchase of these items grew notably during the second half of the eighteenth century, particularly in the urban area of Murcia. The consumption of such commodities was marginal in Cartagena; only 5.5 per cent with respect to the size of the population studied, and it did not occur in rural areas at all.

The analysis of both groups of commodities, textiles made of 'indiana' and chinaware and goods from China is a crucial example for comparing patterns of consumption between urban and rural areas. It is important to make such a distinction in order to understand what the real channels of diffusion of luxury goods were.[1] Both groups of commodities are urban and, therefore, it is at first easy to establish that they are mainly purchased in urban areas. However, the results show that textiles made of 'indiana' were in fact more popular in rural areas of the Kingdom of Murcia, mainly those from Cartagena, than in urban places – see Appendix G and H, pp. 287, 313. The main reason could be the final decision of consumers, in which the role of peddlers in changing consumer habits was crucial. The villages of Cartagena developed and popularized the demand for goods, especially calicoes or 'indianas', which were fairly affordable by the large middle-lower social group. Certainly, the presence of peddlers and the second-hand market and the cost of transportation to interior areas would mean that the consumption of this commodity was higher in neighbouring rural areas of the port of Cartagena. On the other hand, chinaware and articles from China are commodities linked with exotic and exquisite tastes; therefore the elite groups were the selective clientele for the purchase of such goods due to the high prices. Thus, the consumer was not a passive agent in his/her choices for attractive durable goods. Some important features of items such as basic information about the commodity as well as the

---

[1]   Schuurman, A., 'From Citizen to Consumer to Citizen-Consumer? The Development of the Welfare State and the Consumer Society', in Moerbeek, H., Niehof, A. and Ophem, J. van (eds), *Changing Families and their Lifestyles* (Wageningen: Wageningen Academic Publisher, Mansholt publication series 5, 2007). Smart Martin, A., *Buying into the World of Goods: Early Consumers in Backcountry Virginia* (Baltimore: Johns Hopkins University Press, 2008).

price and quality tended to shape the taste of consumers.[2] Hence, purchasers of
fancy commodities were eager to acquire more of these in a compulsive way.
The structure of networks – see Map 8.1 – to distribute goods from the city to
rural communities was crucial in the process of creating in consumers compulsive
behaviour to buy goods not only for covering basic necessities.

Such merchant networks fostered the demand-side. The interconnection of the
maritime area of Cartagena with both rural and urban areas of the entire Kingdom
contributed to changing consumer behaviour. Peddlers were crucial economic
agents in such networks. Although they left very little archival evidence of their
activity, the 'Catastro de la Ensenada' shows the importance of this noteworthy
economic group throughout the territory – see Maps 8.1 and 8.2. Despite the
drawbacks to this map – especially due to the ambiguity of the 'Catastro de la
Ensenada' – it is still helpful to show how this plan covers important areas of the
region – the maritime zone of Cartagena as well as inner zones.

In the second half of the eighteenth century, the consumption of chocolate-
pots, coffee-pots, tea-pots or buffets, mirrors or porcelains by the large middle
social group was higher in urban areas, especially Murcia, than in rural areas.
The use of new household furniture had important connotations related with the
acquisition of new lifestyles. For instance the use of buffets entailed changes in the
distribution of the domestic space, especially with the introduction of the 'estrado'
– a platform in where buffets were located. The presence of chocolate-, coffee-
and tea-pots meant that dietary habits and the taste for consuming such beverages
were widespread among society during the second half of the eighteenth century
– see Appendix G and H, pp. 287, 313. Through these results we can see the
circulation of these commodities and how they were progressively enjoyed by the
large social middle group: chocolate-pots and utensils such as 'jicaras' [bowls] and
'salvillas' [trays] had a predominant position by comparison to tea- and coffee-
pots. Certainly, this feature can be explained by the almost inexistent culture
of drinking tea in Spain during that period. Coffee progressively took hold in
household expenditures. The drinking of chocolate was very popular in the late
seventeenth century and eighteenth century, especially during the second half, a
'boom' in its consumption took place among all levels of society.

Commodities that appear to have been less spread among social groups were
porcelains, books and clocks, which were authentic luxury goods representing a
very high lifestyle that only the upper classes could enjoy. Their diffusion in rural
areas was smaller than in urban zones as they were luxury commodities related
to elegant lifestyles. Between 3 per cent and 9 per cent of books and clocks were
consumed in rural areas of Murcia and Cartagena. Porcelains were barely present

---

[2]   Berg, M. and Clifford, H., 'Selling Consumption in the Eighteenth Century.
Advertising and Trade Card in Britain and France', *Cultural and Social History* (1998),
vol. 4, no. 2, pp. 145–70. From the same authors: *Consumers and Luxury. Consumer
Culture in Europe, 1650–1850* (Manchester and New York: Manchester University Press,
1999).

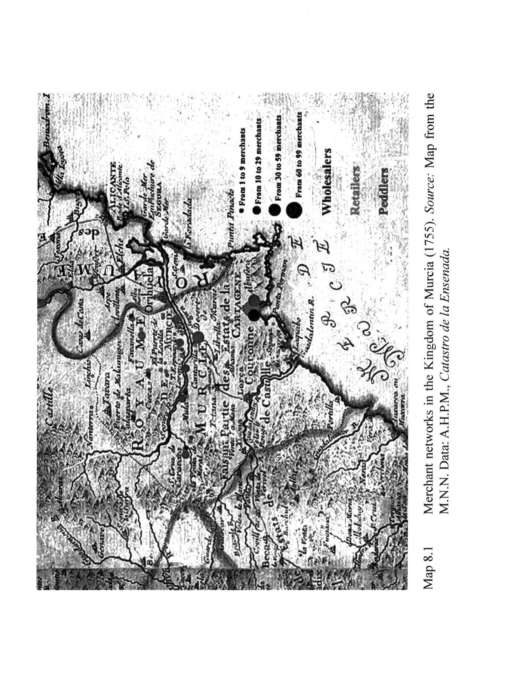

Map 8.1   Merchant networks in the Kingdom of Murcia (1755). *Source:* Map from the M.N.N. Data: A.H.P.M., *Catastro de la Ensenada.*

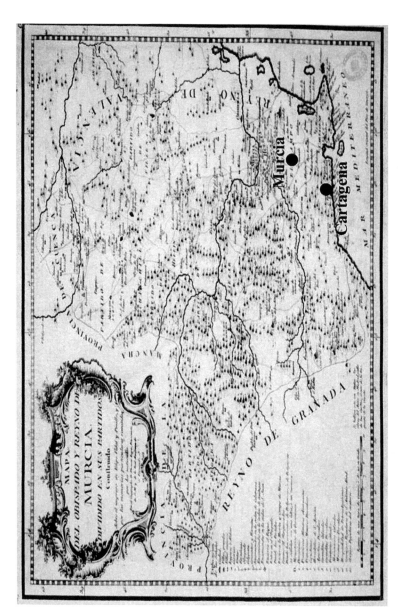

Map 8.2   The Kingdom of Murcia in the eighteenth century. *Source:* Map from A.H.P.M.

in the urban area of Cartagena during the second half of the century, but were found in 5 per cent of homes of rural local elites in the population studied. The urban population of Murcia purchased higher levels of porcelains according to the lists found in inventories – see Appendix G and H, pp. 287, 313. Clocks were more popular than books during the eighteenth century, especially during the second half. The rising tendency to possess clocks refers to the acquisition of new technologies to measure time, being an exclusive activity of small elite groups. The circulation of such items as well as books was related with the diffusion of knowledge and new tastes, by means of books.

The consumption of clothes related to the 'majo's' garments, which inspired some changes in consumer behaviour during the eighteenth century, as a traditional attire, is not necessary linked with urban and upper-class people – see Appendix F, G, H, I, pp. 279, 287, 313, 321. Making a comparison between the levels of consumption of fancy costumes, items mostly related to urban and rich people, and 'basquiñas', garments linked more with rural and ordinary people, it can be affirmed that both goods circulated indistinctively among different social groups, as well as rural and urban areas. In most cases the 'basquiñas' started to be more popular among middle and lower social groups, while the elite began to acquire this commodity later. So, the idea that the 'majo' attire was used first by lower social groups can be confirmed, as from the results of our inventories there is clearly a higher level of consumption of traditional goods by ordinary people. Once this traditional clothing became fashionable, local elites felt the attraction toward the acquisition of popular styles. The consumption of traditional clothes, related to 'majo' outfit, was more popular than foreign or French commodities in the Kingdom of Murcia. The 'basquiña' is found in both urban and rural areas, and its usage increased during the second half of the eighteenth century – see Appendix F, G, H, I, pp. 279, 287, 313, 321.

The tendency to use gold and silver buckles to decorate jackets, shoes and hairstyles was quite widespread in middle-upper social groups, especially during the second half of the eighteenth century, when their usage increased notably in both urban and rural areas of Cartagena and Murcia. Concerning the consumption of another article of the 'majo' outfit such as the 'cofia' [hair net] as well as mantillas, which would be expected to be found in rural inventories, we find that it is also highly consumed by urban high social groups as can be seen in Appendix F, G, H, I, pp. 279, 287, 313, 321.

Some goods identified with the 'majo' fashion, as well as goods related to the taste for French fashion, were used by middle social groups in both rural and urban areas, a fact that a priori we might not have expected. So, there was a progressive consumption of different French commodities as well as the desire for traditional clothing, and this was a way to channel modernity in which we can see that it is wrong to affirm that town and village correspond respectively with modernity and tradition. Surely, cities are major places in which the development of modern social patterns is faster than rural areas, but also villages and small towns channel such a transition to modernity as we can see through the higher volumes of consumption of new clothing in rural areas of Cartagena.

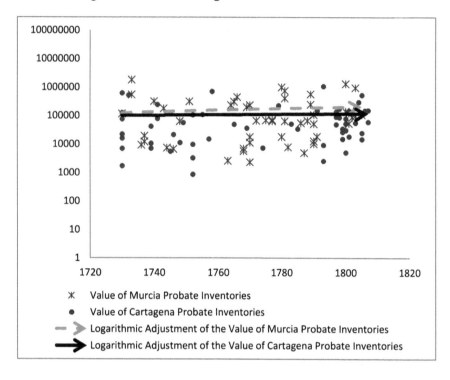

Chart 8.1   Valuation of urban probate inventories of the Kingdom of Murcia (1730–1808). *Source:* A.H.P.M. Value: 'Reales'.

Certainly a major consequence of the progressive increase of the household income, which was caused by the increase in working hours and the economic resources of the household unit, was a rise in the wealth accumulated by an individual during his lifetime, allowing the middle social groups to enjoy more goods. This provoked a social 'democratization' in consumption. This group of commodities, which we have described, were most likely introduced and consumed in society before the eighteenth century, but not to the same degree. In Charts 8.1 and 8.2 the value of inventories in the Kingdom of Murcia has been deflated according to Castilian prices for the period 1730–1808.[3] As we are dealing with two different periods in the sample of inventories, I have considered it appropriate to use 1745–50 as an index year of the first period, and 1785–90 for the second. In Chart 8.1 I have calculated the value of probate inventories for urban areas of Murcia and Cartagena. In general, the value of patrimonies in Murcia and Cartagena inventories remains

  [3]   See Reher, D.S. and Ballesteros, S., 'Precios y salarios', pp. 101–51.

steady, while some growth of the value in the second half of the eighteenth century for the inventories of the urban area of Murcia takes place. In contrast, Chart 8.2 shows that there is a growing tendency of the value of inventories in both Murcia and Cartagena rural communities during the entire century. This could explain the better standards of living of rural social groups, which were able to afford the consumption of commodities related to comfort, luxury and better lifestyles, and the fact that some goods such as clothing made of 'indianas' were more spread in rural than urban areas.

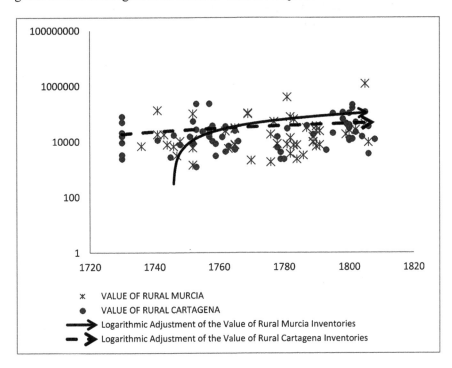

Chart 8.2   Valuation of rural probate inventories of the Kingdom of Murcia (1730–1808). *Source:* A.H.P.M. Value: 'Reales'.

8.2. Introduction of New Fashions through Dowries: Women as Potential Consumers

The presence of a multitude of fancy objects such as dresses, white lingerie, fans, jewellery and mirrors in the dowries of urban and rural women is proof of women's attitudes towards the acquisition of new fashions during the second half of the eighteenth century. These features were related to the new socio-cultural trends of modern civilization. There is a particular connection between real practices and the ideas expressed by writers of the period, who took special notice of the appearance of new decorative ornaments worn by women. The dowry reveals the arrival of new fashions in which women were the main consumers. It is interesting to note the lists of objects symbolising new lifestyles and changes in patterns of consumption which appear in such sources.[4]

Regarding the analysis of dowries, I have followed the same methodology as for the probate inventories, collecting a group of 66 records covering different social groups of varying level of wealth and dividing them into two periods: from 1730 to 1769 and from 1770 to 1808 – see Tables 8.1 and 8.2. I have examined the circulation of particular items, analysing the total value of the dowry, which gives us a view of the individual's level of wealth when the bride and the groom constituted the new family unit by means of the goods provided at the time of the marriage.

Table 8.1   Sample of dowries according to social groups in the City of Murcia (1730–1808)

Social Status	1730/69	1770/1808
Local oligarchy	5	5
Merchants	6	5
Landowners	3	3
Master Artisans' wives	4	4
Professionals	2	2
Artisans	5	5
Yeomen	9	8
Total	34	32 = 66

Source: A.H.P.M., protocols.

Table 8.2   Distribution of dowries according to wealth levels in the City of Murcia (1730–1808)

Total Inventory Valuation (Sample = 66)	No. of Dowries (1730–69)	No. of Dowries (1770–1808)
0>1500	8	2
1500>3000	12	5
3000>8000	7	13
>8000	7	12
TOTAL	34	32

The value of the dowries has been deflated according to the Reher-Ballesteros's index.
Source: A.H.P.M., protocols. Reher, D.S. and Ballesteros, S., 'Precios y salarios', pp. 101–51.

---

    [4]   See Zarandieta Arenas, F., 'Riqueza y consumo'; Torras, J., Duran, M. and Torra, L., 'El ajuar'; Romanelli, R., 'Donne'; Ago, R., *Il gusto delle cose*; García Fernández, M., 'Los bienes dotales'; from the same author: 'Vestirse y vestir la casa. El consumo de productos textiles en Valladolid (1700–1860)', *Obradoiro de Historia Moderna*, no. 14, 2005, p. 160.

For centuries women have been associated with inconsistency and change.[5] In the Enlightenment period, theories were developed to explain fondness of women for frivolities and novel items. The goods listed in dowries reflect the tastes and desires not only of the bride, but also of her family. Surely, dowries showed family values, but with the introduction of some specific goods and materials, they were also challenging family traditions. This attraction to novelties meant that merchants considered women as potential consumers who could buy the objects they offered. Items such as accessories, jewels and fashionable clothes were thus given priority by merchants seeking potential customers.

An imminent result of the increase in consuming such adornments was the individual's acquisition of refined manners. This personal attitude had a very important social expression in the public sphere, where women manifested their refinement and good taste, as well as their belonging to a higher social level. They showed off their fine manners at social gatherings or by participating in walks and promenades in the avenues and parks of urban areas, in which the cultures of appearance as well as the new modern civility were taking hold.[6] The superfluous female garments, as well as domestic decorations as innovative elements, were also interconnected with traditional goods. Tradition and modernity coexisted in the late eighteenth century. Changes occurred in external attire faster than household items as shown by contemporary fashion magazines, the growth of retail sales, mannequins and other ways to draw consumers into shops.[7] Such processes were based on the growth of cities, improvements in communications, the variety of items available on the supply-side, merchandising systems as well as emulation in consumption, provoking an increase in the demand-side. The wide variety of textiles, as demonstrated in previous pages, as well as the introduction of goods by means of the dowry, also fostered shifts in material culture.

The image of the 'new woman' made a profound appearance in European society,[8] though moralists attacked and denounced this new image. The moralists promoted and reinforced the opinion that body ornaments, such as jewellery or head embellishments, were more characteristic of prostitutes than Christian

---

[5]   Jones, J., '*Coquettes* and *Grisettes*. Women Buying and Selling in Ancien Regime Paris', in De Grazia, V. and Furlough, E. (eds), *The Sex of Things*, pp. 25–53.

[6]   In Rafaella Sarti's work is reiterated that the position of women changed across time, due to the development of a growing distinction between public and private spheres: *Europe at Home. Family and Material Culture, 1500–1800* (New Haven, CT: Yale University Press, 2002).

[7]   See the magazine: *La moda elegante ilustrada: periódico de las familias* (Madrid: 1842–1927). Oriol Ronquillo, J., *Diccionario de materia mercantil, industrial y agrícola*, 4 vols. (Barcelona: Imprenta de D.A. Gaspar, 1851–57).

[8]   Kaplan, M.A. (ed.), *The Marriage Bargain: Women and Dowries in European History* (New York: Harrington Park Press, 1985).

women of virtue.[9] The Jesuit priest Pedro Calatayud wrote in 1739 about the use of the wig as an evil symbol filled with vice: 'despojos de otra cabeza muerta, acaso llena de enfermedades y condenada al infierno'.[10] Women's dress styles and fashions were condemned in sermons by preachers, who continuously encouraged people to break their attraction to such superficial things. They denounced the lavish consumption of embellishments such as fans, collars and high-heeled shoes, which were identified with vanity and desire, and argued that they went against proper Catholic behaviour.[11] As a result of such zealous critics, treatises on dress styles appeared, manifesting the incompatibility of arrogance and pity, expressing a repulsion for the vain women who dared to visit churches in such outfits. Jesuit priests described, sometimes with very sensual imagery, the arrogant behaviour of such women:

> El torpe adorno de rostro y cabeza de una mujer, el calzado provocativo, el escote inmodesto; por que una mujer brillante con coloridos y afeites en su semblante es un ídolo o una Venus adornada ... la cual, a manera de una pava real, engreído el cuello y llena la pompa y vanidad en el ruedo de sus plumas vistosas, convida y despierta el apetito del hombre a lujuriar.

Concerning women's new attitudes, European writers followed the same trend as Spanish preachers. The French philosopher Antoine Leonard Thomas wrote in his *Essays on the Character, the Morals, and the Intelligence of Women* (1772):

> Naturellement plus sensible, elles ont plus besoin d'un objet qui sans cesse occupe leur ame ... Moins occuppées & moins actives, elles ont plus le temps de contempler ... Plus frappées par les yeux, elles goûtent plus l'appareil des cérémonies & des temples ...[12]

This was an idea which tended to exaggerate reality as it is necessary to take into consideration the socio-cultural and economic framework. First of all, there was strong propaganda, in Spain and other European territories, through religious

---

[9]   Callahan, W.J. and Higgs, D. (eds), *Church and Society in Catholic Europe of the Eighteenth Century* (Cambridge, [Eng.]; New York: Cambridge University Press, 1979).

[10]   B.N., mss. 6006–6008. Calatayud, P., *Doctrinas prácticas que solía explicar en sus misiones el V.P. Pedro de Calatayud*, Doctrina VI, Parte II, Tratado X, T. III, pp. 416–7.

[11]   Kamen, H., 'Nudité et Contre-réforme', in Redondo, A. (ed.), *Le corps dans la société espagnole des XVIe et XVIIe siècles* (Paris: ed. Publications de la Sorbonne, 1990), pp. 297–307.

[12]   Antoine-Leonard Thomas, *Essai sur le caràctere, les moeurs, et l'esprit des femmes* (Paris: Moutard, 1772), p. 111–14. For the case of Protestant Europe, see De Vries, J., 'Luxury and Calvinism/Luxury and Capitalism: Supply and Demand for Luxury Goods in the Seventeenth-century Dutch Republic', *The Journal of the Walters Art Gallery*, vol. 57, Place and Culture in Northern Art (1999), pp. 73–85.

treatises and sermons against this new female behaviour.[13] Thus, religious dogma had as its primary aim the reinvention of women in accordance with Catholic tradition.[14] We should also note that women have always been represented through men's writings. Sometimes those writings offered a contradictory appraisal, caught between attraction and repulsion or admiration and hostility.[15] The only way to embrace virtue was either through marriage or by entering a convent. Women who did not follow this path were labelled as sinful. This group was attacked because such women were more passionate about excessive French fashions[16] and extravagant clothes than embracing modest virtues.

This was the cultural framework of the strong criticisms against women's behaviour. In addition, there was an important economic component that explains the increase in female purchases. This particular fascination for new and compulsive consumption depended on a family's level of income. However, the consumption of certain goods such as fans is also seen in dowries of a modest value as well as dowries of middle income groups as we can see in Table 8.3. In other words, the fascination for the purchase of frivolities, for which women were being denounced, was more in relation to the wealth of the household and its capacity to accumulate savings in order to afford a wide range of items. Dowries were also related to marital and family alliances. Moreover, they have a strong component related to 'vicarious consumption'.

I have calculated the percentage of the usage of particular goods listed in dowries, in relation to the levels of wealth of different social groups. The percentage has been estimated over the total sample of dowries – see Table 8.3. It can be seen that fans could be afforded by the middle social group, although the data show that purchases of this item were not very significant. Thus, its consumption was more notable in middle-upper social groups, offering proof that ordinary people also participated in the acquisition of new fashions. The consumption of this type of commodity was not only possible for rich people; however, rich classes conspicuously acquired these items to display power and splendor. During the eighteenth century, the fan was a very important element in the composition of female dress styles. The fan, handled in an expert manner, had a repertoire of hidden messages in which women could express 'amorous intents'.[17] Women, as

---

[13]   Burke, P., 'How to Be a Counter-Reformation Saint', in Von Greyerz, K. (ed.), *Religion and Society in Early Modern Europe, 1500–1800* (Boston: Allen and Unwin, 1984). Barnes-Karol, G., 'Religious Oratory in a Culture of Control', in Cruz, A.J. and Perry, M.E., *Culture and Control in Counter-Reformation Spain* (Minneapolis and Oxford: University of Minnesota, 1992).

[14]   López Cordón, M.V., 'Predicación e inducción política en el siglo XVIII: Fray Diego José de Cádiz', *Hispania*, no. 138 (1978), pp. 71–120. Chartier, R., *Cultural History: Between Practices and Representations* (Cambridge: Polity Press in association with Blackwell, 1988).

[15]   Delumeau, J., *Le péché et la peur* (Paris: ed. Fayard, 1983), p. 471.

[16]   Sarrailh, J., *La España ilustrada*, p. 380.

[17]   See Martin Gaite, *Usos Amorosos*, pp. 25–63.

consumers, and foreigners as mediators in the introduction of new fashions, were
strongly attacked by the Establishment:

> En ninguna otra cosa ha introducido más el capricho de la moda, valiéndose de
> ésta las naciones extranjeras para causar infinitos dispendios en la nuestra, al
> mismo tiempo que los da por bien empleados una señora para hacerse aire en
> diciembre.[18]

The main argument used to denounce such fashions was that the conspicuous
consumption of commodities, introduced by foreigners, was the cause of
profound and foolish economic waste, simply to satisfy women's caprice
for useless items. Behind the use of frivolous objects such as the fan, a sort
of 'subliminal language' was introduced into society. Smiles, confidences,
insolences and obscene sights were presented through 'the language of the fan'
in social gatherings. The fan, as a decorative garment, represented the debate on
solving the economic problems of the nation. This is proof that the moral debate
about whether or not it was appropriate for a member of a Catholic nation to
wear superficial clothing was simply used to hide the difficulties which the state
encountered to generate economic resources.[19] Likewise, I have analysed the
appearance of jewellery such as collars and rings in dowries, as well as mirrors
and white lingerie. The consumption of jewellery indicates the preference
toward displaying a refined image in public. In the sample of dowries we can see
that during the second half of the eighteenth century, groups with a middle level
of income widely enjoyed the consumption of collars and rings – see Table 8.3
– especially groups with modest dowries. This can be explained by the growing
value of dowries during the second half of the eighteenth century, revealing an
increase in the buying power of social groups with lower and middle levels of
income – see Charts 8.3 and 8.4. This also happened with the consumption of
white lingerie made of linen and silk, which was greatly consumed in society.
The acquisition of mirrors is found less in our sample, however they do appear
in the entire range of dowries, but not in those whose value is between 1,500 and
3,000 'reales' – see Table 8.3. The consumption of this item was quite significant,
showing an increase of interest in care for individual appearance, which became
an obsession. People wanted to consume it conspicuously in order to look good
in the public eye.

---

[18]   Terreros y Pando, E., *Diccionario castellano, con las voces de las ciencias y artes
y sus correspondientes en las tres lenguas, francesa, italiana y latina* (4 vols., Madrid,
1786–93), vol. 1, artículo: 'Abanico'.
[19]   Callahan, W.J., 'Utility, Material Progress and Morality in Eighteenth-century
Spain', in Fritz, P. and Williams, D. (eds), *The Triumph of Culture. Eighteenth Century
Perspectives* (Toronto: Hakkert, 1972), pp. 359–60.

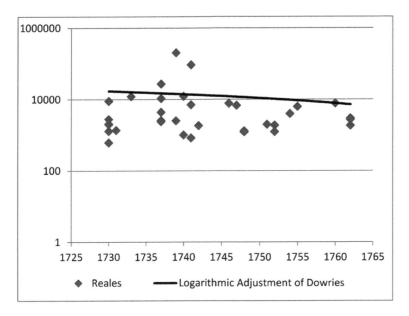

Chart 8.3   Value of dowries of the City of Murcia (1730–69)

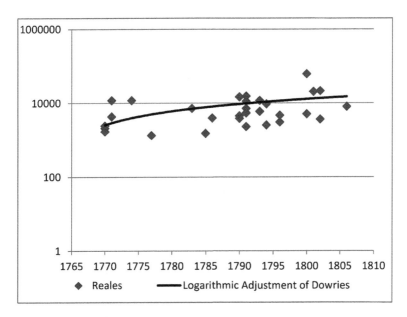

Chart 8.4   Value of dowries of the City of Murcia (1770–1808). The value of the dowries has been deflated according to the Reher-Ballesteros's index. *Source:* A.H.P.M., protocols. Reher, D.S. and Ballesteros, S., 'Precios y salarios', pp. 101–51, 1993.

Table 8.3   Frequency of selected goods in dowries of Murcia (1730–1808)

Total Dowry Valuation (Sample = 66)		'Enaguas' [white lingerie] (1730–69) (%)	'Enaguas' [white lingerie] (1770–1808) (%)	Fans (1730–69) (%)	Fans (1770–1808) (%)	Rings (1730–69) (%)	Rings (1770–1808) (%)	Collars (1730–69) (%)	Collars (1770–1808) (%)	Mirrors (1730–69) (%)	Mirrors (1770–1808) (%)
	1730/69	1770/1808									
0 > 1500 = 8*	2*	37.50	50.00	0.00	0.00	12.50	0.00	0.00	0.00	12.50	50.00
1500 > 3000 = 12*	5*	91.66	60.00	33.33	20.00	25.00	40.00	16.66	60.00	8.33	0.00
3000 > 8000 = 7*	13*	100.00	61.53	71.42	23.07	71.42	30.76	42.85	30.76	71.42	7.69
> 8000 = 7*	12*	57.14	83.33	0.00	0.00	28.57	41.66	42.85	0.00	42.85	16.66
TOTAL = 34*	32*	73.52	68.75	26.47	12.50	32.35	34.37	23.52	21.87	29.41	12.50

Source: A.H.P.M., protocols. *Number of Dowries.

Conclusions

The analysis of probate inventories shows the gradual diffusion in the consumption of durable and semi-durable goods in urban and rural families as well as households with different levels of wealth. There was certainly an interest in consuming exotic and foreign goods filling new consumer needs, but at the same time the display of some types of goods, in public life, caused a social backlash, because those goods were the symbol of social transgressions against traditional lifestyles. Therefore, in eighteenth-century Spanish literature, as well as political texts such as letters, prohibitions or pamphlets, we find the major platform for traditional voices that were imposing barriers against the conversion of the national territory into a 'melting pot' composed of both national and foreign human, economic, material and cultural capital. There was a progressive process of building up of social stereotypes and prejudices such as the French model of the 'petimetre' with the aim of preserving the traditional Spanish aesthetic order and values. The Spanish statement was feeding the social repulsion and hatred towards the acquisition of French fashions and attitudes. However, the acquisition and diffusion of fashion has more complex components such as the creation of new needs, the desire for renovation and the social aspiration of being distinguished in the public arena. Certainly, there was a taste for French commodities and a wide range of luxury and household furniture that were satisfying these needs, especially middle social class necessities, as a feature of the new consumer behaviour. Such tastes were prompted by the French trade networks established in south-eastern Spain, which acted as 'vicarious consumers' by introducing new patterns of consumption, as well as foreign values.

The major socio-economic agents that stimulated and created the new demand for textiles and luxury and colonial commodities were merchants. In south-eastern Spain during the eighteenth century, an industrious revolution did not occur as most of the commodities consumed by all social groups, especially those by ordinary people, who enjoyed a wide variety of goods, came from the market. Such goods did not provoke an increase in the productive forces of both artisan and agrarian groups, as the regional economy depended on goods from external markets, neither was there a direct policy by both national and local administrations to improve the technology of the backward system imposed by craft guilds. In addition, these agents stimulated the 'democratization' or 'popularization' of commodities, which did not flow from the top to the bottom in the social hierarchy. Instead new fashions, in general, and the social diffusion of certain goods, in particular, followed a diverse social trend, which demonstrate that McKendrick's apriorism related to the 'trickle-down' corresponds to a more complex social process.

PART V
General Conclusions

The attainment of new customs and habits occurred under certain social conditions, especially in the urban area, where the significance of prestige and ostentation among classes was stronger than in rural areas. The urban sphere was the space for social differentiation, mainly because it was the place where the oligarchy lived. In addition, modes of dressing and new elaborate interior decorations played an important role, as these new consumer features implied conditions of external exhibition of power and civility as well as the enjoyment of a better lifestyle.[1]

The extravagance and folly that took place in the market in connection with the consumption of certain objects had a high symbolic value. During the eighteenth century in Spain, new patterns of consumption were emerging, inspiring the display of ostentation through new fancy objects due to a rise in the purchases of goods that the middle social classes could afford. Thus the cultural history of appearances is in relation with the social practices and the status of the different social groups.

The 'industrious revolution' theory, examined through the data, shows the different ways in which commodities penetrated the household economy of social groups with diverse levels of income. Hence, the essential questions that were posed by the agents of the marketplace were:

- What should be produced?
- What should be consumed?
- What should be distributed?

The historians' focus need to be addressed to observe how the different ideological models coexisted and competed in order to regulate consumer behaviour by the Spanish government, mixing reality and imaginary worlds in an attempt to shape the ideal state. The struggle represented by the 'petimetre' and 'majo' stereotypes is a good example of the confrontation between traditional and modern societies, creating an imaginary world in which consumers were the main social actors of a modern economic order. The 'macaroni' and 'dandy' phenomenon, which took place in the British territory, as well as the new independent British American colonies, constitute the most outstanding evidence that such socio-cultural models

---

[1] Roche, D., *La culture*, p. 3.

did not emerge exceptionally in European regions, but were also a cultural trend integrated in the international movement of the upcoming modern era.

Fashion itself was the main vehicle through which commercial agents initially wanted to stimulate their business and political institutions. On the other hand, they reinforced traditional national values by stereotyping the people who were enchanted by foreign cultures and fashions, which circulated transculturally among European, Asian and American regions, as perverse and transgressive. The intervention of the state on how people should dress, behave and lead their patterns of consumption exerted a very important influence on dislocating foreign merchant businesses in the Spanish Mediterranean during the late eighteenth and early nineteenth centuries. The path to achieve a new economic stage is identified by how the supply- and demand-sides stimulate the economy. But if either the supply- or the demand-side are affected by means of political interventions such as bans, rules of prohibition on consumption and the identification of both human and material foreign capitals as demonic and perverse, then the main consequence is the disruption of the stimulating forces that make the economy grow.

In south-eastern Spain during the eighteenth and early nineteenth centuries there was a transition towards a new order on consumption, the household unit was the main hub of that activity. Middle social groups increasingly spent their budgets on commodities of traditional industries and also raised the demand for commodities from markets such as the Mediterranean, Atlantic and Asian, thus making consumption, in particular, and the economy, in general, more global. From the sample of probate inventories we can state that there was no 'consumer revolution' or consumer boom in south-eastern Spain, especially if we take into account the fact that a large group of the lower working class such as urban workers, the poor or peddlers are the social classes for which we rarely find an inventory in the archive of protocols of the Kingdom of Murcia. However, a progressive acquisition of consumer goods certainly took place, accelerating changes in fashion among society in the early days of modern consumerism by shaping new consumer behaviour during the late eighteenth and early nineteenth centuries. Furthermore, as Fernando Ramos Palencia has demonstrated for other Castilian territories, the household consumption depreciation rates increased gradually, the life expectancy of these goods fell and the replacement rates rose.[2] As mentioned above, urban areas absorbed more rapidly the demand for the bulk of items commercialized in the import-export market, and thus cities, rather than rural areas, were the main places where household consumption was more pronounced.

The key elements which encouraged the growth in the demand for durable and semi-durable goods were: income; the marginal rise of purchasing power, especially among middle and upper-middle groups; the shift of the population from subsistence agriculture to a market economy, urban areas being the main nuclei; and the drop-off related to the price of manufactured textiles and agricultural prices. This progressive expansion of household consumption could

---

[2]   Ramos Palencia, F. and Nicolini, E.A, 'A New Method', pp. 145–77.

lead us to deduce that standards of living and comfort grew steadily. This is caused by the increase of private expenditure on luxury goods, those related to interior decorations, clothing, as well as beverages such as coffee, chocolate and tea. The group of commodities of clothing was in relation with the consumption of a large variety of textiles, as they were the main sector in which family budgets were spent.

Did an industrious revolution really occur as the consumption of certain goods by middle-lower social groups such as artisans and peasants increased during the eighteenth century? Examining the results shown in the data of our sample of probate inventories, it could be deduced that surely the consumption for goods that came from the market increased in households of south-eastern Spain. But this did not provoke an increase on the productive forces of local artisan and agrarian groups of the territory; although from the demand-side in some social groups we could find certain symptoms of an industrious revolution. However, that appreciation is motivated by the changes on consumer behaviour, shifts that in other countries such as north-western Europe – England and Low Countries – accelerated the process for the industrial revolution as an upper stage of economic development. But in southern Europe, in particular south-eastern Spain, through the empirical analysis probate inventories, it can be said that middle social groups increased their expenditure on commodities that improved their lifestyles. This can be also explained by the fact of the favourable eighteenth-century conjuncture when prices were more stable, fuelling their desires, expectations and choices for a wide range of items. There was no 'obvious breakthrough' indicating an industrious revolution. The number of working hours probably did not increase as the artisan sector was constrained by the political institution's rules and the technological lack illustrated by the decrease in the possession of looms and artefacts.

Nevertheless, levels of consumption grew and the shift in the allocation and transaction networks was only due to the growth and integration of markets from local to global scale. Likewise, it would seem plausible that the expansion of the market, the intensifying of commercial exchange and the progressive integration of the south-eastern Spanish market facilitated the consumption of durable goods among the population. Simultaneously, these factors stimulated industrial and financial activities in the Kingdom of Murcia, especially in its main urban regions: Murcia and Cartagena.

To examine whether the industrious revolution and 'trickle-down' effect took place in south-eastern Spain I have analysed the circulation of certain products in order to observe the social channels of diffusion. In other words, within such an approach it is possible to establish whether such circulation starts from a concrete social group and moves to a different group without following a trend from top to bottom in the social hierarchy, causing a variant in the socio-economic forces that stimulate demand. This issue is very difficult to analyse. However, this approach, to analyse the industrious revolution and 'trickle-down' effect through the study of the social circulation of commodities, offers completely different findings than have been offered to date. The analysis of different trends of circulation of goods in social groups, with different levels of wealth, is an innovative element of our study. Thus, McKendrick's theory does not always correspond with the social reality. Jan de Vries did not establish a particular trend of social diffusion in the consumption of products. His idea was that the industrious revolution took place among middle and lower social groups, without considering the influence of elite groups on possible economic changes on consumer behaviour.

One of the most important features of this research, to establish the trends of social diffusion in the circulation of products, is the analysis of the key role played by merchants. Foreign trade groups settled in south-eastern Spain, mainly composed by French dealers, created an integrated community by shaping a solid social network. The social relations and businesses among such dealers were based on trust, co-national values, family unions, as well as by those sharing the same occupation. This allowed them to establish a socio-economic circuit by which they could undertake commercial ventures and fulfil their deals through a credit system based on transparency and the intermediation of brokers.

Hence, the creation of commercial networks in the western Mediterranean area, among French dealers established in south-eastern Spain and southern France, with Marseille as the main European gateway through which a high number of goods were exported and re-exported to European countries shaped a new consumer behaviour. This trade circuit made it possible not only to acquire products from the Mediterranean market, but also products from the Near East as well as the Atlantic region. Textiles, colonial commodities, such as coffee, tea, sugar, opium, cacao or chocolate, as well as exotic commodities, such as porcelains from China, became the material objects of a global demand and trans-national market. The Mediterranean areas of Spain were not excluded from this international and global process, especially taking into account the impossibility of national industries to produce goods to satisfy new consumer needs.

As we have shown in Part III, the total imports of products that entered the Spanish Mediterranean ports were higher than exports. This commercial circuit activated the consumption of commodities in south-eastern Spain, mainly in the areas of Murcia and Cartagena, rather than the local factors of production. In addition, we must add to this factor other notable features that stimulated the demand in the Kingdom of Murcia such as the very low prices of the wholesale market, from Marseille to Spain, which were affordable and stimulated the purchases by dealers, who thus sold high volumes of merchandise as reflected in the indexes of the 'Bourse de Marseille'. We must consider other important factors such as the steady increase of the purchasing power among the populations of Murcia and Cartagena, as well as the shifts in fashions and tastes that make the goods introduced by foreign dealers more desirable. As we have shown in our sample of probate inventories (see Appendices), all these features made the introduction of social transformations possible through the consumption of foreign and unusual goods, in some social groups, creating a social backlash among traditional groups, but at the same time breaking certain socio-cultural prejudices among the groups that consumed such goods.

Therefore, it is has been demonstrated that merchants were the 'vicarious consumers' that stimulated local demand: firstly by introducing their products as the main consumers, and secondly by encouraging new desires to purchase such goods among the local population. Cartagena and Murcia were important sites for the reception of goods traded from the international market, which means that the availability and consumption of those commodities grew. A substitution process did not occur to replace the high volume of imports, and the south-eastern Spanish economy was dependent on foreign trade. In addition, merchant families, as well as artisans and agrarian groups of south-eastern Spain, like most commercial and working-class areas of the Spanish Mediterranean territory, were more concerned about their properties, such as workshops, trade houses and companies, land and labour tools, rather than increasing productivity to produce commodities, through the household labour, with goods that came from the market.

International models of consumption as well as global trade contributed to changing social patterns of consumption and shaping the behaviour of modern consumers, who acted as individual agents going against the social norms and mores dictated by the state. Through such attitudes, individuals challenged the socio-economic policies of the government, putting aside bans, rules and all the political apparatus, whose aim was to control national consumption. Consequently, the real visualization of tradition and modernity has been deconstructed in our research, by observing that individuals, as autonomous consumers, were not involved in the political discourse, which emphasized *what* they should consume and *how*. This has been demonstrated through the analysis of probate inventories and dowries, which are the material evidence of the 'real' products consumed by the different social classes, as well as their expectations.

Appendix A

Testing the 'Industrious Revolution' Theory through Craftsmen in the Kingdom of Murcia (1730–1808)

Tables begin on next page.

Testing the 'industrious revolution' through the consumption of French commodities in the probate inventories of the Kingdom of Murcia (1730–1808)

	1730/69					
SAMPLE (=*135)	**Textiles made of 'bretaña' (%)**	**'Briaçu' (%)**	**Buffets (%)**	**'Cabriolé' (%)**	**Textiles made of 'cambray' (%)**	**Textiles made of 'crea' (%)**
Craftsmen (=37)	2.85	2.85	45.71	0.00	8.57	8.57
Rest of population (=98)	4.12	2.06	32.98	1.03	3.09	8.24
TOTAL	**3.78**	**2.27**	**36.36**	**0.75**	**4.54**	**8.33**
	1770/1808					
SAMPLE (=*138)	**Textiles made of 'bretaña' (%)**	**'Briaçu' (%)**	**Buffets (%)**	**'Cabriolé' (%)**	**Textiles made of 'cambray' (%)**	**Textiles made of 'crea' (%)**
Craftsmen (=37)	0.00	0.00	28.57	8.57	0.00	11.42
Rest of population (=101)	1.00	1.00	25.00	4.00	1.00	10.00
TOTAL	**0.74**	**0.74**	**25.92**	**5.18**	**0.74**	**10.37**

SOCIAL GROUPS

SOCIAL GROUPS

Testing the 'industrious revolution' through the consumption of French commodities in the probate inventories of the Kingdom of Murcia (1730–1808)

	SAMPLE (=*135)	'Desavillé' (%)	Textiles made of 'duray' (%)	Items with the French 'trade-mark' (%)	'Pompadour' (%)	Textiles made of 'tripé' (%)	Textiles made of 'trué' (%)
				1730/69			
SOCIAL GROUPS	Craftsmen (=37)	0.00	0.00	14.28	0.00	0.00	5.71
	Rest of population (=98)	0.00	0.00	14.43	1.03	1.03	8.24
	TOTAL	0.00	0.00	14.39	0.75	0.75	7.57
	SAMPLE (=*138)	'Desavillé' (%)	Textiles made of 'duray' (%)	Items with the French 'trade-mark' (%)	'Pompadour' (%)	Textiles made of 'tripé' (%)	Textiles made of 'trué' (%)
				1770/1808			
SOCIAL GROUPS	Craftsmen (=37)	8.57	14.28	8.57	0.00	5.71	20.00
	Rest of population (=101)	3.00	4.00	16.00	0.00	6.00	6.00
	TOTAL	4.44	6.66	14.07	0.00	5.92	9.62

Testing the 'industrious revolution' through the consumption of 'majo' attire in the probate inventories of the Kingdom of Murcia (1730–1808)

		'Basquiña' [top petticoat] (%)	'Chal' [shawl] (%)	'Chaqueta' [jacket] (%)	'Cofia' [hair net] (%)	'Jubon' [doublet] (%)	Mantilla (%)	'Trajes' [suits] (%)
	SAMPLE (=*135)				1730/69			
SOCIAL GROUPS	Craftsmen (=37)	34.28	0.00	0.00	2.85	20.00	34.28	2.85
	Rest of population (=98)	25.77	0.00	1.03	3.09	24.74	12.37	1.03
	TOTAL	**28.03**	**0.00**	**0.75**	**3.03**	**23.48**	**18.18**	**1.51**
	SAMPLE (=*138)				1770/1808			
SOCIAL GROUPS	Craftsmen (=37)	51.42	2.85	8.57	17.14	25.71	45.71	2.85
	Rest of population (=101)	41.00	0.00	6.00	8.00	14.00	34.00	1.00
	TOTAL	**43.70**	**0.74**	**6.66**	**10.37**	**17.03**	**37.03**	**1.48**

Testing the 'industrious revolution' through the consumption of household furniture in the probate inventories of the Kingdom of Murcia (1730–1808)

			1730/69			
	SAMPLE (=*135)	**Porcelains (%)**	**Mirrors (%)**	**Household cloth made of 'indiana' (%)**	**Items from China (%)**	**Chinaware (%)**
SOCIAL GROUPS	**Craftsmen (=37)**	8.57	42.85	31.42	0.00	0.00
	Rest of population (=98)	5.15	26.80	23.71	4.12	2.06
	TOTAL	**6.06**	**31.06**	**25.75**	**11.76**	**5.88**
			1770/1808			
	SAMPLE (=*138)	**Porcelains (%)**	**Mirrors (%)**	**Household cloth made of 'indiana' (%)**	**Items from China (%)**	**Chinaware (%)**
SOCIAL GROUPS	**Craftsmen (=37)**	2.85	57.14	62.85	5.71	5.71
	Rest of population (=101)	4.00	38.00	59.00	11.00	8.00
	TOTAL	**3.70**	**42.96**	**66.66**	**9.62**	**7.40**

Testing the 'industrious revolution' through the consumption of household furniture in the probate inventories of the Kingdom of Murcia (1730–1808)

SOCIAL GROUPS	1730/69		
	SAMPLE (=*135)	Clocks (%)	Books (%)
	Craftsmen (=37)	8.57	8.57
	Rest of population (=98)	6.18	4.12
	TOTAL	6.81	5.30
SOCIAL GROUPS	1770/1808		
	SAMPLE (=*138)	Clocks (%)	Books (%)
	Craftsmen (=37)	17.14	8.57
	Rest of population (=101)	16.00	9.00
	TOTAL	16.29	8.88

Testing the 'industrious revolution' through the consumption of household furniture in the probate inventories of the Kingdom of Murcia (1730–1808)

	SAMPLE (=*135)	Coffee-pots (%)	Tea-pots (%)	Chocolate-pots (%)	'Jicaras' [bowls] (%)	'Salvillas' [trays] (%)	Cups (%)
				1730/69			
SOCIAL GROUPS	Craftsmen (=37)	2.85	0.00	40.00	11.42	25.71	5.71
	Rest of population (=98)	2.06	0.00	27.83	6.18	19.58	7.21
	TOTAL	**2.27**	**0.00**	**31.06**	**7.57**	**21.21**	**6.81**

	SAMPLE (=*138)	Coffee-pots (%)	Tea-pots (%)	Chocolate-pots (%)	Jicaras' [bowls] (%)	'Salvillas' [trays] (%)	Cups (%)
				1770/1808			
SOCIAL GROUPS	Craftsmen (=37)	2.85	0.00	57.14	14.28	22.85	5.71
	Rest of population (=101)	11.00	2.00	60.00	14.00	26.00	9.00
	TOTAL	**8.88**	**1.48**	**59.25**	**14.07**	**25.18**	**8.14**

Appendix B

Testing the 'Industrious Revolution' Theory through Yeomen in the Kingdom of Murcia (1730–1808)

Tables begin on next page.

Testing the 'industrious revolution' through the consumption of French commodities in the probate inventories of the Kingdom of Murcia (1730–1808)

		Textiles made of 'bretaña' (%)	'Briaçu' (%)	Buffets (%)	'Cabriolé' (%)	Textiles made of 'cambray' (%)	Textiles made of 'crea' (%)
	1730/69						
	SAMPLE (=*135)						
SOCIAL GROUPS	Yeomen (=38)	0.00	0.00	15.78	0.00	0.00	2.63
	Rest of population (=97)	5.31	3.19	44.68	1.06	6.38	10.63
	TOTAL	**3.78**	**2.27**	**36.36**	**0.75**	**4.54**	**8.33**
	1770/1808						
	SAMPLE (=*138)						
SOCIAL GROUPS	Yeomen (=40)	0.00	0.00	10.25	0.00	0.00	5.12
	Rest of population (=98)	1.04	1.04	32.29	7.29	1.04	12.50
	TOTAL	**0.74**	**0.74**	**25.92**	**5.18**	**0.74**	**10.37**

Testing the 'industrious revolution' through the consumption of French commodities in the probate inventories of the Kingdom of Murcia (1730–1808)

		1730/69					
SOCIAL GROUPS	SAMPLE (=*135)	'Desavillé' (%)	Textiles made of 'duray' (%)	Items with the French 'trade-mark' (%)	'Pompadour' (%)	Textiles made of 'tripé' (%)	Textiles made of 'truè' (%)
	Yeomen (=38)	0.00	0.00	0.00	0.00	0.00	2.63
	Rest of population (=97)	0.00	0.00	20.21	1.06	1.06	9.57
	TOTAL	0.00	0.00	14.39	0.75	0.75	7.57
		1770/1808					
SOCIAL GROUPS	SAMPLE (=*138)	'Desavillé' (%)	Textiles made of 'duray' (%)	Items with the French 'trade-mark' (%)	'Pompadour' (%)	Textiles made of 'tripé' (%)	Textiles made of 'truè' (%)
	Yeomen (=40)	0.00	0.00	2.56	0.00	5.12	0.00
	Rest of population (=98)	6.25	9.37	18.75	0.00	6.25	13.54
	TOTAL	4.44	6.66	14.07	0.00	5.92	9.62

Testing the 'industrious revolution' through the consumption of 'majo' attire in the probate inventories of the Kingdom of Murcia (1730–1808)

1730/69

SOCIAL GROUPS	SAMPLE (=*135)	'Basquiña' [top petticoat] (%)	'Chal' [shawl] (%)	'Chaqueta' [jacket] (%)	'Cofia' [hair net] (%)	'Jubon' [doublet] (%)	Mantilla (%)	'Trajes' [suits] (%)
	Yeomen (=38)	21.05	0.00	0.00	0.00	23.68	7.89	0.00
	Rest of population (=97)	30.85	0.00	1.06	4.25	23.40	22.34	2.12
	TOTAL	28.03	0.00	0.75	3.03	23.48	18.18	1.51

1770/1808

SOCIAL GROUPS	SAMPLE (=*138)	'Basquiña' [top petticoat] (%)	'Chal' [shawl] (%)	'Chaqueta' [jacket] (%)	'Cofia' [hair net] (%)	'Jubon' [doublet] (%)	Mantilla (%)	'Trajes' [suits] (%)
	Yeomen (=40)	41.02	0.00	0.00	0.00	12.82	25.64	0.00
	Rest of population (=98)	44.79	1.04	9.37	14.58	18.75	41.66	2.08
	TOTAL	43.70	0.74	6.66	10.37	17.03	37.03	1.48

Testing the 'industrious revolution' through the consumption of household furniture in the probate inventories of the Kingdom of Murcia (1730–1808)

	SAMPLE (=*135)	Porcelains (%)	Mirrors (%)	Household cloth made of 'indiana' (%)	Items from China (%)	Chinaware (%)
SOCIAL GROUPS	Yeomen (=38)	2.63	5.26	7.89	0.00	0.00
	Rest of population (=97)	7.44	41.48	32.97	4.25	2.12
	TOTAL	**6.06**	**31.06**	**25.75**	**11.76**	**5.88**

	SAMPLE (=*138)	Porcelains (%)	Mirrors (%)	Household cloth made of 'indiana' (%)	Items from China (%)	Chinaware (%)
SOCIAL GROUPS	Yeomen (=40)	5.12	10.25	43.58	0.00	0.00
	Rest of population (=98)	3.12	56.25	66.66	13.54	10.41
	TOTAL	**3.70**	**42.96**	**66.66**	**9.62**	**7.40**

Testing the 'industrious revolution' through the consumption of household furniture in the probate inventories of the Kingdom of Murcia (1730–1808)

		Clocks (%)	Books (%)
SOCIAL GROUPS	**1730/69**		
	SAMPLE (=*135)		
	Yeomen (=38)	0.00	0.00
	Rest of population (=97)	9.57	7.44
	TOTAL	**6.81**	**5.30**
SOCIAL GROUPS	**1770/1808**		
	SAMPLE (=*138)		
	Yeomen (=40)	0.00	0.00
	Rest of population (=98)	22.91	12.50
	TOTAL	**16.29**	**8.88**

Testing the 'industrious revolution' through the consumption of household furniture in the probate inventories of the Kingdom of Murcia (1730–1808)

		Coffee-pots (%)	Tea-pots (%)	Chocolate-pots (%)	'Jicaras' [bowls] (%)	'Salvillas' [trays] (%)	Cups (%)
	1730/69						
SOCIAL GROUPS	SAMPLE (=*135)						
	Yeomen (=38)	0.00	0.00	7.89	2.63	2.63	0.00
	Rest of population (=97)	3.19	0.00	40.42	9.57	28.72	9.57
	TOTAL	2.27	0.00	31.06	7.57	21.21	6.81
	1770/1808						
SOCIAL GROUPS	SAMPLE (=*138)	Coffee-pots (%)	Tea-pots (%)	Chocolate-pots (%)	'Jicaras' [bowls] (%)	'Salvillas' [trays] (%)	Cups (%)
	Yeomen (=40)	0.00	0.00	30.76	2.56	2.56	0.00
	Rest of population (=98)	12.50	2.08	70.83	18.75	34.37	11.45
	TOTAL	8.88	1.48	59.25	14.07	25.18	8.14

Appendix C

Testing the 'Trickle-down' Theory through the Oligarchy in the Kingdom of Murcia (1730–1808)

Tables begin on next page.

Testing the 'trickle-down' through the consumption of French commodities in the probate inventories of the Kingdom of Murcia (1730–1808)

		Textiles made of 'bretaña' (%)	'Briaçu' (%)	Buffets (%)	'Cabriolé' (%)	Textiles made of 'cambray' (%)	Textiles made of 'crea' (%)
	SAMPLE (=*135)			**1730/69**			
SOCIAL GROUPS	Local oligarchy (=17)	12.50	0.00	68.75	6.25	6.25	12.50
	Rest of population (=118)	2.58	2.58	31.89	0.00	4.31	7.75
	TOTAL	**3.78**	**2.27**	**36.36**	**0.75**	**4.54**	**8.33**
	SAMPLE (=*138)			**1770/1808**			
SOCIAL GROUPS	Local oligarchy (=17)	0.00	6.25	50.00	18.75	0.00	0.00
	Rest of population (=121)	0.84	0.00	22.68	3.36	0.84	11.76
	TOTAL	**0.74**	**0.74**	**25.92**	**5.18**	**0.74**	**10.37**

Testing the 'trickle-down' through the consumption of French commodities in the probate inventories of the Kingdom of Murcia (1730–1808)

	SAMPLE (=*135)	'Desavillé' (%)	Textiles made of 'duray' (%)	Items with the French 'trade-mark' (%)	'Pompadour' (%)	Textiles made of 'tripé' (%)	Textiles made of 'trué' (%)
	1730/69						
SOCIAL GROUPS	Local oligarchy (=17)	0.00	0.00	37.50	6.25	6.25	18.75
	Rest of population (=118)	0.00	0.00	11.20	0.00	0.00	6.03
	TOTAL	**0.00**	**0.00**	**14.39**	**0.75**	**0.75**	**7.57**

	SAMPLE (=*138)	'Desavillé' (%)	Textiles made of 'duray' (%)	Items with the French 'trade-mark' (%)	'Pompadour' (%)	Textiles made of 'tripé' (%)	Textiles made of 'trué' (%)
	1770/1808						
SOCIAL GROUPS	Local oligarchy (=17)	6.25	6.25	43.75	0.00	6.25	12.50
	Rest of population (=121)	4.20	6.72	10.08	0.00	5.88	9.24
	TOTAL	**4.44**	**6.66**	**14.07**	**0.00**	**5.92**	**9.62**

Testing the 'trickle-down' through the consumption of 'majo' attire in the probate inventories of the Kingdom of Murcia (1730–1808)

	1730/69						
SAMPLE (=*135)	'Basquiña' [top petticoat] (%)	'Chal' [shawl] (%)	'Chaqueta' [jacket] (%)	'Cofia' [hair net] (%)	'Jubon' [doublet] (%)	Mantilla (%)	'Trajes' [suits] (%)
SOCIAL GROUPS Local oligarchy (=17)	37.50	0.00	6.25	12.50	18.75	31.25	6.25
Rest of population (=118)	26.72	0.00	0.00	1.72	24.13	16.37	0.86
TOTAL	28.03	0.00	0.75	3.03	23.48	18.18	1.51
	1770/1808						
SAMPLE (=*138)	'Basquiña' [top petticoat] (%)	'Chal' [shawl] (%)	'Chaqueta' [jacket] (%)	'Cofia' [hair net] (%)	'Jubon' [doublet] (%)	Mantilla (%)	'Trajes' [suits] (%)
SOCIAL GROUPS Local oligarchy (=17)	37.50	0.00	0.00	18.75	6.25	37.50	0.00
Rest of population (=121)	44.53	0.84	7.56	9.24	18.48	36.97	1.68
TOTAL	43.70	0.74	6.66	10.37	17.03	37.03	1.48

Testing the 'trickle-down' through the consumption of household furniture in the probate inventories of the Kingdom of Murcia (1730–1808)

	SAMPLE (=*135)	Porcelains (%)	Mirrors (%)	Household cloth made of 'indiana' (%)	Items from China (%)	Chinaware (%)
				1730/69		
SOCIAL GROUPS	Local oligarchy (=17)	0.00	37.50	37.50	27.27	9.09
	Rest of population (=118)	6.89	30.17	24.13	0.86	0.86
	TOTAL	6.06	31.06	25.75	11.76	5.88

	SAMPLE (=*138)	Porcelains (%)	Mirrors (%)	Household cloth made of 'indiana' (%)	Items from China (%)	Chinaware (%)
				1770/1808		
SOCIAL GROUPS	Local oligarchy (=17)	6.25	50.00	75.00	43.75	37.50
	Rest of population (=121)	3.36	42.01	57.98	5.04	3.36
	TOTAL	3.70	42.96	66.66	9.62	7.40

Testing the 'trickle-down' in consuming household furniture in the probate inventories of the Kingdom of Murcia (1730–1808)

		1730/69		
	SAMPLE (=*135)		Clocks (%)	Books (%)
SOCIAL GROUPS	Local oligarchy (=17)		31.25	12.50
	Rest of population (=118)		3.44	4.31
	TOTAL		**6.81**	**5.30**
		1770/1808		
	SAMPLE (=*138)		Clocks (%)	Books (%)
SOCIAL GROUPS	Local oligarchy (=17)		43.75	31.25
	Rest of population (=121)		12.60	5.88
	TOTAL		**16.29**	**8.88**

Testing the 'trickle-down' through the consumption of household furniture in the probate inventories of the Kingdom of Murcia (1730–1808)

		Coffee-pots (%)	Tea-pots (%)	Chocolate-pots (%)	'Jicaras' [bowls] (%)	'Salvillas' [trays] (%)	Cups (%)
	SAMPLE (=*135)			**1730/69**			
SOCIAL GROUPS	Local oligarchy (=17)	6.25	0.00	43.75	12.50	62.50	6.25
	Rest of population (=118)	1.72	0.00	29.31	6.89	15.51	6.89
	TOTAL	**2.27**	**0.00**	**31.06**	**7.57**	**21.21**	**6.81**
	SAMPLE (=*138)			**1770/1808**			
SOCIAL GROUPS	Local oligarchy (=17)	37.50	6.25	87.5	43.75	62.50	25.00
	Rest of population (=121)	5.04	0.84	55.46	10.08	20.16	5.88
	TOTAL	**8.88**	**1.48**	**59.25**	**14.07**	**25.18**	**8.14**

Appendix D

Testing the 'Trickle-down' Theory through the Merchants in the Kingdom of Murcia (1730–1808)

Tables begin on next page.

Testing the 'trickle-down' through the consumption of French commodities in the probate inventories of the Kingdom of Murcia (1730–1808)

	1730/69						
SAMPLE (=*135)	Textiles made of 'bretaña' (%)	'Briaçu' (%)	Buffets (%)	'Cabriolé' (%)	Textiles made of 'cambray' (%)	Textiles made of 'crea' (%)
Merchants (=16)	6.66	6.66	13.33	0.00	6.66	20.00
Rest of population (=119)	3.41	1.70	39.31	0.85	4.27	6.83
TOTAL	**3.78**	**2.27**	**36.36**	**0.75**	**4.54**	**8.33**

	1770/1808						
SAMPLE (=*138)	Textiles made of 'bretaña' (%)	'Briaçu' (%)	Buffets (%)	'Cabriolé' (%)	Textiles made of 'cambray' (%)	Textiles made of 'crea' (%)
Merchants (=17)	5.55	0.00	16.66	5.55	5.55	11.11
Rest of population (=121)	0.00	0.85	27.35	5.12	0.00	10.25
TOTAL	**0.74**	**0.74**	**25.92**	**5.18**	**0.74**	**10.37**

SOCIAL GROUPS

SOCIAL GROUPS

Testing the 'trickle-down' through the consumption of French commodities in the probate inventories of the Kingdom of Murcia (1730–1808)

1730/69

	SAMPLE (=*135)	'Desavillé' (%)	Textiles made of 'duray' (%)	Items with the French 'trade-mark' (%)	'Pompadour' (%)	Textiles made of 'tripé' (%)	Textiles made of 'trué' (%)
SOCIAL GROUPS	Merchants (=16)	0.00	0.00	40.00	0.00	0.00	13.33
	Rest of population (=119)	0.00	0.00	11.11	0.85	0.85	6.83
	TOTAL	**0.00**	**0.00**	**14.39**	**0.75**	**0.75**	**7.57**

1770/1808

	SAMPLE (=*138)	'Desavillé' (%)	Textiles made of 'duray' (%)	Items with the French 'trade-mark' (%)	'Pompadour' (%)	Textiles made of 'tripé' (%)	Textiles made of 'trué' (%)
SOCIAL GROUPS	Merchants (=17)	0.00	11.11	16.66	0.00	5.55	5.55
	Rest of population (=121)	5.12	5.98	13.67	0.00	5.98	10.25
	TOTAL	**4.44**	**6.66**	**14.07**	**0.00**	**5.92**	**9.62**

Testing the 'trickle-down' through the consumption of 'majo' attire in the probate inventories of the Kingdom of Murcia (1730–1808)

SOCIAL GROUPS	1730/69								
SAMPLE (=*135)	'Basquiña' [top petticoat] (%)	'Chal' [shawl] (%)	'Chaqueta' [jacket] (%)	'Cofia' [hair net] (%)	'Jubon' [doublet] (%)	Mantilla (%)	'Trajes' [suits] (%)
Merchants (=16)	46.66	0.00	0.00	6.66	33.33	13.33	0.00
Rest of population (=119)	25.64	0.00	0.85	2.56	22.22	18.80	1.70
TOTAL	28.03	0.00	0.75	3.03	23.48	18.18	1.51

SOCIAL GROUPS	1770/1808								
SAMPLE (=*138)	'Basquiña' [top petticoat] (%)	'Chal' [shawl] (%)	'Chaqueta' [jacket] (%)	'Cofia' [hair net] (%)	'Jubon' [doublet] (%)	Mantilla (%)	'Trajes' [suits] (%)
Merchants (=17)	38.88	0.00	22.22	11.11	11.11	27.77	5.55
Rest of population (=121)	44.44	0.85	4.27	10.25	17.94	38.46	0.85
TOTAL	43.70	0.74	6.66	10.37	17.03	37.03	1.48

Testing the 'trickle-down' through the consumption of household furniture in the probate inventories of the Kingdom of Murcia (1730–1808)

			1730/69			
SOCIAL GROUPS	SAMPLE (=*135)	Porcelains (%)	Mirrors (%)	Household cloth made of 'indiana' (%)	Items from China (%)	Chinaware (%)
	Merchants (=16)	20.00	60.00	46.66	0.00	0.00
	Rest of population (=119)	4.27	27.35	23.07	3.41	1.70
	TOTAL	**6.06**	**31.06**	**25.75**	**11.76**	**5.88**
			1770/1808			
SOCIAL GROUPS	SAMPLE (=*138)	Porcelains (%)	Mirrors (%)	Household cloth made of 'indiana' (%)	Items from China (%)	Chinaware (%)
	Merchants (=17)	0.00	72.22	55.55	5.55	0.00
	Rest of population (=121)	4.27	38.46	60.68	10.25	8.54
	TOTAL	**3.70**	**42.96**	**66.66**	**9.62**	**7.40**

Testing the 'trickle-down' through the consumption of household furniture in the probate inventories of the Kingdom of Murcia (1730–1808)

	1730/69		
	SAMPLE (=*135)	**Clocks (%)**	**Books (%)**
SOCIAL GROUPS	Merchants (=16)	6.66	0.00
	Rest of population (=119)	6.83	5.98
	TOTAL	**6.81**	**5.30**

	1770/1808		
	SAMPLE (=*138)	**Clocks (%)**	**Books (%)**
SOCIAL GROUPS	Merchants (=17)	16.66	11.11
	Rest of population (=121)	16.23	8.54
	TOTAL	**16.29**	**8.88**

Testing the 'trickle-down' through the consumption of household furniture in the probate inventories of the Kingdom of Murcia (1730–1808)

SOCIAL GROUPS	SAMPLE (=*135)	Coffee-pots (%)	Tea-pots (%)	Chocolate-pots (%)	'Jicaras' [bowls] (%)	'Salvillas' [trays] (%)	Cups (%)
				1730/69			
	Merchants (=16)	0.00	0.00	53.33	13.33	20.00	13.33
	Rest population (=119)	2.56	0.00	28.20	6.83	21.36	5.98
	TOTAL	2.27	0.00	31.06	7.57	21.21	6.81
SOCIAL GROUPS	SAMPLE (=*138)	Coffee-pots (%)	Tea-pots (%)	Chocolate-pots (%)	'Jicaras' [bowls] (%)	'Salvillas' [trays] (%)	Cups (%)
				1770/1808			
	Merchants (=17)	16.66	0.00	72.22	5.55	33.33	11.11
	Rest of population (=121)	7.69	1.70	57.26	15.38	23.93	7.69
	TOTAL	8.88	1.48	59.25	14.07	25.18	8.14

Consumption of Selected Commodities in the Kingdom of Murcia by the Value of Probate Inventories (1730–1808)

Sample of probate inventories by wealth Groups in the Kingdom of Murcia (1730–1808)

Total inventory valuation (Sample = 273)	No. of inventories (1730–69)	No. of inventories (1770–1808)
No. evaluated	34	13
0 > 10,000	35	28
10,000 > 50,000	35	43
50,000 > 100,000	10	23
> 100,000	21	31
TOTAL	135	138

Tables continue on next page.

Consumption of household furniture by wealth groups in the Kingdom of Murcia (1730–1808)

Total inventory valuation (Sample = 273)	Coffee-pots (%) (1730–69)	Coffee-pots (%) (1770–1808)	Chocolate-pots (%) (1730–69)	Chocolate-pots (%) (1770–1808)	Tea-pots (%) (1730–69)	Tea-pots (%) (1770–1808)	'Salvillas' [trays] (%) (1730–69)	'Salvillas' [trays] (%) (1770–1808)	'Jícaras' [bowls] (%) (1730–69)	'Jícaras' [bowls] (%) (1770–1808)	Cups (%) (1730–69)	Cups (%) (1770–1808)
No. evaluated	2.94	7.69	29.41	30.76	0.00	0.00	35.29	15.38	8.82	15.38	8.82	15.38
0 > 10,000	0.00	0.00	17.14	35.71	0.00	0.00	2.85	10.71	2.85	3.57	2.85	3.57
10,000 > 50,000	0.00	2.32	25.71	44.18	0.00	0.00	8.57	9.30	0.00	20.93	2.85	2.32
50,000 > 100,000	10.00	4.34	20.00	82.60	0.00	0.00	20.00	43.47	0.00	17.39	10.00	8.69
> 100,000	0.00	32.25	61.90	83.87	0.00	6.45	42.85	48.38	9.52	22.58	14.28	16.12
TOTAL	1.48	9.42	29.62	56.52	0.00	1.44	20.00	24.63	4.44	16.66	6.66	7.97

Consumption of household furniture by wealth groups in the Kingdom of Murcia (1730–1808)

Total inventory valuation (Sample = 273)	Items from China (%) (1730–69)	Items from China (%) (1770–1808)	Chinaware (%) (1730–69)	Chinaware (%) (1770–1808)	Items made of 'indiana' (%) (1730–69)	Items made of 'indiana' (%) (1770–1808)	Porcelains (%) (1730–69)	Porcelains (%) (1770–1808)	Mirrors (%) (1730–69)	Mirrors (%) (1770–1808)
No. evaluated	2.94	0.00	2.94	0.00	17.64	38.46	8.82	0.00	47.05	23.07
0 > 10,000	0.00	0.00	0.00	0.00	11.42	46.42	8.57	3.57	17.14	21.42
10,000 > 50,000	0.00	2.32	0.00	2.32	25.71	48.83	5.71	2.32	20.00	30.23
50,000 > 100,000	0.00	4.34	0.00	0.00	10.00	65.21	0.00	8.69	20.00	56.52
> 100,000	14.28	35.48	4.76	25.80	57.14	90.32	0.00	3.22	47.61	74.19
TOTAL	2.96	9.42	1.48	6.52	23.70	59.42	5.92	3.62	30.37	42.02

Consumption of household furniture by wealth groups in the Kingdom of Murcia (1730–1808)

Total inventory valuation (Sample = 273)	Books (%) (1730–69)	Books (%) (1770–1808)	Clocks (%) (1730–69)	Clocks (%) (1770–1808)
No. evaluated	11.76	7.69	14.70	0.00
0 > 10,000	2.85	0.00	0.00	0.00
10,000 > 50,000	0.00	2.32	0.00	9.30
50,000 > 100,000	0.00	13.04	0.00	21.73
> 10,0000	4.76	22.58	23.80	41.93
TOTAL	**4.44**	**8.69**	**7.40**	**15.94**

Consumption of French commodities by wealth groups in the Kingdom of Murcia (1730–1808)

Total inventory valuation (Sample = 273)	Items made of 'bretaña' (%) (1730–69)	Items made of 'bretaña' (%) (1770–1808)	'Briaçu' (%) (1730–69)	'Briaçu' (%) (1770–1808)	Buffets (%) (1730–69)	Buffets (%) (1770–1808)	'Cabriolé' (%) (1730–69)	'Cabriolé' (%) (1770–1808)	Items made of 'cambray' (%) (1730–69)	Items made of 'cambray' (%) (1770–1808)	Items made of 'crea' (%) (1730–69)	Items made of 'crea' (%) (1770–1808)
No. evaluated	5.88	0.00	2.94	7.69	29.41	15.38	0.00	0.00	11.76	0.00	17.64	0.00
0 > 10,000	0.00	0.00	0.00	0.00	22.85	14.28	0.00	3.57	2.85	0.00	0.00	7.14
10,000 > 50,000	2.85	0.00	2.85	0.00	37.14	9.30	0.00	2.32	0.00	0.00	8.57	9.30
50,000 > 100,000	0.00	4.34	0.00	0.00	40.00	39.13	0.00	4.34	0.00	0.00	0.00	13.04
> 100,000	9.52	0.00	4.76	0.00	57.14	48.38	4.76	12.90	4.76	3.22	9.52	16.12
TOTAL	**3.70**	**0.72**	**2.22**	**0.72**	**34.81**	**24.63**	**0.74**	**5.07**	**4.44**	**0.72**	**8.14**	**10.14**

Consumption of French commodities by wealth groups in the Kingdom of Murcia (1730–1808)

Total inventory valuation (Sample = 273)	'Desavillé' (%) (1730–69)	'Desavillé' (%) (1770–1808)	Items made of 'duray' (%) (1730–69)	Items made of 'duray' (%) (1770–1808)	Items with the French 'trade-mark' (%) (1730–69)	Items with the French 'trade-mark' (%) (1770–1808)	Textiles made of 'pompadour' (%) (1730–69)	Textiles made of 'pompadour' (%) (1770–1808)	Textiles made of 'tripé' (%) (1730–69)	Textiles made of 'tripé' (%) (1770–1808)	Textiles made of 'true' (%) (1730–69)	Textiles made of 'true' (%) (1770–1808)
No. evaluated	0.00	0.00	0.00	7.69	17.64	30.76	0.00	0.00	0.00	0.00	11.76	7.69
0 > 10,000	0.00	3.57	0.00	3.57	5.71	3.57	0.00	0.00	0.00	7.14	2.85	3.57
10,000 > 50,000	0.00	2.32	0.00	6.97	2.85	6.97	0.00	0.00	0.00	4.65	5.71	2.32
50,000 > 100,000	0.00	4.34	0.00	17.39	0.00	4.34	0.00	0.00	0.00	8.69	0.00	21.73
> 100,000	0.00	6.45	0.00	0.00	47.61	32.25	4.76	0.00	4.76	6.45	14.28	16.12
TOTAL	0.00	3.62	0.00	6.52	14.07	13.76	0.74	0.00	0.74	5.79	7.40	9.42

Consumption of 'majo's attire' by wealth groups in the Kingdom of Murcia (1730–1808)

Total inventory valuation (Sample = 273)	'Basquiñas' [top petticoats] (%) (1730–69)	'Basquiñas' [top petticoats] (%) (1770–1808)	'Chal' [shawl] (%) (1730–69)	'Chal' [shawl] (%) (1770–1808)	'Chaquetas' [jackets] (%) (1730–69)	'Chaquetas' [jackets] (%) (1770–1808)	'Cofias' [hair nets] (%) (1730–69)	'Cofias' [hair nets] (%) (1770–1808)	'Jubon' [doublet] (%) (1730–69)	'Jubon' [doublet] (%) (1770–1808)	Man-tillas (%) (1730–69)	Man-tillas (%) (1770–1808)	'Trajes' [suits] (%) (1730–69)	'Trajes' [suits] (%) (1770–1808)
No. evaluated 0 > 10,000	23.52	30.76	0.00	0.00	2.94	7.69	5.88	0.00	26.47	0.00	17.64	23.07	0.00	0.00
0 > 10,000	31.42	32.14	0.00	0.00	0.00	3.57	0.00	3.57	8.57	3.57	8.57	28.57	0.00	0.00
10,000 > 50,000	17.14	39.53	0.00	0.00	0.00	4.65	0.00	6.97	0.00	9.30	20.00	27.90	0.00	0.00
50,000 > 100,000	30.00	56.52	0.00	0.00	0.00	8.69	0.00	21.73	20.00	21.73	0.00	52.17	0.00	4.34
> 100,000	38.09	51.61	0.00	3.22	0.00	9.67	9.52	16.12	23.80	9.67	38.09	48.38	9.52	3.22
TOTAL	26.66	42.75	0.00	0.72	0.74	6.52	2.96	10.14	14.07	9.42	17.77	36.23	1.48	1.44

Appendix F

Social Diffusion of Selected Commodities in the Kingdom of Murcia (1730–1808)

Tables begin on next page.

Social diffusion of French commodities in the probate inventories of the Kingdom of Murcia (1730–1808)

1730/69

SOCIAL GROUPS / SAMPLE (=*135)	Textiles made of 'bretaña' (%)	'Briaçu' (%)	Buffets (%)	'Cabriolé' (%)	Textiles made of 'cambray' (%)	Textiles made of 'crea' (%)
Local oligarchy	12.50	0.00	68.75	6.25	6.25	12.50
Merchants	6.66	6.66	13.33	0.00	6.66	20.00
Landowners	0.00	4.34	47.82	0.00	0.00	4.34
Master artisans	8.33	8.33	41.66	0.00	16.66	16.66
Professionals	20.00	0.00	40.00	0.00	20.00	20.00
Artisans	0.00	0.00	47.82	0.00	4.34	4.34
Yeomen	0.00	0.00	15.78	0.00	0.00	2.63
TOTAL	**3.78**	**2.27**	**36.36**	**0.75**	**4.54**	**8.33**

1770/1808

SOCIAL GROUPS / SAMPLE (=*138)	Textiles made of 'bretaña' (%)	'Briaçu' (%)	Buffets (%)	'Cabriolé' (%)	Textiles made of 'cambray' (%)	Textiles made of 'crea' (%)
Local oligarchy	0.00	6.25	50.00	18.75	0.00	0.00
Merchants	5.55	0.00	16.66	5.55	5.55	11.11
Landowners	0.00	0.00	41.66	0.00	0.00	20.83
Master artisans	0.00	0.00	36.36	0.00	0.00	18.18
Professionals	0.00	0.00	0.00	0.00	0.00	33.33
Artisans	0.00	0.00	25.00	12.50	0.00	8.33
Yeomen	0.00	0.00	10.25	0.00	0.00	5.12
TOTAL	**0.74**	**0.74**	**25.92**	**5.18**	**0.74**	**10.37**

Social diffusion of French commodities in the probate inventories of the Kingdom of Murcia (1730–1808)

1730/69

SOCIAL GROUPS — SAMPLE (=*135)	'Desavillé' (%)	Textiles made of 'duray' (%)	Items with the French 'trade-mark' (%)	'Pompadour' (%)	Textiles made of 'tripe' (%)	Textiles made of 'true' (%)
Local oligarchy	0.00	0.00	37.50	6.25	6.25	18.75
Merchants	0.00	0.00	40.00	0.00	0.00	13.33
Landowners	0.00	0.00	4.34	0.00	0.00	4.34
Master artisans	0.00	0.00	16.66	0.00	0.00	16.66
Professionals	0.00	0.00	20.00	0.00	0.00	20.00
Artisans	0.00	0.00	13.04	0.00	0.00	0.00
Yeomen	0.00	0.00	0.00	0.00	0.00	2.63
TOTAL	**0.00**	**0.00**	**14.39**	**0.75**	**0.75**	**7.57**

1770/1808

SOCIAL GROUPS — SAMPLE (=*138)	'Desavillé' (%)	Textiles made of 'duray' (%)	Items with the French 'trade-mark' (%)	'Pompadour' (%)	Textiles made of 'tripe' (%)	Textiles made of 'true' (%)
Local oligarchy	6.25	6.25	43.75	0.00	6.25	12.50
Merchants	0.00	11.11	16.66	0.00	5.55	5.55
Landowners	4.16	4.16	12.50	0.00	8.33	12.50
Master artisans	0.00	18.18	9.09	0.00	0.00	27.27
Professionals	33.33	0.00	66.66	0.00	0.00	0.00
Artisans	12.50	12.50	8.33	0.00	8.33	16.66
Yeomen	0.00	0.00	2.56	0.00	5.12	0.00
TOTAL	**4.44**	**6.66**	**14.07**	**0.00**	**5.92**	**9.62**

Social diffusion of 'majo' attire in the probate inventories of the Kingdom of Murcia (1730–1808)

1730/69

	SAMPLE (=*135)	'Basquiña' [top petticoat] (%)	'Chal' [shawl] (%)	'Chaqueta' [jacket] (%)	'Cofia' [hair net] (%)	'Jubon' [doublet] (%)	Mantilla (%)	'Trajes' [suits] (%)
SOCIAL GROUPS	Local oligarchy	37.50	0.00	6.25	12.50	18.75	31.25	6.25
	Merchants	46.66	0.00	0.00	6.66	33.33	13.33	0.00
	Landowners	13.04	0.00	0.00	0.00	26.08	4.34	0.00
	Master artisans	25.00	0.00	0.00	0.00	16.66	25.00	0.00
	Professionals	20.00	0.00	0.00	0.00	20.00	20.00	0.00
	Artisans	39.13	0.00	0.00	4.34	21.73	39.13	4.34
	Yeomen	21.05	0.00	0.00	0.00	23.68	7.89	0.00
	TOTAL	**28.03**	**0.00**	**0.75**	**3.03**	**23.48**	**18.18**	**1.51**

1770/1808

	SAMPLE (=*138)	'Basquiña' [top petticoat] (%)	'Chal' [shawl] (%)	'Chaqueta' [jacket] (%)	'Cofia' [hair net] (%)	'Jubon' [doublet] (%)	Mantilla (%)	'Trajes' [suits] (%)
SOCIAL GROUPS	Local oligarchy	37.50	0.00	0.00	18.75	6.25	37.50	0.00
	Merchants	38.88	0.00	22.22	11.11	11.11	27.77	5.55
	Landowners	41.66	0.00	4.16	8.33	25.00	41.66	0.00
	Master artisans	45.45	0.00	9.09	9.09	36.36	36.36	9.09
	Professionals	66.66	0.00	33.33	33.33	0.00	100.00	0.00
	Artisans	54.16	4.16	8.33	20.83	20.83	50.00	0.00
	Yeomen	41.02	0.00	0.00	0.00	12.82	25.64	0.00
	TOTAL	**43.70**	**0.74**	**6.66**	**10.37**	**17.03**	**37.03**	**1.48**

Social diffusion of household furniture in the probate inventories of the Kingdom of Murcia (1730–1808)

1730/69

SAMPLE (=*135)		Porcelains (%)	Mirrors (%)	Household cloth made of 'indiana' (%)	Items from China (%)	Chinaware (%)
SOCIAL GROUPS	Local oligarchy	0.00	37.50	37.50	27.27	9.09
	Merchants	20.00	60.00	46.66	0.00	0.00
	Landowners	4.34	30.43	26.08	0.00	0.00
	Master artisans	16.66	41.66	33.33	0.00	0.00
	Professionals	0.00	40.00	20.00	33.33	33.33
	Artisans	4.34	43.47	30.43	0.00	0.00
	Yeomen	2.63	5.26	7.89	0.00	0.00
	TOTAL	**6.06**	**31.06**	**25.75**	**11.76**	**5.88**

1770/1808

SAMPLE (=*138)		Porcelains (%)	Mirrors (%)	Household cloth made of 'indiana' (%)	Items from China (%)	Chinaware (%)
SOCIAL GROUPS	Local oligarchy	6.25	50.00	75.00	43.75	37.50
	Merchants	0.00	72.22	55.55	5.55	0.00
	Landowners	4.16	41.66	75.00	8.33	4.16
	Master artisans	0.00	72.72	54.54	9.09	9.09
	Professionals	0.00	100.00	66.66	33.33	33.33
	Artisans	4.16	50.00	66.66	4.16	4.16
	Yeomen	5.12	10.25	43.58	0.00	0.00
	TOTAL	**3.70**	**42.96**	**66.66**	**9.62**	**7.40**

Social diffusion of household furniture in the probate inventories of the Kingdom of Murcia (1730–1808)

	SAMPLE (=*135)	Books (%)	Clocks (%)
SOCIAL GROUPS	Local oligarchy	12.50	31.25
	Merchants	0.00	6.66
	Landowners	4.34	0.00
	Master artisans	16.66	0.00
	Professionals	20.00	0.00
	Artisans	4.34	13.04
	Yeomen	0.00	0.00
	TOTAL	5.30	6.81
	SAMPLE (=*138)	Books (%)	Clocks (%)
SOCIAL GROUPS	Local oligarchy	31.25	43.75
	Merchants	11.11	16.66
	Landowners	4.16	16.66
	Master artisans	18.18	27.27
	Professionals	33.33	66.66
	Artisans	4.16	12.50
	Yeomen	0.00	0.00
	TOTAL	8.88	16.29

Social diffusion of household furniture in the probate inventories of the Kingdom of Murcia (1730–1808)

1730/69

SAMPLE (=*135)	Coffee-pots (%)	Tea-pots (%)	Chocolate-pots (%)	'Jicaras' [bowls] (%)	'Salvillas' [trays] (%)	Cups (%)
Local oligarchy	6.25	0.00	43.75	12.50	62.50	6.25
Merchants	0.00	0.00	53.33	13.33	20.00	13.33
Landowners	0.00	0.00	26.08	0.00	8.69	13.04
Master artisans	0.00	0.00	33.33	25.00	25.00	8.33
Professionals	20.00	0.00	60.00	20.00	60.00	20.00
Artisans	4.34	0.00	43.47	4.34	26.08	4.34
Yeomen	0.00	0.00	7.89	2.63	2.63	0.00
TOTAL	2.27	0.00	31.06	7.57	21.21	6.81

1770/1808

SAMPLE (=*138)	Coffee-pots (%)	Tea-pots (%)	Chocolate-pots (%)	'Jicaras' [bowls] (%)	'Salvillas' [trays] (%)	Cups (%)
Local oligarchy	37.50	6.25	87.50	43.75	62.50	25.00
Merchants	16.66	0.00	72.22	5.55	33.33	11.11
Landowners	4.16	0.00	75.00	16.66	33.33	4.16
Master artisans	0.00	0.00	63.63	18.18	27.27	9.09
Professionals	33.33	33.33	100.00	33.33	33.33	66.66
Artisans	4.16	0.00	54.16	12.50	20.83	4.16
Yeomen	0.00	0.00	30.76	2.56	2.56	0.00
TOTAL	8.88	1.48	59.25	14.07	25.18	8.14

SOCIAL GROUPS

Appendix G

Comparing and Contrasting Areas: Social Diffusion of Selected Commodities in the Urban and Rural Places of Murcia and Cartagena Testing all Social Groups (1730–1808)

Tables begin on next page.

Social diffusion of French commodities in the probate inventories of Murcia (1730–1808)

1730/69

	SAMPLE (=*135)	Textiles made of 'bretaña' (%)	'Briaçu' (%)	Buffets (%)	'Cabriolé' (%)	Textiles made of 'cambray' (%)	Textiles made of 'crea' (%)
SOCIAL GROUPS	Local oligarchy	9.09	0.00	72.72	9.09	9.09	18.18
	Merchants	0.00	0.00	0.00	0.00	14.28	28.57
	Landowners	0.00	0.00	0.00	0.00	0.00	0.00
	Master artisans	16.66	16.66	33.33	0.00	33.33	33.33
	Professionals	33.33	0.00	33.33	0.00	33.33	33.33
	Artisans	0.00	0.00	80.00	0.00	0.00	20.00
	Yeomen	0.00	0.00	50.00	0.00	0.00	0.00
	TOTAL	8.82	2.94	47.05	2.94	14.70	23.52

1770/1808

	SAMPLE (=*138)	Textiles made of 'bretaña' (%)	'Briaçu' (%)	Buffets (%)	'Cabriolé' (%)	Textiles made of 'cambray' (%)	Textiles made of 'crea' (%)
SOCIAL GROUPS	Local oligarchy	0.00	11.11	66.66	33.33	0.00	0.00
	Merchants	0.00	0.00	20.00	0.00	20.00	0.00
	Landowners	0.00	0.00	40.00	0.00	0.00	40.00
	Master artisans	0.00	0.00	66.66	0.00	0.00	16.66
	Professionals	0.00	0.00	0.00	0.00	0.00	0.00
	Artisans	0.00	0.00	57.14	0.00	0.00	14.28
	Yeomen	0.00	0.00	0.00	0.00	0.00	25.00
	TOTAL	0.00	2.77	47.22	11.11	2.77	13.88

Social diffusion of French commodities in the probate inventories of the rural area of Murcia (1730–1808)

SOCIAL GROUPS	SAMPLE (=*135)	Textiles made of 'bretaña' (%)	'Briaçu' (%)	Buffets (%)	'Cabriolé' (%)	Textiles made of 'cambray' (%)	Textiles made of 'crea' (%)
Local oligarchy	1730/69	0.00	0.00	50.00	0.00	0.00	0.00
Merchants		50.00	0.00	0.00	0.00	0.00	50.00
Landowners		0.00	0.00	42.85	0.00	0.00	0.00
Master artisans		0.00	0.00	0.00	0.00	0.00	0.00
Professionals		0.00	0.00	100.00	0.00	0.00	0.00
Artisans		0.00	0.00	0.00	0.00	0.00	0.00
Yeomen		0.00	0.00	16.66	0.00	0.00	5.55
TOTAL		3.33	0.00	26.66	0.00	0.00	6.66

SOCIAL GROUPS	SAMPLE (=*138)	Textiles made of 'bretaña' (%)	'Briaçu' (%)	Buffets (%)	'Cabriolé' (%)	Textiles made of 'cambray' (%)	Textiles made of 'crea' (%)
Local oligarchy	1770/1808	0.00	0.00	100.00	0.00	0.00	0.00
Merchants		50.00	0.00	50.00	0.00	0.00	0.00
Landowners		0.00	0.00	40.00	0.00	0.00	20.00
Master artisans		0.00	0.00	0.00	0.00	0.00	0.00
Professionals		0.00	0.00	0.00	0.00	0.00	0.00
Artisans		0.00	0.00	0.00	0.00	0.00	0.00
Yeomen		0.00	0.00	10.00	0.00	0.00	0.00
TOTAL		3.03	0.00	21.21	0.00	0.00	3.03

Social diffusion of French commodities in the probate inventories of Cartagena (1730–1808)

1730/69

	Textiles made of 'bretaña' (%)	'Briaçu' (%)	Buffets (%)	'Cabriolé' (%)	Textiles made of 'cambray' (%)	Textiles made of 'crea' (%)
SAMPLE (=*135)						
Local oligarchy	33.33	0.00	66.66	0.00	0.00	0.00
Merchants	0.00	16.66	33.33	0.00	0.00	0.00
Landowners	0.00	0.00	66.66	0.00	0.00	0.00
Master artisans	0.00	0.00	50.00	0.00	0.00	0.00
Professionals	0.00	0.00	0.00	0.00	0.00	0.00
Artisans	0.00	0.00	45.45	0.00	9.09	0.00
Yeomen	0.00	0.00	0.00	0.00	0.00	0.00
TOTAL	**3.33**	**3.33**	**43.33**	**0.00**	**3.33**	**0.00**

1770/1808

	Textiles made of 'bretaña' (%)	'Briaçu' (%)	Buffets (%)	'Cabriolé' (%)	Textiles made of 'cambray' (%)	Textiles made of 'crea' (%)
SAMPLE (=*138)						
Local oligarchy	0.00	0.00	0.00	0.00	0.00	0.00
Merchants	0.00	0.00	9.09	0.00	0.00	18.18
Landowners	0.00	0.00	20.00	0.00	0.00	0.00
Master artisans	0.00	0.00	0.00	0.00	0.00	20.00
Professionals	0.00	0.00	0.00	0.00	0.00	50.00
Artisans	0.00	0.00	0.00	50.00	0.00	16.66
Yeomen	0.00	0.00	0.00	0.00	0.00	0.00
TOTAL	**0.00**	**0.00**	**5.88**	**8.82**	**0.00**	**14.70**

SOCIAL GROUPS

Social diffusion of French commodities in the probate inventories of the rural area of Cartagena (1730–1808)

1730/69

SOCIAL GROUPS	SAMPLE (=*135)	Textiles made of 'bretaña' (%)	'Briaçu' (%)	Buffets (%)	'Cabriolé' (%)	Textiles made of 'cambray' (%)	Textiles made of 'crea' (%)
	Local oligarchy	0.00	0.00	0.00	0.00	0.00	0.00
	Merchants	0.00	0.00	0.00	0.00	0.00	0.00
	Landowners	0.00	7.69	46.15	0.00	0.00	7.69
	Master artisans	0.00	0.00	50.00	0.00	0.00	0.00
	Professionals	0.00	0.00	0.00	0.00	0.00	0.00
	Artisans	0.00	0.00	28.57	0.00	0.00	0.00
	Yeomen	0.00	0.00	12.50	0.00	0.00	0.00
	TOTAL	**0.00**	**2.63**	**28.94**	**0.00**	**0.00**	**2.63**

1770/1808

SOCIAL GROUPS	SAMPLE (=*138)	Textiles made of 'bretaña' (%)	'Briaçu' (%)	Buffets (%)	'Cabriolé' (%)	Textiles made of 'cambray' (%)	Textiles made of 'crea' (%)
	Local oligarchy	0.00	0.00	0.00	0.00	0.00	0.00
	Merchants	0.00	0.00	0.00	0.00	0.00	0.00
	Landowners	0.00	0.00	55.55	0.00	0.00	22.22
	Master artisans	0.00	0.00	0.00	0.00	0.00	0.00
	Professionals	0.00	0.00	0.00	0.00	0.00	0.00
	Artisans	0.00	0.00	25.00	0.00	0.00	0.00
	Yeomen	0.00	0.00	13.33	0.00	0.00	6.66
	TOTAL	**0.00**	**0.00**	**28.12**	**0.00**	**0.00**	**9.37**

Social diffusion of French commodities in the probate inventories of Murcia (1730–1808)

1730/69

SOCIAL GROUPS	SAMPLE (=*135)	'Desavillé' (%)	Textiles made of 'duray' (%)	Items with the French 'trade-mark' (%)	'Pompadour' (%)	Textiles made of 'tripé' (%)	Textiles made of 'true' (%)
	Local oligarchy	0.00	0.00	45.45	9.09	9.09	18.18
	Merchants	0.00	0.00	57.14	0.00	0.00	28.57
	Landowners	0.00	0.00	0.00	0.00	0.00	0.00
	Master artisans	0.00	0.00	33.33	0.00	0.00	33.33
	Professionals	0.00	0.00	33.33	0.00	0.00	33.33
	Artisans	0.00	0.00	40.00	0.00	0.00	0.00
	Yeomen	0.00	0.00	0.00	0.00	0.00	0.00
	TOTAL	**0.00**	**0.00**	**44.11**	**2.94**	**2.94**	**20.58**

1770/1808

SOCIAL GROUPS	SAMPLE (=*138)	'Desavillé' (%)	Textiles made of 'duray' (%)	Items with the French 'trade-mark' (%)	'Pompadour' (%)	Textiles made of 'tripé' (%)	Textiles made of 'true' (%)
	Local oligarchy	0.00	0.00	66.66	0.00	11.11	22.22
	Merchants	0.00	0.00	20.00	0.00	0.00	0.00
	Landowners	0.00	20.00	40.00	0.00	20.00	40.00
	Master artisans	0.00	33.33	0.00	0.00	0.00	33.33
	Professionals	0.00	0.00	0.00	0.00	0.00	0.00
	Artisans	0.00	28.57	0.00	0.00	14.28	14.28
	Yeomen	0.00	0.00	25.00	0.00	0.00	0.00
	TOTAL	**0.00**	**13.88**	**27.77**	**0.00**	**8.33**	**19.44**

Social diffusion of French commodities in the probate inventories of the rural area of Murcia (1730–1808)

1730/69

SOCIAL GROUPS	SAMPLE (=*135)	'Desavillé' (%)	Textiles made of 'duray' (%)	Items with the French 'trade-mark' (%)	'Pompadour' (%)	Textiles made of 'tripé' (%)	Textiles made of 'trué' (%)
	Local oligarchy	0.00	0.00	0.00	0.00	0.00	0.00
	Merchants	0.00	0.00	0.00	0.00	0.00	0.00
	Landowners	0.00	0.00	0.00	0.00	0.00	0.00
	Master artisans	0.00	0.00	0.00	0.00	0.00	0.00
	Professionals	0.00	0.00	0.00	0.00	0.00	0.00
	Artisans	0.00	0.00	0.00	0.00	0.00	0.00
	Yeomen	0.00	0.00	0.00	0.00	0.00	0.00
	TOTAL	**0.00**	**0.00**	**0.00**	**0.00**	**0.00**	**0.00**

1770/1808

SOCIAL GROUPS	SAMPLE (=*138)	'Desavillé' (%)	Textiles made of 'duray' (%)	Items with the French 'trade-mark' (%)	'Pompadour' (%)	Textiles made of 'tripé' (%)	Textiles made of 'trué' (%)
	Local oligarchy	0.00	50.00	50.00	0.00	0.00	0.00
	Merchants	0.00	50.00	0.00	0.00	50.00	50.00
	Landowners	0.00	0.00	0.00	0.00	20.00	0.00
	Master artisans	0.00	0.00	0.00	0.00	0.00	0.00
	Professionals	0.00	0.00	0.00	0.00	0.00	0.00
	Artisans	0.00	0.00	0.00	0.00	0.00	0.00
	Yeomen	0.00	0.00	0.00	0.00	10.00	0.00
	TOTAL	**0.00**	**6.06**	**3.03**	**0.00**	**12.12**	**3.03**

Social diffusion of French commodities in the probate inventories of Cartagena (1730–1808)

1730/69

SOCIAL GROUPS	SAMPLE (=*135)	'Desavillé' (%)	Textiles made of 'duray' (%)	Items with the French 'trade-mark' (%)	'Pompadour' (%)	Textiles made of 'tripé' (%)	Textiles made of 'trué' (%)
	Local oligarchy	0.00	0.00	33.33	0.00	0.00	33.33
	Merchants	0.00	0.00	33.33	0.00	0.00	0.00
	Landowners	0.00	0.00	0.00	0.00	0.00	0.00
	Master artisans	0.00	0.00	0.00	0.00	0.00	0.00
	Professionals	0.00	0.00	0.00	0.00	0.00	0.00
	Artisans	0.00	0.00	0.00	0.00	0.00	0.00
	Yeomen	0.00	0.00	0.00	0.00	0.00	0.00
	TOTAL	**0.00**	**0.00**	**10.00**	**0.00**	**0.00**	**3.33**

1770/1808

SOCIAL GROUPS	SAMPLE (=*138)	'Desavillé' (%)	Textiles made of 'duray' (%)	Items with the French 'trade-mark' (%)	'Pompadour' (%)	Textiles made of 'tripé' (%)	Textiles made of 'trué' (%)
	Local oligarchy	20.00	0.00	0.00	0.00	0.00	0.00
	Merchants	0.00	9.09	18.18	0.00	0.00	0.00
	Landowners	20.00	0.00	20.00	0.00	0.00	0.00
	Master artisans	0.00	0.00	20.00	0.00	0.00	20.00
	Professionals	50.00	0.00	100.00	0.00	0.00	0.00
	Artisans	16.66	16.66	33.33	0.00	0.00	33.33
	Yeomen	0.00	0.00	0.00	0.00	0.00	0.00
	TOTAL	**11.76**	**5.88**	**23.52**	**0.00**	**0.00**	**8.82**

Social diffusion of French commodities in the probate inventories of the rural area of Cartagena (1730–1808)

1730/69

SAMPLE (=*135)	'Desavillé' (%)	Textiles made of 'duray' (%)	Items with the French 'trade-mark' (%)	'Pompadour' (%)	Textiles made of 'tripé' (%)	Textiles made of 'trué' (%)
Local oligarchy	0.00	0.00	0.00	0.00	0.00	0.00
Merchants	0.00	0.00	0.00	0.00	0.00	0.00
Landowners	0.00	0.00	0.00	0.00	0.00	7.69
Master artisans	0.00	0.00	0.00	0.00	0.00	0.00
Professionals	0.00	0.00	0.00	0.00	0.00	0.00
Artisans	0.00	0.00	14.28	0.00	0.00	0.00
Yeomen	0.00	0.00	0.00	0.00	0.00	6.25
TOTAL	**0.00**	**0.00**	**2.63**	**0.00**	**0.00**	**5.26**

1770/1808

SAMPLE (=*138)	'Desavillé' (%)	Textiles made of 'duray' (%)	Items with the French 'trade-mark' (%)	'Pompadour' (%)	Textiles made of 'tripé' (%)	Textiles made of 'trué' (%)
Local oligarchy	0.00	0.00	0.00	0.00	0.00	0.00
Merchants	0.00	0.00	0.00	0.00	0.00	0.00
Landowners	0.00	0.00	0.00	0.00	0.00	11.11
Master artisans	0.00	0.00	0.00	0.00	0.00	0.00
Professionals	0.00	0.00	0.00	0.00	0.00	0.00
Artisans	12.50	0.00	0.00	0.00	12.50	12.50
Yeomen	0.00	0.00	0.00	0.00	0.00	0.00
TOTAL	**3.12**	**0.00**	**0.00**	**0.00**	**3.12**	**6.25**

SOCIAL GROUPS

Social diffusion of 'majo' attire in the probate inventories of Murcia (1730–1808)

1730/1769

	SAMPLE (=*135)	'Basquiña' [top petticoat] (%)	'Chal' [shawl] (%)	'Chaqueta' [jacket] (%)	'Cofia' [hair net] (%)	'Jubon' [doublet] (%)	Mantilla (%)	'Trajes' [suits] (%)
SOCIAL GROUPS	Local oligarchy	45.45	0.00	9.09	18.18	27.27	36.36	9.09
	Merchants	42.85	0.00	0.00	14.28	42.85	14.28	0.00
	Landowners	0.00	0.00	0.00	0.00	0.00	0.00	0.00
	Master artisans	33.33	0.00	0.00	0.00	33.33	33.33	0.00
	Professionals	33.33	0.00	0.00	0.00	33.33	33.33	0.00
	Artisans	60.00	0.00	0.00	20.00	60.00	40.00	0.00
	Yeomen	50.00	0.00	0.00	0.00	50.00	0.00	0.00
	TOTAL	**44.11**	**0.00**	**2.94**	**11.76**	**38.23**	**29.41**	**2.94**

1770/1808

	SAMPLE (=*138)	'Basquiña' [top petticoat] (%)	'Chal' [shawl] (%)	'Chaqueta' [jacket] (%)	'Cofia' [hair net] (%)	'Jubon' [doublet] (%)	Mantilla (%)	'Trajes' [suits] (%)
SOCIAL GROUPS	Local oligarchy	33.33	0.00	0.00	22.22	0.00	44.44	0.00
	Merchants	20.00	0.00	0.00	0.00	20.00	0.00	0.00
	Landowners	60.00	0.00	0.00	20.00	40.00	40.00	0.00
	Master artisans	83.33	0.00	16.66	16.66	66.66	50.00	16.66
	Professionals	0.00	0.00	0.00	0.00	0.00	0.00	0.00
	Artisans	57.14	0.00	0.00	28.57	57.14	57.14	0.00
	Yeomen	50.00	0.00	0.00	0.00	75.00	50.00	0.00
	TOTAL	**50.00**	**0.00**	**2.77**	**16.66**	**38.88**	**41.66**	**2.77**

Social diffusion of 'majo' attire in the probate inventories of the rural area of Murcia (1730–1808)

1730/1769

	SAMPLE (=*135)	'Basquiña' [top petticoat] (%)	'Chal' [shawl] (%)	'Chaqueta' [jacket] (%)	'Cofia' [hair net] (%)	'Jubon' [doublet] (%)	Mantilla (%)	'Trajes' [suits] (%)
SOCIAL GROUPS	Local oligarchy	50.00	0.00	0.00	0.00	0.00	50.00	0.00
	Merchants	50.00	0.00	0.00	0.00	50.00	0.00	0.00
	Landowners	14.28	0.00	0.00	0.00	57.14	14.28	0.00
	Master artisans	0.00	0.00	0.00	0.00	0.00	0.00	0.00
	Professionals	0.00	0.00	0.00	0.00	0.00	0.00	0.00
	Artisans	0.00	0.00	0.00	0.00	0.00	0.00	0.00
	Yeomen	22.22	0.00	0.00	0.00	38.88	11.11	0.00
	TOTAL	23.33	0.00	0.00	0.00	40.00	13.33	0.00

1770/1808

	SAMPLE (=*138)	'Basquiña' [top petticoat] (%)	'Chal' [shawl] (%)	'Chaqueta' [jacket] (%)	'Cofia' [hair net] (%)	'Jubon' [doublet] (%)	Mantilla (%)	'Trajes' [suits] (%)
SOCIAL GROUPS	Local oligarchy	100.00	0.00	0.00	50.00	50.00	50.00	0.00
	Merchants	50.00	0.00	0.00	50.00	50.00	50.00	0.00
	Landowners	40.00	0.00	0.00	0.00	80.00	20.00	0.00
	Master artisans	0.00	0.00	0.00	0.00	0.00	0.00	0.00
	Professionals	0.00	0.00	0.00	0.00	0.00	100.00	0.00
	Artisans	0.00	0.00	0.00	0.00	33.33	33.33	0.00
	Yeomen	25.00	0.00	0.00	0.00	10.00	20.00	0.00
	TOTAL	30.30	0.00	0.00	6.06	27.27	27.27	0.00

Social diffusion of 'majo' attire in the probate inventories of Cartagena (1730–1808)

1730/69

SAMPLE (=*135)	'Basquiña' [top petticoat] (%)	'Chal' [shawl] (%)	'Chaqueta' [jacket] (%)	'Cofia' [hair net] (%)	'Jubon' [doublet] (%)	Mantilla (%)	'Trajes' [suits] (%)
Local oligarchy	0.00	0.00	0.00	0.00	0.00	0.00	0.00
Merchants	50.00	0.00	0.00	0.00	16.66	16.66	0.00
Landowners	33.33	0.00	0.00	0.00	33.33	0.00	0.00
Master artisans	25.00	0.00	0.00	0.00	0.00	25.00	0.00
Professionals	0.00	0.00	0.00	0.00	0.00	0.00	0.00
Artisans	45.45	0.00	0.00	0.00	9.09	54.54	9.09
Yeomen	50.00	0.00	0.00	0.00	0.00	0.00	0.00
TOTAL	36.66	0.00	0.00	0.00	10.00	26.66	3.33

1770/1808

SAMPLE (=*138)	'Basquiña' [top petticoat] (%)	'Chal' [shawl] (%)	'Chaqueta' [jacket] (%)	'Cofia' [hair net] (%)	'Jubon' [doublet] (%)	Mantilla (%)	'Trajes' [suits] (%)
Local oligarchy	20.00	0.00	0.00	0.00	0.00	20.00	0.00
Merchants	45.45	0.00	36.36	9.09	0.00	36.36	9.09
Landowners	20.00	0.00	0.00	0.00	0.00	40.00	0.00
Master artisans	0.00	0.00	0.00	0.00	0.00	20.00	0.00
Professionals	100.00	0.00	50.00	50.00	0.00	100.00	0.00
Artisans	66.66	16.66	33.33	33.33	0.00	66.66	0.00
Yeomen	0.00	0.00	0.00	0.00	0.00	0.00	0.00
TOTAL	38.23	2.94	17.64	11.76	0.00	41.17	2.94

SOCIAL GROUPS

Social diffusion of 'majo' attire in the probate inventories of the rural area of Cartagena (1730–1808)

1730/69

SAMPLE (=*135)	'Basquiña' [top petticoat] (%)	'Chal' [shawl] (%)	'Chaqueta' [jacket] (%)	'Cofia' [hair net] (%)	'Jubon' [doublet] (%)	Mantilla (%)	'Trajes' [suits] (%)
Local oligarchy	0.00	0.00	0.00	0.00	0.00	0.00	0.00
Merchants	0.00	0.00	0.00	0.00	0.00	0.00	0.00
Landowners	7.69	0.00	0.00	0.00	7.69	0.00	0.00
Master artisans	0.00	0.00	0.00	0.00	0.00	0.00	0.00
Professionals	0.00	0.00	0.00	0.00	0.00	0.00	0.00
Artisans	14.28	0.00	0.00	0.00	14.28	14.28	0.00
Yeomen	12.50	0.00	0.00	0.00	6.25	6.25	0.00
TOTAL	**10.52**	**0.00**	**0.00**	**0.00**	**7.89**	**5.26**	**0.00**

1770/1808

SAMPLE (=*138)	'Basquiña' [top petticoat] (%)	'Chal' [shawl] (%)	'Chaqueta' [jacket] (%)	'Cofia' [hair net] (%)	'Jubon' [doublet] (%)	Mantilla (%)	'Trajes' [suits] (%)
Local oligarchy	0.00	0.00	0.00	0.00	0.00	0.00	0.00
Merchants	0.00	0.00	0.00	0.00	0.00	0.00	0.00
Landowners	44.44	0.00	11.11	11.11	0.00	55.55	0.00
Master artisans	0.00	0.00	0.00	0.00	0.00	0.00	0.00
Professionals	0.00	0.00	0.00	0.00	0.00	0.00	0.00
Artisans	62.50	0.00	0.00	12.50	0.00	37.50	0.00
Yeomen	60.00	0.00	0.00	0.00	0.00	26.66	0.00
TOTAL	**56.25**	**0.00**	**3.12**	**6.25**	**0.00**	**37.50**	**0.00**

Social diffusion of household furniture in the probate inventories of Murcia (1730–1808)

		Porcelains (%)	Mirrors (%)	Household cloth made of 'indiana' (%)	Items from China (%)	Chinaware (%)
1730/69						
SAMPLE (=*135)	Local oligarchy	0.00	45.45	36.36	27.27	9.09
SOCIAL GROUPS	Merchants	42.85	57.14	28.57	0.00	0.00
	Landowners	0.00	0.00	0.00	0.00	0.00
	Master artisans	16.66	33.33	16.66	000	0.00
	Professionals	0.00	66.66	33.33	33.33	33.33
	Artisans	0.00	100.00	20.00	0.00	0.00
	Yeomen	0.00	50.00	50.00	0.00	0.00
	TOTAL	**11.76**	**55.88**	**29.41**	**11.76**	**5.88**
1770/1808						
SAMPLE (=*138)	Local oligarchy	11.11	55.55	88.88	77.77	66.66
SOCIAL GROUPS	Merchants	0.00	60.00	40.00	20.00	0.00
	Landowners	20.00	80.00	80.00	40.00	20.00
	Master artisans	0.00	66.66	33.33	0.00	0.00
	Professionals	0.00	0.00	0.00	0.00	0.00
	Artisans	14.28	57.14	85.71	14.28	14.28
	Yeomen	25.00	25.00	2500	0.00	0.00
	TOTAL	**11.11**	**58.33**	**63.88**	**30.55**	**22.22**

Social diffusion of household furniture in the probate inventories of the rural area of Murcia (1730–1808)

1730/69

SOCIAL GROUPS — SAMPLE (=*135)	Porcelains (%)	Mirrors (%)	Household cloth made of 'indiana' (%)	Items from China (%)	Chinaware (%)
Local oligarchy	0.00	50.00	0.00	0.00	0.00
Merchants	0.00	50.00	50.00	0.00	0.00
Landowners	0.00	42.85	28.57	0.00	0.00
Master artisans	0.00	0.00	0.00	0.00	0.00
Professionals	0.00	0.00	0.00	0.00	0.00
Artisans	0.00	0.00	0.00	0.00	0.00
Yeomen	5.55	5.55	5.55	0.00	0.00
TOTAL	3.33	20.00	13.33	0.00	0.00

1770/1808

SOCIAL GROUPS — SAMPLE (=*138)	Porcelains (%)	Mirrors (%)	Household cloth made of 'indiana' (%)	Items from China (%)	Chinaware (%)
Local oligarchy	0.00	50.00	100.00	0.00	0.00
Merchants	0.00	50.00	50.00	0.00	0.00
Landowners	0.00	20.00	20.00	0.00	0.00
Master artisans	0.00	0.00	0.00	0.00	0.00
Professionals	0.00	100.00	0.00	0.00	0.00
Artisans	0.00	0.00	0.00	0.00	0.00
Yeomen	0.00	5.00	30.00	0.00	0.00
TOTAL	0.00	15.15	30.30	0.00	0.00

Social diffusion of household furniture in the probate inventories of Cartagena (1730–1808)

1730/69

	SAMPLE (=*135)	Porcelains (%)	Mirrors (%)	Household cloth made of 'indiana' (%)	Items from China (%)	Chinaware (%)
SOCIAL GROUPS	Local oligarchy	0.00	0.00	66.66	0.00	0.00
	Merchants	0.00	66.66	66.66	0.00	0.00
	Landowners	0.00	0.00	0.00	0.00	0.00
	Master artisans	25.00	25.00	75.00	0.00	0.00
	Professionals	0.00	0.00	0.00	0.00	0.00
	Artisans	0.00	36.36	36.36	0.00	0.00
	Yeomen	0.00	0.00	0.00	0.00	0.00
	TOTAL	3.33	30.00	43.33	0.00	0.00

1770/1808

	SAMPLE (=*138)	Porcelains (%)	Mirrors (%)	Household cloth made of 'indiana' (%)	Items from China (%)	Chinaware (%)
SOCIAL GROUPS	Local oligarchy	0.00	40.00	40.00	0.00	0.00
	Merchants	0.00	81.81	63.63	0.00	0.00
	Landowners	0.00	40.00	100.00	0.00	0.00
	Master artisans	0.00	80.00	80.00	20.00	20.00
	Professionals	0.00	100.00	100.00	50.00	50.00
	Artisans	0.00	83.33	50.00	0.00	0.00
	Yeomen	0.00	0.00	0.00	0.00	0.00
	TOTAL	0.00	70.58	67.64	5.88	5.88

Social diffusion of household furniture in the probate inventories of the rural area of Cartagena (1730–1808)

1730/69

SAMPLE (=*135)	Porcelains (%)	Mirrors (%)	Household cloth made of 'indiana' (%)	Items from China (%)	Chinaware (%)
Local oligarchy	0.00	0.00	0.00	0.00	0.00
Merchants	0.00	0.00	0.00	0.00	0.00
Landowners	7.69	30.76	30.76	0.00	0.00
Master artisans	0.00	100.00	0.00	0.00	0.00
Professionals	0.00	0.00	0.00	0.00	0.00
Artisans	14.28	14.28	28.57	0.00	0.00
Yeomen	0.00	0.00	6.25	0.00	0.00
TOTAL	**5.26**	**18.42**	**18.42**	**0.00**	**0.00**

1770/1808

SAMPLE (=*138)	Porcelains (%)	Mirrors (%)	Household cloth made of calico	Items from China (%)	Chinaware (%)
Local oligarchy	0.00	0.00	0.00	0.00	0.00
Merchants	0.00	0.00	0.00	0.00	0.00
Landowners	0.00	33.33	88.88	0.00	0.00
Master artisans	0.00	0.00	0.00	0.00	0.00
Professionals	0.00	0.00	0.00	0.00	0.00
Artisans	0.00	37.50	87.50	0.00	0.00
Yeomen	6.66	13.33	66.66	0.00	0.00
TOTAL	**3.12**	**25.00**	**78.12**	**0.00**	**0.00**

SOCIAL GROUPS

Social diffusion of household furniture in the probate inventories of Murcia (1730–1808)

	1730/69		
	SAMPLE (=*135)	Clocks (%)	Books (%)
SOCIAL GROUPS	Local oligarchy	36.36	9.09
	Merchants	0.00	0.00
	Landowners	0.00	0.00
	Master artisans	0.00	33.33
	Professionals	0.00	33.33
	Artisans	40.00	20.00
	Yeomen	0.00	0.00
	TOTAL	17.64	14.70

	1770/1808		
	SAMPLE (=*138)	Clocks (%)	Books (%)
SOCIAL GROUPS	Local oligarchy	66.66	55.55
	Merchants	0.00	0.00
	Landowners	0.00	0.00
	Master artisans	16.66	33.33
	Professionals	0.00	0.00
	Artisans	0.00	0.00
	Yeomen	0.00	0.00
	TOTAL	19.44	19.44

Social diffusion of household furniture in the probate inventories of the rural area of Murcia (1730–1808)

SOCIAL GROUPS	1730/69		
	SAMPLE (=*135)	Clocks (%)	Books (%)
Local oligarchy		0.00	0.00
Merchants		0.00	0.00
Landowners		0.00	14.28
Master artisans		0.00	0.00
Professionals		0.00	0.00
Artisans		0.00	0.00
Yeomen		0.00	0.00
TOTAL		**0.00**	**3.33**

SOCIAL GROUPS	1770/1808		
	SAMPLE (=*138)	Clocks (%)	Books (%)
Local oligarchy		50.00	0.00
Merchants		50.00	0.00
Landowners		20.00	0.00
Master artisans		0.00	0.00
Professionals		0.00	0.00
Artisans		0.00	0.00
Yeomen		0.00	0.00
TOTAL		**9.09**	**0.00**

Social diffusion of household furniture in the probate inventories of Cartagena (1730–1808)

	1730/69		
	SAMPLE (=*135)	Clocks (%)	Books (%)
SOCIAL GROUPS	Local oligarchy	33.33	33.33
	Merchants	16.66	0.00
	Landowners	0.00	0.00
	Master artisans	0.00	0.00
	Professionals	0.00	0.00
	Artisans	9.09	0.00
	Yeomen	0.00	0.00
	TOTAL	10.00	3.33

	1770/1808		
	SAMPLE (=*138)	Clocks (%)	Books (%)
SOCIAL GROUPS	Local oligarchy	0.00	0.00
	Merchants	18.18	18.18
	Landowners	40.00	20.00
	Master artisans	40.00	0.00
	Professionals	100.00	50.00
	Artisans	33.33	16.66
	Yeomen	0.00	0.00
	TOTAL	29.41	14.70

Social diffusion of household furniture in the probate inventories of the rural area of Cartagena (1730–1808)

	1730/69		
	SAMPLE (=*135)	Clocks (%)	Books (%)
SOCIAL GROUPS	Local oligarchy	0.00	0.00
	Merchants	0.00	0.00
	Landowners	0.00	0.00
	Master artisans	0.00	0.00
	Professionals	0.00	0.00
	Artisans	0.00	0.00
	Yeomen	0.00	0.00
	TOTAL	**0.00**	**0.00**

	1770/1808		
	SAMPLE (=*138)	Clocks (%)	Books (%)
SOCIAL GROUPS	Local oligarchy	0.00	0.00
	Merchants	0.00	0.00
	Landowners	11.11	0.00
	Master artisans	0.00	0.00
	Professionals	0.00	0.00
	Artisans	12.50	0.00
	Yeomen	0.00	0.00
	TOTAL	**6.25**	**0.00**

Social diffusion of household furniture in the probate inventories of Murcia (1730–1808)

SOCIAL GROUPS	SAMPLE (=*135)	Tea-pots (%)	Coffee-pots (%)	Chocolate-pots (%)	'Jicaras' [bowls] (%)	'Salvillas' [trays] (%)	Cups (%)
				1730/69			
	Local oligarchy	0.00	9.09	54.54	18.18	72.72	9.09
	Merchants	0.00	0.00	28.57	14.28	28.57	28.57
	Landowners	0.00	0.00	0.00	0.00	0.00	0.00
	Master artisans	0.00	0.00	50.00	16.66	33.33	16.66
	Professionals	0.00	33.33	66.66	33.33	66.66	33.33
	Artisans	0.00	0.00	100.00	20.00	80.00	0.00
	Yeomen	0.00	0.00	50.00	0.00	0.00	0.00
	TOTAL	0.00	5.88	55.88	17.64	52.94	14.70

SOCIAL GROUPS	SAMPLE (=*138)	Tea-pots (%)	Coffee-pots (%)	Chocolate-pots (%)	'Jicaras' [bowls] (%)	'Salvillas' [trays] (%)	Cups (%)
				1770/1808			
	Local oligarchy	11.11	44.44	77.77	55.55	77.77	33.33
	Merchants	0.00	0.00	100.00	0.00	80.00	20.00
	Landowners	0.00	0.00	60.00	20.00	60.00	0.00
	Master artisans	0.00	0.00	83.33	33.33	33.33	16.66
	Professionals	0.00	0.00	0.00	0.00	0.00	0.00
	Artisans	0.00	0.00	57.14	28.57	28.57	0.00
	Yeomen	0.00	0.00	75.00	0.00	25.00	0.00
	TOTAL	2.77	11.11	75.00	27.77	52.77	13.88

Social diffusion of household furniture in the probate inventories of the rural area of Murcia (1730–1808)

1730/69

SOCIAL GROUPS	SAMPLE (=*135)	Tea-pots (%)	Coffee-pots (%)	Chocolate-pots (%)	'Jicaras' [bowls] (%)	'Salvillas' [trays] (%)	Cups (%)
	Local oligarchy	0.00	0.00	50.00	0.00	0.00	0.00
	Merchants	0.00	0.00	100.00	50.00	0.00	0.00
	Landowners	0.00	0.00	57.14	0.00	0.00	28.57
	Master artisans	0.00	0.00	0.00	0.00	0.00	0.00
	Professionals	0.00	0.00	0.00	0.00	0.00	0.00
	Artisans	0.00	0.00	0.00	0.00	0.00	0.00
	Yeomen	0.00	0.00	11.11	5.00	0.00	0.00
	TOTAL	0.00	0.00	30.00	6.06	0.00	6.66

1770/1808

SOCIAL GROUPS	SAMPLE (=*138)	Tea-pots (%)	Coffee-pots (%)	Chocolate-pots (%)	'Jicaras' [bowls] (%)	'Salvillas' [trays] (%)	Cups (%)
	Local oligarchy	0.00	50.00	100.00	100.00	100.00	50.00
	Merchants	0.00	0.00	50.00	50.00	50.00	0.00
	Landowners	0.00	0.00	80.00	14.28	20.00	0.00
	Master artisans	0.00	0.00	0.00	0.00	0.00	0.00
	Professionals	0.00	0.00	100.00	0.00	0.00	0.00
	Artisans	0.00	0.00	66.66	0.00	0.00	0.00
	Yeomen	0.00	0.00	20.00	0.00	0.00	0.00
	TOTAL	0.00	3.03	42.42	13.33	12.12	3.03

Social diffusion of household furniture in the probate inventories of Cartagena (1730–1808)

	SAMPLE (=*135)	Tea-pots (%)	Coffee-pots (%)	Chocolate-pots (%)	'Jicaras' [bowls] (%)	'Salvillas' [trays] (%)	Cups (%)
				1730/69			
SOCIAL GROUPS	Local oligarchy	0.00	0.00	0.00	0.00	66.66	0.00
	Merchants	0.00	0.00	66.66	0.00	16.66	0.00
	Landowners	0.00	0.00	33.33	0.00	33.33	0.00
	Master artisans	0.00	0.00	25.00	40.00	0.00	0.00
	Professionals	0.00	0.00	100.00	0.00	100.00	0.00
	Artisans	0.00	0.00	45.45	0.00	18.18	9.09
	Yeomen	0.00	0.00	0.00	0.00	0.00	0.00
	TOTAL	0.00	0.00	40.00	5.88	23.33	3.33

	SAMPLE (=*138)	Tea-pots (%)	Coffee-pots (%)	Chocolate-pots (%)	'Jicaras' [bowls] (%)	'Salvillas' [trays] (%)	Cups (%)
				1770/1808			
SOCIAL GROUPS	Local oligarchy	0.00	20.00	100.00	0.00	20.00	0.00
	Merchants	0.00	27.27	63.63	0.00	9.09	9.09
	Landowners	0.00	20.00	80.00	66.66	60.00	20.00
	Master artisans	0.00	0.00	40.00	0.00	20.00	0.00
	Professionals	50.00	5000	100.00	100.00	50.00	100.00
	Artisans	0.00	16.66	50.00	9.09	50.00	16.66
	Yeomen	0.00	0.00	0.00	0.00	0.00	0.00
	TOTAL	2.94	20.58	67.64	13.33	29.41	14.70

Social diffusion of household furniture in the probate inventories of the rural area of Cartagena (1730–1808)

1730/69

SOCIAL GROUPS / SAMPLE (=*135)	Tea-pots (%)	Coffee-pots (%)	Chocolate-pots (%)	'Jicaras' [bowls] (%)	'Salvillas' [trays] (%)	Cups (%)
Local oligarchy	0.00	0.00	0.00	0.00	0.00	0.00
Merchants	0.00	0.00	0.00	0.00	0.00	0.00
Landowners	0.00	0.00	7.69	0.00	7.69	7.69
Master artisans	0.00	0.00	0.00	0.00	50.00	0.00
Professionals	0.00	0.00	0.00	0.00	0.00	0.00
Artisans	0.00	14.28	0.00	0.00	0.00	0.00
Yeomen	0.00	0.00	0.00	0.00	6.25	0.00
TOTAL	**0.00**	**2.63**	**2.63**	**0.00**	**7.89**	**2.63**

1770/1808

SOCIAL GROUPS / SAMPLE (=*138)	Tea-pots (%)	Coffee-pots (%)	Chocolate-pots (%)	'Jicaras' [bowls] (%)	'Salvillas' [trays] (%)	Cups (%)
Local oligarchy	0.00	0.00	0.00	0.00	0.00	0.00
Merchants	0.00	0.00	0.00	0.00	0.00	0.00
Landowners	0.00	0.00	77.77	0.00	11.11	0.00
Master artisans	0.00	0.00	0.00	0.00	0.00	0.00
Professionals	0.00	0.00	0.00	0.00	0.00	0.00
Artisans	0.00	0.00	50.00	0.00	0.00	0.00
Yeomen	0.00	0.00	33.33	6.66	0.00	0.00
TOTAL	**0.00**	**0.00**	**50.00**	**3.12**	**3.12**	**0.00**

Appendix H

Comparing and Contrasting Areas: Social Diffusion of Selected Commodities in the Urban and Rural Places of Murcia and Cartagena Testing All Population of the Sample (1730–1808)

Tables begin on next page.

Frequency of ownership of selected goods (French commodities) in the urban and rural areas of Murcia and Cartagena (1730–69)

Place		No. of inventories	Textiles made of 'bretaña' (%)	'Briaçu' (%)	Buffets (%)	'Cabriolé' (%)	Textiles made of 'cambray' (%)	Textiles made of 'crea' (%)
Murcia area	Urban	34	8.82	2.94	47.05	2.94	14.70	23.52
	Rural	32	3.33	0.00	26.66	0.00	0.00	6.66
Cartagena area	Urban	31	3.33	3.33	43.33	0.00	3.33	0.00
	Rural	38	0.00	2.63	28.94	0.00	0.00	2.63

Source: Protocols of the Archivo Historico Provincial de Murcia

Frequency of ownership of selected goods (French commodities) in the urban and rural areas of Murcia and Cartagena (1770–1808)

Place		No. of inventories	Textiles made of 'bretaña' (%)	'Briaçu' (%)	Buffets (%)	'Cabriolé' (%)	Textiles made of 'cambray' (%)	Textiles made of 'crea' (%)
Murcia area	Urban	34	0.00	2.77	47.22	11.11	2.77	13.88
	Rural	32	3.03	0.00	21.21	0.00	0.00	3.03
Cartagena area	Urban	31	0.00	0.00	5.88	8.82	0.00	14.70
	Rural	38	0.00	0.00	28.12	0.00	0.00	9.37

Source: Protocols of the Archivo Historico Provincial de Murcia

Frequency of ownership of selected goods (French commodities) in the urban and rural areas of Murcia and Cartagena (1730–69)

	Place	No. of inventories	'Desavillé' (%)	Textiles made of 'duray' (%)	Items with the French 'trade-mark' (%)	'Pompadour' (%)	Textiles made of 'tripé' (%)	Textiles made of 'trué' (%)
Murcia area	Urban	34	0.00	0.00	44.11	2.94	2.94	20.58
	Rural	32	0.00	0.00	0.00	0.00	0.00	0.00
Cartagena area	Urban	31	0.00	0.00	10.00	0.00	0.00	3.33
	Rural	38	0.00	0.00	2.63	0.00	0.00	5.26

Source: Protocols of the Archivo Historico Provincial de Murcia

Frequency of ownership of selected goods (French commodities) in the urban and rural areas of Murcia and Cartagena (1770–1808)

	Place	No. of inventories	'Desavillé' (%)	Textiles made of 'duray' (%)	Items with the French 'trade-mark' (%)	'Pompadour' (%)	Textiles made of 'tripé' (%)	Textiles made of 'trué' (%)
Murcia area	Urban	34	0.00	13.88	27.77	0.00	8.33	19.44
	Rural	32	0.00	6.06	3.03	0.00	12.12	3.03
Cartagena area	Urban	31	11.76	5.88	23.52	0.00	0.00	8.82
	Rural	38	3.12	0.00	0.00	0.00	3.12	6.25

Source: Protocols of the Archivo Historico Provincial de Murcia

Frequency of ownership of selected goods ('majo's' outfit) in the urban and rural areas of Murcia and Cartagena (1730–69)

	Place	No. of inventories	'Basquiña' [top petticoat] (%)	'Chal' [shawl] (%)	'Chaqueta' [jacket] (%)	'Cofia' [hair net] (%)	'Jubon' [doublet] (%)	Mantilla (%)	'Traje' [suit] (%)
Murcia area	Urban	34	44.11	0.00	2.94	11.76	38.23	29.41	2.94
	Rural	32	23.33	0.00	0.00	0.00	40.00	13.33	0.00
Cartagena area	Urban	31	36.66	0.00	0.00	0.00	10.00	26.66	3.33
	Rural	38	10.52	0.00	0.00	0.00	7.89	5.26	0.00

Source: Protocols of the Archivo Historico Provincial de Murcia

Frequency of ownership of selected goods ('majo's' outfit) in the urban and rural areas of Murcia and Cartagena (1770–1808)

	Place	No. of inventories	'Basquiña' [top petticoat] (%)	'Chal' [shawl] (%)	'Chaqueta' [jacket] (%)	'Cofia' [hair net] (%)	'Jubon' [doublet] (%)	Mantilla (%)	'Traje' [suit] (%)
Murcia area	Urban	38	50.00	0.00	2.77	16.66	38.88	41.66	2.77
	Rural	32	30.30	0.00	0.00	6.06	27.27	27.27	0.00
Cartagena area	Urban	36	38.23	2.94	17.64	11.76	0.00	41.17	2.94
	Rural	32	56.25	0.00	3.12	6.25	0.00	37.50	0.00

Source: Protocols of the Archivo Historico Provincial de Murcia

Frequency of ownership of selected goods (household furniture) in the urban and rural areas of Murcia and Cartagena (1730–69)

	Place	No. of inventories	Mirrors (%)	Bedclothes and furniture clothes made of 'indiana' (%)	Porcelains (%)	Items from China (%)	Chinaware (%)
Murcia area	Urban	34	55.88	29.41	11.76	11.76	5.88
	Rural	32	20.00	13.33	3.33	0.00	0.00
Cartagena area	Urban	31	30.00	43.33	3.33	0.00	0.00
	Rural	38	18.42	18.42	5.26	0.00	0.00

Source: Protocols of the Archivo Historico Provincial de Murcia

Frequency of ownership of selected goods (household furniture) in the urban and rural areas of Murcia and Cartagena (1770–1808)

	Place	No. of inventories	Mirrors (%)	Bedclothes and furniture clothes made of 'indiana' (%)	Porcelains (%)	Items from China (%)	Chinaware (%)
Murcia area	Urban	38	58.33	63.88	11.11	30.55	22.22
	Rural	32	15.15	30.30	0.00	0.00	0.00
Cartagena area	Urban	36	70.58	67.64	0.00	5.88	5.88
	Rural	32	25.00	78.12	3.12	0.00	0.00

Source: Protocols of the Archivo Historico Provincial de Murcia

Frequency of ownership of selected goods (household furniture) in the urban and rural areas of Murcia and Cartagena (1730–69)

	Place	No. of inventories	Clocks (%)	Books (%)
Murcia area	Urban	34	17.64	14.70
	Rural	32	0.00	3.33
Cartagena area	Urban	31	10.00	3.33
	Rural	38	0.00	0.00

Source: Protocols of the Archivo Historico Provincial de Murcia

Frequency of ownership of selected goods (household furniture) in the urban and rural areas of Murcia and Cartagena (1770–1808)

	Place	No. of inventories	Clocks (%)	Books (%)
Murcia area	Urban	38	19.44	19.44
	Rural	32	9.09	0.00
Cartagena area	Urban	36	29.41	14.70
	Rural	32	6.25	0.00

Source: Protocols of the Archivo Historico Provincial de Murcia

Frequency of ownership of selected goods (household furniture) in the urban and rural areas of Murcia and Cartagena (1730–69)

	Place	No. of inventories	Chocolate-pots (%)	Coffee-pots (%)	Tea-pots (%)	'Jicaras' [bowls] (%)	'Salvillas' [trays] (%)	Cups (%)
Murcia area	Urban	34	55.88	5.88	0.00	17.64	52.94	14.70
	Rural	32	30.00	0.00	0.00	6.06	0.00	6.66
Cartagena area	Urban	31	40.00	0.00	0.00	5.88	23.33	3.33
	Rural	38	2.63	2.63	0.00	0.00	7.89	2.63

Source: Protocols of the Archivo Historico Provincial de Murcia

Frequency of ownership of selected goods (household furniture) in the urban and rural areas of Murcia and Cartagena (1770–1808)

	Place	No. of inventories	Chocolate-pots (%)	Coffee-pots (%)	Tea-pots (%)	'Jicaras' [bowls] (%)	'Salvillas' [trays] (%)	Cups (%)
Murcia area	Urban	38	75.00	11.11	2.77	27.77	52.77	13.88
	Rural	32	42.42	3.03	0.00	13.33	12.12	3.03
Cartagena area	Urban	36	67.64	20.58	2.94	13.33	29.41	14.70
	Rural	32	50.00	0.00	0.00	3.12	3.12	0.00

Source: Protocols of the Archivo Historico Provincial de Murcia

Appendix I

Analysing the Volume of Consumption: Durable Commodities of Social Groups in the Kingdom of Murcia (1730–1808)

Number of items consumed per social rank in the Kingdom of Murcia (1730–1808)

A. – Household furniture

Table A.1　　　Number of coffee-pots

Social groups (*sample=273)	1730–50 (n. items)	1751–70 (n. items)	1771–90 (n. items)	1791–1808 (n. items)
Local oligarchy (=34)	–	1	5	21
Merchants (=33)	–	–	–	–
Landowners (=46)	–	–	1	–
Master artisans (=22)	–	–	–	–
Professionals (=8)	1	–	–	2
Artisans (=52)	–	–	1	4
Yeomen (=78)	–	–	–	–
Total (=273)	1	1	7	27 = 36

Source: A.H.P.M.　*Number of probate inventories

Table A.2　　　Number of chocolate-pots

Social groups (*sample=273)	1730–50 (n. items)	1751–70 (n. items)	1771–90 (n. items)	1791–1808 (n. items)
Local oligarchy (=34)	12	11	24	27
Merchants (=33)	6	2	7	14
Landowners (=46)	3	5	9	25
Master artisans (=22)	3	5	7	4
Professionals (=8)	3	4	–	5
Artisans (=52)	16	5	9	10
Yeomen (=78)	–	4	5	7
Total (=273)	43	36	61	92 = 232

Table A.3   Number of tea-pots

Social groups (*sample=273)	1730–50 (n. items)	1751–70 (n. items)	1771–90 (n. items)	1791–1808 (n. items)
Local oligarchy (=34)	–	–	1	–
Merchants (=33)	–	–	–	–
Landowners (=46)	–	–	–	–
Master artisans (=22)	–	–	–	–
Professionals (=8)	–	–	–	7
Artisans (=52)	–	–	–	–
Yeomen (=78)	–	–	–	–
Total (=273)	–	–	1	7 = 8

Table A.4   Number of 'jicaras' [bowls]

Social groups (*sample=273)	1730–50 (n. items)	1751–70 (n. items)	1771–90 (n. items)	1791–1808 (n. items)
Local oligarchy (=34)	–	88	464	275
Merchants (=33)	1	6	–	–
Landowners (=46)	–	–	3	34
Master artisans (=22)	21	12	42	–
Professionals (=8)	20	–	–	26
Artisans (=52)	10	12	6	22
Yeomen (=78)	–	2	–	4
Total (=273)	52	120	515	361 = 1048

Table A.5   Number of 'salvillas' [trays]

Social groups (*sample=273)	1730–50 (n. items)	1751–70 (n. items)	1771–90 (n. items)	1791–1808 (n. items)
Local oligarchy (=34)	11	8	16	12
Merchants (=33)	3	3	10	1
Landowners (=46)	1	1	3	3
Master artisans (=22)	2	2	5	1
Professionals (=8)	2	2	–	3
Artisans (=52)	4	4	3	6
Yeomen (=78)	6	1	–	–
Total (=273)	29	21	37	26 = 113

Table A.6   Number of cups

Social groups (*sample=273)	1730–50 (n. items)	1751–70 (n. items)	1771–90 (n. items)	1791–1808 (n. items)
Local oligarchy (=34)	–	37	247	–
Merchants (=33)	–	15	–	4
Landowners (=46)	1	2	–	4
Master artisans (=22)	–	12	1	–
Professionals (=8)	28	–	–	21
Artisans (=52)	1	–	–	51
Yeomen (=78)	–	–	–	–
Total (=273)	30	66	248	80 = 424

Table A.7   Number of items from China

Social groups (*sample=273)	1730–50 (n. items)	1751–70 (n. items)	1771–90 (n. items)	1791–1808 (n. items)
Local oligarchy (=34)	–	94	270	114
Merchants (=33)	–	–	–	–
Landowners (=46)	–	–	–	3
Master artisans (=22)	–	–	–	–
Professionals (=8)	40	–	–	17
Artisans (=52)	–	–	–	3
Yeomen (=78)	–	–	–	–
Total (=273)	40	94	270	137 = 541

Table A.8   Number of Chinaware

Social groups (*sample=273)	1730–50 (n. items)	1751–70 (n. items)	1771–90 (n. items)	1791–1808 (n. items)
Local oligarchy (=34)	3	94	282	112
Merchants (=33)	–	–	–	2
Landowners (=46)	–	–	–	4
Master artisans (=22)	–	–	–	4
Professionals (=8)	40	–	–	13
Artisans (=52)	–	–	–	3
Yeomen (=78)	–	–	–	–
Total (=273)	43	94	282	138 = 557

Table A.9   Number of household cloth made of 'indiana'

Social groups (*sample=273)	1730–50 (n. items)	1751–70 (n. items)	1771–90 (n. items)	1791–1808 (n. items)
Local oligarchy (=34)	4	10	31	28
Merchants (=33)	13	4	23	–
Landowners (=46)	–	10	8	93
Master artisans (=22)	6	7	5	5
Professionals (=8)	1	–	–	–
Artisans (=52)	3	17	36	16
Yeomen (=78)	1	2	22	30
Total (=273)	28	50	125	172 = 375

Table A.10   Number of porcelains

Social groups (*sample=273)	1730–50 (n. items)	1751–70 (n. items)	1771–90 (n. items)	1791–1808 (n. items)
Local oligarchy (=34)	–	–	3	–
Merchants (=33)	–	8	–	–
Landowners (=46)	1	–	–	8
Master artisans (=22)	1	1	–	–
Professionals (=8)	–	–	–	–
Artisans (=52)	–	1	1	–
Yeomen (=78)	1	2	–	1
Total (=273)	3	12	4	9 = 28

Table A.11   Number of mirrors

Social groups (*sample=273)	1730–50 (n. items)	1751–70 (n. items)	1771–90 (n. items)	1791–1808 (n. items)
Local oligarchy (=34)	9	3	–	7
Merchants (=33)	14	447	1	–
Landowners (=46)	3	4	8	7
Master artisans (=22)	5	3	1	12
Professionals (=8)	–	–	1	3
Artisans (=52)	21	14	3	11
Yeomen (=78)	–	3	2	1
Total (=273)	52	474	16	41 = 583

Table A.12   Number of books

Social groups (*sample=273)	1730–50 (n. items)	1751–70 (n. items)	1771–90 (n. items)	1791–1808 (n. items)
Local oligarchy (=34)	4	1	97	11
Merchants (=33)	–	–	–	–
Landowners (=46)	4	–	–	–
Master artisans (=22)	4	25	2	2
Professionals (=8)	–	1	–	–
Artisans (=52)	–	4	–	–
Yeomen (=78)	–	–	–	–
Total (=273)	12	31	99	13 = 155

Table A.13   Number of clocks

Social groups (*sample=273)	1730–50 (n. items)	1751–70 (n. items)	1771–90 (n. items)	1791–1808 (n. items)
Local oligarchy (=34)	3	2	11	6
Merchants (=33)	2	–	1	1
Landowners (=46)	–	–	3	–
Master artisans (=22)	–	–	1	3
Professionals (=8)	–	–	–	5
Artisans (=52)	2	1	–	6
Yeomen (=78)	–	–	–	–
Total (=273)	7	3	16	21 = 47

B. – French commodities

Table B.1   Number of textiles made of 'bretaña'

Social groups (*sample=273)	1730–50 (n. items)	1751–70 (n. items)	1771–90 (n. items)	1791–1808 (n. items)
Local oligarchy (=34)	9	–	–	–
Merchants (=33)	3	–	1	–
Landowners (=46)	–	–	–	–
Master artisans (=22)	12	–	–	–
Professionals (=8)	2	–	–	–
Artisans (=52)	–	–	–	–
Yeomen (=78)	–	–	–	–
Total (=273)	26	–	1	– = 27

Table B.2   Number of 'briaçu'

Social groups (*sample=273)	1730–50 (n. items)	1751–70 (n. items)	1771–90 (n. items)	1791–1808 (n. items)
Local oligarchy (=34)	1	1	–	–
Merchants (=33)	–	–	–	–
Landowners (=46)	–	1	–	–
Master artisans (=22)	–	1	–	–
Professionals (=8)	–	–	–	–
Artisans (=52)	–	–	–	–
Yeomen (=78)	–	–	–	–
Total (=273)	1	3	–	– = 4

Table B.3   Number of buffets

Social groups (*sample=273)	1730–50 (n. items)	1751–70 (n. items)	1771–90 (n. items)	1791–1808 (n. items)
Local oligarchy (=34)	31	10	22	10
Merchants (=33)	11	–	3	1
Landowners (=46)	10	8	7	6
Master artisans (=22)	6	–	7	–
Professionals (=8)	–	1	1	–
Artisans (=52)	24	10	7	2
Yeomen (=78)	2	5	3	1
Total (=273)	84	34	50	20 = 188

Table B.4   Number of 'cabriolé'

Social groups (*sample=273)	1730–50 (n. items)	1751–70 (n. items)	1771–90 (n. items)	1791–1808 (n. items)
Local oligarchy (=34)	–	1	5	–
Merchants (=33)	–	–	1	–
Landowners (=46)	–	–	–	–
Master artisans (=22)	–	–	–	–
Professionals (=8)	–	–	–	–
Artisans (=52)	–	–	2	1
Yeomen (=78)	–	–	–	–
Total (=273)	–	1	8	1 = 10

Table B.5   Number of textiles made of 'cambray'

Social groups (*sample=273)	1730–50 (n. items)	1751–70 (n. items)	1771–90 (n. items)	1791–1808 (n. items)
Local oligarchy (=34)	–	18	–	–
Merchants (=33)	–	6	18	–
Landowners (=46)	–	–	–	–
Master artisans (=22)	2	5	–	–
Professionals (=8)	1	–	–	–
Artisans (=52)	–	1	–	–
Yeomen (=78)	–	–	–	–
Total (=273)	3	30	18	– = 51

Table B.6   Number of textiles made of 'crea'

Social groups (*sample=273)	1730–50 (n. items)	1751–70 (n. items)	1771–90 (n. items)	1791–1808 (n. items)
Local oligarchy (=34)	1	1	–	–
Merchants (=33)	16	17	–	9
Landowners (=46)	–	2	1	12
Master artisans (=22)	1	15	4	11
Professionals (=8)	1	–	–	2
Artisans (=52)	5	–	3	26
Yeomen (=78)	–	2	6	–
Total (=273)	24	37	14	60 = 135

Table B.7   Number of 'desavillé'

Social groups (*sample=273)	1730–50 (n. items)	1751–70 (n. items)	1771–90 (n. items)	1791–1808 (n. items)
Local oligarchy (=34)	–	–	–	2
Merchants (=33)	–	–	–	–
Landowners (=46)	–	–	3	–
Master artisans (=22)	–	–	–	–
Professionals (=8)	–	–	–	3
Artisans (=52)	–	–	2	–
Yeomen (=78)	–	–	–	–
Total (=273)	–	–	5	5 = 10

Table B.8   Number of textiles made of 'duray'

Social groups (*sample=273)	1730–50 (n. items)	1751–70 (n. items)	1771–90 (n. items)	1791–1808 (n. items)
Local oligarchy (=34)	–	2	–	–
Merchants (=33)	–	1	–	1
Landowners (=46)	–	–	–	1
Master artisans (=22)	–	–	1	1
Professionals (=8)	–	–	–	–
Artisans (=52)	–	–	4	–
Yeomen (=78)	–	–	–	–
Total (=273)	–	3	5	3 = 11

Table B.9   Number of items with the French 'trade-mark'

Social groups (*sample=273)	1730–50 (n. items)	1751–70 (n. items)	1771–90 (n. items)	1791–1808 (n. items)
Local oligarchy (=34)	50	18	32	19
Merchants (=33)	84	69	–	8
Landowners (=46)	–	1	1	4
Master artisans (=22)	1	6	–	4
Professionals (=8)	10	26	–	5
Artisans (=52)	7	–	–	4
Yeomen (=78)	–	19	–	–
Total (=273)	152	139	33	44 = 368

Table B.10   Number of 'pompadour'

Social groups (*sample=273)	1730–50 (n. items)	1751–70 (n. items)	1771–90 (n. items)	1791–1808 (n. items)
Local oligarchy (=34)	–	2	–	–
Merchants (=33)	–	–	–	–
Landowners (=46)	–	–	–	–
Master artisans (=22)	–	–	–	–
Professionals (=8)	–	–	–	–
Artisans (=52)	–	–	–	–
Yeomen (=78)	–	–	–	–
Total (=273)	–	2	–	– = 2

Table B.11 Number of textiles made of 'tripé'

Social groups (*sample=273)	1730–50 (n. items)	1751–70 (n. items)	1771–90 (n. items)	1791–1808 (n. items)
Local oligarchy (=34)	–	1	7	–
Merchants (=33)	–	–	3	–
Landowners (=46)	–	–	2	2
Master artisans (=22)	–	–	–	–
Professionals (=8)	–	–	–	–
Artisans (=52)	–	–	4	–
Yeomen (=78)	–	–	2	–
Total (=273)	–	1	18	2 = 21

Table B.12 Number of textiles made of 'trué'

Social groups (*sample=273)	1730–50 (n. items)	1751–70 (n. items)	1771–90 (n. items)	1791–1808 (n. items)
Local oligarchy (=34)	1	33	19	–
Merchants (=33)	–	14	6	–
Landowners (=46)	–	1	8	4
Master artisans (=22)	11	–	4	–
Professionals (=8)	12	–	–	–
Artisans (=52)	43	1	–	–
Yeomen (=78)	–	1	–	–
Total (=273)	67	50	37	4 = 158

C. – 'Majo' attire

Table C.1 Number of 'basquiña' [top petticoat]

Social groups (*sample=273)	1730–50 (n. items)	1751–70 (n. items)	1771–90 (n. items)	1791–1808 (n. items)
Local oligarchy (=34)	14	8	10	4
Merchants (=33)	6	7	8	12
Landowners (=46)	3	2	7	13
Master artisans (=22)	4	3	6	3
Professionals (=8)	2	–	–	4
Artisans (=52)	8	8	12	11
Yeomen (=78)	3	7	12	9
Total (=273)	40	35	55	56 = 186

Table C.2   Number of 'chal' [shawl]

Social groups (*sample=273)	1730–50 (n. items)	1751–70 (n. items)	1771–90 (n. items)	1791–1808 (n. items)
Local oligarchy (=34)	–	–	–	–
Merchants (=33)	–	–	–	–
Landowners (=46)	–	–	–	–
Master artisans (=22)	–	–	–	–
Professionals (=8)	–	–	–	–
Artisans (=52)	–	–	–	6
Yeomen (=78)	–	–	–	–
Total (=273)	–	–	–	6 = 6

Table C.3   Number of 'chaqueta' [jacket]

Social groups (*sample=273)	1730–50 (n. items)	1751–70 (n. items)	1771–90 (n. items)	1791–1808 (n. items)
Local oligarchy (=34)	1	–	–	–
Merchants (=33)	–	–	–	6
Landowners (=46)	–	–	–	2
Master artisans (=22)	–	–	–	1
Professionals (=8)	–	–	–	1
Artisans (=52)	–	–	–	3
Yeomen (=78)	–	–	–	–
Total (=273)	1	–	–	13 = 14

Table C.4   Number of 'cofia' [hair net]

Social groups (*sample=273)	1730–50 (n. items)	1751–70 (n. items)	1771–90 (n. items)	1791–1808 (n. items)
Local oligarchy (=34)	–	2	2	2
Merchants (=33)	–	38	2	2
Landowners (=46)	–	–	–	2
Master artisans (=22)	–	–	2	–
Professionals (=8)	–	–	–	2
Artisans (=52)	–	1	4	20
Yeomen (=78)	–	–	–	–
Total (=273)	–	41	10	28 = 79

Table C.5   Number of 'jubon' [doublet]

Social groups (*sample=273)	1730–50 (n. items)	1751–70 (n. items)	1771–90 (n. items)	1791–1808 (n. items)
Local oligarchy (=34)	3	8	–	–
Merchants (=33)	8	7	11	–
Landowners (=46)	3	2	–	8
Master artisans (=22)	2	15	12	–
Professionals (=8)	–	2	–	–
Artisans (=52)	2	1	10	1
Yeomen (=78)	3	6	2	3
Total (=273)	21	41	35	12 = 109

Table C.6   Number of mantilla

Social groups (*sample=273)	1730–50 (n. items)	1751–70 (n. items)	1771–90 (n. items)	1791–1808 (n. items)
Local oligarchy (=34)	7	7	12	13
Merchants (=33)	3	1	2	13
Landowners (=46)	–	5	10	38
Master artisans (=22)	4	1	7	9
Professionals (=8)	2	–	1	7
Artisans (=52)	5	9	13	4
Yeomen (=78)	1	3	11	28
Total (=273)	22	26	56	112 = 216

Table C.7   Number of 'traje' – [suit]

Social groups (*sample=273)	1730–50 (n. items)	1751–70 (n. items)	1771–90 (n. items)	1791–1808 (n. items)
Local oligarchy (=34)	2	–	–	–
Merchants (=33)	–	–	–	1
Landowners (=46)	–	–	–	–
Master artisans (=22)	–	–	5	–
Professionals (=8)	–	–	–	–
Artisans (=52)	4	–	–	–
Yeomen (=78)	–	–	–	–
Total (=273)	6	–	5	1 = 12

Glossary

Ajamis: blue cotton drape. It was one of the most popular fibres commercialized from the routes of Alep.

Aman: blue drapes from Alep.

Antioche: blue and white drapes from the trade scales of Alep.

Basquiña [top petticoat]: smock used by women to go out the street. Nowadays, is used as a garment of traditional regional costumes.

Battanonis: white cotton drape from the routes of Alep.

Briaçu: French garment knotted with silver buckles as described in probate inventories of the Kingdom of Murcia.

Buffet: French furniture, composed of tables and desk which became popular in Spain during the eighteenth century.

Cabriolé: its origins comes from the French voice 'cabriolet', as a cloak with sleeves in both sides to take out the arms. It was a garment used by men and women. 'Cabriolet' could be also a light two-wheeled carriage with a hood, drawn by one horse.

Caissie: cotton textiles from the Levant market.

Calico: originally from India, a fine cotton cloth painted in attractive flowery motif designs. Its exotic name recalled the Indian town of Calicut. It was the general term used by Europeans to refer to cottons exported from India.

Cambray: Fabric made of linen or cotton, thinner and brighter than the 'holanda' textile. It was similar to the light and thin 'quintin' from Brittany. Its name comes from the French city of Cambrai in which this textile was elaborated.

Chal [shawl]: a piece of fabric worn by women over shoulders or head.

Cofia [hair net]: Used by women and men to put up their hair. Men's 'cofias' were made of cloth or net with a tassel or a pompom. Women's 'cofias' were more ornate, could be made of cloth with lace on top and a decorated net. Also, women's 'cofias' had tassels or pompoms.

Crea: white fabric made of thin linen. It was a very popular material, which was used to make shirts and sheets. Its origin was from the French city of León, Brittany, in where the 'creas leonas' were made.

Currutaco: a person who fastidiously cares about the use of fashions.

Demitte: white and dyed drape made of cotton from the commercial routes of Smyrna, Egypt, Seyde and Cyprus.

Desavillé: similar to the English 'negligee', lingerie made of thin knotted fabrics and laces.

Dorures fines: silk textiles whose origin is China. During the eighteenth century it was unknown in Europe. This fabric was also made of satin, embellished with gold and silver flowers made of paper cut in long and narrow threads.

Duray or Duroi: as it appears in probate inventories from Murcia and Cartagena, is a carded-woollen fabric from Holland, whose prime origin is England, and later it was introduced to Amiens, France, in the eighteenth century, from where it was exported to Spain in high quantities.

Escamitte: white cotton drape from the trade routes of the Levant.

Etamine: sort of silk 'jaspée' [marbled] or 'virée' [with double silk layers]. It was imported from the East Indies to Marseille, a silk of 2 ells long and 7/16 wide.

Etoffe: silk drapes from Persia, the East Indies and China.

Indiana: cotton fabric printed with colourful designs. They were printed on white cotton cloth imitating the calico textiles from India. This fibre was elaborated in Spain, mainly in the Catalonian area.

Indienne: block-printed calico, originally made in India but from the 1670s in Europe.

Jubon [doublet]: a man's short, close-fitting padded jacket, worn from the fourteenth to the eighteenth centuries.

Livre tournois: French currency whose value was based on silver or gold. It was a monetary unit of account used in France in the medieval and the early modern periods.

Manouf: cotton textiles from the Levant market.

Mantilla: a typical Spanish lace or scarf, which composed the 'majo' outfit, worn by women over the head and shoulders. Women wore white or dark coloured veils or 'mantilla' and they decorated their hair with 'peineta', little combs.

Mousseline: lightweight cotton from India; much like muslin.

Muslin: fine and semi-transparent high-quality cotton cloth with origins in the Iraqi town of Mosul. The cloth itself was woven in India, especially the district of Bengal.

Pompadour: French high-quality fabric with bright colours.

Real: The real [meaning: 'royal', plural: reales] was a unit of currency in Spain for several centuries after the mid-1300s, but changed in value relative to other units introduced. The 'real de plata fuerte' was introduced in 1737 at a value of 2½ reales de vellón or 85 maravedíes. This real was the standard, issued as coins until the early nineteenth century. The gold escudo was worth 16 reales de plata fuerte.

Soleil: division of the French 'livre tournois', [1 'livre tournois' = 20 French 'soleils'].

Tejido casero: textile elaborated in peasant and artisans households.

Tejido de la tierra: typical textile from a certain region manufactured by the household labour.

Tejido del país: fabric typical from a given territory manufactured by the household labour.

Tejidos basto y ordinario: fabrics with rough or harsh texture typical in working-class households.

Tisú: silk fabric interwoven with threads of gold or silver from both sides of the textile.

Toiles blanches: white drapes from Side, Alep and Egypt, traded in Levantine routes.

Toiles de montagne: drapes of heavy quality from Side, Alep and Egypt, traded in Levantine routes.

Toiles diverses: drapes of varied origin and they could be dyed or white.

Trué: fabric made of white and thin linen, whose name was taken by the French city of Troyes from the region of Champagne.

Bibliography

Manuscript Sources

A.C.C.M. Fonds Roux-Frères, Manifestes des navires entrés à Marseille (1757–71), Référence: L. IX, 1024.

A.C.C.M, L. IX, 739, lettre du 3 février 1764.

A.C.C.M., L. IX, 773, Lettre d' A. Geoffroy, procureur de J.-J. Badaraque, 17 février 1775.

A.C.C.M., L. IX, 773–775, Lettres des divers correspondants à Alep.

A.C.C.M., L. IX, 870, Fonds Roux-Frères. Correspondant à l'étranger. Espagne.

A.C.C.M, L. IX, Fonds Roux.

A.C.C.M., Reference: Serie H, 71. Commerce avec l' Espagne (1700–49). Prohibition de marchandises venant d' Angleterre.

A.C.C.M., Référence: Serie H, 73, Commerce avec l' Espagne (1776–91).

A.C.C.M., Statistique. Serie I. Article 29, I.30, I.24, I.31.

A.H.P.M., protocol 771, 991, 1077, 1187, 2352, 2378, 2694, 2703, 2787, 2804, 2811, 2946, 3122, 3970, 4281, 4228, 4222, 5492, 5487, 6214, 11375.

A.H.P.M., Respuestas Particulares al Catastro de la Ensenada (1752–55), Hacienda, L. 3845.

A.M.C., Libro no. 8 de entrada de embarcaciones francesas (1795–98).

A.M.L., Cartas de Antonio Martín de Lorca, S. II, 19.

A.M.L., S. II, 19, Cartas de Antonio Martín de Lorca.

A.M.M., Belluga, L., *Carta Pastoral que el Obispo de Cartagena escribe a los fieles de su diócesis a cada uno en lo que le toca, para que todos concurran a que se destierre la profanidad de los trages y varios e intolerables abusos que ahora nuevamente se han introducido* (Murcia, 1711).

A.M.M., Belluga, L., *Carta sobre trages y honestidad de costumbres* (Murcia, 1715).

A.M.M., Charles' III Census of Foreigners, 1764.

A.M.M., Correo Literario de Murcia, Octubre de 1793.

B.N., Clavijo y Fajardo, J., *Antología de El pensador* [Texto impreso], 1763 Biblioteca básica canaria; 10, El Pensador, M 6091–1989, I, pensamiento VII, pp. 9, 10, 17, 18.

B.N., mss. 6006–6008. Calatayud, P., *Doctrinas prácticas que solía explicar en sus misiones el V.P. Pedro de Calatayud*, Doctrina VI, Parte II, Tratado X, T. III, pp. 416–7.

C.D.M.T., CA 118, *Pragmática sanción contra los trages y otras cosas* (Madrid, 1729).

C.D.M.T., CA 155, *Ordenanzas para los fabricantes de Indianas de Cataluña*, 1767.

C.D.M.T., CA 168, *Notificación de la Real Orden prohibiendo la entrada de muselinas*, Barcelona, 1770.

C.D.M.T., CA 299, Don Lucas Campoo y Otazu, *Sermón contra el lujo y la profanidad en los vestidos y adornos de las mujeres cristianas* (Málaga, 1781).

C.D.M.T., CA 360, *Copia de una bula de su santidad Pio VII sobre la modestia en el vestir*, 1801, Roma.

C.D.M.T., CA 361, *Discurso sobre el lujo de las señoras y proyecto de un traje nacional*, Madrid, Imprenta Real, 1788.

C.D.M.T., CA, Don Felipe Rojo de Flores, *Una juiciosa satira contra la profanidad, y luxo con varias noticias historicas relativas a los trages y adornos*, Madrid, Imprenta Real, 1794.

Printed Primary Sources

Antoine-Leonard Thomas, *Essai sur le caràctere, les moeurs, et l'esprit des femmes* (Paris: Moutard, 1772).

La moda elegante ilustrada: periódico de las familias (Madrid: 1842–1927).

The Correspondence of Jeremy Bentham: 1752–1776 (ed. Timothy L.S. Sprigge. London: Athlone Press, 1968), pp. 362–5. Print. *Electronic Enlightenment*, ed. Robert McNamee et al. Vers. 2.1. 2010 (University of Oxford. 2 June 2010). <http://0-www.e-enlightenment.com.biblio.eui.eu/item/bentjeOU0010362_1key001cor>. © Electronic Enlightenment Project, Bodleian Library, University of Oxford, 2008–2010. All rights reserved. Distributed by Oxford University Press.

The Macaroni and Theatrical Magazine, or Monthly Register (October, 1772): 1.

Secondary Sources

Abel, W., *Agricultural Fluctuations in Europe* (London: Menthuen, 1980).

Acemoglu, D., Johnson S. and Robinson J., 'The Rise of Europe: Atlantic Trade, Institutional Change, and Economic Growth', *The American Economic Review*, vol. 95, no. 3 (June, 2005), pp. 546–79.

Adams, C., *A Taste for Comfort and Status. A Bourgeois Family in Eighteenth-Century France* (Pennsylvania: The Pennsylvania State University Press University Park, 2000).

Adshead, S.A.M, *Material Culture in Europe and China, 1400–1800* (New York and London: St Martin's Press and Macmillan, 1997).

Ago, R., 'Oltre la dote: I beni femminile', in Groppi, A., *Storia delle donne in Italia. Il lavoro delle donne* (Bari: Editori Laterza, 1996), pp. 164–82.

——, *Il gusto delle cose. Una storia degli oggetti nella Roma del Seicento* (Roma: Donzelli Editore, 2006).

Allen, C.A., 'India in the Great Divergence', in Hatton, T.J., O'Rourke, K.H. and Taylor, A.M. (eds), *The New Comparative Economic History: Essays in Honor of Jeffrey G. Williamson* (Cambridge, MA: MIT Press, 2007), pp. 9–32.

Alvarez Barrientos, J., 'La civilización como modelo de vida en el Madrid del siglo XVIII', *RDTP*, LVI, 1 (2001), pp. 142–62.

Álvarez de Miranda, P., *Palabras e ideas: el léxico de la Ilustración temprana en España (1680–1760)* (Madrid: Real Academia Española, 1992).

Amalric, J.P., 'Franceses en tierras de España. Una presencia mediadora en el Antiguo Régimen', Villar García, M.B. and Pezzi Cristobal, P. (eds), *Los extranjeros en la España Moderna* (Málaga: Junta de Andalucía, 2003), vol. 1, pp. 23–38.

Amelang, J.S., *Honored Citizens of Barcelona: Patrician Culture and Class Relations, 1490–1714* (Princeton, NJ: Princeton University Press, 1986).

Anderson, B., *Imagined Communities: Reflections on the Origin and Spread of Nationalism* (London: Verso, 1983).

——, 'Introduction', in Balakrishnan, G., *Mapping the Nation* (London: Verso in association with *New Left Review*, 1996), pp. 1–16.

Anderson, M., Berchhofer, F. and Gershuny, J., 'Introduction', in Anderson, Berchhofer and Gershuny (eds), *The Social and Political Economy of the Household* (Oxford: Oxford University Press, 1994), pp. 1–16.

Andioc, R., *Teatro y sociedad en el Madrid del siglo XVIII* (Valencia: Fundación Juan March, Editorial Castalia, 1976).

Anes Álvarez de Castrillón, G., *Economía e Ilustración en la España del siglo XVIII* (Barcelona: Ariel, 1981).

——, 'Coyuntura económica e Ilustración', in Rico Manrique, F. (ed.), *Historia y critica de la literatura española* (4 vols), t. 1, Caso González, J.M. (ed.), *Ilustración y Neoclasicismo* (Barcelona: Crítica, 1983), pp. 49–58.

Antoine-Leonard Thomas, *Essai sur le caràctere, les moeurs, et l'esprit des femmes* (Paris: Moutard, 1772).

Aranguren, J.L., *Moral y sociedad: La moral social española en el s. XIX* (Madrid: Cuadernos para el Diálogo, 1970).

Asthor, E., 'Recent Research on Levantine Trade', *Journal of European Economic History*, II (1973), 187–206, XIV (1985).

Auslander, L., 'The Gendering of Consumer Practices in Nineteenth-Century France', in De Grazia, V. and Furlough, E. (eds), *The Sex of Things. Gender Consumption in Historical Perspective* (Berkeley: University of California Press, 1996), pp. 79–112.

Banks, K.J., *Chasing Empire across the Sea: Communications and the State in the French Atlantic, 1713–1763* (Montreal and Kingston: MacGill Queen's University Press, 2002).

Barnes-Karol, G., 'Religious Oratory in a Culture of Control', in Cruz, A.J. and
     Perry, M.E., *Culture and Control in Counter-Reformation Spain* (Minneapolis-
     Oxford: University of Minnesota, 1992).
Bartolomei, A., 'Paiements commerciaux et profits bancaires: les usages de la
     lettre de change (1780–1820)', *Rives Méditerranéennes* [En ligne], Jeunes
     chercheurs (2007), mis en ligne le 15 octobre 2008, Consulté le 10 mars 2010.
     URL: http://rives.revues.org/101.
Baskes, J., *Indian, Merchants and Markets. A Reinterpretation of the Repartimiento
     and Spanish-Indian Economic Relations in Colonial Oaxaca, 1750–1821*
     (Stanford: Stanford University Press, 2000).
Batchelor, R., 'On the Movement of Porcelains. Rethinking the Birth of Consumer
     Society as Interactions of Exchange Networks, 1600–1750', in Brewer, J. and
     Trentmann, F. (eds), *Consuming Cultures, Global Perspectives. Historical
     Trajectories, Transnational Exchanges* (Oxford and New York: Berg, 2006),
     pp. 95–121.
Baulant, M., 'Enquête sur les inventaires après décès autour de Meaux aux
     XVIIe–XVIIIe siècles', in Schuurman, A. and Walsh, L.S. (eds), *Material Culture:
     Consumption, Life-Style, Standard of Living, 1500–1900* (Milan: Eleventh
     International Economic History Congress, September, 1994), pp. 141–8.
Baulant, M., Piponnier, F., Tryantafyllidou-Baladié, Y. and Veinstein, G.,
     'Problématique et méthode comunes aux corpus présentés par les chercheurs
     de l'E.H.E.S.S. de Paris', in Schuurman, A. and Walsh, L.S. (eds), *Material
     Culture: Consumption, Life-Style, Standard of Living, 1500–1900* (Milan:
     Eleventh International Economic History Congress, September, 1994),
     pp. 141–8, pp. 115–26.
Beaumarchais, Pierre-Agustin Caron de, *Ouvres complètes de Beaumarchais*,
     Preface de Edouard Fournier (Paris: Laplace, Sánchez et Cie, 1876).
——, *Le mariage de Figaro*, Préface de Pierre Larthomas (Paris: editions
     Gallimard, 1984).
Becker, G., 'A Theory of the Allocation of Time', *The Economic Journal*, 75
     (1965), pp. 493–517.
Benson, K., 'Indigo Production in the Eighteenth-Century', *Hispanic American
     Historical Review*, vol. XLIV, 2 (1964).
Berg, M., 'Commerce and Creativity in Eighteenth-century Birmingham', in Berg,
     M., *Markets and Manufacture in Early Industrial Europe* (London and New
     York: Routledge, 1991), pp. 173–201.
——, 'In Pursuit of Luxury: Global History and British Consumer Goods in the
     Eighteenth-Century', *Past and Present*, no. 182 (February, 2004), pp. 85–142.
——, *Luxury and Pleasure in Eighteenth-Century Britain* (Oxford: Oxford
     University Press, 2005).
Berg, M. and Clifford, H., 'Selling Consumption in the Eighteenth-Century.
     Advertising and Trade Card in Britain and France', *Cultural and Social
     History*, vol. 4, no. 2 (1998), pp. 145–70.

——, *Consumers and Luxury. Consumer Culture in Europe, 1650–1850* (Manchester and New York: Manchester University Press, 1999).

Berg, M. and Eger, E., 'The Rise and Fall of Luxury Debates', in Berg, M. and Eger, E. (eds), *Luxury in the Eighteenth Century. Debates, Desires and Delectable goods* (New York: Palgrave Macmillan, 2003), pp. 7–27.

Bergasse, L. and Rambert A.G. *Histoire du commerce de Marseille*. t. IV. *De 1559 a 1660. De 1660 à 1789* (Paris: Libraire Plon, 1954).

Berndt, E. and Christensen, L., 'The Translog Function and the Substitution of Equipment, Structures, and Labour in US Manufacturing, 1929–1968', *Journal of Econometrics*, vol. 1, no. 1 (1973), pp. 81–114.

——, 'The Internal Structure of Functional Relationships: Separability, Substitution, and Aggregation', *The Review of Economic Studies*, vol. 40, no. 3 (July, 1973), pp. 403–10.

Bibiloni Amengual, A., 'Mallorca i els ports europeus: la comercialització de l'oli (1667–1702)', *Randa*, no. 25 (1989), pp. 17–46.

Bolufer, M., *Mujeres e Ilustración. La construcción de la feminidad en la España del siglo XVIII* (Valencia: Institucio Alfons el Magnanim, 1998).

——, 'Transformaciones culturales. Luces y sombras', in *Historia de las mujeres en España y America Latina II*, Morant, I. (dir.), Ortega, M., Lavrin, A. and Pérez Cantó, P. (eds) (Madrid: Cátedra, 2005), pp. 479–510.

——, 'De madres a hijas, de padres a hijos: familia y transmisión moral (ss. XVII–XVIII)', in Pérez García, M. and Bestard, J. (eds), *Familia, Valores y Representaciones* (Murcia: Universidad de Murcia, 2010), pp. 217–38.

Born, W., 'Scarlet', *Ciba Review*, I (March, 1938).

Borsay, P., *The English Urban Renaissance. Culture and Society in the Provincial Town, 1660–1770* (Oxford: Oxford University Press, 1989).

Boserup, E., *The Conditions of Agricultural Growth* (Chicago: University of Chicago Press, 1965).

Boucher, F., *Histoire du costume en occident de l'antiquité à nous jours* (Paris: Flammarion, 1965).

Boulanger, P., 'Marseille, escale des soies à l'orée du XVIIIe siècle', in *Marseille sur les routes de la soie*, Actes de la table ronde organisée par la Chambre de Commerce et d'Industrie Marseille-Provence et l'Université de Provence (Marseille: Chambre de Commerce et d'Industrie Marseille-Provence, 2001), pp. 47–65.

Bourdieu, P., *La distinction. Critique sociale du jugement* (Paris: Les editions de minuit, 1979).

Boutin-Arnaud, M.N. and Tasmadjian, S., *Le vêtement* (Paris: Éditions Nathan, 1997).

Bowen, H.V., *The Business of the Empire: the East India Company and the Imperial Britain, 1756–1833* (Cambridge: Cambridge University Press, 2006).

Braude, B., 'International Competition and Domestic Cloth in the Ottoman Empire, 1500–1650: a Study in Underdevelopment', *Review Fernand Braudel Center* 2/3 (1979), pp. 437–51.

Braudel, F., *Civilisation matérielle, économie, capitalisme, XVᵉ–XVIIIᵉ siècle. Les structures du quotidien: le impossible et le impossible* (Tome I, Paris: Armand Colin, 1979).

———, *Les structures du quotidien. Civilisation matérielle, économie et capitalisme XVᵉ–XVIIIᵉ siècle* (Paris: Armand Colin, 1979).

Brewer, J., *The Error of Our Ways: Historians and the Birth of Consumer Society*, Working Paper 12 (June, 2004), www.consume.bbk.ac.uk.

Brewer, J. and Bermingham, A., *The Consumption of Culture, 1600–1800: Image, Object, Text* (London and New York: Routledge, 1995).

Brewer, J. and Porter, R., *Consumption and the World of Goods* (London and New York: Routledge, 1993).

Brewer, J. and Staves, S., *Early Modern Conceptions of Property* (London and New York: Routledge, 1994).

Brewer, J. and Trentmann, F., 'Introduction. Space, Time and Value in Consuming Cultures', in Brewer, J. and Trentmann, F., *Consuming Cultures, Global Perspectives. Historical Trajectories, Transnational Exchanges* (Oxford and New York: Berg ed., 2006), pp. 1–17.

Broadberry, S. and Gupta, B., 'The Early Modern Great Divergence: Wages, Prices and Economic Development in Europe and Asia, 1500–1800', *Economic History Review*, 59/1 (2006), pp. 2–31.

Burke, P., 'How to Be a Counter-Reformation Saint', in Von Greyerz, K. (ed.), *Religion and Society in Early Modern Europe, 1500–1800* (Boston: Allen and Unwin, 1984).

———, 'Res et verba: Conspicuous Consumption in the Early Modern World', in Brewer, J. and Porter, R., *Consumption and the World of Goods* (London and New York: Routledge, 1993).

———, *Varieties of Cultural History* (Ithaca, NY: Cornell University Press, 1997).

Burnet, J., *Liquid Pleasures, a Social History of Drinks in Modern Britain* (London: Taylor and Francis, 1999).

Buti, G., 'Marseille, l'Espagne et la soie au XVIIIe siècle', in *Marseille sur les routes de la soie*, Actes de la table ronde organisée par la Chambre de Commerce et d'Industrie Marseille-Provence et l'Université de Provence (Marseille: Chambre de Commerce et d'Industrie Marseille-Provence, 2001), pp. 229–53.

Cadalso, J., *Cartas Marruecas* (Madrid: edition José Miguel Caso, Colección Austral, 1999).

Callahan, W.J., 'Utility, Material Progress and Morality in Eighteenth-Century Spain', in Fritz, P. and Williams, D. (eds), *The Triumph of Culture. Eighteenth Century Perspectives* (Toronto: Hakkert, 1972), pp. 359–60.

Callahan, W.J. and Higgs, D. (eds), *Church and Society in Catholic Europe of the Eighteenth-Century* (Cambridge [Eng.] and New York: Cambridge University Press, 1979).

Campbell, C., *The Romantic Ethic and the Spirit of Modern Consumerism* (Oxford: Blackwell, 1987).

Carrière, Ch., *Négotians Marsellais au XVIIIe siècle. Contribution à l'étude des économies maritimes* (Marseille: Institut Historique de Provence, 1973).

——, *Richesse du passé marseillais. Le port mondial au XVIIIe siècle* (Marseille: Chambre de Commerce et d'Industrie de Marseille, 1979).

Castle, T., *Masquerade and Civilization: the Carnivalesque in Eighteenth-Century English Culture and Fiction* (Stanford, California: Stanford University Press, 1986).

Cecere, G., 'L' "Oriente d' Europa": un' idea in movimento (sec. XVIII). Un contributo cartografico', *Cromohs*, 8 (2003): 1–25, in Atti del seminario internazionale: *Immagini d'Italia e d'Europa nella letteratura e nella documentazione di viaggio nel XVIII e nel XIX secolo* (edited online: http://www.cromohs.unifi.it/8_2003/cecere.html).

Cerutti, S., 'Estrategias de grupo y estrategias de oficio: el gremio de sastres de Turin a finales del s. XVIII y principios del XVIII', in López, V. and Nieto, J.A. (eds), *El trabajo en la encrucijada. Artesanos urbanos en la Europa de la Edad Moderna* (Madrid: Historia Social, 1996), pp. 70–112.

Chacón Jiménez, F. and Hernández Franco J. (eds), *Poder, Familia y consanguinidad en la España del Antiguo Régimen* (Barcelona: Anthropos Editorial del Hombre, 1992).

Chamberlayne, John, *The Natural History of Coffee, Chocolate, Thee, 1682. The Making of the Modern World* (London: Printed for Christopher Wilkinson, 1682 – Gale, Cengage L, UC Berkeley Library, 2008), pp. 17–19.

Chapman, S.D. and Chassagne, S., *European Textile Printers in the Eighteenth-Century. A Study of Peel and Oberkampf* (London: Heinemann Educational Books, 1981).

Chartier, R., *Cultural History: Between Practices and Representations* (Cambridge: Polity Press in association with Blackwell, 1988).

——, *Culture écrite et société: l'ordre des livres, XIVe–XVIIIe siècle* (Paris: Albin Michel, 1996).

Chaudhuri, K.N., *The Trading World of Asia and the English East India Company 1660–1760* (Cambridge: Cambridge University Press, 1978).

Cheung, H. and Mui, L., *Shops & Shopkeeping in Eighteenth-Century England* (London: Routledge, 1989).

Christol, C., *L'industrie chapelière dans le haut vallée de l'Aude aux XIXe et XXe siècles* (Toulouse: Mémoire de maîtrise réalisé sous la direction de Rémy Pech, Université de Toulouse II-Le Mirail, 1995).

Clarence-Smith, W.G., *Cocoa and Chocolate, 1765–1914* (London: Routledge, 2000).

——, 'The Spread of Coffee Cultivation in Asia, from the Seventeenth to the Early Nineteenth-Century', in Tuchscherer, M. (ed.), *Le commerce du café avant l'ère des plantations colonials* (Cairo: Institut français d'archéologie orientale, 2001), pp. 371–84.

——, 'The Global Consumption of Hot Beverages, c. 1500 to c. 1900', in Nützenadel, A. and Trentmann, F. (eds), *Food and Globalization. Consumption,*

Markets and Politics in the Modern World (London: Cultures of Consumption Series, 2008), pp. 37–55.

Clark, G. and Vand Der Weerf, 'Work in Progress? The Industrious Revolution', *Journal of Economic History*, 58, no. 3 (1998), 830–43.

Clark, H.C., 'Commerce, the Virtues and the Public Sphere in the Early Seventeenth-century France', *French Historical Studies*, vol. 21, no. 3 (Summer, 1998), pp. 415–40.

Clavero, B., *Mayorazgo: propiedad feudal en Castilla, 1369–1836* (Madrid: Siglo XXI, 1974).

Clunas, C., *Pictures and Visuality in Early Modern China* (Princeton: Princeton University Press, 1997).

——, 'Modernity Global and Local: Consumption and the Rise of the West', *The American Historical Review*, vol. 104, no. 5. (December, 1999), pp. 1503.

Coe, S.D. and Coe, M.D., *The True History of Chocolate* (London: Thames and Hudson Ltd, 1996).

Corneo, G. and Jeanne, O., 'Conformism, Snobbism, and Conspicuous Consumption', *Journal of Public Economics*, 66 (1997), pp. 55–71.

——, 'Segmented Communication and Fashionable Behaviour', *Journal of Economic Behaviour and Organization*, 39 (1999), pp. 371–85.

Crépon, M., *Paysages en mouvement, transports et perception de l'espace (XVIIIᵉ-XIXᵉ)* (Paris: Gallimard, 2005).

Crespo Solana, A., *América desde otra frontera. La Guayana holandesa (Surinam): 1680–1795* (Madrid: Consejo Superior de Investigaciones Científicas, 2006).

Cruz, J., 'Propiedad urbana y sociedad en Madrid, 1749–1774', in *Revista de Historia Económica*, no. 2 (1990), pp. 239–69.

——, 'Elites, Merchants, and Consumption in Madrid at the End of the Old Regime', in Schuurman, A.J. and Walsh, L.S. (eds), *Material Culture: Consumption, Life-Style, Standard of Living, 1500–1900* (Milan: Eleventh International Economic History Congress, September, 1994), pp. 137–56.

——, *Gentleman, Bourgeois and Revolutionaries. Political Change and Cultural Persistence among the Spanish Dominant Groups, 1750–1850* (New York: Cambridge University Press, 1996).

——, 'La construcción de una nueva identidad liberal en el Madrid del siglo XIX: el papel de la cultura material en el hogar', *Revista de Historia Económica* (2003), pp. 181–206.

Cuenca Esteban, J.J., 'Comparative Patterns of Colonial Trade: Britain and its Rivals', in Prados de la Escosura, L. (ed.), *Exceptionalism and Industrialization: Britain and its European Rivals, 1688–1815* (Cambridge: Cambridge University Press, 2004), pp. 35–66.

Dale, S.F., *Indian Merchants and Eurasian Trade, 1600–1750* (Cambridge: Cambridge University Press, 1994), pp. 46–55.

Dalhgren, B., *La grana cochinilla* (México: UNAM, 1990).

Davidoff, L. and Hall, C., *Family Fortunes: Men and Women of the English Middle Class 1780–1850* (London: Hutchinson, 1987).

Dávila Corona, R.M., Duran y Pujol, M. and García Fernández, M., *Diccionario histórico de telas y tejidos. Castellano-Catalán* (Valladolid: Junta de Castilla y León, Consejería de Cultura y Turismo, 2004).

Davis, R., *Aleppo and Devonshire Square. English Traders in the Levant in the Eighteenth Century* (London: Macmillan, 1967).

De Alzate y Ramírez, J.A., *Memoria sobre la naturaleza, cultivo y beneficio de la grana* (Mexico: Archivo General de la Nación, 2001).

De Grazia, 'Changing Consumption Regimes', in De Grazia, V. and Furlough, E. (eds), *The Sex of Things. Gender Consumption in Historical Perspective* (Berkeley: University of California Press, 1996), pp. 12–24.

——, 'Introduction', in De Grazia, V. and Furlough, E. (eds), *The Sex of Things. Gender Consumption in Historical Perspective* (Berkeley: University of California Press, 1996), pp. 1–10.

De Isla, J.F., *Historia del famoso predicador Fray Gerundio de Campazas, alias Zotes* (Madrid: Gredos editorial, 1992).

De Long, J.B. and Shleifer, A., 'Princes and Merchants: European City Growth before the Industrial Revolution', *Journal of Law and Economics*, vol. 36, no. 2 (October, 1993), pp. 671–702.

De Roy, L., *L'emprunt linguistique* (Paris: Édition les Belles-Lettres, 1956).

De Vos, P., 'Natural History and the Pursuit of Empire in Eighteenth-Century Spain', *Eighteenth-century Studies*, vol. 40, no. 2 (Winter, 2007), pp. 209–39.

De Vries, J., *The Dutch Rural Economy in the Golden Age, 1500–1700* (New Haven: Yale University Press, 1974).

——, 'The Decline and Rise of the Dutch Economy, 1675–1750', in Saxonhouse A.G. and Wridley, G. (eds), *Technique, Spirit and Form in the Making of Modern Economic: Essays in Honour of William N. Parker* (Greenwich: JAI Press, 1984), pp. 149–89.

——, 'Between the Purchasing Power and the World of Goods: Understanding the Household Economy in the Early Modern Europe', in Brewer, J. and Porter, R. (eds), *Consumption and the World of Goods* (London; New York: Routledge, 1993), pp. 107–8.

——, 'The Industrial Revolution and the Industrious Revolution', *The Journal of Economic History*, vol. 54, no. 2 (June, 1994), pp. 249–70.

——, 'Luxury and Calvinism/Luxury and Capitalism: Supply and Demand for Luxury Goods in the Seventeenth-century Dutch Republic', *The Journal of the Walters Art Gallery*, vol. 57, Place and Culture in Northern Art (1999), pp. 73–85.

——, 'Connecting Europe and Asia: A Quantitative Analysis of Cape-Route Trade, 1497–1795', in Flynn, D.O., Giraldez, A. and Von Glanhn, R. (eds), *Global Connections and Monetary History, 1470–1800*, 2003 (London: Ashgate, 2003), pp. 35–106.

——, 'Luxury in the Dutch Golden Age in Theory and Practice', in Berg, M. and Eger, E. (eds), *Luxury in the Eighteenth Century. Debates, Desires and Delectable Goods* (New York: Palgrave Macmillan, 2003), pp. 41–56.

——, *The Industrious Revolution. Consumer Behavior and the Household Economy, 1650 to the Present* (Cambridge: Cambridge University Press, 2008).

De Vries, J. and Van der Woude, Ad., *The First Modern Economy: Success, Failure, and Perseverance of the Dutch Economy, 1500–1815* (Cambridge: Cambridge University Press, 1997).

Deaton, A., 'Demand Analysis', in Griliches, Z. and Intriligator, M. (eds), *Handbook of Econometrics* (Amsterdam: North Holland, 1994).

Deaton, A. and Muellbauer, J., *Economics and Consumer Behaviour* (New York: Cambridge University Press, 1980).

Delgado Ribas, J.M., 'El algodón engaña: algunas reflexiones en torno a la demanda americana en el desarrollo de la indianería catalana', *Manuscrits: Revista d'Història Moderna*, no. 11 (1993), pp. 61–84.

Delille, G., *Le maire et le prieur: pouvoir central et pouvoir local en Méditerranée occidentale, XVe–XVIIIe Siècle* (Rome: Ecole française de Rome; Paris: Editions de l'Ecole des Hautes Études en Sciences Sociales, 2003).

Delumeau, J., *Le péché et la peur* (Paris: ed. Fayard, 1983).

Demerson, P., *María Francisca de Sales Portocarrero, Condesa de Montijo. Una figura de la Ilustración* (Madrid: Editora Nacional, 1975).

Doria, P.M., *Lettere e ragionamenti* (Naples: Biblioteca Regia Monacensis, 1741).

Duplessis, R.S., *Transitions to Capitalism in Early Modern Europe* (Cambridge: Cambridge University Press, 1997).

——, 'Cottons Consumption in the Seventeenth and Eighteenth-century North Atlantic', in Riello, G. and Parthasarathi, P. (eds), *The Spinning World. A Global History of Cotton Textiles, 1200–1850* (London: Oxford University Press, 2008), pp. 227–46.

Dusenberry, J.S., *Income, Saving and the Theory of Consumer Behaviour* (Cambridge, MA: Harvard University Press, 1949).

Egnal, M., *New World Economies: The Growth of the Thirteenth Colonies and Early Canada* (New York: Oxford University Press, 1998).

Epstein, S.R., *Freedom and Growth: The Rise of States and Markets in Europe, 1300–1750* (London: Routledge, 2000).

Escobedo Romero, R., 'El contrabando transpirenaico y el monopolio de tabacos español durante el s. XVIII', in Minovez, J.M. and Poujade, P. (eds), *Circulation des marchandises et réseaux commerciaux dans les Pyrénées (XIII–XIX siècles)* (Toulouse: CNRS-Université de Toulouse Le Mirail, 2005), pp. 119–32.

Eymard-Beamelle, M.J., 'Les tissus de soie ouvrée à Marseille (XVIIe–XVIIIe s.)', in *Marseille sur les routes de la soie*, Actes de la table ronde organisée par la Chambre de Commerce et d'Industrie Marseille-Provence et l'Université de Provence (Marseille: Chambre de Commerce et d'Industrie Marseille-Provence, 2001), pp. 1–46.

Fairchilds, C., 'The Production and Marketing of Populuxe Goods in Eighteenth-century Paris', in Brewer, J. and Porter, R. (eds), *Consumption and the World of Goods* (London and New York: Routledge, 1993), pp. 228–48.

Faroqhi, S., 'Ottoman Cotton Textiles. The Story of a Success that did not Last, 1500–1800', in Riello, G. and Parthasarathi, P. (eds), *The Spinning World. A Global History of Cotton Textiles, 1200–1850* (London: Oxford University Press, 2008), pp. 89–103.

Fenández de Pinedo, Fernández, E. and Bilbao, L.M., 'Exportación de lanas, trashumancia y ocupación del espacio en Castilla durante los siglos XVI, XVII y XVIII', in García Martín, P. and Sánchez Benito, J.M. (eds), *Contribución a la historia de la trashumancia en España* (Madrid: Ministerio de Agricultura, Pesca y Alimentación, 1996), pp. 343–62.

Fernández Pérez, P. and Sola-Corbacho, J.C., 'Regional Identity, Family, and Trade in Cadiz and Mexico City in the Eighteenth-Century', *Journal of Early Modern History* 8: 3–4 (2004): 358–85.

Ferrier, R.W., 'The Armenians and the East India Company in Persia in the Seventeenth and Early Eighteenth Centuries', *The Economic History Review*, 2nd series, vol. XXVI, no. 1 (1973), pp. 38–62.

——, 'An English View of Persian Trade in 1618', *Journal of the Economic and Social History of the Orient*, vol. XIX, part. II (1976), pp. 182–214.

Figueroa, M.F., 'La 'expedición' de la naturaleza americana: sobre unos gustos metropolitanos y algunas recolecciones coloniales', *Anuario de Historia de América Latina*, 45 (2008), pp. 297–324.

Fine, B. and Leopold, E., 'Consumerism and the Industrial Revolution', *Social History*, no. 15 (1990), pp. 151–79.

Fisher, J., 'The Imperial Response to "Free trade": Spanish Imports from Spanish America, 1778–1796', *Journal of Latin America Studies*, vol. 17, no. 1 (May, 1985), pp. 35–78.

Floor, W., 'Economy and Society: Fibres, Fabrics, Factories', in Bier, C. (ed.), *Woven from the Soul, Spun from the Heart: Textile Arts of Safavit and Qajar Iran 16th–17th centuries* (Washington DC: Textile Museum, 1987), pp. 20–32.

Floyd, S.T., 'The Indigo Merchants: Promoter of Central American Economic Development, 1750–1808', *Business Historic Review*, vol. XXXIX, 11 (1965), pp. 466–88.

Fontana, J., *El comercio exterior de Barcelona en la 2ª mitad del siglo XVII, (1664–1699) a través de las importaciones y exportaciones registradas en su puerto* (Barcelona: Universitat de Barcelona. Facultat de Filosofia i Lletres, 1956).

——, 'La Desamortización de Mendizábal y sus antecedentes', in García Sanz, A. and Garrabou, R. (eds), *Historia agraria de la España Contemporánea*, vol. 1: *Cambio social y nuevas formas de propiedad (1800–1850)* (Barcelona: Crítica, 1985), pp. 219–244.

——, 'Nivel de vida, calidad de vida: un intento de estado de la cuestión y algunas reflexiones', in *Actas del XV Simposi d'Analisi Econòmica. Nivells de vida a*

Espanya, ss. XIX i XX (Barcelona: Universitat Autònoma de Barcelona, 1990), pp. 1–12.

Franch Benavent, R., *Crecimiento comercial y enriquecimiento burgués en la Valencia del siglo XVIII* (Valencia: Institut Alfons el Magnànim, 1986).

——, 'El papel de los extranjeros en las actividades artesanales y comerciales del Mediterráneo español durante la Edad Moderna', in Villar García and Pezzi Cristóbal, P. (eds), *Los extranjeros en la España Moderna* (Málaga: Junta de Andalucía, 2003), vol. 1, p. 39–72.

Friedman, M., *The Theory of the Consumption Function* (Princeton: Princeton University Press, 1957).

Friis, A., *Alderman Cockayne's Project and the Cloth trade* (London: Oxford University Press, 1927).

Fukusawa, K., *Toilerie et commerce du Levant d'Alep à Marseille* (Paris: CNRS, 1987).

Gabaccia, D.R., *Italy's Many Diasporas* (London: UCL Press, 2000).

Gabaccia, D.R., Iacovetta F. and Ottanelli F., 'Laboring across National Borders: Class, Gender, and Militancy in the Proletarian Mass Migrations', *International Labor and Working-class History*, no. 66, New Approaches to Global Labor History (Fall, 2004), pp. 57–77.

Gallego Abaroa, E., 'La educación de las mujeres en los discursos ilustrados', *Mediterráneo económico*, no. 9 (2006), pp. 83–94.

Galloway, P.R., 'A Reconstruction of the Population of North Italy from 1650 to 1881. Using Annual Inverse Projection with Comparisons to England, France, and Sweden', *European Journal of Population/Revue Européenne de Démographie*, vol. 10, no. 3 (September, 1994), pp. 223–74.

García Fernández, M., 'Los bienes dotales en la ciudad de Valladolid, 1700–1850. El ajuar doméstico y la evolución del consumo y la demanda', in Torras Elías, J. and Yun Casalilla, B., *Consumo, condiciones de vida y comercialización. Cataluña y Castilla, ss. XVII–XIX* (Valladolid: Junta de Castilla y León, 1999), pp. 133–58.

——, *Comunidad extranjera y puerto privilegiado: los británicos en Cádiz en el siglo XVIII* (Cádiz: Universidad de Cádiz, Servicio de Publicaciones, 2005).

——, 'Vestirse y vestir la casa. El consumo de productos textiles en Valladolid (1700–1860)', *Obradoiro de Historia Moderna*, no. 14, 2005, pp. 141–74.

García Fernández, M. and Yun Casalilla, B., 'Pautas de consumo, estilos de vida y cambio político en las ciudades castellanas a fines del Antiguo Régimen. Sobre algunas perspectivas del crecimiento económico desde la perspectiva de la demanda', in Fortea Pérez, J.I. (ed.), *Imágenes de la diversidad. El mundo urbano en la Corona de Castilla (ss. XVI–XVIII)* (Santander: Universidad de Cantabria, 1997), pp. 245–82.

García Fuentes, L., *El comercio español con América (1650–1700)* (Sevilla: Diputación Provincial de Sevilla, 1980).

García Mercadal, J., *Viajes de extranjeros por España y Portugal. In Siglo XVIII*, vol. III, (Madrid: ed. Aguilar, 1962), p. 563.

García Sanz, A., 'Estructuras agrarias y reformismo ilustrado en la España del siglo XVIII', in *Estructuras agrarias y reformismo ilustrado en la España del siglo XVIII* (Madrid: ed. Ministerio de Agricultura, Pesca y Alimentación, 1989), pp. 629–38.

Garnot, B., *Un déclin. Chartres au XVIIIe siècle* (Paris: Editions de L.T.H.S., 1991).

Gauci, P., *Emporium of the Worlds. The Merchants of London 1660–1800* (London: Hambledom Continuum, 2007).

Gellner, E., *Thought and Change* (London: Weidenfeld & Nicolson, 1972).

——, *Nations and Nationalism* (Ithaca, NY: Cornell University Press, 2008).

Giddens, A., *Modernity and self-identity* (Cambridge: Cambridge University Press, 1991)

Gilboy, E.W., *Wages in Eighteenth Century England* (Cambridge: Cambridge University Press, 1932).

Gladwell, M., *The Tipping Point: How Little Things Can Make a Big Difference* (Boston, MA: Little Brown, 2000).

Glamann, K., *Dutch-Asiatic Trade 1620–1740* (Copenhagen and LaHave: Nijhoff, 1958).

Gleason, Ph., 'Identifying Identity: A Semantic History', *Journal of American History*, 69/4 (1983), pp. 910–31.

Gonzalbo, P., *Familias novohispanas: siglos XVI al XIX* (Mexico, D.F.: Seminario de Historia de la Familia; Centro de Estudios Históricos, Colegio de México, 1991).

Greif, A., *Institutions and the Path to the Modern Economy: Lessons from Medieval Trade* (Cambridge and New York: Cambridge University Press, 2006).

Gruzinski, S., *La colonisation de l'imaginaire: sociétés indigènes et occidentalisation dans le Mexique espagnol, 16ᵉ–18ᵉ siècle* (Paris: Gallimard, 1988).

Gunder Frank, A., 'The Development of Underdevelopment', and 'Economic Dependence, Class Structure, and Underdevelopment Policy', in Cockroft, J.D., Gunder Frank, A. and Johnson, D.J. (eds), *Dependence and Underdevelopment* (New York: Doubleday, 1972), pp. 3–46.

Habermas, J., *The Structural Transformation of the Public Sphere. An Inquiry into a Category of Bourgeois Society* (Great Britain: Polity Press, 1989).

Haidt, R., 'Luxury, Consumption and Desire: Theorizing the *Petimetra*', *Arizona Journal of Hispanic Cultural Studies*, vol. 3 (1999), pp. 35–50.

Hamilton, E.J., *American Treasure and the Price Revolution in Spain, 1501–1650* (Cambridge: Harvard University Press, 1934).

——, 'The Role of Monopoly in the Overseas Expansion and Colonial Trade of Europe before 1800', *American Economic Review* (1948), 38 (2), pp. 33–53.

——, *War and Prices in Spain, 1651–1800* (Cambridge, MA: Harvard University Press, 1974).

Hancock, D., *Citizens of the World. London Merchants and the Integration of the British Atlantic Community, 1735–1785* (Cambridge: Cambridge University Press, 1995).

——, 'The Trouble with Networks: Managing the Scots' Early-Modern Madeira Trade', *Business History Review*, 79 (2005), pp. 467–91.

Haudrère, P., *La compagnie française des Indes au XVIIIe siècle (1719–1795)*, 4 vols (Paris: Librairie de l'Inde, 1989), vol. 1.

Hayek, F., *The Constitution of Liberty* (Chicago: University of Chicago Press, 1960).

Herr, R., *España y la revolución del siglo XVIII* (Madrid: ed. Aguilar, 1964).

Hesse, C., *The Other Enlightenment: How French Women Became Modern* (Princeton: Princeton University Press, 2001).

Hobsbawm, E., 'Introduction: Inventing Traditions', in Hobsbawm, E. and Ranger, T. (eds), *The Invention of Tradition* (Cambridge [Cambridgeshire] and New York: Cambridge University Press, 1983), pp. 1–14.

Hobsbawm, E. and Ranger, T. (eds), *The Invention of Tradition* (Cambridge [Cambridgeshire] and New York: Cambridge University Press, 1983).

Houghton, H., *La cochinilla. Memoria demostrativa de las causas que han producido la decadencia de este renglón de comercio en los últimos años. Publicada por la Sociedad Eonómica de Amigos del País de Gran Canaria* (Gran Canaria: Imprenta de la Verdad, 1887).

Hudson, P., 'The Limits of Wool and the Potential Cotton in the Eighteenth and Early Nineteenth Centuries', in Riello, G. and Parthasarathi, P. (eds), *The Spinning World. A Global History of Cotton Textiles, 1200–1850* (London: Oxford University Press, 2008), pp. 327–50.

Israel, J.I., *The Dutch Republic: its Rise, Greatness and Fall 1477–1806. Volume I: The Oxford History of Early Modern Europe* (New York: Oxford University Press, 1995).

——, *Radical Enlightenment. Philosophy and the Making of Modernity 1650–1750* (Oxford: Oxford University Press, 2001).

Janos, A.C., 'The Politics of Backwardness in Continental Europe, 1780–1945', *World Politics*, vol. 41, no. 3 (April, 1989), pp. 325–58.

Jones, A., *Wealth of Nation to Be* (New York: Columbia University Press, 1980).

Jones, J., '*Coquettes* and *Grisettes*. Women Buying and Selling in Ancien Regime Paris', in De Grazia, V. and Furlough, E. (eds), *The Sex of Things. Gender Consumption in Historical Perspective* (Berkeley: University of California Press, 1996), pp. 25–53.

Kamen, H., *The War of Succession in Spain, 1700–15* (Bloomington: Indiana University Press, 1969).

——, 'Nudité et Contre-réforme', in Redondo, A. (ed.), *Le corps dans la société espagnole des XVIe et XVIIe siècles* (Paris: ed. Publications de la Sorbonne, 1990), pp. 297–307.

Kaplan, M.A. (ed.), *The Marriage Bargain: Women and Dowries in European History* (New York: Harrington Park Press, 1985).

Kaplan, S.L., *Provisioning Paris: Merchants and Millers in the Grain and Flour Trade during the Eighteenth Century* (Ithaca: Cornell University Press, 1984).

Keirn, T., 'Parliament, Legislation and the Regulation of English Textile Industries, 1689–1714', in Davison, L., Hitchcock, T. and Shoemakers, R.D. (eds), *Stilling the Grumbling Hive: the Response to Social and Economic Problems in England, 1689–1750* (Stroud: Allen Sutton Press, 1992), pp. 1–24.

Keynes, J.M., *The General Theory of Employment, Interest and Money* (London: Macmillan, 1936).

Krauss, W., *Aufklärung III. Deutschland und Spanien* (Berlin: ed. Gruyter, 1996).

Kriedte, P., Medick, H. and Schlumbohm, J., 'Proto-industrialization: bilan et perspectives. Démographie, structure sociale et industrie à domicile modern', in Leboutte, R. (ed.), *Proto-industrialization. Recherches récentes et nouvelles perspectives* (Gèneve: Librairie Droz S.A., 1996), pp. 29–71.

Langle de Paz, T., 'Beyond the Canon: New Documents on the Feminist Debate in Early Modern Spain', *Hispanic Review*, vol. 70, no. 3 (Summer, 2002), pp. 393–420.

Larrére, C., *L' invention de la economie au XVIIIe siècle du droit natural á la physiocratie* (Paris: Prosses Universitaires de France, 1992), pp. 95–140.

Laslett, P. and Wall, R. (eds), *Household and Family in Past Time* (Cambridge: Cambridge University Press, 1972).

Le café en Méditerranée. Histoire, anthropologie, économie XVIIIe–XXe siècle. Actes de la Table ronde de l'Institut de Recherches Méditerranéennes et de la Chambre de Commerce et d'Industrie de Marseille (Marseille: Institut de Recherches Méditerranéennes, Université de Provence, 1980).

Le Roy Ladurie, E., 'L' histoire immobile', *Annales. Economies, Sociétés, Civilizations*, 29 (1974): 673–92.

Lee, R.L., 'Cochineal Production and Trade in New Spain to 1600', *The Americas*, vol. 4, no. 4 (April, 1948), pp. 449–73.

Leira, A., *Vestido hecho a la inglesa*, Museo del Traje (Madrid: Museo del Traje, 2008).

Lemeunier, G. and Pérez Picazo, M.T., 'Comercio y comerciantes catalanes en la crisis del Antiguo Régimen murciano', *Primer Congrés d' Història Moderna de Catalunya* (vol. 1, Barcelona: Universidad de Barcelona, 1984), pp. 747–56.

——, 'Les français en Murcie sous l'Ancien Régime (v. 1700–v. 1850). Des migrations populaires au grand commerce', in *Les Français en Espagne a l'époque moderne (XVIe.–XVIIIe. Siècles)* (Paris: CNRS, 1990), pp. 111–39.

Lemire, B., 'Domesticating the Exotic: Floral Culture and the East India Calico Trade with England, c. 1600–1800', *Textile*, 1/1 (2003), pp. 65–85.

——, 'Revising the Historical Narrative: India Europe, and the Cotton Trade, c. 1300–1800', Riello, G. and Parthasarathi, P. (eds), *The Spinning World. A Global History of Cotton Textiles, 1200–1850* (London: Oxford University Press, 2008), pp. 205–26.

Lencina Pérez, X., 'Los inventarios post-mortem en el estudio de la cultura material y el consumo. Propuesta metodológica. Barcelona, siglo XVII', in

Torras Elías, J. and Yun Casalilla, B. (eds), *Consumo, condiciones de vida y comercialización. Cataluña y Castilla, ss. XVII–XIX* (Valladolid: Junta de Castilla y León, 1999), pp. 41–59.

Levi, G., 'Comportements, ressources, procès: avant la "révolution" de la consommation', in Revel, J. (ed.), *Jeux d'échelles. La micro-analyse à l'experience* (Paris: Hautes Études, Gallimard Le Seuil, 1996), pp. 187–207.

Levi Martin, J., 'The Myth of the Consumption-Oriented Economy and the Rise of the Desiring Subject', *Theory and Society*, 28 (1999), pp. 187–207.

Levine, D., 'Consumer Goods and Capitalist Modernization', *Journal of Interdisciplinary History*, 22 (1991), p. 67–77.

Llombart, V., *Campomanes, economista y político de Carlos III* (Madrid: Alianza Universidad Editorial, 1992).

López Cordón, M.V., 'Predicación e inducción política en el siglo XVIII: Fray Diego José de Cádiz', *Hispania*, no. 138 (1978), pp. 71–120.

——, 'Familia, sexo y género en la España Moderna', *Studia Histórica. Historia Moderna*, vol. 18 (1998), pp. 105–34.

Lupo, S., 'Inertie épistolaire et audace négociante au XVIIIᵉ siècle', *Rives Méditerranéennes*, 27 (2007), mis en ligne le 27 juin 2008, Consulté le 10 mars 2010. URL: http://rives.revues.org/2063.

Lynch, K.A., *Individuals, Families, and Communities in Western Europe* (Cambridge: Cambridge University Press, 1983).

McCabe, I.B., *The Sha's Silk for Europe Silver: The Eurasian Trade of the Julfan Armenians in Sfavid Iran and India (1530–1750)* (Atlanta: Scholars Press, 1999).

——, 'Global Trading Ambitions in Diaspora: The Armenians and their Eurasian Silk Trade, 1530–1750', in McCabe, I.B., Harlaftis, G. and Minoglou, I. (eds), *Diaspora Entrepreneurial Networks: Four Centuries of History* (Oxford: Berg, 2005), pp. 27–49.

McCants, A., 'Petty Debts and Family Networks. The Credit Markets of Widows and Wives in Eighteenth-Century Amsterdam', in Lemire, B., Pearson, R. and Campbell G. (eds), *Women and Credit. Researching the Past, Refiguring the Future* (Oxford: Berg Publishers, 2001), pp. 33–50.

——, 'Poor Consumers as Global Consumers: the Diffusion of Tea and Coffee Drinking in the Eighteenth-Century', *Economic History Review*, 61/S1 (2008), pp. 172–200.

McCusker, J.J. and Gravesteijn, C., *The Beginning of Commercial and Financial Journalism. The Commodity Price Currents, Exchange Rate Currents and Money Currents of Early Modern Europe* (Amsterdam: Neha, 1991).

McKendrick, N., 'The Consumer Revolution of Eighteenth-century England', in McKendrick, N., Brewer, J. and Plumb, J.H. (eds), *The Birth of a Consumer Society. The Commercialization of Eighteenth-century England* (London: Europe Publications, 1982), pp. 9–33.

Malamina, P., *Il lusso dei contadini. Consumi e industrie nella campagne toscane del Sei e Settecento* (Bolonia: Il Mulino, 1990).

Malamud Rikles, C., 'El comercio colonial del siglo XVIII visto como suma del comercio vía Andalucía y del comercio directo europeo', *Journal of Iberian and Latin American Economic History*, año no. 1, no. 2 (1983), pp. 307–22.

Mandeville, B., *The Fable of the Bees, or Private Vices, Public Benefits, 1723*, Douglas Garmen, ed. (London: Wishart and Company, 1934).

Martín Corrales, E., 'Comerciantes malteses e importaciones catalanas de algodón (1728–1804)', in *Actas del I coloquio internacional hispano-maltés de Historia* (Madrid: Ministerio de Asuntos Exteriores, 1991), pp. 119–62.

——, 'La importación de telas de algodón levantino y los inicios del estampado en Cataluña', *Revista de Historia Industrial*, 6 (1994), pp. 47–74.

——, *Comercio de Cataluña con el Mediterráneo musulmán: el comercio con los 'enemigos de la fe'* (Barcelona: Bellaterra, 2001).

——, 'Marseille, Échelle des Toiles Levantines pour l'Espagne, XVIIᵉ et XVIIIᵉ siècles', *Rives méditerranéennes*, 29 (2008), pp. 61–78.

Martin Gaite, C., *Los usos amorosos del dieciocho en España* (Madrid: Siglo XXI, 1972).

Martín Rodríguez, M., 'Andalucía: Luces y sombras de una industrialización interrumpida', in Nadal Oller, J. and Carreras, A. (eds), *Pautas regionales de la industrialización española (siglos XIX Y XX)* (Barcelona: Ariel, 1990), pp. 349–51.

Martínez Shaw, C., 'Los orígenes de la industria algodonera catalana y el comercio colonial', in Tortella Casares, G. and Nadal J. (eds), *Agricultura, comercio colonial y crecimiento económico en la España contemporánea: actas del Primer Coloquio de Historia Económica de España* (Barcelona: Ariel, 1974), pp. 243–67.

——, 'La Cataluña del siglo XVIII bajo el signo de la expansión', in Fernández Díaz, R. (ed.), *España en el siglo XVIII: homenaje a Pierre Vilar* (Barcelona: Crítica, 1985), pp. 55–131.

Maruri Villanueva, R., *La burguesía mercantil santanderina, 1700–1850* (Santander: Asamblea Regional de Camtabria, D.L., 1990).

——, 'Vestir el cuerpo, vestir la casa. El consumo de textiles en la burguesía mercantil de Santander, 1750–1850', in Torras Elías, J. and Yun Casalilla, B. (eds), *Consumo, condiciones de vida y comercialización. Cataluña y Castilla, ss. XVII–XIX* (Valladolid: Junta de Castilla y León, 1999), pp. 159–82.

Maruri Villanueva, R. and Hoyo Aparicio, A., 'Pautas de consumo textil en una sociedad rural: Liébana (Cantabria), 1760–1860', *Revista de Historia Económica*, Año XXI (2003), no. extraordinario, pp. 107–39.

Masson, P., *Histoire du commerce français dans le Levant au XVIIᵉ siècle* (Paris: Hachette, 1986).

Matthee, R., *The Politics of Trade Safavd Iran: Silk for Silver, 1600–1730* (Cambridge: Cambridge University Press, 1999).

Mauro, F., *Histoire du café* (Paris: Editions Desjonquères, 1991).

Mazzaoui, M.F., 'The First European Cotton Industry. Italy and Germany, 1100–1800', in Riello, G. and Parthasarathi, P. (eds), *The Spinning World. A Global History of Cotton Textiles, 1200–1850* (London: Oxford University Press, 2008), pp. 63–88.

Melón Jiménez, M.A., 'Algunas consideraciones en torno a la crisis de la transhumancia en Castilla', *Studia Historica. Historia Moderna*, n. 8 (1990), pp. 61–89.

Miller, L.E., 'Paris-Lyon-Paris: Dialogue in the Design and Distribution of Patterned Silks in the Eighteenth-Century', in Fox, R. and Turner, A.J. (eds), *Luxury Trades and Consumerism in Ancien Régime Paris: Studies in the History of the Skilled Workforce* (Farnham: Ashgate, 1998), pp. 139–68.

Modigliani, F., *The Collected Papers of Franco Modigliani*, (eds) A. Abel and S. Johnson (Cambridge, MA: MIT Press, 1980–89).

Modigliani, F. and Brumberg, R., 'Utility Analysis and the Consumption Function: an Interpretation of Cross-Section Data', in Kurihara, K., *Post-Keynesian Economics* (New Brunswick: Rutgers University Press, 1954).

Mokyr, J., 'Demand vs. Supply in the Industrial Revolution', *Journal of Economic History*, 37 (1977), pp. 981–1008.

——, 'Is There Still Life in the Pessimist Case? Consumption during the Industrial Revolution, 1790–1850', *Journal of Economic History*, XLVIII (1998), pp. 69–92.

Montesquieu, Charles de Secondat, baron de, *Persian Letters*, 1721 (translated by Mr. Orzell, [Dublin]: London printed, and Dublin re-printed by S. Powell, for P. Crampton, 1731, third edition).

Montgomery, M., *Printed Textiles: English and American Cottons and Linens, 1700–1850* (New York: Viking Press, 1970).

Montojo y Montojo, V. and Maestre de San Juan Pelegrin, F., 'Los comerciantes de Cartagena y su actividad comercial en Huéscar en la segunda mitad del s, XVII', in Díaz López, J.P (ed.), *Campesinos, nobles y mercaderes. Huéscar y el Reino de Granada en los ss. XVI y XVII* (Granada: Ayuntamiento de Huéscar, 2005), pp. 93–109.

——, 'El Comercio Cartagenero en el Siglo XVIII', en Rubio Paredes, J.Mª (ed.), *Cartagena Puerto de Mar en el Mediterráneo* (Cartagena: Autoridad Portuaria, 2007).

Morant, I., *Discursos de la vida buena. Matrimonio, mujer y sexualidad en la literatura humanista* (Madrid: Catedra, 2002).

Moreno Claverías, B., 'La burguesía local de las letras y los negocios a través de los inventarios post-mortem. El Penedés del siglo XVIII', in Torras Elías, J. and Yun Casalilla, B. (eds), *Consumo, condiciones de vida y comercialización. Cataluña y Castilla, ss. XVII–XIX* (Valladolid: Junta de Castilla y León, 1999), pp. 71–88.

Morineau, M., 'Flottes de commerce et trafics français en Méditerranée au XVIIe siècle', *XVIIe Siècle*, 86–7 (1970), pp. 135–71.

Morley, D. 'Cultural Transformations: The Politics of Resistence', in Harris, R. and Thornham, M. (eds), *Media Studies. A Reader* (New York: New York University Press, 2000), pp. 471–81.

Murcott, A., Mennell, S. and van Otterloo, A.H. *The Sociology of Food* (Aldershot: Sage Publications, 1992).

Muset i Pons, A., *Catalunya i el mercat español al segle XVIII: Els traginers i els negociants de Calaf i Copons* (Barcelona: ed. Abadía de Montserrat, 1997).

Nadal i Farregas, J., *Comercio exterior y subdesarrollo. La política comercial y sus repercusiones en las relaciones hispano-británicas de 1772 a 1914* (Madrid: Instituto de Estudios Fiscales, 1978).

Nahoum-Grappe, V., 'La estética: ¿máscara táctica, estrategia o identidad petrificada?', in Duby, G. and Perrot, M. (eds), *Historia de las Mujeres en el Occidente. Los grandes cambios del siglo y la nueva mujer* (Madrid: ed. Taurus, 2006), pp. 122–41.

Nenadic, S., 'Middle-Rank Consumers and Domestic Culture in Edinburgh and Glasgow 1720–1840', *Past and Present*, no. 145 (November 1994), pp. 122–56.

Norton, R., *Mother Clap's Molly House: The Gay Subculture in England, 1700–1830* (London: GMP, 1992).

——, 'The Macaroni Club: Homosexual Scandals in 1772', *Homosexuality in Eighteenth-Century England: A Sourcebook* (19 December 2004, updated 11 June 2005) <http://rictornorton.co.uk/eighteen/macaroni.htm>.

Noyes, D., 'La Maja Vestida. Dress as resistance to Enlightenment in Late-18th-Century Madrid', *Journal of American Folklore*, 111 (440) (Spring, 1998), pp. 197–217.

O'Brien, P., 'Mercantilism and Imperialism in the Rise and Decline of the Dutch and British Empire, 1688–1815', *De Economist*, 148 (2000), pp. 469–501.

——, 'Historiographical Traditions and Modern Imperatives for the Restoration of Global History', *Journal of Global History* (2006), 1, pp. 3–39.

——, 'The Geopolitics of a Global Industry: Eurasian Divergence and the Mechanization of Cotton Textile Production in England', in Riello, G. and Parthasarathi, P. (eds), *The Spinning World. A Global History of Cotton Textiles, 1200–1850* (London: Oxford University Press, 2008), pp. 351–65.

O'Brien, P.K., Griffith, T. and Hunt, Ph., 'Political Components of the Industrial Revolution: English Cotton Textile Industry, 1660–1774', *Economic History Review*, 46/3 (1991), pp. 395–423.

Oliva Melgar, J.M., *Cataluña y el comercio privilegiado con América en el siglo XVIII: la Real Compañía de Comercio de Barcelona a Indias* (Barcelona: Universidad de Barcelona, 1987).

Oliva Melgar, J.M. and Martínez Shaw, C., 'El sistema atlántico español (siglos XVII–XIX): presentación', in Martínez Shaw C. and Oliva Melgar J.M. (eds), *El sistema atlántico español (siglos XVII–XIX)* (Madrid: ed. Marcial Pons, 2005), pp. 11–18.

Olivier, J.M., 'Les exportations transpyrénéennes d'horlogerie franco-suisse et d'articles de Paris vers l'Espagne (XVIIIe–XIXe siècles)', in Minovez, J. and Poujade, P. (eds), *Circulation des marchandises et réseaux commerciaux dans les Pyrénées (XIII–XIX siècles)* (Toulouse: CNRS-Université de Toulouse Le Mirail, 2005), pp. 31–8.

Oriol Ronquillo, J., *Diccionario de materia mercantil, industrial y agrícola*, 4 vols, (Barcelona: Imprenta de D.A. Gaspar 1851–57).

Ormrod, D., *The Rise of Commercial Empires. England and the Netherlands in the Age of Mercantilism, 1650–1770* (Cambridge: Cambridge University Press, 2003).

Özmucur, S. and Pamuk, S., 'Did European Commodity Prices Converge during 1500–1800?', in Hatton, T.J., O'Rourke, K.H. and Taylor, A.M. (eds), *The New Comparative Economic History: Essays in Honor of Jeffrey G. Williamson* (Cambridge, MA: MIT Press, 2007), pp. 59–86.

Pagano De Divitiis, G., *Mercanti inglesi nell'Italia del seicento: navi, traffici, egemonie* (Venezia: Marsilio editori, 1990).

Panzac, D., *La caravane maritime. Marins européens et marchands ottomans en Méditerranée (1680–1830)* (Paris: CNRS, 2004).

Paris, R., *Histoire du commerce de Marseille de 1660 à 1789, vol. 5, Le Levant* (Paris: ed. Gaston Rambert, 1957).

Parker, G. and Kagan, R. (eds), *Spain, Europe, and the Atlantic World: Essays in Honour of John H. Elliott* (Cambridge [England] and New York, NY, USA: Cambridge University Press, 1995).

Parthasarathi, P., 'Cotton Textiles in the Indian Subcontinent, 1200–1800', in Riello, G. and Parthasarathi, P. (eds), *The Spinning World. A Global History of Cotton Textiles, 1200–1850* (London: Oxford University Press, 2008), pp. 17–41.

Passama, J., *La chapellerie toulosaine au XIXe siècle* (Mémoire de maîtrise réalisé sous la direction de Jean-Marc Olivier, Université de Toulouse 2-Le Mirail, 2002).

Pedro Rodríguez, Conde de Campomanes, *Apéndice a la educación popular de los artesanos y su fomento*, 5 vols (Madrid: Imprenta de D. Antonio de Sancha, 1775–77).

Pennell, S., 'Consumption and Consumerism in Early Modern England', *The Historical Journal*, vol. 42, no. 2 (June, 1999), pp. 549–64.

Perdices, L. and Reeder, J., *Biblioteca de los economistas españoles de los siglos XVI, XVII y XVIII de Manuel Colmeiro* (Madrid: Real Academia de Ciencias Morales y Políticas, 2005).

Pérez López, C., *Estadística Aplicada a través de Excel* (Madrid: Universidad Complutense, 2002).

Pérez Picazo, M.T., *El proceso de modernización de la región murciana (ss. XVI–XIX)* (Murcia: Editora Regional de Murcia, 1984).

——, 'Crecimiento agrícola y relaciones de mercado en la España del siglo XVIII', in *Estructuras agrarias y reformismo ilustrado en la España del s. XVIII* (Madrid: Ministerio de Agricultura, 1989), pp. 47–61.

Peristiany, J.G. (ed.), *Mediterranean Family Structures* (Cambridge [Eng.] and New York: Cambridge University Press, 1976).

——, *Dote y matrimonio en los países mediterráneos* (Madrid: Centro de Investigaciones Sociológicas, 1987).

Perkins, H., *The Origins of Modern English Society* (London: Routledge and Kegan Paul, 1968).

Peyrot, J., 'Marseille, porte d'entrée des soies aux XVIIe et XVIIIe siècles', in *Marseille sur les routes de la soie*, Actes de la table ronde organisée par la Chambre de Commerce et d'Industrie Marseille-Provence et l'Université de Provence (Marseille: Chambre de Commerce et d'Industrie Marseille-Provence, 2001), pp. 61–76.

Phillips, C.R., *The Treasure of the San José: Death at Sea in the War of the Spanish Succession* (Baltimore: The Johns Hopkins University Press, 2007).

Pijning, E., 'Passive Resistance: Portuguese Diplomacy of Contraband Trade during King John V's Reign (1705–1750)', *Arquipelago-Historia*, 2ª serie, II (1997), pp. 171–91.

Piqueras, J., *La agricultura valenciana de exportación y su formación histórica* (Madrid: Ministerio de Agricultura, 1985).

Pomeranz, K., *The Great Divergence: China, Europe and the Making of the Modern World Economy* (Princeton: Princeton University Press, 2000).

Pomeranz, K. and Topik, S., *The World that Trade Created: Society, Culture and the World Economy, 1400 to the Present* (New York: M.E. Sharpe: 1999).

Poni, C., 'Normas y pleitos: el gremio de zapateros de Bolonia en el s. XVIII', in López, V. and Nieto, J.A. (eds), *El trabajo en la encrucijada. Artesanos urbanos en la Europa de la Edad Moderna* (Madrid: Historia Social, 1996), pp. 153–78.

Portier, R., 'Goût', in Delon, M. (dir.), *Dictionnaire européen des Lumières* (Paris: P.U.F., 1997).

Prance, G. and Nesbitt, M. (eds), *The Cultural History of Plants* (New York: Routledge, 2005).

Price, J.M., *France and Chesapeake. A History of the French Tobacco Monopoly, 1674–1791*, 2 vols. (Ann Arbor: University of Michigan Press, 1973).

Radeff, A., *Du café dans le chaudron. Économie globale d'Ancien Régime. Suisse Occidentale, Franche-Comté et Savoie* (Lausanne: Société d'Histoire de la Suisse Romande, 'Mémoires et documents', 1996).

Rambert, G. (ed.), *Histoire du commerce de Marseille*, 8 vols (Paris: Plon, 1949–66), vol. 1.

Ramos Palencia, F., 'Una primera aproximación al consumo en el mundo rural castellano a través de los inventarios post-mortem: Palencia, 1750–1840', in Torras Elías, J. and Yun Casalilla, B. (eds), *Consumo, condiciones de vida y comercialización. Cataluña y Castilla, ss. XVII–XIX* (Valladolid: Junta de Castilla y León, 1999), pp. 107–32.

——, *Pautas de consumo familiar y mercado en la Castilla preindustrial. El consumo de bienes duraderos y semiduraderos en Palencia, 1750–1850* (Facultad de Ciencias Económicas y Empresariales, Departamento de Historia e Instituciones Económicas y Economía Aplicada, Universidad de Valladolid, unpublished PhD, 2001).

——, 'La demanda de textiles en las familias castellanas del Antiguo Régimen: ¿aumento del consumo sin revolución industrial?', *Revista de Historia Económica*, no. Extraordinario, Año XXI (2003), pp. 141–80.

Ramos Palencia, F. and Nicolini, E.A., 'A New Method for Estimating the Money Demand in Pre-Industrial Economies: Probate Inventories and Spain in the Eighteenth-Century', *European Review of Economic History*, 14 (2009), pp. 145–77.

Rauser, A., 'Hair, Authenticity, and the Self-Made Macaroni', *Eighteenth-Century Studies*, vol. 38, no. 1, Hair (Fall, 2004), pp. 101–17.

Raveux, O., 'Espaces et tecnologiques dans la France méridionale d'ancien régime: l'example de l'indiennage marseillais (1648–1793)', *Annales du Midi*, 116/246 (2004), pp. 155–70.

——, 'The Birth of a New European Industry. L' Indiennage in Seventeenth-century Marseilles', in Riello, G. and Parthasarathi, P. (eds), *The Spinning World. A Global History of Cotton Textiles, 1200–1850* (London: Oxford University Press, 2008), pp. 291–306.

——, 'Entre réseau communautaire international et intégration locale: la colonie marseillaise des marchands arméniens de la Nouvelle-Djoulfa (Ispahan), 1669–1695', *Revue d'histoire moderne et contemporaine*, no. 59–1 (Paris: Belin, 2012), pp. 83–102.

Reher, D.S., 'Family Ties in Western Europe: Persistent Contrasts', *Population and Development Review*, vol. 24, no. 2 (June, 1998), pp. 203–34.

Reher, D.S. and Ballesteros, S., 'Precios y salarios en Castilla la Nueva: la construcción de un índice de salarios reales', *Revista de Historia Económica* (XI) (1993), no. 1, pp. 101–51.

Riello, G., 'The Globalization of Cotton Textiles: India Cottons, Europe and the Atlantic World, 1600–1800', in Riello, G. and Parthasarathi, P. (eds), *The Spinning World. A Global History of Cotton Textiles, 1200–1850* (London: Oxford University Press, 2008), pp. 261–87.

Ringrose, D., 'European Economic Growth: Comments on the Noth-Thomas Theory', *The Economic History Review*, vol. 26, no. 2 (1973), pp. 285–92.

——, *Spain, Europe and the 'Spanish Miracle', 1700–1900* (Cambridge: Cambridge University Press, 1996), pp. 135–62.

Roche, D., *La culture des apparences. Une histoire du vêtement XVIIe–XVIIIe siècle* (Paris: Fayard, 1989).

——, *Humeurs vagabondes. De la circulation des hommes et de l'utilité des voyages* (Paris: Fayard, 2003).

——, 'Circolazione delle idée, mobilità dele persone: continuità e rotture', in Visceglia, M.A., *Le radici storiche dell'Europa. L'età moderna* (Roma: ed. Viella, 2007), pp. 127–40.

Romanelli, R., 'Donne e patrimonio', in Groppi, A. (ed.), *Storia delle donne in Italia. Il lavoro delle donne* (Bari: Editori Laterza, 1996), pp. 345–67.

Rosenthal, J.L., 'Credit Markets and Economic Change in Southeastern France 1630–1788', *Explorations in Economic History*, 30 (1993), pp. 129–57.

Rostow, W.W., *The Stages of Economic Growth: a Non-Communist Manifesto* (3rd edition, Cambridge: Cambridge University Press, 1990).

Rothstein, N., 'The Calico Campaign of 1719–1721', *East London Papers*, 7 (1964), pp. 3–21.

Rousseau, *Discours sur l'économie politique* (Geneve: Chez Emanuel du Villard, 1758).

Roux, F. Ch., *Les Echelles de Syrie et de Palestine au XVIIIe siècle* (Paris: Paul Geuthner, 1928).

Ruíz Gómez, F., *Fábricas textiles en la industrialización de Cantabria* (Santander: Universidad de Cantabria-Textil Santanderina, 1998).

Rule, J., *The Vital Century: England's Developing Economy, 1714–1815* (London; New York: Longman, 1992).

Sahlins, P., *Boundaries. The Making of France and Spain in the Pyrenées* (Berkeley: University of California Press, 1989).

Sala Valldaura, J.M., 'Gurruminos, petimetres, abates y currutacos en el teatro breve del siglo XVIII', *Revista de Literatura* (julio–diciembre, vol. LXXI), no. 142, pp. 429–60.

Salas Auséns, J.A., *En busca del dorado. Inmigración francesa en la España de la Edad Moderna* (Bilbao: Universidad del País Vasco, 2009).

Sánchez-Blanco Parody, F., *Europa y el pensamiento español del siglo XVIII* (Madrid: Alianza Universal Editorial, 1991).

Sánchez Silva, C. and Suárez Bosa, M., 'Evolución de la producción y el comercio mundial de la grana cochinilla, siglos XVI–XIX', *Revista de Indias* (2006), vol. LXVI, no. 237, pp. 473–90.

Sarrailh, J., *La España ilustrada de la segunda mitad del siglo XVIII* (Madrid: ed. F.C.E., 1957).

Sarti, R., *Europe at Home. Family and Material Culture, 1500–1800* (New Haven, CT: Yale University Press, 2002).

Schama, S., *The Embarrassment of Riches* (New York: Knopf, 1985).

Schuurman, A., 'Probate inventories: research issues, problems and results', in Van der Woude, A. and Schuurman, A. (eds), *Probate Inventories. A New Source for the Historical Study of Wealth, Material Culture and Agricultural Development* (Utrecht: Hes Publishers, 1980), pp. 19–31.

——, 'From Citizen to Consumer to Citizen-Consumer? The Development of the Welfare State and the Consumer Society', in Moerbeek, H., Niehof, A. and Ophem, J. van (eds), *Changing Families and their Lifestyles* (Wageningen: Wageningen Academic Publisher, Mansholt publication series 5, 2007).

Sempere y Guarinos, J., *Historia del lujo y las leyes suntuarias de España* (Madrid: Impr. Real, 1788).

Seton-Watson, H., *Nations and States: an Enquiry into the Origins of Nations and the Politics of Nationalism* (London: Methuen, 1977).

Shammas, C., 'The Eighteenth-Century English Diet and Economic Change', *Explorations in Economic History*, 21 (1982), pp. 254–69.

——, *The Pre-Industrial Consumer in England and America* (Oxford: Clarendon Press, 1990).

——, 'The Revolutionary Impact of European Demand for Tropical Goods', in Morgan, K. and McCusker, J.J. (eds), *The Early Modern Atlantic Economy* (Cambridge: Cambridge University Press, 2000), pp. 163–85.

Shephard, E.J. Jr, 'Movilidad social y geográfica del artesanado en el siglo XVIII: estudio de la admisión a los gremios de Dijon, 1700–90', in López, V. and Nieto, J.A. (eds), *El trabajo en la encrucijada. Artesanos urbanos en la Europa de la Edad Moderna* (Madrid: Historia Social, 1996), pp. 37–69.

Sicknger, R.L., 'Regulation or Ruination: Parliament's Consistent Pattern of Mercantilist Regulation of the English Textile Trade, 1660–1800', *Parliamentary History*, 19/2 (2000), pp. 211–32.

Siddle, D.J., 'Migration as a Strategy of Accumulation: Social and Economic Change in Eighteenth-century Savoy', *The Economic History Review*, New Series, vol. 50, no. 1 (February, 1997), pp. 1–20.

Simmel, G., 'Fashion', *International Quarterly*, 10 (1904), pp. 130–155.

Slicher van Bath, B.H., *The Agrarian History of Western Europe, 500–1850* (London: Edward Arnold, 1963).

Smart Martin, A., *Buying into the World of Goods: Early Consumers in Backcountry Virginia* (Baltimore: Johns Hopkins University Press, 2008).

Smith, R.S., 'Indigo Production and Trade in Colonial Guatemala', *HAHR*, vol. XXXIX, 2 (1959).

——, 'English Economic Thought in Spain, 1775–1848', *South Atlantic Quarterly*, vol. 67 (1968), pp. 306–37.

Steensgard, N., *The Asian Trade revolution of the Seventeenth-century. The East India Companies and the Decline of the Caravan Trade* (Chicago: University of Chicago Press, 1973).

Stein, S.J. and Stein B., *Apogee of Empire. Spain and New Spain in the Age of Charles III* (Baltimore and London: John Hopkins University Press, 2003).

Styles, J., 'Product Innovation in Early Modern London', *Past and Present*, 168 (2000), pp. 124–69.

——, *The Dress of People. Everyday Fashion in Eighteenth-Century England* (New Haven and London: Yale University Press, 2007).

——, 'What Were Cottons for in the Early Industrial Revolution', in Riello, G. and Parthasarathi, P. (eds), *The Spinning World. A Global History of Cotton Textiles, 1200–1850* (London: Oxford University Press, 2008), pp. 307–26.

Subirá, J., ''Petimetría' y 'Majismo' en la literatura', *Revista de Literatura* (October–December 1954): 267–85.

Svendsen, L., *Fashion. A Philosophy* (London: ed. Reaktion Books, 2006).

Tékénian, Ch. D., 'Marseille, la Provence et les arméniens', *Mémoire de l'Institut Historique de Provence* (1929), pp. 5–65.

Terreros y Pando, E., *Diccionario castellano, con las voces de las ciencias y artes y sus correspondientes en las tres lenguas, francesa, italiana y latina*, 4 vols (Madrid: Imprenta de la Viuda de Ibarra, Hijos y Compañia, 1786–93), vol. 1, artículo: 'Abanico'.

Thirsk, J., *Economic Policy and Projects. The Development of a Consumer Society in Early Modern England* (Oxford: Clarendon Press, 1978).

Thomas, H., *Beaumarchais en Sevilla* (Barcelona: ed. Planeta, 2008).

Thompson, J.K.J., *Clermont-de-Lodève 1633–1789. Fluctuations in the Prosperity of a Languedocian Cloth-Making Town* (Cambridge: Cambridge University Press, 1982).

——, *A Distinctive Industrialization. Cotton in Barcelona (1728–1832)* (Cambridge: Cambridge University Press, 1992).

Tomlinson, J.A., *Francisco Goya: The Tapestry Cartoons and Early Career at the Court of Madrid* (Cambridge: Cambridge University Press, 1989).

Toribio de Benavente (Montolinía), *Historia de los Indios de Nueva España* (Mexico: Salvador Chávez Hayhoe, 1941).

Torra Fernández, L., 'Pautas de consumo textil en la Cataluña del siglo XVIII. Una visión a partir de los inventarios post-mortem', in Torras Elías, J. and Yun Casalilla, B. (eds), *Consumo, condiciones de vida y comercialización. Cataluña y Castilla, ss. XVII–XIX* (Valladolid: Junta de Castilla y León, 1999), pp. 89–105.

Torras, J., Duran, M. and Torra, L., 'El ajuar de la novia. El consumo de tejidos en los contratos matrimoniales de una localidad catalana, 1600–1800', in Torras Elías, J. and Yun Casalilla, B. (eds), *Consumo, condiciones de vida y comercialización. Cataluña y Castilla, ss. XVII–XIX* (Valladolid: Junta de Castilla y León, 1999), pp. 61–70.

Torras Elías, J. and Yun Casalilla, B. (eds), *Consumo, condiciones de vida y comercialización. Cataluña y Castilla, ss. XVII–XIX* (Valladolid: Junta de Castilla y León, 1999).

Trevor-Roper, H., 'The Invention of Tradition: the Highland Tradition of Scotland', in Hobsbawm, E. and Ranger, T. (eds), *The Invention of Tradition* (Cambridge [Cambridgeshire] and New York: Cambridge University Press, 1983), pp. 15–42.

Trivellato, F., *Cross-Cultural Trade in the Early Modern Period* (New Haven: Yale University Press, 2009).

Tryantafyllidou-Baladié, Y., 'Le marché de la soie au Proche-Orient et son importance pour les industries françaises du XVIIe au XIXe siècle: le rôle du port de Marseille', in *Marseille sur les routes de la soie*, Actes de la table ronde organisée par la Chambre de Commerce et d'Industrie Marseille-Provence et l'Université de Provence (Marseille: Chambre de Commerce et d'Industrie Marseille-Provence, 2001), pp. 282–300.

Van der Woude, A. and Schuurman, A. (eds), *Probate Inventories. A New Source for the Historical Study of Wealth, Material Culture and Agricultural Development* (Utrecht: Hes Publishers, 1980).

Vasallo, C., *Corsairing to Commerce. Maltese Merchants in XVIII-Century Spain* (Valleta: Malta University Publishers, 1997).

Veblen, T., *The Theory of the Leisure Class. An Economic Study of the Institutions* (New York: The Modern Library, 1934), pp. 102–3.

Veinstein, G., 'Commercial Relations between India and the Ottoman Empire (Late Fifteenth to Late Eighteenth-Centuries): A Few Notes and Hypothesis', in Chaudhury, S. and Morineau, M. (eds), *Merchants, Companies and Trade: Europe and Asia in the Early Modern Era* (Cambridge: Cambridge University Press, 1999), pp. 95–115.

Vermaut, J., 'Structural Transformation in a Textile Centre: Bruges from Sixteenth to the Nineteenth-Century', in Van der Wee, H. (ed.), *The Rise and Decline of Urban Industries in Italy and the Low Countries (Late Middle Ages-Early Modern Times)* (Louvain: Louvain University Press, 1988), pp. 187–206.

Viazzo, P.P., 'What's so Special about the Mediterranean?', *Continuity and Change*, 18 (2003), pp. 111–37.

Vicente, M.V. *Clothing the Spanish Empire: Families and Calico Trade in the Early Modern Atlantic World* (New York: Palgrave Macmillan, 2006).

Vickery, A., 'Women and the World of Goods: a Lancashire Consumer and her Possessions, 1751–1781', in Brewer, J. and Porter, R., *Consumption and the World of Goods* (London and New York: Routledge, 1993), pp. 274–301.

Villard, M., 'Aspects des industries de la soie en Languedoc aux XVIIe et XVIII siècle', in *Marseille sur les routes de la soie*, Actes de la table ronde organisée par la Chambre de Commerce et d'Industrie Marseille-Provence et l'Université de Provence (Marseille: Chambre de Commerce et d'Industrie Marseille-Provence, 2001), pp. 177–93.

Visceglia, M.A., 'I consumi in Italia in età moderna', in Romano, R. (ed.), *Storia dell'economia italiana. Tomo II. L'età moderna: verso la crisi* (Turin: Einaudi editore, 1991), pp. 219–23.

Walker, G., *Política española y comercio colonial, 1700–1789* (Barcelona: Editorial Ariel, 1979).

Wallerstein, I., *Modern World System. 2: Mercantilism and the Consolidation of the European World-Economy, 1600–1750* (New York: Academic Press, 1980).

Wallerstein, I, Decdeli, H. and Kasaba, R., 'The Incorporation of the Ottoman Empire into the World-Economy', in Slamo Iu-nan, H. (ed.), *The Ottoman Empire and the World Economy* (Cambridge: Cambridge University Press, 1987), pp. 88–100.

Walton, W., 'Feminine Hospitality in the Bourgeois Home of Nineteenth-Century Paris', *Proceedings of the Western Society for French History*, 14 (1987), pp. 197–203.

Weatherill, L., *Consumer Behavior and Material Culture in Britain, 1660–1760* (London and New York: Routledge, 1988).

——, 'The Meaning of Consumer Behaviour in Late Seventeenth-and Early Eighteenth Century England', in Brewer, J. and Porter, R., *Consumption and the World of Goods* (London and New York: Routledge, 1993), pp. 206–27.

Withers, Ch. W.J., 'Geography, Natural History and the Eighteenth-Century Enlightenment: Putting the World in Place', *History Workshop Journal*, no. 39 (Spring, 1995), pp. 136–63.

Wolff, L., *Inventing Eastern Europe: The Map of Civilization on the Mind of the Enlightenment* (Stanford, California: Stanford University Press, 1994).

Wright, H.R.C., *Free Trade and Protection in the Netherlands, 1816–1830* (Cambridge: Cambridge University Press, 1955).

Yun Casalilla, B., 'Peasant Material Culture in Castile (1750–1900): Some Proposals', in Schuurman, A.J. and Walsh, L.S. (eds), *Material Culture: Consumption, Life-Style, Standard of Living, 1500–1900* (Milan: Eleventh International Economic History Congress, September, 1994), pp. 125–36.

——, 'Perspectivas para la investigación en historia económica y social de Palencia: Consumo y redes de comercialización', in Calleja González, M.V. (ed.), *Actas del III Congreso de Historia de Palencia* (Palencia: Diputación Provincial de Palencia, 1995), pp. 56–8.

——, 'La historia económica por el lado de la demanda y el consumo: unas reflexiones generales', in Torras Elías, J. and Yun Casalilla, B. (eds), *Consumo, condiciones de vida y comercialización. Cataluña y Castilla, ss. XVII–XIX* (Valladolid: Junta de Castilla y León, 1999), pp. 9–26.

——, 'Consumi, società e mercati: verso uno spazio economico europeo', in Visceglia, M.A., *Le radici storiche dell'Europa. L'età moderna* (Roma: ed. Viella, 2007, pp. 85–103.

Zarandieta Arenas, F., 'Riqueza y consumo en la Baja Extremadura en el s. XVII. Análisis a través de las cartas de dote', *Historia Agraria*, 21 (Agosto 2000), pp. 63–97.

Index

Modern Economic and Social History Series

General Editor
Derek H. Aldcroft, University Fellow, Department of Economic and
Social History, University of Leicester, UK

Derek H. Aldcroft
Studies in the Interwar European Economy
1 85928 360 8 (1997)

Michael J. Oliver
Whatever Happened to Monetarism?
Economic Policy Making and Social Learning in the United Kingdom
Since 1979
1 85928 433 7 (1997)

R. Guerriero Wilson
Disillusionment or New Opportunities?
The Changing Nature of Work in Offices,Glasgow 1880–1914
1 84014 276 6 (1998)

Roger Lloyd-Jones and M.J. Lewis with the assistance of M. Eason
Raleigh and the British Bicycle Industry
An Economic and Business History, 1870–1960
1 85928 457 4 (2000)

Barry Stapleton and James H. Thomas
Gales
A Study in Brewing, Business and Family History
0 7546 0146 3 (2000)

Derek H. Aldcroft and Michael J. Oliver
Trade Unions and the Economy: 1870–2000
1 85928 370 5 (2000)

Ted Wilson
Battles for the Standard
Bimetallism and the Spread of the Gold Standard in the Nineteenth Century
1 85928 436 1 (2000)

Patrick Duffy
The Skilled Compositor, 1850–1914
An Aristocrat Among Working Men
0 7546 0255 9 (2000)

Robert Conlon and John Perkins
Wheels and Deals
The Automotive Industry in Twentieth-Century Australia
0 7546 0405 5 (2001)

Sam Mustafa
Merchants and Migrations
Germans and Americans in Connection, 1776–1835
0 7546 0590 6 (2001)

Bernard Cronin
Technology, Industrial Conflict and the Development of Technical
Education in 19th-Century England
0 7546 0313 X (2001)

Andrew Popp
Business Structure, Business Culture and the Industrial District
The Potteries, c. 1850–1914
0 7546 0176 5 (2001)

Scott Kelly
The Myth of Mr Butskell
The Politics of British Economic Policy, 1950–55
0 7546 0604 X (2002)

Michael Ferguson
The Rise of Management Consulting in Britain
0 7546 0561 2 (2002)

Alan Fowler
Lancashire Cotton Operatives and Work, 1900–1950
A Social History of Lancashire Cotton Operatives in the Twentieth Century
0 7546 0116 1 (2003)

John F. Wilson and Andrew Popp (eds)
Industrial Clusters and Regional Business Networks in England, 1750–1970
0 7546 0761 5 (2003)

John Hassan
The Seaside, Health and the Environment in England and Wales since 1800
1 84014 265 0 (2003)

Marshall J. Bastable
Arms and the State
Sir William Armstrong and the Remaking of British Naval Power, 1854–1914
0 7546 3404 3 (2004)

Robin Pearson
Insuring the Industrial Revolution
Fire Insurance in Great Britain, 1700–1850
0 7546 3363 2 (2004)

Andrew Dawson
Lives of the Philadelphia Engineers
Capital, Class and Revolution, 1830–1890
0 7546 3396 9 (2004)

Lawrence Black and Hugh Pemberton (eds)
An Affluent Society?
Britain's Post-War 'Golden Age' Revisited
0 7546 3528 7 (2004)

Joseph Harrison and David Corkill
Spain
A Modern European Economy
0 7546 0145 5 (2004)

Ross E. Catterall and Derek H. Aldcroft (eds)
Exchange Rates and Economic Policy in the 20th Century
1 84014 264 2 (2004)

Armin Grünbacher
Reconstruction and Cold War in Germany
The Kreditanstalt für Wiederaufbau (1948–1961)
0 7546 3806 5 (2004)

Till Geiger
Britain and the Economic Problem of the Cold War
The Political Economy and the Economic Impact of the
British Defence Effort, 1945–1955
0 7546 0287 7 (2004)

Anne Clendinning
Demons of Domesticity
Women and the English Gas Industry, 1889–1939
0 7546 0692 9 (2004)

Timothy Cuff
The Hidden Cost of Economic Development
The Biological Standard of Living in Antebellum Pennsylvania
0 7546 4119 8 (2005)

Julian Greaves
Industrial Reorganization and Government Policy in Interwar Britain
0 7546 0355 5 (2005)

Derek H. Aldcroft
Europe's Third World
The European Periphery in the Interwar Years
0 7546 0599 X (2006)

James P. Huzel
The Popularization of Malthus in Early Nineteenth-Century England
Martineau, Cobbett and the Pauper Press
0 7546 5427 3 (2006)

Richard Perren
Taste, Trade and Technology
The Development of the International Meat Industry since 1840
978 0 7546 3648 9 (2006)

Roger Lloyd-Jones and M.J. Lewis
Alfred Herbert Ltd and the British Machine Tool Industry,
1887–1983
978 0 7546 0523 2 (2006)

Anthony Howe and Simon Morgan (eds)
Rethinking Nineteenth-Century Liberalism
Richard Cobden Bicentenary Essays
978 0 7546 5572 5 (2006)

Espen Moe
Governance, Growth and Global Leadership
The Role of the State in Technological Progress, 1750–2000
978 0 7546 5743 9 (2007)

Peter Scott
Triumph of the South
A Regional Economic History of Early Twentieth Century Britain
978 1 84014 613 4 (2007)

David Turnock
Aspects of Independent Romania's Economic History with
Particular Reference to Transition for EU Accession
978 0 7546 5892 4 (2007)

David Oldroyd
Estates, Enterprise and Investment at the Dawn of the Industrial Revolution
Estate Management and Accounting in the North-East of England, c.1700–1780
978 0 7546 3455 3 (2007)

Ralf Roth and Günter Dinhobl (eds)
Across the Borders
Financing the World's Railways in the Nineteenth and Twentieth Centuries
978 0 7546 6029 3 (2008)

Vincent Barnett and Joachim Zweynert (eds)
Economics in Russia
Studies in Intellectual History
978 0 7546 6149 8 (2008)

Raymond E. Dumett (ed.)
Mining Tycoons in the Age of Empire, 1870–1945
Entrepreneurship, High Finance, Politics and Territorial Expansion
978 0 7546 6303 4 (2009)

Peter Dorey
British Conservatism and Trade Unionism, 1945–1964
978 0 7546 6659 2 (2009)

Shigeru Akita and Nicholas J. White (eds)
The International Order of Asia in the 1930s and 1950s
978 0 7546 5341 7 (2010)

Myrddin John Lewis, Roger Lloyd-Jones, Josephine Maltby
and Mark David Matthews
Personal Capitalism and Corporate Governance
British Manufacturing in the First Half of the Twentieth Century
978 0 7546 5587 9 (2010)

John Murphy
A Decent Provision
Australian Welfare Policy, 1870 to 1949
978 1 4094 0759 1 (2011)

Robert Lee (ed.)
Commerce and Culture
Nineteenth-Century Business Elites
978 0 7546 6398 0 (2011)

Martin Cohen
The Eclipse of 'Elegant Economy'
The Impact of the Second World War on Attitudes to Personal
Finance in Britain
978 1 4094 3972 1 (2012)

Gordon M. Winder
The American Reaper
Harvesting Networks and Technology, 1830–1910
978 1 4094 2461 1 (2012)

Julie Marfany
Land, Proto-Industry and Population in Catalonia, c. 1680–1829
An Alternative Transition to Capitalism?
978 1 4094 4465 7 (2012)

Lucia Coppolaro
The Making of a World Trading Power
The European Economic Community (EEC) in the GATT Kennedy Round
Negotiations (1963–67)
978 1 4094 3375 0 (2013)

Ralf Roth and Henry Jacolin (eds)
Eastern European Railways in Transition
Nineteenth to Twenty-first Centuries
978 1 4094 2782 7 (2013)

For Product Safety Concerns and Information please contact our
EU representative GPSR@taylorandfrancis.com Taylor & Francis
Verlag GmbH, Kaufingerstraße 24, 80331 München, Germany